INDEPENDENT MEMBER

A MAN ABOUT TOWN

BALLADS FOR BROADBROWS

BOMBER GIPSY AND OTHER POEMS

GENERAL CARGO

HALF HOURS AT HELLES

LEAVE MY OLD MORALE ALONE

INDEPENDENT MEMBER

LAUGHING ANN AND OTHER POEMS

HOLY DEADLOCK

MILD AND BITTER

LITTLE RAYS OF MOONSHINE

PLAIN JANE

SHE-SHANTIES

SIREN SONG

SIP! SWALLOW!

TANTIVY TOWERS

THE AYES HAVE IT

THE HOUSE BY THE RIVER

THE OLD FLAME

THE SECRET BATTLE

THE WATER GIPSIES

THE WHEREFORE AND THE WHY

"TINKER TAILOR"

TOPSY

UNCOMMON LAW

WHAT A WORD!

Books by A. P. Herbert

Independent Member

By A. P. Herbert

1951

DOUBLEDAY & COMPANY, INC., GARDEN CITY, NEW YORK

WITH LOVE AND APOLOGIES TO MY DEAR WIFE,
WHO FOR FOURTEEN YEARS (OUT OF THIRTY-FIVE)
HAS HAD TO LIVE WITH A MEMBER OF PARLIAMENT

AUTHOR'S NOTE: I thank the Controller of His Majesty's Stationery Office for his courteous permission to reprint some extracts from speeches made in the House of Commons.

I thank the Admiralty, the Library of the House of Commons, and the Port of London Authority for correcting my recollections on many points.

Wherever I thought that descriptions of private meetings or conversations might possibly offend, I have sought, and obtained, the consent of the persons concerned, and I thank them all.

Some passages have been extracted from articles or verses in *Punch,* the *Sunday Graphic*, and the *Daily Telegraph*, and I thank the proprietors for their permission to print them again.

Finally, my warm thanks to Mrs. Joan Clark, my excellent secretary, who, having helped to fight so many of my battles, has had the horrid task of typing all of them.

A. P. H.

Contents

1. 'RARE AND REFRESHING'   1
2. 'INTO PARLIAMENT HE MUST GO'   20
3. I GO HOME   30
4. MAIDEN SPEECH   33
5. GOOD BOY   40
6. THE TORTURE CHAMBER   47
7. PRIVATE FRIDAYS   62
8. BETTING, FRUSTRATION, ETC.   70
9. THE MARRIAGE BILL   73
10. THE POPULATION (STATISTICS) BILL   86
11. MUNICH   90
12. 1939   99
13. 'SAY IT IN "PUNCH"!'   102
14. WAR   108
15. A TAX ON BOOKS   131
16. IN THE NAVY   134
17. THE BATTLE OF LAMBETH BRIDGE   142
18. NAVIGATION AS A VICE   146
19. MIND AGAINST MINES   152
20. SOME NAVAL OCCASIONS   158

21. THE MAIN BRACE   161
22. THE HORSE'S NAVEL   165
23. THE THAMES PREPARES   170
24. 'WAIT TILL TUESDAY'   172
25. MR. CHURCHILL RECITES   192
26. LESS NONSENSE   195
27. FLYING THE ATLANTIC   198
28. NEWFOUNDLAND   202
29. LABRADOR   219
30. MARY'S FIRST ATTEMPT   237
31. 'GOODWILL' AT WESTMINSTER   244
32. THE OVENS ALIGHT   249
33. A CRITIC IN THE BLITZ   252
34. THE THAMES ATTACKS   255
35. THE TIME OF 'DOODLE-BUGS'   261
36. MONTY IN ACTION   270
37. BIG BANGS   285
38. UP THE NORTH SEA—BUT WHY?   288
39. V.E. DAY—AND AFTER   296
40. TO LÜNEBURG   300
41. 'DEMOB'   304
42. THE RUDE PARLIAMENT   308
43. BILLS ON THE FLOOR   312
44. A TALE OF BRAVERY   316
45. SNUB FOR KING JAMES   324
46. TO THE ARGENTINE   328
47. 'WE COULD NOT RISK IT'   336
48. WRITING TO 'THE TIMES'   344
49. LAST OF THE BURGESSES   352
50. SWAN SONG   357

INDEPENDENT MEMBER

1. 'Rare and Refreshing'

My first official contact with the British Parliament was at Bow Street Police Court, where, on 17 May 1934, I laid an information against the Kitchen Committee of the House of Commons for selling 'liquor' without a licence. That may remind you of the opening sentence in the *Memoirs of Harriette Wilson:* 'I shall not say why and how I became, at the age of fifteen, the mistress of the Earl of Craven.' I shall not be quite so reticent: but I will not inflict upon you the full story of that first venture. Not that I am ashamed of it. I think it was a good adventure. It failed, as I have often failed, because I trusted too much to my own sense of logic, and far too much to that of my countrymen.

It was not done for fun or fame, as many suggested. I could have thought of many cheaper and safer ways of winning fame or fun than by a lone legal assault on the House of Commons, with all the resources of the Crown against me and only a few good friends behind me. It would not have been very useful 'publicity' to receive a severe wigging from the High Court, or even to be laughed out of court by the Magistrates. As for 'fun,' it is one thing to talk big in club or pub: it is quite another, I can assure you, to go to dreary Bow Street on a Monday morning, to watch the week-end 'drunk and disorderlies' pass swiftly before the Magistrate, and realize that you have come there to prosecute, in effect, the House of Commons, a deed that no man has attempted before.[1]

One or two papers did kindly acknowledge this. That not very frivolous organ the *Law Times* said, at the end of it all:

He made a brave attempt to make the House of Commons feel the pressure of the Licensing Laws which it has itself created. He failed but . . . it has doubtless helped to draw public attention to laws which many feel, with Mr. Herbert, are unduly oppressive in operation and are apparently based on an estimate of an Englishman's self-control which may in the past have been justified but is no longer so since the advent of other pastimes and the spread of education.

'The particular question' the learned organ continued 'was one quite open to argument.' Not even my view of the law was as crazy as it sounds. Grubbing about in Erskine May[2] and the famous cases in constitutional law, I had independently formed the opinion that the sale of 'liquor' without a licence in the House of Commons (elsewhere a very serious crime) could not be defended in a court of law. I discussed, in the *Daily Telegraph*, the possibility of getting the matter tested, and I was told by many learned men that the notion was ridiculous, for I should at once be committed to the Clock Tower for contempt of Parliament, or breach of privilege. And indeed, it is laid down in Erskine May that it is a breach of privilege to institute legal proceedings against any Member or servant of the House for any act done in accordance with the instructions or customs of the House.

Then, by accident, I heard of the case of *Williamson* v. *Norris* (1899, 1 Q.B., 7). I secured from Messrs. Todd, Dennes, and Lamb, solicitors, the papers in the case, and, after further researches, I learned that better men had come to the same conclusion many years before.

On 21 January 1897, Sir Wilfrid Lawson, M.P., the celebrated 'Temperance' Reformer, put a question to the Attorney-General,

---

[1]Charles Bradlaugh brought numerous civil actions against the Sergeant-at-Arms and other officers of the House. This was the first criminal information against it.

[2]Sir T. Erskine May's *Parliamentary Practice*, accepted as the highest authority.

Sir Richard Webster (afterwards Lord Alverstone and Lord Chief Justice of England).

Sir Richard replied:

I have carefully looked into the matter, and I have come to the conclusion that the sale of intoxicating liquor, as at present carried on in the precincts of the House, is not in accordance with the law. (*Loud laughter.*)

I am, however, clearly of the opinion that the provisions of the Licensing Acts cannot be applied, and are wholly unsuitable to the circumstances of the case. (*Renewed laughter.*)

I am in communication with my right hon. friends the Home Secretary and the Chancellor of the Exchequer as to what steps had best be taken. My present opinion is that a short Act should be passed exempting the Houses of Parliament from the operation of the Licensing and Excise laws.

On 17 February 1897, a Licensing Exemption (Houses of Parliament) Bill was ordered to be read a first time and printed. It was introduced by Lord Stanley, Mr. W. Redmond, and two other members of the Kitchen Committee, and drafted with the assistance of the Attorney-General.

There were three inconclusive second reading debates: the session came to an end, and the Bill died an unnatural death.

The Kitchen Committee, I gather, 'owing to the attitude of the teetotallers,' decided not to reintroduce their Bill, and to leave it to those who had asked questions to test the matter in the courts.

Sir Wilfrid Lawson accepted the challenge, and the case of *Williamson* v. *Norris* (1899, 1 Q.B., 7) followed. Sir Wilfrid, being himself a Member, could not, I suppose, proceed directly himself, or proceed against another Member, without exposing himself to odium, or possibly punishment for breach of privilege. So he sent hired men into the House to consume whisky and collect evidence, and they informed against the humble barman, Norris.

Bow Street was not afraid of the House of Commons. The Magistrate, Sir Franklin Lushington, accepted jurisdiction and issued a summons without hesitation. But he found for the defence and there was an appeal to the High Court—the Lord Chief Justice and Mr. Justice Wills—on a point of law.

The Lord Chief Justice held that the charge against the barman failed on the technical point that he was only a servant of the Kitchen Committee and therefore was not responsible for the offence, if any. But he went out of his way to say this:

I am far—very far—from being satisfied that no offence has been committed . . . by those by whose authority the sale takes place . . . I am not at all impressed by the argument that because many of the provisions of the Licensing Acts cannot be worked with reference to the House of Commons therefore the Acts do not apply.

In face of this doubt, the very grave doubt which exists, it is obvious that an appeal should be made to the Legislature to legalize and regulate what is going on, if Parliament thinks it expedient that the sale of liquor should take place within the precincts of Parliament.

Nothing was done in the matter by the Legislature, however, except, from time to time, to make more severe the laws restricting the citizens' refreshment.

On this encouraging authority, I decided to proceed. But why? Why, you may say, this Puritanical attempt to make the House of Commons, where you had so many friends, go dry? But that was not the notion. The good old *Morning Post* saw deeper, and said more shrewdly:

THE MORAL OF THE JOKE

. . . Mr. Herbert, being a humane man, . . . in truth would have felt deeply shocked had he succeeded in cramping hospitality and transporting our legislators to gaol. He is perfectly ready to grant Members supply if they will fairly redress the nation's grievances: and may the demonstration he has staged help to impress the conscience of the House! . . .

That was the fond, fantastic hope—that, if we won, it might, sooner or later, lead to better laws for the people.

But then, in this unimportant area of life, why worry about that? 'The whole thing,' said a 'progressive' paper, 'seems to us to be a great waste of time and money.'

Through all my little 'public life' I have been deafened by two contradictory injunctions. One is 'Stick to your last!' and the other is 'Stick to someone else's last!' When I fought for higher Civil List

Pensions, Mr. Neville Chamberlain said, 'Say it in *Punch!*' When I fought for saner Divorce Laws, they said: 'You should not spend your time and ability on trifles like this. Consider Poverty, and Unemployment, and the State of Europe.' But, when I tried to speak for the Mercantile Marine, I was shooed away like a trespasser by Mr. Shinwell and the Seamen's Union. And when I fought for the independence of Newfoundland I was reminded by certain folk across the Atlantic that I was a 'funny' man.

No complaints. We all think that every other dog is barking up the wrong tree. The truth is, there are so many trees that any good dog should be allowed to choose his own. I thought in those days that there were quite enough dogs under the obvious trees. Nothing is easier—or safer—than to make a reputation by constantly crying aloud that the poor are too numerous and ought to have more money (I have done a little of it myself). It was not so safe, in those days, to fight for a liberal reform of the Marriage, Divorce, Licensing, Betting, Sunday, and Public Entertainment Laws. No man could do that without incurring the suspicion that he was a libertine, drunkard, gambler, and atheist, and was seeking only to extend his own opportunities for self-indulgence. Though I had been happily married for twenty-one years and had four fine children, I heard that my book, *Holy Deadlock*, dedicated to my wife, was, by some foolish people, interpreted as a personal complaint of some sort. Under such trees in the forest of Home Affairs I had done most of my ineffective barking. It was better, I thought, for those of us who have neither the powers of supermen nor the position of dictators to try to get a few small things done than to vapour vainly about the woes of the world. But the earnest apostles of Civil Liberty, who were always agonizing about an election in Bulgaria or the presence of two policemen at a Communist meeting in Hoxton, cared nothing for my kind of 'Civil Liberty,' and thought that I was wasting my time and talents. They hated Hitler (as I did), but seemed to delight in 'Dora.'[3] Very well. Each dog to his tree. I had made a great study of

[3]Pet name for the Defence of the Realm Act, and, later, any unpopular interference with liberty.

these tricky, unpopular themes (they are not so unpopular now). I was tired of saying 'Something ought to be done,' and was eager to do something. The Sunday Cinemas Act (a halfhearted, illogical, and indeed unjust extension of liberty) had been brought about by the action of a common informer. I had already done what I could about the Divorce Laws by writing a book; and I had, thank God, no reason or desire to go to law about that. But here, in the gracious garden of public refreshment, one of the little bees in my bonnet might make itself heard at last.

We needed funds, we needed lawyers, we needed 'evidence.' I was not, as my friend Lady Astor at once assumed, financed by 'the Trade.' On the contrary, the only paper which consistently poured cold water on me was the brewers' own organ; and the 'Trade,' I was told, were racked with virginal fears that people might suspect them of complicity in my obscene activities. A few personal friends contributed, and when we went to Bow Street our fighting fund was £105—not a lot for the job.

Two old Oxford friends, (Sir) Walter Monckton, K.C., and Henry Strauss, M.P. (now a K.C. too), agreed to plead the cause, without fee, and were instructed by my neighbour Mr. (now Sir) George Bull, son of Sir William, so long the sunny Member for South Hammersmith. Harry Strauss did very ably the long preliminary work of choosing the target, preparing the ammunition, and laying the guns. I had, I think, the worst part, collecting 'evidence.' I had determined to do this necessary but uncongenial job myself, and to do it openly—not, that is, to send in hired clerks or detectives.

It was very difficult, and many times I thought with sympathy of the police-officers who have to do this kind of work. For, though one may be persuaded that one is saving the nation, it is difficult to shake off the sensation of being a spy. The police, I suppose, do not suffer that sensation so keenly as I did, even when they are spying on harmless offenders against our most fantastic laws; and the police have no complicated problems of taste and friendship to worry them.

I should explain here that I had to get evidence of a sale of 'intoxicating liquor' not only to a member of the public but to a Member of Parliament, for it was thought that the defence might seek to make a distinction between the two,[4] and a decision which deprived the Press Gallery but not the legislators of refreshment would not have been welcome to me.

Now, to get evidence of a sale to the public I had only to walk into the public bar and order a drink. I had been for two years secretary to that fine man Sir Leslie (later Lord Justice) Scott, and knew my way about. But it was not so simple as it sounds. I was, even then (though this may surprise you), a respecter of Parliament, and, like all good citizens, I am impressed by the outward symbols of law and power and venerable institutions. The Houses of Parliament have a great capacity for commanding awe. I have known many men to go into the Palace of Westminster boldly despising the 'talking-shop' and the 'politicians,' but to come out in an almost reverent frame of mind. I do not know whether it is the Gothic arches or the frescoes, or the faint ecclesiastical smell (disinfectant, I believe), or the numerous policemen, or the gold-chained messengers, or the statue of Mr. Gladstone, the marble floor below, the roving echoes above—or simply the apprehension of an indestructible solidity which the good Englishman ought to have in that place. But there is something there which might cause the boldest prosecutor to draw back.

And the technique of detective-work, I found, is not acquired at once. When I order a drink I am generally talking, I pull a handful of change out of my pocket and do not notice how much I pay, what time it is, whether the other fellow has a gin and French or a gin and mixed, or even, sometimes, the appearance of the barmaid. All these things must be carefully noted, and afterwards written down by the sleuth on duty; but I made three or four visits and bought many drinks before I learned to concentrate upon their criminal aspect.

But the 'sale to a Member' presented graver problems. Many of my friends in the House expressed interest and even goodwill, until it appeared that I was seriously determined to carry the thing through; and then they became alarmed. Polite but nervous inquiries

---

[4] "I do not know on what grounds any action could lie. No outsiders can obtain anything unless they are accompanied by a Member.'—Sir Park Goff. But he forgot the Press, and many others.

followed the departure of the wine-waiter—'You're not collecting evidence to-night, I hope?' I would explain, of course, that I had no intention of dragging the name of any host of mine into this affair without his knowledge and consent; the legislator's face would then lighten, and we would begin again to denounce the Licensing Laws. I enjoyed three or four excellent meals in the House about this time but could not secure the very small co-operation we required. There was no question of the Member having to give evidence. He was asked only to permit me, as his guest, to say in a test case that I had seen him buy a bottle of wine. But each man thought, I suppose, that he would be branded as a conspirator against his own House. The House is very like a club or school, and it would be 'letting the school down.' Some thought that I was right and might win, so that every obstacle ought to be put in my way. The notion that if I was right I ought to prevail, because it meant that the mighty House of Commons was behaving wrongly, I did not find anywhere—except in Lord Hugh Cecil. He, as a great constitutional lawyer, thought that I had raised an important constitutional point, which ought to be settled: and, being afraid of nobody, he gave me some assistance. We solemnly visited the public bar together one morning, and I reluctantly drank a whisky and soda at twenty past eleven: but this evidence was secured in the wrong Session or for some other reason was held to be valueless. Elsewhere I found a complete absence of conscience or respect towards the Licensing Laws. The laws might or might not be good for the poor, but it was laughable to suggest that they should be observed by the Members.[5] I agree. But when you find such an attitude among the law-givers it is a fair deduction that the laws are bad.

Well, these enjoyable meals gave me some interesting glimpses of political psychology, but carried the case no farther. The only course now was to catch a strange Member drinking in the public bar, where the obligations of a guest would not constrain me. So on 10 April 1934, with Mr. George Izzard, the lively landlord of the

---

[5]'As a member of the Kitchen Committee I can only say that we have carried on for some time without anyone interfering and we shall carry on till some one does.'

Sir Nicholas Grattan-Doyle, M.P.

Doves Inn at Hammersmith, as a 'corroborative' witness, I penetrated the doomed citadel again.

I chose that day because the Licensing (Standardization of Hours) Bill was being discussed in Standing Committee. This was a Private Members' Bill to end the silliness and scandal of pubs and restaurants closing at ten o'clock in one borough and ten-thirty or eleven-thirty in the rest, so that there was a mad rush from borough to borough, and the cause of temperance was not assisted. In 1949—and all credit to the present Government—this was put right at last; but observe that it had taken fifteen years.

The Strangers' Bar was then close to the Committee Room, upstairs, and if we had to explain what we were doing in the House we could truthfully say that we were interested in the passage of the Bill and had attended the Committee in the public seats. (I had, in fact, been present at one of the meetings of its promoters.)

In the Committee Room Mr. Isaac Foot was on his feet, making, I thought, an intemperate speech against the poor little Bill (which, by the way, was killed at last, I think by the Government). Beside Mr. Foot sat my friend Lady Astor, and Mr. Rhys Davies. Lady Astor made a friendly face at me, fixed her sharp eyes on George Izzard, and spotted at once (as she told me later) a member of 'the Trade.' That morning she was in fighting form, interjecting, flinging taunts and making queer gestures across the table at a row of well-behaved Etonians in top-hats, Tory supporters of the Bill. Mr. Foot was reading a letter which he had received from a social worker in Leeds protesting against the Bill. When he had finished this ill-expressed communication and announced that that was the sort of reason why this infamous measure should not be passed into law, one of the young men in top-hats asked politely, 'Is that letter signed?' Mr. Isaac Foot made this astonishing reply: 'No, it is not signed, but it bears upon the face of it all the marks of authenticity.' The young men in top-hats laughed at that; Lady Astor cried some insult at them, the terms of which I forget, and made a gesture signifying very clearly that in her opinion the Bill's supporters had no brains. 'Well,' I thought, 'this is a very queer method of deciding whether the pubs in Kensington ought to close at the same time as the pubs at Knightsbridge.' And Mr. Izzard, who had not witnessed such a scene before, was genuinely shocked. When Mr. Foot sat down Mr. Rhys Davies made another speech against the Bill.

I had not thought before of challenging the 'Temperance' Group to provide me with my 'evidence,' but their behaviour towards this Bill and its supporters moved me not only to indignation but to action. In the luncheon interval I waited for Lady Astor in the corridor.

I like and admire Lady Astor: she is courageous and witty and kind, and a good fighter. I had enjoyed her hospitality and her fun, and I should enjoy her conversation if I could have more share in it.

We always shout at each other. The moment she sees me she shouts, 'Hullo, here's the brewers' friend!' And I shout back the first thing that comes into my head. Unhappily, the good lady will not listen to more than the first four words of any sentence that I can frame. It is hard work, but entertaining. She greeted me with her customary gusto and the remark that she supposed I was in the pay of the brewers. I had heard before that she said this of me (she could not believe that anyone could disagree with her upon this subject except for a sinister reason); I had sent her a special message to say that I had never had a penny from the brewers, and denied it in the Press. So I told her now that it was naughty of her to say it again. But by the time I finished saying that she was sentences ahead, roaring away on another tack, and saying that she did not really mind the beer so much as the brewers and their malign 'political influence.' I tried to tell her that, to my personal knowledge, this pathetic little Bill was not the wicked invention of the brewers but the independent work of some young private Members, whose only purpose was to make our arrangements a little more orderly and our law a little less of a laughing-stock. She would not listen, and we passed down the stairs together, both talking at once, and exchanging abuse, like two fish-porters, in the friendliest way.

In the Members' Lobby she paused for an instant, and I said, 'It's all very well, Nancy. You're very bold upstairs against the pleasures of the people, but I notice that you've said nothing about my campaign against the House of Commons.'

Lady Astor said—and, to do her justice, I must emphasize this—

'Well, as a matter of fact, I agree with you. I think it's rotten that there should be one law outside and another law in here.'

I said, 'Well, take me into that bar and stand me a drink, and I'll use it as evidence.' (There was then a small bar off the Lobby.) She said, 'No, I've got a luncheon-party. I must go. Come and have some lunch.'

I said, 'Thanks, but I've got a friend waiting for me——'

'I saw him. One of the Trade.'

'And I must get my evidence. Come on,' I urged her, 'it won't take a minute.'

She said, 'Well, I *would*. But I really must go now. I can't. But Isaac Foot will—— Isaac, give Mr. Herbert a drink.'

Mr. Isaac Foot was now standing near. He said in a friendly way, 'I can't—because of my Templar's vow. But Rhys Davies will.' And he called to Mr. Rhys Davies, who was then entering the bar, 'Give Mr. Herbert a drink.'

Mr. Rhys Davies assented, I forget in what terms, and I followed him into 'Annie's' little bar. And there and then I might have got my 'evidence' in the most attractive form, provided by one of the three fanatical opponents of the little Bill upstairs. But some soft scruple intervened. I had not met this worthy Welshman before; he did not, I thought, know anything about me; and, though he was one of the enemy, I thought that he should have fair warning. So I said, 'I must warn you, sir, that any drink you give me will be taken down and used in evidence against you.'

He said, 'Oh well, if there's going to be any blahther in the newspapers I'll have none of it.' Then, with a grand gesture to the barmaid, 'Give the gentleman a ginger beer!'

My attempt to get the Temperance Party to assist me in suppressing the consumption of 'alcohol' in the Mother of Parliaments had failed, as I expected, but it was fun. And, if I had been in their place, I do not think, as a Member, that I should have done differently. Here is a nest that no bird wants to foul.

Well, I returned to the public bar, and George Izzard and I bought from my old friend Doris (still serving in the Strangers' Smoking Room) the historic 'glass of lager beer and glass of gin and vermouth' which are mentioned in 1 K.B. (1935), on page 595.

But there were no Members present; and as to a 'sale to a Member' we were no farther advanced. So, at six-thirty on the evening of the same day (prosecuting the House of Commons is a whole-time job), I returned to the Palace of Westminster and captured at the water-hole a Member I did not know, drinking beer in a top-hat.

Meanwhile, we had given fair warning in *The Times* and *Telegraph*. We had decided to go for the big game, the sixteen Members of the Kitchen Committee, and Mr. Bradley, the Refreshment Manager, and not, as in the former case, make poor Doris the defendant. My advisers now sent a formal, respectful but cunningly worded letter to the Chairman of the Kitchen Committee (Sir John Ganzoni), setting out, with the authorities, the legal position, as it appeared to us, and concluding with the respectful hope that the Kitchen Committee's arrangements could be brought within the law without legal proceedings; which, in view of the dignity of the House of Commons, we should undertake with reluctance. We had a formal receipt: we waited patiently but never had a reply. Nobody put a Question to the Attorney-General. Officially, there was silence: though privately I received many friendly warnings about the Clock Tower. The House of Commons, like a gigantic 'bottle party,'[6] sat dumb and defiant, challenging the accusers to come on. So we went on.

We had our evidence, our tackle, all in order, but not enough money. Later our £105 increased to £120. But if we went to the High Court, the Attorney-General, I was told, might cost me £100 a day. The estimates of costs varied, for the proceedings might take various turns. The whole bill, they said, might come to £700 or £800. And we had £105. But we went on.

On the first day there were so few citizens at Bow Street, and so many policemen, that I had to keep reminding myself that I was the prosecutor and not the defendant. But this unease passed off at last, for we made three visits in all. It became like going to the office. The policemen got to know me, and they would say: 'Good morning, Mr. Herbert. Best of luck!'

On the first day Mr. Fry said that the Chief Metropolitan Magistrate wished to hear our application himself another day. But now

[6]A night-club of dubious legality.

the glove was on the ground. The Kitchen Committee woke up at last; two or three of them made statements; one muttered vaguely about 'Royal Palaces,' and the Chairman told a newspaper man: 'We have been advised by the Law Officers of the Crown that the position is perfectly proper.'

Tuesday, 22 May, was the day after the Whitsun holiday, and the drunks were a little more numerous. 'Pay ten shillings, or one day.' . . . The last reveller stumbled out of court, and my counsel, Mr. Strauss, was opening another alcoholic case.

I thought we were off at last, but we were stopped in the first stride. The Chief Metropolitan Magistrate, Sir Rollo Graham-Campbell, said he had consulted the text-books, and was in doubt: 'Were the Kitchen Committee, Members of the House of Commons, carrying out duties entrusted to them by the House, under the control of the House, in a way long practised and approved by the House, amenable in this matter to the jurisdiction of the Court?'

Harry Strauss, with a formidable battery of books and all the authorities in his head, was ready to join battle at once, but it was decided to accept an adjournment so that Walter Monckton, K.C., could be brought into action. We trickled into Bow Street again.

We had not been shooed out of court as the authors of a 'frivolous' application, and that was something to show. On the contrary, the Chief Magistrate gave many signs that he took a very serious view of the affair. But the 'doubts' about his jurisdiction were disturbing and unexpected. My counsel were prepared for him to find against us at the trial of the case, but then there would be an appeal (by case stated) to the High Court. (Two bites at the cherry only—for there would be no appeal from the Divisional Court.) But they did not think that Sir Rollo, however reluctant to try the House of Commons, would decline jurisdiction, with the precedent of *Williamson* v. *Norris* and the strong observations of Lord Russell to fortify him. If he did, that was not necessarily the last word: for we could apply to the High Court for a writ of *mandamus* ('We command you'). But if we obtained our writ (or rule?) we should then have to come back to Bow Street for the summonses and the trial, and then, if defeated, go up to the High Court again. Four bites at the cherry. And I still had only £105.

Friday, 25 May. One minute it was 'Pay ten shillings, or one day,' and the next it was the Bill of Rights (1689), *The Case of Sir John Eliot* (1629), *Stockdale* v. *Hansard* (1839), *Bradlaugh* v. *Gossett* (1883), and so on. Walter Monckton talked till one-fifteen, and a masterly performance it was. But he made no impression. Sir Rollo said:

Mr. Monckton, I am very much indebted to you for your interesting and learned argument. Having regard to the fact that in certain circumstances I may have to try this matter, I think it very desirable that I should say nothing more on this occasion than this, that so far you have not satisfied me that I have jurisdiction to issue the processes for which you ask.

By saying so little, as I understand the matter, he at least left the road indubitably open for us to go to the High Court for a *mandamus*. But I still had only £105.

That day the Chairman of the Kitchen Committee made another statement to the Press. He said that after the magistrate's decision he 'should have thought that Mr. Herbert might well let the matter drop.'

But on 7 June we made our first visit to the High Court. This was, I imagine, like reaching the centre court at Wimbledon at last after obscure combats at humbler tournaments. There was more pomp, no drunks, and fewer policemen. The name of our case had expanded importantly—it was now *Rex* v. *Sir Rollo Graham-Campbell*—ex parte *Herbert,* and I felt at least that I was getting my money's worth. We obtained without difficulty two 'rules *nisi* for orders in the nature of *mandamus'*—one of which would call upon Sir Rollo to 'show cause' why the summonses for which I had applied should not be issued. My counsel were ready, if necessary, to cite authorities from twenty-two large law-books, and these were slowly assembled in the corridor. It was desirable that for each of the three judges a copy of each of the twenty-two volumes should be available, and the usher was busily collecting them from the shelves in his own and adjacent courts. In the end, I believe, he secured the full complement less two: so that there were eighty-six books ready for battle. Not one of them was used.

'You may have your rule, at your peril,' said the Lord Chief Justice. He was an old friend; we had often spoken 'after dinner' in succession, and he was always very kind to me. What he said now, I believe, was the customary phrase on such occasions, meaning that 'costs' might 'follow the event,' though the Press and public supposed it was a special warning directed to my impious person. The reporters, busily writing, did not, as I did, at that moment, look up and catch his Lordship's eye. If it had been any but the Lord Chief Justice's eye, I should have said that, at those words, I saw a, without doubt, involuntary wink.

We had to wait five months for our fifth visit to the courts: and that was just a year after I obtained my 'evidence.' For the comfort of Temperance Reformers I should add that ordinary licensing victuallers and managers of clubs are brought to justice with much more expedition.

On 12 December 1934 we 'came on' again in the spacious court of the Lord Chief Justice, and for the first time, after twelve months of skirmishing, we met the enemy. They were represented by the Attorney-General, Sir Thomas Inskip, and Mr. Wilfrid (the late Mr. Justice) Lewis, 'showing cause,' and carrying, I observed with interest, some numbers of *Punch* in their bundles of papers (I never discovered what these were for).

My own leading counsel, Mr. Monckton, unhappily was deeply embroiled in some railway inquiry, and having given an undertaking to his important clients that he would not leave their business (while it lasted) for any other, he could not be with us. I was sorry, for, apart from his great powers of advocacy, it is a joy to listen to him; but Mr. Strauss most ably and bravely led the attack instead, and I am sure that, substantially, it made no difference.

The day before, Lord Hewart, like an eagle disturbed from its eyrie, had descended on the House of Lords and there made a most vigorous and even angry oration about the conduct of the Lord Chancellor, the Lord Chancellor's office, the proposal to form a Ministry of Justice, the insidious encroachments of bureaucracy, the treatment of Lord Justice Slesser by the Master of the Rolls, an alleged failure to show proper respect to his own high office, and other important matters. The House of Lords had adjourned in an unusual state of excitement and alarm: for Lord Hewart had threatened that if a certain course were not taken he would adjourn his Court early every day and fight the Bill (whose name and purpose I forget) 'line by line.' The morning papers had 'splashed' this event, and a very distinguished barrister said to me in court, 'You have chosen a good day—his lordship being at daggers drawn with almost every authority.' I said that Fate could hardly have chosen a less auspicious date for the presentment before the Lord Chief Justice of a criminal charge against the House of Commons.

'You may be right,' said the barrister, and returned to his place.

The case went on till the morning of the third day. The proceedings began with a crackle of legal wit, very enjoyable.

THE ATTORNEY-GENERAL: The House cannot be regarded as a Government Department.

THE LORD CHIEF JUSTICE: I hope that you will be able to say that a few years hence.

Some said that there were too many jokes. But most of them amounted to a judicial derision of the Licensing Laws, and I felt that they, not I, were being laughed out of court. The Lord Chief Justice would not have joked if the charge had been the distribution of obscene literature or narcotic drugs in the Lower House. In other words, he was proclaiming as publicly as the House of Commons that the Licensing Laws did not, in all particulars, deserve respect. So I was grateful to his Lordship for his levity.

Mr. Justice Avory made no jokes. He sat quiet and attentive on Lord Hewart's right, an ivory mask, the tip of his tongue slipping out and in like a lizard's. Suddenly, on the second day, like a bird on the lawn, he raised his head, fixed sharp eyes upon counsel, and darted at a passage in the judgment of Lord Denman in *Stockdale* v. *Hansard*:

The Commons of England are not invested with more power and dignity by their legislative character than by that which they have as the grand inquest of the nation. All the privileges that can be required for the energetic discharge of the duties inherent in that high trust are conceded without a murmur or a doubt.

As I had come to court at great trouble and expense to make a loud murmur and express a powerful doubt, I was not myself much impressed by the latter part of this pronouncement. And I should have liked to put the vital question whether the uncontrolled consumption of 'intoxicating liquor' could properly be said to be *required* for the energetic discharge of Parliament's duties, remembering that the fundamental assumption of the Licensing Acts is that 'intoxicants' are injurious to the discharge of any man's duties.

But I felt at once that the Court had found what they were seeking, and indeed the Lord Chief Justice made this passage the keystone of his judgment. But Mr. Strauss nobly battled on with *Sir John Eliot* and the rest. (Sir John Eliot's case seemed [to us] to show clearly that an ordinary crime committed in the House would not be withdrawn from the ordinary course of criminal justice.) I wearied, at last, I confess, of *Sir John Eliot* and *Mr. Topham*, unanswerable though they seemed to be. From the moment of Mr. Justice Avory's intervention, I was sure that we should 'go down.'

The Lord Chief Justice, deliberate and weighty, courteous and complimentary to my counsel and myself, was 'clearly of opinion that these rules should be discharged' (which does not mean, as you might suppose, 'carried out' or 'completed,' but 'cancelled').

The Magistrate was entitled to say on the material before him, that in the matter complained of the House of Commons was acting collectively in a matter which fell within the area of the internal affairs of the House, and, that being so, any tribunal might well feel, on the authorities, an invincible reluctance to interfere. To take the opposite course might conceivably be, in proceedings of a somewhat different character from these, after the various stages of these proceedings had been passed, to make the House of Lords the arbiter of the privileges of the House of Commons.

More than that, with the greatest respect for the observations of my illustrious predecessor, Lord Russell, C.J., in *Williamson* v. *Norris*, it appears to me that the bulk of the Licensing Acts are quite inapplicable to the House of Commons.

Mr. Justice Avory said:

I wish to call attention to the argument presented by the Attorney-General in *Williamson* v. *Norris*, when he said . . . etc. Later he said

'It is clear that many of the provisions of the Licensing Acts could not possibly be made applicable to the House of Commons.' I wish to adopt that argument as part of my judgment in this case.

It is true that Lord Russell, C.J., in *Williamson* v. *Norris* said '. . . I am not at all impressed by the argument that because many of the provisions of the Licensing Acts cannot be worked with reference to the House of Commons, therefore those Acts do not apply.' In my view those words do not amount even to *dicta*. At the most they amount to an expression of doubt. Speaking with the most profound respect for even an expression of doubt by Lord Russell of Killowen I have come to the conclusion that the argument addressed to the Court by the Attorney-General in that case ought to have prevailed, and that, it being impracticable and impossible to apply the general provisions of the Licensing (Consolidation) Act 1910 to the House of Commons, it is equally impracticable and impossible to apply s. 65, sub-s. 1, which forbids the sale of liquor without a licence . . .

Mr. Justice Swift 'had nothing to add.'

There followed the little, but, to one person at least, enthralling Drama of Costs.

My Fighting Fund, I think, that morning, was £115. I had little hope of obtaining further support for a cause already lost. Our own bill, I knew, was in the region of £160 (and a very reasonable bill too). But now I should, presumably, have to pay for the other side as well. We had occupied the Attorney-General and his junior for three days, to say nothing of the activities of the Treasury Solicitor. My solicitor had roughly estimated the full costs upon the other side at £500. Not even in that moment, I can truthfully say, did I regret our exploit: but I listened with some anxiety to the following passage (which does not appear in the Law Reports):

MR. WILFRID LEWIS (*for the Commons*): Your Lordship will discharge the rules with costs?

THE LORD CHIEF JUSTICE (*bless him!*): Are you really asking for costs, Mr. Lewis? We have had, and I imagine you have had, *a rare and refreshing* diversion from the ordinary routine of this Court.

MR. WILFRID LEWIS: I was instructed to ask for costs, my Lord . . .

THE LORD CHIEF JUSTICE (*after some discussion with Mr. Justice Avory*): Mr. Wilfrid Lewis, we quite appreciate your difficulty, and you never raise a difficulty, if I may say so, without reason, but we have come to the conclusion . . . that although these rules ought to be discharged there ought to be no costs.

MR. WILFRID LEWIS: If your Lordship pleases.

THE LORD CHIEF JUSTICE (*God bless him!*): May I add the expression of a hope—it can be no more than that—that the funds of the Kitchen Committee may be of use, and, if not those funds, then perhaps the matter ultimately may not prove to be beyond the scope of a supplementary estimate.

With these warming words my little revolution came to an end— as most English revolutions end, with a joke. I was courteously treated, and fairly heard: I was shown to be wrong and have no complaints. My total bill was £165—of which, very properly, I had to find £45. I thought myself fortunate to suffer no more. I do not think anyone again will prosecute the House of Commons for £45.

Observe that throughout the case, as we had predicted, nothing was heard of the 'Royal Palace' argument. The decision rested squarely on Parliamentary privilege, so that if the House is burned down again and Parliament sits in the Albert Hall the Licensing Acts will still not apply.

There should be, of course, a memorial plaque to me in some Smoking Room or bar, for through my rash act the liberties of the faithful Commons were proclaimed and freed from doubt by the High Court of Justice, and established for ever.

Little did I think that day that, within a year, both Harry Strauss and I would be Members of the House of Commons ourselves, and enjoying the privileges we had so righteously assailed.

2. 'Into Parliament He Must Go'

A procession of accidents[1] led, or perhaps pushed, me into Parliament.

Three weeks before the General Election of 1935 I had no more thought of standing for Parliament than I had of exploring the North Pole. But one day in October my lively friend Mr. Sidney Rogerson, of Imperial Chemical Industries, sent me an invitation, I do not quite know why, to go up to Billingham and see the opening of the new coal-into-oil plant by Mr. Ramsay MacDonald. I went, I do not quite know why, and on the special train an old Oxford man passed and paused at Lord Melchett's table where I sat. I did not know him; I do not think we were introduced, but I happened to hear his name. That chain of chances changed the course of my life.

I had often thought that I should like to be in Parliament and try to tackle some of the things, especially divorce reform, about which, as a writer, I was interminably abusing 'the politicians.' But I was not, I thought (and still think), fitted for an ordinary territorial constituency: I was not a strong party man, and could afford neither the money nor the time. But I had sometimes secretly entertained ambitious, almost impious thoughts, about that great prize, an Oxford University seat. When certain eminent political friends said,

[1]Related more fully in *The Ayes Have It* (Methuen).

'You ought to come into the House, my boy,' I would say 'All right, if you give me Oxford University,' and we would laugh heartily at the notion. The great Lord Hugh Cecil and Professor Oman were then strongly entrenched; and, in any case, what chance had a professional humourist, with queer opinions about divorce and drink, of entering that citadel of the Church of England?

But now Professor Oman was to retire; and after much discussion (and, I had heard, some unpleasantness) a new candidate, Professor C. R. M. Cruttwell, had been adopted by the Conservative 'Caucus.' I had said to my secret heart that now, if ever, with a new candidate and dissension in the citadel, would be the time to attempt a breach. But unless by chance I had met this Oxford man on this unpremeditated expedition to Billingham I should not have done anything about it. For one thing, I had not the faintest notion how to begin. For another thing, I rather agreed with Gilbert Frankau, who was sitting at the same table and in the morning gave me a great lecture about wasting my time on odd corners of politics. I should be writing novels, he said, not articles about divorce. I said I thought he was quite right: I would mend my ways. And I meant it.

Then along came this Oxford man. We talked a little about the Oxford situation and the new candidate, and I said to him: 'Would there be any chance for an Independent, do you think?' 'What does one do?' 'Must one have a Committee?' 'Must you have taken your degree?' (I had never taken mine), and so on. He seemed to think the procedure would not be difficult. The trouble would be to obtain the addresses of the electors in the short time remaining (less than three weeks) before nomination day. He did not encourage me. I said, 'Well, if you meet any young man who would help me, ask him to let me know.' We had a large lunch at Billingham, and I thought no more about it.

Next week, to my surprise, a young man rang me up from Oxford —Mr. Francis Pakenham,[2] a lively and learned tutor of Christ Church—and he asked me if I meant business about the election. I said I was blowed if I knew. He came to see me with my friend Mr. Peter Fleming. They were flattering and enthusiastic. They thought I should not get more than half a dozen votes in Oxford itself, but

[2]Now Lord Pakenham, Labour.

that would not matter, for there were only 700 there, out of the 22,000. There was a new register, and B.A.s had votes now, so that it was a younger register. They thought that hockey Blues by the thousand would support me, and some of the 3,000 ladies, for poor Mr. Cruttwell was a bachelor. But the keener they became the more dubious was I. The whole thing now seemed absurd, impertinent, and dangerous. I should probably lose my deposit, and I could not spare £150. If I were defeated it would be 'another of Mr. Herbert's publicity stunts,' and if I were elected, how was I to keep up my work and feed the family? Besides, I liked a quiet life, and I hated making speeches—except after dinner to a small company.

But I said I would think it over, and meanwhile I would try to draft an Election Address and see how it looked.

This, I perceived, would be the crux of the question. The University electors are scattered over the country, and vote by post. They cannot be addressed at meetings, or canvassed at the front door. They cannot be swept away by oratory or good looks, loud-speakers or posters. The Election Address is the one approach to them. It is one of the big remaining opportunities for the power of the pen, and a professional writer, we thought, should make the most of it. I had seen the somewhat dreary Address of the two official Conservatives —or, rather, of the 'Caucus,' for it was not signed by either of the candidates, but by a number of Heads of Houses and other eminent persons on their behalf; so that any elector was entitled to say that he had not the smallest notion what the new candidate, Mr. Cruttwell, thought about anything. This was not the fault of Mr. Cruttwell, who had my sympathy from first to last. It was the way things were done then, and had been done for a very long time. But after that all the candidates wrote long personal Addresses.

I sat down next day and composed an Address, which afterwards received some praise. But I was not to know that then, and the more I wrote the less I liked it. At least, I thought, it was a good intellectual exercise for a spasmodic journalist to be compelled to display all his political beliefs in one basket. It is, and I commend it as an exercise to every citizen. One discovers how few the eggs are and of what irregular shapes and sizes. Very soon I ceased to think of my Address as a practical affair for public use. Three parts through I very nearly stopped, and I remember, as I threw the sheets across, apologizing to my secretary for wasting her time. But I explained to her the intellectual exercise theory; she said she didn't mind; and we laboured on.

When we had done, it was the longest Election Address in political history—or so I suppose: nearly 5,000 words. I read it through and liked a few passages; but, as a whole, I thought it was impossible. And I was pleased. For this, I said, would let me out of the mess. I had made an effort; I had had a useful and a chastening exercise, but nobody at Oxford or anywhere else would urge me to stand for Parliament when they had read a page or two of *this*. I sent it off and had a more cheerful evening.

But at Oxford the document was approved, except for a word or two, and there we were, sliding down the slope again. There was still a small hope that I might be saved from this preposterous enterprise by the difficulty of getting the electors' addresses. I went up to Oxford and crept about, feeling like a burglar surveying the scene of a contemplated coup. One immediate task was to collect the signatures of at least twelve voters for the nomination paper. This was not easy in Oxford, for nearly all my friends among the dons were 'wedded' either to the official Conservatives or the Labour candidate, Mr. J. L. Stocks. But I had not one Head of a House behind me (though privately Mr. H. A. L. Fisher wished me well), no Committee (indeed, I never had a Committee),[3] no office or organization, and none of the usual appurtenances—not even the addresses of the 22,000 electors. And it was only a few days before nomination day, which was Friday, 4 November.

So that, even as I secured my nominators' signatures, I assured my friends that there was little real danger of their being mixed up in politics. They looked at me a little queerly, I thought. The few political friends whom I consulted in London just laughed in a friendly way; and I do not blame them. They thought I was about to make a free gift of £150 to the University,[4] and there was a bet to that effect in the betting book at All Souls.

---

[3]This has advantages. If nobody has ever expressed its confidence in you, nobody can get together and say it has lost confidence in you.

[4]In University Elections the forfeited deposit went to the University Chest.

Well, I did not make any large wagers on my chances, but I did know—or thought I knew—something that was hidden from these wise men, and this is relevant to the main story. I believed that the country parsons, as a whole, were not so hidebound or timid, even upon my suspect causes, as tradition said. Through my work on *Punch* I had for many years had much correspondence with clergymen, schoolmasters, dons, civil servants, and all those respectable ranks which presumably make up the University vote. That year, through my 'Word War' in *Punch,* I had had about 1,000 letters from friendly strangers of this kind. As for divorce and the Church, I had formed even then, from various signs, the opinion that the majority of churchmen were ready and even eager for a reasonable reform. And I thought that more of them might be with me on some of my minor causes, the preservation of pedestrians and quiet, of the English (and the Latin) language, for example, than would be against me on the bigger things.

Still, with good reason, I think, I wavered. So many people stand for Parliament at the General Election that to the others it may not seem to matter much whether they stand or not. But, if you have already two or three lines of activity, and are not rich, it must always be a big choice to set out upon another. Then, on the Tuesday, the faithful and indefatigable Frank Pakenham secured from somewhere a set of addresses, believed to be fairly up-to-date. *Now* we had to make up our minds; and that evening at Hammersmith we debated all things at a meeting of my Council, Executive Committee, and General Staff—namely, my wife and a neighbour, Mr. Frank Bluff. My wife says that I have done so many odd things that she is always resigned for the next, and she thought, wisely, that I had got the political itch so badly that it must be obeyed. We decided to go ahead.

But how? The Election Addresses of the other candidates were in print, with official 'parties' behind them and organized workers ready to dispatch them. Ours was in type, waiting for the word 'Go' at a printing works at Chichester, of which Frank Bluff was a director. The addresses of the electors were at Oxford. So were the voting papers. We were at Hammersmith. Our 'workers' were nowhere. All the professional addressing firms were overflowing with election business. Time was short.

But my wife and Mr. Bluff were grand organizers. On the Wednesday morning we told the printers to start the machines. On Thursday, 3 November, my candidature was announced—or, as I felt, confessed. Friday, 4 November, was nomination day. And by the following Wednesday morning, seven days from zero hour, my wordy Address had been posted to all the 22,000 electors—though a great many of them had thoughtlessly moved and so escaped us.

This was no mean feat for a scratch organization of amateurs. It was all done in the old nursery at home, by my wife and family, friends, neighbours, and kindly strangers who rang up and offered their aid. I have often marvelled at the free, fiery and selfless toil that people will devote to pushing someone else into Parliament; but in this wild enterprise it impressed me more than ever. Still, it was fun; and those who say that they have no use for politics do not realize what fun they miss, if it is only the fun of the fight and the communal excitement of the team. Day and night, with intervals for sausages or sandwiches, they ploughed through that interminable card-index and transcribed the names of those innumerable clergymen. 'Another rector,' the girls would sigh. 'What a hope!' and some of them put the clergymen as high as 30 per cent of the total. But, as I have said, that did not frighten me so much as many. In fact, in that week, of the hundred letters of support I received, about twenty-five were signed by clergymen, and gratefully I record that fact. And, by the way, I had practised no deception on the clergy. For in my Address I said, upon Divorce:

If His Majesty's Government do not, as they should, accept the responsibility for this reform, I shall myself do what I can.

At last the slag-heaps of envelopes were ready. Frank Pakenham brought the voting forms from Oxford and Frank Bluff the great bales of Addresses from Chichester. And the Second Phase of the Operation began—the Folding of the Forms and the Filling of the Envelopes.

Meanwhile, on the Friday, my wife and I went up to Oxford for the nominations, as I thought it would be the respectful duty of a candidate to do. My 'agent,' Frank Pakenham, and my chief nominator, Mr. Gilbert Vassall, met us in the Broad. The celebrated athlete and schoolmaster was still a little bewildered, I think, to find himself involved in politics: but he put on his cap, hood, and gown, I handed over my £150, in notes, and guiltily we advanced upon the Clarendon Building.

I found, with some surprise, that I was the only candidate present. While I was secretary to Sir Leslie Scott, I had seen many nomination days at the Town Hall of Liverpool. All the candidates for all the ten divisions would be there, with their agents and supporters, and a crowd of spectators. T. P. O'Connor would make a sly little speech of thanks to the Returning Officer; he would reply, and one felt that something important and serious had been done, the offer by a number of citizens of their services to the State. But at Oxford University, the home of solemnity and ritual, the candidates, it seemed, did not trouble to appear: the dons who represented them gave their names and addresses to the Vice-Chancellor, deposited their £150, and that was all. This did not matter to me; indeed, it gave me hope, for it was a sign of sleepiness in the citadel. A tradition of inevitable success had led to lazy behaviour. Two champions were chosen by the High Priest, as it were; their Election Address was written by somebody else; somebody else attended both the nominations and the counting. They were elected almost automatically and had little to do but take the train to Westminster.

Well, I have no wish to introduce any alien excitement into the monastic calm of a University election. But I determined that, as often as I should have the temerity to stand again, I should at least think it right to present myself both at the nomination and the counting, if only as a kind of formal acknowledgment of the high honour I was asking the University to give me.

Beyond that, Heaven forbid that I should augment the labours of the University candidate, which are so beautifully few. The rest of the 'campaign' consisted of one speech, and one short letter to *The Times*. I am not even sure that it was proper to make the speech. The undergraduate Conservative Association kindly invited and urged me to address a meeting at the Union. Lord Hugh Cecil had declined a similar invitation on the ground that the burgesses by tradition ought not to speak about general politics in Oxford; but Mr. Cruttwell, they said, had addressed them at one of the hotels. It was cheering to have the support of the young men; and in the special circumstances I thought that I had better accept. But I had not spoken at the Union since 1913, and the prospect of addressing bright and critical youth in that difficult place was alarming. Peter Fleming, Eric Linklater (who had, in vain, made a similar assault on the Scottish Universities), and one or two other good friends came up with me. I heard that the young men were highly critical now, and generally stamped after forty minutes, no matter how distinguished the visitor. I was terrified, as I always was at the Union. The building was packed, upstairs and down—though there were only about three voters in the audience, for undergraduates have no votes. They permitted me to harangue them for a full hour without stamping, and the speech, I believe, was successful, though slightly deplorable. I made some irreverent fun of All Souls College, in terms which I will not repeat, for All Souls, I gather, have generously forgiven me. But the boys seemed to like it.

The whole 'campaign' had cost me about £100. But the deposit might go after that. Frank Bluff inquired in the City about the possibilities of insuring against the loss of that £150. He could get no better rate than £25 per cent—or £37 10s. in all. I said I thought better of my chances than that, and we did no business.

I went up to Oxford for the counting. It was raining there, as usual, and I wandered forlornly about the streets, wondering why I had got myself into this mess.

Neither of the Conservative candidates was present at the counting. I thought this was odd, for I had never failed to face a First Night, much as I detest them. But at the Clarendon Building I met Mr. J. L. Stocks, the Socialist candidate, whom I never met before or after. He seemed charming.

This was worse than a First Night. I felt, as authors do, seeing the stalls fill up and the critics come in, that I was an alien who had thrust himself into a strange land and deserved what was coming to him. I was the only person in the room not in academic dress. The Vice-Chancellor, the Registrar, one or two Heads of Houses, and dons I did not know—including one lady—Mr. Stocks, the representatives of the other candidates and my own, Mr. Roy Harrod, don, Frank Pakenham and all were in hoods and gowns. Technically, I was not even a member of the University, for I had never taken my degree. Certainly I had no vote. Yet I was putting myself forward to be a burgess, Parliamentary voice of this great place. I felt very properly small.

I have elsewhere attempted to describe the working of the Single Transferable Vote, and the way the votes were counted and transferred that day. To my great astonishment I was second all the way, and the final result was:

Cecil	7,365	Elected
Herbert	5,206	Elected
Cruttwell	3,697	
Stocks	2,776	

And poor Mr. Cruttwell, an official Conservative candidate, though third in the final reckoning, *lost his deposit;* and some highly surprised Fellow of All Souls lost a bet. This was very bad luck, I thought. But, for reasons which I cannot explain, a candidate, to save his deposit, had to get one-eighth of the *first preferences,* which Mr. Stocks, but not Mr. Cruttwell, had done.

But let me remark, to the credit of this system, that the result was declared under two hours from the closing of the poll.

We filed out, a rather silent party. I still felt more guilty than elated; and I was sorry for the three dons who represented the 'Caucus' and had to go and break the news.

Mr. Stocks charmingly congratulated me, and I remember he said: 'Well, now I hope you'll do something about the Divorce Laws.'

The Registrar was kind too, but he added, 'Well, now I hope you'll take your degree.'

With Frank Pakenham I slunk out into the night, feeling much more like a naughty schoolboy than a Parliamentary representative of the oldest University.

I did take my degree—at the first opportunity. Indeed, I took two, both B.A. and M.A., to the sound of some good-humoured hilarity among the young.

It gives me pleasure to say that the first and most generous letter of congratulation I received came from Mr. Cruttwell, the Principal of Hertford, who was the victim in many ways of an unpredictable and undeserved misfortune. My election, naturally, caused some dismay in many quarters of Oxford: but I must add that, ever since, I have received nothing but courtesy, hospitality, and kindness.

And perhaps I may conclude this section of the story with an extract from a letter from Lord Hugh Cecil, the Senior Burgess. I wrote to congratulate him on his election and to ask for certain advice. He replied (and I do not think he would mind my repeating this, for it is an example of that frank and fearless sincerity which has won for him universal respect) :

Dear Mr. Herbert,
Thank you for your very kind congratulations. I wish I could recipro-
cate them, but sincerity obliges me to say that I deeply and keenly regret, on public grounds, your election to the University seat.

He had in mind (I presume and hope) the question of divorce, on which he feels as strongly as all the Cecils.

I liked·that. I knew where I was. But there followed two pages of careful and particular advice about the customs governing a burgess, and, ever after, in the House, he treated me as if I were a favourite son.

3. I Go Home

And now, for the last time, it is 'Who goes home?'

Parliament decided, by the Representation of the People Act, 1948, that after the end of the Parliament of 1945 the Universities should be represented at Westminster no more. In 1950, then, this humble Burgess for Oxford University, with eleven others, was flung out of the House of Commons, not by the enraged electorate, not to comply with any popular mandate or even any party programme, but to please some of his colleagues in the House of Commons, with many of whom he had been working amicably for fourteen years.

'Well,' I thought to myself, during those debates, 'perhaps I have been wasting my time.' A sad thought: for fourteen years is a long time in the life of a writer. Indeed, I cannot think of many professional writers who have been a Member of Parliament so long. Before my election I had written two successful novels, and—who knows?—I might have written more. But since that day I have not written one real book. Mr. Churchill, unique person, finds time to write major works and save the nation as well. But little, comparatively, though my Parliamentary doings have been, I have not in all these years been able to write anything more substantial than a few musical plays. 'Parliament,' it has been well said, 'is a place where you can neither rest nor work.' When I went in, there was a laughable legend that the author-M.P. could sit in the Library and write, emerging now and then when the Division Bell rang. But in my early days I was always too busy with my little campaigns to think of writing. You can spend so many hours in that place being busy but getting little done. And it is not only the Chamber, the Committee, or the massive correspondence of every morning that takes the time. Public life spreads like a rash over a man. If an unlikely person like myself is mad enough to leave the quiet of his study for the rumpus of politics, people do not say considerately: 'This man must have enough to do already. And he has his own living to earn. Let us leave him alone.' They say—or seem to say—'This man is fair game. He has time to do anything for nothing.' Before you know where you are, you are on all the committees in London, and are expected to make a witty speech whenever you have a meal.

Still—if this is not too pompous—I did not go into the House for fun, or professional gain, and I have no complaints about my Parliamentary episode (I never thought of it as a career). Provided, that is, that something has been done worth doing, that some small mark has been left upon the sands. But if one thought the time had been wasted; if one might as well have stayed in the study, spinning novels and money, like the sensible men, that would be depressing indeed. And if I, who have had perhaps better fortune than most, go out regretful, or even dubious, how can I urge others like me to go in, as I often do? So I thought I would go back to the beginning, look through the Official Report, and remind myself what things a mere back-bencher said and did, and feel again, perhaps, the urge of old campaigns. 'Remind myself'—yes, for one forgets what speeches one made almost as easily as other men do. Here and there in *Hansard* I have come across passages under my name which, but for the record, I would have sworn I never spoke. These researches may or may not justify to myself and to my constituents the way in which I have used my time. I shall be still more happy if they help to justify the University franchise, in which I strongly believe, and the incursion of the occasional artist (if I may presume so far) into politics. I am sure that there should be more of these, men who can speak with the knowledge of the producer, as well as the zest of the artist, when such subjects as a Books Tax, the Entertainments Duty, the 'Civic Theatre,' or the newsprint supply come up. I was very sorry that Mr. J. B. Priestley was not elected in 1945, though I do not always agree with him. I wish that Sir Malcolm Sargent were a Member, and Mr. T. S. Eliot, and Mr. Harold Nicolson. Mr. Nicolson, of course, has stood three times, and been elected once, in the ordinary way, but he would have been the ideal University Member. One strong objection to the abolition of the University seats is that it blocks a highly appropriate approach for such good and useful counsellors.

It is all very well to say, as Mr. Crossman said, that 'the professor should go through the ordinary rough and tumble and behave like an ordinary democrat.' The hard fact is that very few artists or professors, because they are what they are, feel themselves fit to face the 'ordinary rough and tumble' or are likely to be elected if they do. If you want to feed the birds you do not insist that they walk in at the front door.

Well, Mr. Churchill and his men have said that if they are returned to power, they will restore the University seats. That day, if any writer, musician, painter, architect, doctor or don thinks of offering himself for election, I hope that in these pages he may find some encouragement. He will certainly find some Awful Warnings. For I intend to expose some of the episodes where I know that I was naughty as faithfully as those where I felt that I was a fine fellow. And here and there, Young Man, you may pick up a practical hint or two about the Parliamentary game.

4. Maiden Speech

Indeed, I must begin with an Awful Warning: *Do not be in too great a hurry to make your Maiden Speech.* The traditions, and the tricks, of the House of Commons are not learned in a day. You should sit quiet for a time, and study carefully how things are said and done. This was the friendly advice of all the wise old men, who wished to see me do well, including that very wise old statesman Sir Austen Chamberlain, who said that one should wait for months. But I went mad and roared into action on the second day of the new Parliament. I was not quite so rash, perhaps, as William Cobbett. It is a tradition that the maiden speech should be modest and unprovocative, so that he who follows may compliment you with real goodwill, and no Member will be tempted to tear your first offering to pieces. William Cobbett opened fire on his first evening in the House, and, having listened to a debate in which all the swells had taken part, he rose and said: 'Mr. Speaker, it appears to me that since I have been sitting here I have heard a great deal of vain and unprofitable conversation.'

One cause of too much boldness in the new-comer may be fear. The thought of the first plunge is so alarming that there is a natural itch to 'get it over.' A man may be well accustomed to addressing large audiences on the platform or at the dinner-table, but will still think with panic of speaking in the House, of which the great Macaulay said, 'There is not a more terrible audience in the world.' The bold Disraeli called it 'the most chilling and nerve-destroying audience in the world.' Then he may have heard the stories of famous failures. Lord North's son gave this account of his maiden effort:

I brought out two or three sentences, when a mist seemed to rise before my eyes. I then lost my recollection, and could see nothing but the Speaker's wig, which swelled and swelled and swelled till it covered the whole House. I then sank back on my seat and never attempted another speech, but quickly accepted the Chiltern Hundreds.[1]

Mr. Whiteside, the Irish Member, was also affected by the wig, and said that when he saw the Speaker's wig surrounded by blue flames he knew it was time to sit down.

Many new Members have had to sit down without saying a word, like Mr. Gibson Craig. 'He rose,' wrote Disraeli, 'stared like a stuck pig and said nothing. His friends cheered; he stammered; all cheered; then there was a dead and awful pause, and then he sat down, and that was his performance.' Addison, the famous essayist, failed, and made but one attempt to speak. Steele was howled down by the Tories with cries of 'The Tatler!' because he had made fun of them. 'He fancies,' they said, 'that because he can scribble he can address an assembly of gentlemen. Out upon him!' Parnell was painfully nervous and could only stammer out a few barely intelligible sentences. After Sheridan's 'maiden' a reporter said, 'You had much better have stuck to your former pursuits.' Mr. Gladstone's maiden speech was reported thus: 'Mr. Gladstone made a few remarks which were not audible in the Gallery.'

No wonder, then, that the New Boy is afraid; and no wonder the Old Boys advise him to wait. But I had come in determined to introduce a Divorce Bill (and others) in Private Members' time.

---

[1] A Member cannot resign his seat, but in the old days the acceptance of 'an office of profit under the Crown' legally vacated his seat, and the office of steward, or bailiff, of His Majesty's Three Chiltern Hundreds of Stoke, Desborough, and Burnham is nominally an office of profit under the Crown. In fact, no profit is attached to it, and when the next Member wants to get out the steward retires. It is no longer necessary for Members to resign when they accept real offices of profit, that is, become Ministers. Odd, but English.

The Prime Minister, Mr. Baldwin, had announced on the first day that the Government proposed to take all the time of the House till Christmas. No Bills but Government Bills could be introduced before the New Year. 'The Government consider,' he said, 'that as the House has met so soon after the General Election and so near to Christmas, it will be more convenient to Members, and will give them more time to think out suitable Bills, if we postpone the ballot till we meet in the New Year.'

This was not wildly unreasonable, maybe; but I chose to make of it a *casus belli*. My precious causes had languished so long that I was in the mood to object to the tiniest loss of time—no bad mood, perhaps, for a reformer. Ignoring a warning message from Speaker Fitzroy himself, and the urgent advice of my friend and counsellor, William Mabane, clutching an old copy of Mr. Holford Knight's Matrimonial Causes Bill, on the back of which I had scribbled some notes, I rose up, like one intent on suicide, and spoke as follows:

I rise with more than the usual trepidation because I know I am doing an unusual thing, and therefore I shall not ask the usual indulgence of this House. I rise with no moral hesitation whatever, on a point of principle, on a point of conscience. I am the Junior Burgess of the University of Oxford, the elected mouthpiece of innumerable clergymen; the trumpet—or second trumpet—of 20,000 bachelors of arts; and I have been sent here, I do believe at a very unusual election, by my constituents largely to stop, or try to stop, the kind of thinking that is behind this Motion. The Prime Minister, I understand, is taking away from us private Members what he says is only one Friday, and he has mentioned three reasons why that is good. First he says that he understands there is no objection among the Opposition Whips. In my comparative inexperience I wonder what that has to do with it in any way. Is it not a contradiction in terms that the Whips, who are the symbols and the officers of the machine, the slavery, the organization— whatever you like to call it—should be able to barter and give away the free time of private Members which, *ex hypothesi*, is not theirs to give? Secondly, the Prime Minister made what is, I suppose, the oldest excuse for the oldest offence. He says it is 'only a little one.' It is only one Friday. Well, it is true that there are fifty-two Fridays in the year, but how many Fridays are there in the year of the private Member? Last year there were none at all. This year I do not know if there will be four or five, six, seven, or eight, but at any rate whatever the figure is, one will be quite a high proportion of it. I understand it is not only a question of this particular Friday, but during this unspecified period we shall not be able even to have our private Bills printed, and even I know that that is a very formidable and important weapon in the armoury of one who tries to educate opinion.

Thirdly, the Prime Minister used what I thought was the most extraordinary reason of all when he said that this was being done for the benefit of the victims, because back-benchers and private Members, being uncivilized, backward, and unintelligent, had not had the time to prepare their contributions to the safety of the country and the legislation of the future. I seem to remember that that was the excuse put forward by Signor Mussolini to defend his descent upon the Ethiopians. I hope the Prime Minister will not think that all private Members are quite so deficient in imaginative and constructive power as that. At any rate, in answer to that point, let me tell him that I have in my hand a Bill which I am ready to introduce next Friday, or on the Friday after, or on all the Fridays, until it is passed into law; and I swear that it shall be passed before this Parliament is over.[2] (*Laughter.*) Hon. Members laugh. But I must remind them that all the serious politicians laughed when I disclosed my obscene designs upon my almost virgin University. They said that with my extraordinary opinions I ought to go to Hoxton, to the taverns, to the race-courses of our land, and hope perhaps to scramble together a discreditable vote or two, but that to go to Oxford, the citadel of Christian enlightenment and the stronghold of orthodoxy, a constituency with more parsons to the square vote than any other constituency besides—this was lunacy. However, I went on, and the walls of Jericho fell down. Therefore, I would ask hon. Members in the north-east corner of the House to consider again before they laugh at my intentions.

At all events, here is this Bill, and it is not a feeble little Bill. It is called the Matrimonial Causes Bill. It is a Bill to reform the indecent, hypocritical, cruel, and unjust marriage laws of this country. It is a Bill which carries out or is based upon the recommendations of the Majority Report of the Royal Commission which reported twenty-three years ago, and I am ready, as I say, to introduce it next Friday.

In your wise advice to us the other day, Mr. Speaker, you mentioned

[2]This impious vow, which makes me blush when I read it now, was fulfilled in one year and nine months.

the decline of public interest in the proceedings of this House. I was wondering then whether some part of that decline might not be due to the fact that so many high and great problems are discussed in the House which are not understood or understandable by the common people, and that simple human problems such as are dealt with in this Bill, and which the common man does think he understands, are so seldom mentioned here, and when they are mentioned are dismissed as frivolities.

In regard to the other point made by the Prime Minister, about Government time, I have been watching the proceedings of this House for many years with close attention, and I am very tired of hearing that the Government have no time to do this or that. With great respect to the Prime Minister, who quoted it, that seems to be a foolish observation of Mr. John Bright that you cannot drive twenty wagons through Temple Bar. One answer to that is that no man with any sense would attempt such a thing; and another answer is that if any man did desire to drive twenty wagons past this point or another, either he would widen Temple Bar or take some of the wagons round another way. The more I hear about Parliament having no time to do this, that, and the other, the more the Prime Minister and other defenders of liberty and democracy are in danger of driving me towards the camp of my old football captain, the hon. and learned Member for East Bristol (Sir S. Cripps). So many years go by, so many Sessions, so many Parliaments, and nothing is done about these things. If we mention them at General Election time, we are told that we must not trespass upon what are called the major issues. If we mention them after the election, we are told that since they were not mentioned at the election, the Government have no mandate for them. At the beginning of a Parliament the Government have no time to do anything; at the end of a Parliament they have no courage to do anything; and in the middle of a Parliament there is a change of Ministries. We are told that a party Government cannot do this thing, and it seems that a National Government cannot do it, though it would seem to me that if any Government could be fitted for such a task, it would be a National Government, which claims to represent all sections of society.

Indeed, the conclusion seems to be that there is no conceivable combination of political conditions in this great democracy which would ever be favourable for tackling or even discussing these problems; and now, when I come here pledged especially by that great constituency, the most remarkable and unlikely constituency to give this message, the first thing that happens is that the Prime Minister says, 'The first day on which you might move your little Bill is taken away by the Government.' This little Friday, which cannot mean very much to the Government, might mean a great deal to me and to the thousands of unhappy souls who might benefit from this Bill if it were passed into law. (*Laughter.*) I am surprised at hon. Members on the Labour benches laughing; they are always talking to us about the human problems, and I should like to ask them by what feat of political chemistry they can isolate the problem of the slums from the problems of the sexes, the problem of unhappy souls who may live in the grandest house in Park Lane but would still be wretched, because of these laws. How can they dare to say to me that the bricks and mortar questions of housing are important, but not those problems of the home which our marriage laws create?

It is a serious suggestion, that this little Friday should be given—since nobody else seems to have anything particular to do with it—not to me, but to the Commons, so that this great question, which goes not only to the social life of the people but to the roots of relations between Church and State, can be discussed fairly and squarely on Second Reading on the Floor of this House without Whips or trickery and talking out, and all the rest of it.

Sir, I have not come here to make jokes; nor yet to collect an agreeable background for a work of fiction, nor with any personal political ambitions. I have come here to raise my small voice for a large number of small people who think, rightly or wrongly, that a number of small but important things like this are, in the midst of our mighty cares, being thrust aside or wrongfully neglected. If I cannot make that voice effective I will go back to my books and plays. It was never my intention to start my Parliamentary career by dividing the House against His Majesty's Government, with which, on the whole, I am in sympathy. I am prepared to do it upon this point of principle, but apart from that, whatever may be said on the matter, and whatever may happen, I should like to say that I am proud indeed to be standing in this place among the faithful Commons of His Majesty the King.

I did not see any blue flames round the Speaker's wig. I do not think I saw anything much. But—beginner's impudence, no doubt —once I was away I felt more assured than I have ever felt since. Mr. Maxton, who had been warned of my wild intentions by Mr. Mabane, supported me, in terms which made my case sound thoroughly sensible, also Miss Eleanor Rathbone; and we two University Members went into the 'No' Lobby with the Independent Labour Party—'Ayes to the Right, 232; Noes, 5'—a very queer beginning for a representative of Oxford University.

Alone of the swells, Mr. Churchill sought out the naughty boy and complimented me on my 'composure and aplomb.' It was right, he said, for a young Member to take advantage of the chances of procedure to say what was in him. He finished with a characteristic chuckle: 'Call that a maiden speech? It was a brazen hussy of a speech. Never did such a painted lady of a speech parade itself before a modest Parliament.'

5. Good Boy

I was a good boy, then, I see, for some months, and sat quiet till 6 March 1936, duly studying the ways of the place. There was plenty to study in that full five years, which began with Abyssinia and finished with Poland, included the death of one King and the abdication of another. I suppose there are always more giants when one is young, but certainly there were more men I liked to listen to than there are to-day. We have very many good speakers, but only two to whom I would concede the title of 'orator'—Mr. Churchill and Mr. Bevan. Mr. Baldwin, in his homely rugged style a master of the House, could touch the heights now and then, like a farmer bursting into song. Mr. Neville Chamberlain, Chancellor of the Exchequer, was not an attractive speaker, but he had a mind like a chisel and a fine capacity for winding up an argument in short sharp effective sentences, with an admirable economy of words. Sir John Simon, a beacon of lucidity, was always fascinating for his clarity and calm. Sir Austen Chamberlain, in his top-hat,[1] was a sage and lovable voice from the Victorians. Josiah Wedgwood, Arnold Wilson, both a little mad, had

[1]The top-hat, by the way, was no mere affectation or challenge. It had the practical merit, he used to say, of protecting the eyes from the 'top-lighting' in the chamber.

the souls of poets and could move you. 'Geordie' Buchanan could stir the whole House with his tales of mean streets; and Jimmy Maxton, his leader, with his burning eyes and compelling voice, was a natural orator, if ever there was one. The women Members, too, I think, were a better vintage than the women of to-day. They wasted fewer words than the men, worked hard and fought like tigresses. Lady Astor, Mrs. Tate, made battling speeches with wit and fire. Miss Rathbone feared nothing and never gave up, though she had a sad knack of making the men laugh in the wrong place. On the subject of the official statistics concerning maternal and infant mortality, they tell me she said: 'Mr. Speaker, sir, we have ante-natal treatment and we have post-natal treatment, but still we have these appalling figures.' Megan Lloyd George (still there, I am glad to say) speaks with gentle and persuasive grace.

Opposite to Maxton, on the corner seat of the bench where I sat, was Mr. Churchill, still in the wilderness, but tramping on undaunted, undoubting, through the unfriendly sands. And over the other side, perched on the corner of the Front Opposition Bench, was the master orator—David Lloyd George. He was not all that he had been, they said, and what he said, the Smoking Room whispered, was often 'unsound' or 'naughty.' But he impressed me as the greatest 'performer' of all. Not even Mr. Churchill had the same technical and histrionic equipment, the musical voice, the range of tone, the thrilling whisper, the sudden crescendo, the dramatic pause, the rich variety of gesture.

And things were always happening in that Parliament to give the big guns cause for going off and the young men food for anxious study. The old boys used to say that we saw more in those five years than they had seen in fifteen. Three times we took the Oath to His Majesty. There was Mussolini—and 'Midsummer Madness.' We heard Sir Samuel Hoare make his sad resignation speech: we saw Mr. J. H. Thomas make his farewell bow at the Bar. There was Abyssinia, and there was Spain. There was Hitler steadily swelling and advancing, and Churchill trying to make Britain believe it. There was poor Sir Thomas Inskip as Minister for Co-ordination, and Churchill making that heroic series of speeches on Defence, full, not of phrases, but facts and figures. and heard with hardly a cheer from either side. There was Neville Chamberlain sadly renouncing his schemes for social reform and turning his mind and our money to armaments instead. There were the emotional days of Munich and the harrowing weeks that followed. There was rearmament and Prague, the pledge to Rumania and the pledge to Poland. One day in April 1939 Mr. Hore-Belisha moved his resolution for the introduction of peacetime conscription. On that day, by a queer chance, the Oxford Union were discussing a motion 'That this House is in favour of conscription.' Then the Senior Burgess for the University, I thought that on that subject I should hear what the young men had to say. So I 'paired' for the Government and went to Oxford, and heard the young men vote themselves into compulsory service by a big majority. A speech by a young guest called Randolph Churchill had much to do with the result.

And so to war.

Though I attended, rapt and wrung, the big debates on the big affairs, I seldom felt any itch to speak in them. There were quite enough men fighting for the Speaker's eye on these occasions. I was not quite so humble as Edward Gibbon, author of *The Decline and Fall*, who said: 'It is more tremendous than I imagined. The great speakers fill me with despair: the bad ones with terror,' and sat in his place for eight years without opening his mouth. But I like speaking so little—indeed, in the Commons I hate it—that I have never wanted to speak unless I thought there was something to be said or done which was not likely to be provided by anyone else, and that, in such a storehouse of knowledge and experience, might well keep a modest man silent for ever. I had come in with a limited armoury for a limited target and, rightly or wrongly, I would not increase the range.

And I was always busy enough preparing and pushing my own little Bills, which is no mean undertaking. I had no luck in the Private Members' Ballot (I never draw a horse), nor could I, that year, persuade any of the lucky ones to adopt my Marriage Bill (afterwards the Matrimonial Causes Act, 1937), much less my Betting and Bookmakers Bill, an even more alarming topic. But I could still introduce them, and get them printed, though not debated, and to have their names on the Order Paper was a beginning. When you have decided what your law is to be, and got it drafted, it must be examined and passed by the Public Bill Office, friendly but firm. I have often wondered how I got Number 3, the Public Refreshment Bill, 1936, past that barrier, for, though it perfectly expressed my aims and opinions, it must have seemed a little naughty. But here is a bit of it, solemnly printed on the grey-green paper:

A BILL TO

AMEND THE LAWS CONCERNING PUBLIC REFRESHMENT[2]

Whereas it appears that the laws concerning public refreshment are vexatious and unreasonable, and are not well fitted to the good sense of Englishmen and the conditions of the present time.

And whereas it is commonly accepted that England is now to be considered as a part of the continent of Europe, and should so conduct herself in all proper and peaceful affairs: and in this affair it is expedient that she should follow the good and civilized customs of France, which, by reason of the said laws, is now not possible.[3]

ADOPTION OF THE LAWS OF FRANCE

1. The laws of England concerning the provision of public refreshment, including the sale or supply of wine, beer, spirits and the like, shall be made, *mutatis mutandis,* the same as the laws of France.

I was pleased with myself for reviving the 'preamble,' a good old institution almost forgotten. Most Bills have now an 'Explanatory Memorandum,' but this is a very dull document, and must contain nothing 'argumentative.' In a preamble you can let yourself go. Look at the Suspension of the Habeas Corpus Act, 1803:

Whereas a treasonable and rebellious spirit of insurrection now unfortunately exists in Ireland . . .

That tells the Judges, and all who come after, what Parliament had in mind. Nowadays, as often as not, the Courts cannot guess.

'Members,' *The Spectator* said, 'were shocked by the terms of the Public Refreshment Bill.' Yet it only declared, in Parliamentary formula, what I had said so often in speeches and articles outside, that continental arrangements were civilized, and ours were not.

[2]Long title.   [3]Preamble.

At the Lyric Theatre, Hammersmith, where no drinks could be supplied after ten, by order of the Kensington Licensing Justices, the playwright had to construct or cut his second Act so that the interval came not later than nine-fifty. That could not happen in France. My Bill was a declaration of faith—and also of despair. For I saw no hope then of getting the Licensing Laws amended by normal means: and I see none now.

I have often wondered what would have happened if France had accepted Mr. Churchill's offer of common citizenship in 1940. Should we have followed my Bill and taken over the French arrangements? Or would poor France have had to observe our Licensing Laws?

By 1936 I had had so much practice in the preparation of Bills that I was moved to draft a Bill in verse. I did not present it at the Table.

THE SPRING (ARRANGEMENTS) BILL

Whereas in every lawn and bed the plucky crocus lifts his head, and to and fro sweet song-birds go, the names of which we do not know:

Whereas the woods no more are dumb, the Boat Race and the Budget come, the Briton swells his manly chest, his mate, as eager, scrubs the nest, and Spring, with light but lavish hand, is spreading madness o'er the land:

It is expedient—but in rhyme—to legislate for such a time:

Be it enacted, therefore, by our King with Lords and Commons in a fairy ring assembled joyously at Westminster (or any other place that they prefer):

PROVISION FOR SEASON CALLED SPRING

1. (i) It shall be lawful everywhere for citizens to walk on air, to hang their hats upon the trees and wander hatless, if they please: and notwithstanding any cracked provision in a previous Act to give a constable a kiss is not felonious after this.

(ii) All citizens who choose to ride on taxi-tops and not inside: and those who do not use their votes because they're busy painting boats: and any miscreant who hums, instead of doing dismal sums: whoever does a silly thing need only answer ' 'Tis the Spring': and this shall be a good defence in any court with any sense:

Provided that, in late July, this Act, of course, does not apply.

FINANCIAL PROVISIONS

2. *If any person feels he must get out of London* now *or bust, because the Spring is in his bones, but he must work for Mr. Jones, it shall be lawful for the same to give the Treasury his name, and say 'Upon sufficient grounds I want about a hundred pounds': and there shall not be any fuss concerning sums expended thus.*

REPEAL OF REDUNDANT STATUTES

3. Subsection (i) of Section Four of any Act that seems a bore, and all the Acts concerning beer, and every Act that is not clear (always excepting Schedule A), shall be repealed and thrown away.

HOUSE OF COMMONS—REFORM OF PROCEDURE—MUSIC, ETC.

4. (i) There shall be banks of maidenhair arranged about the Speaker's Chair: and roses white and roses red shall hang above the Speaker's head: like some tremendous window-box, the Galleries be gay with phlox: and goldfish, lovely but aloof, shall swim above the glassy roof.

(ii) From now until the First of June all speeches shall be sung (in tune). The Speaker shall determine what hon. Members are in tune, or not.

(iii) When in Committee of Supply the House may hum (but not too high). The Clerk-Assistant-at-the-Table shall choose the key (if he is able).

(iv) A band shall nearly always play (not on the first Allotted Day) behind the Speaker's Chair at three and on the Terrace after tea.

SAVING FOR COMMITTEES

5. On any day in May or June Committees shall adjourn quite soon: Provided, if the cuckoo call, Committees shall not sit at all.

SITTINGS OF THE UPPER HOUSE

6. The House of Lords shall never sit on sunny days till after Whit: and they shall rise, if they have met, when it is foggy, fine or wet.

TERMINATION OF OFFICIAL REPORT

7. (i) Except as hereinafter hinted, *Hansard* shall not again be printed, and, save as in this Act is learned, all previous *Hansards* shall be burned.

(ii) It is a pity, history teaches, to make reports of people's speeches, and afterwards to be unkind, simply because they change their mind.

It is a most disgusting thing to make such comments in the Spring: so, as from when this Act is passed, that day's Report shall be the last.

(iii) And, as respects exceptions, see Subheading (*a*) of Schedule B.

POWERS AND DUTIES OF DEPARTMENTS

8. (i) The Secretary of State for Home Affairs shall now proceed to Rome, to Moscow, Washington, Cathay, or anywhere that's far away, and not return to English skies until the Speaker certifies that Spring has ceased to be a fact under the Moss (Collection) Act.

(ii) Meanwhile o'er all his grim domain a lovely golden girl shall reign: and this delicious creature shall give cosmic parties in the Mall (*paying the bills, if she is dunned, from the Consolidated Fund*). The Civil Service, hand in hand, shall dance in masses down the Strand: and all the Cabinet shall wear wild dandelions in their hair.

(iii) It shall be deemed that everyone has come into the world for fun. This shall be printed on the wall of every office in Whitehall.

PENALTIES FOR CERTAIN EXPRESSIONS

9. (i) No kind of crisis shall excuse a man exploring avenues: no lesser doom does he deserve when he is straining every nerve: and special punishment is earned by those who leave no stone unturned.

(ii) The penalty for each offence shall be elastic but immense.

(iii) A pension shall reward the man who modestly does all he can.

INTERPRETATION

10. (i) The greatest care has been employed to make this measure null and void: not one expression in this Act means anything it means in fact.

(ii) Examples we decline to give: the lawyers, after all, must live.

APPLICATION

11. This Act applies and shall be good where anybody thinks it should:

Provided that, if strong objection should be expressed to any Section, that Section shall not have effect except for those who don't object.

SCHEDULE B (*a*)

Any speech, motion, question, amendment or interruption by
A. P. H.

6. The Torture Chamber

I suppose there are some folk who enjoy speaking in the House of Commons, and rise without a doubt or tremor. It is impossible to tell, for everyone must leap to his feet with the same alacrity if he is to 'catch the eye,' even though he feels like Mr. John Bright: 'I suppose I ought to be ashamed of myself, but the fact is I never rise in the House without a trembling at the knees and a secret wish that somebody else would catch the Speaker's eye and enable me to sit down again.' John Bright had no cause to be ashamed of himself, for the evidence is plentiful that the House of Commons has a formidable quality all its own.

Though the 'maiden' be safely passed, the ghost is not laid. Not long before he died, Sir Austen Chamberlain, to whom the whole House listened with respect, said to me: 'I never rise in the House without a sinking feeling in the pit of my stomach.' He showed me the single sheet of notepaper on which were the 'notes' for a delightful speech he had just delivered. Something, I forget what, was written in large capitals across the middle. I said, 'But you didn't say anything about that, sir?' 'No,' said the Elder Statesman sadly, 'It was the one thing I wanted to say. So I wrote it large like that. But you know how it is. I forgot.'

What hope, then, for the smaller fry? I would not, myself, go quite as far as John Bright; for, once I have stood up, I am eager to be 'called' soon and get it over. But I still dislike the whole business as much as ever.

I have perhaps had more than my fair share of attention and laughter. I can remember a few occasions when I seemed to have the House really with me and felt I was doing pretty well, and a very few when I did almost 'enjoy myself,' as kind friends said afterwards. But nearly always I have had the same feeling of unease and unreality. I am thinking:

Is this really me standing up here and talking this nonsense? Must I go on with it? Why don't I sit down? Am I dropping my voice? Can they hear me in the Gallery? I am not finishing my sentences well. I have left out one of the main things I meant to say, but it is too late to go back now. What are they muttering about on the Front Bench? How am I going to end? Is this really me?

I am two persons, one the dashing centre-forward, and the other a most discontented manager on the side-line.

There is, of course, almost every possible ingredient of unease in that place. An after-dinner speaker or a platform speaker may reasonably expect to have the attention of most of his audience. They are in front of him, and they cannot easily get away. He has a table, or desk, for his notes and papers. Even the 'front-bencher' commands the length of the House and can use the Dispatch Box for his notes and papers—and thumping fist, if necessary. He has a fort; he has a field of fire. The back-bencher, clutching his notes, is like a lonely man standing up in the middle of a public meeting. His audience is all round him, some in front, some behind, some above him, some below—and a great many high up in galleries in a building not highly meritorious for 'acoustics.' An interruption, a sneer, an ironical laugh may hit him from any quarter. And, if he rounds upon the interrupter to the south-west, or the sneerer to the east, he may be reminded that he must address his remarks to the Chair, which lies north. More, unless he is very good, or fairly important—and even if he is—his audience is moving and changing all the time. Members, good friends, it may be, receive urgent telephone messages or 'green cards,' bow to the Speaker, and march out as he approaches his principal, or only, joke. The Minister whom he hopes to convert, or intends to shatter with a deadly jest, is relieved by another Minister and goes out for a cup of tea just before the unanswerable argument or the crushing quip is reached. The Front Opposition Bench, in the same way, are constantly coming and going. There is a procession of Members to the Table, putting down Questions and getting advice from the Clerks. Others go up to the Speaker and engage him in conversation. There is movement everywhere. It is like making a speech in a beehive. And those who remain motionless are not necessarily attentive, or even silent. Ministers and Whips must confer upon the course of the debate, check facts and figures, read documents about something quite different. A Member will come in with a resolution or an amendment to another Bill, to which he is seeking signatures. He goes from friend to friend, and there is a whispered colloquy with each. All this is quite legitimate. Then there will be a few couples having private conversations about their holiday plans, about the party meeting, about the latest scandal, or the by-election, or the pretty girl in the Speaker's Gallery. Behind the orator may be one of those Members who have the habit of muttering a running commentary—'Quite right, too' 'Not with this Government' 'They're *afraid*'—quite friendly, maybe, but maddening. Then there are the professional interrupters, who, if they do not like the speaker or the speech, make it their business to snap at him from time to time—'Nonsense!' 'Rubbish!' 'What about 1926?' 'All very well for you!' and so on. But these may be an advantage to the speaker, since they revive the languishing interest of others. Then there is the formal interruption. No two Members may be on their feet at the same time, but at any moment a Member, half rising, with his rump just airborne, may say: 'May I——' or 'If I may——' The speaker is not bound to 'give way' and sit down—it is a matter of courtesy, but it is generally best, and it is generally done. Again, if he has a telling answer to the interjection, it may assist him. At least it shows that someone is awake and listening. But the interjection, question, or comment may well be devastating, knocking or seeming to knock his whole case from under him. And if he has not got a good answer, though he completes the course with a confident air and does a jaunty jump or two, he will be uneasily aware that he knocked down the big fence in the middle. Here is, perhaps, the fundamental cause of alarm. Whatever jokes may be made about it, the House of Commons is a formidable body, drawn from every class and corner. They may not all be philosophers or senior wranglers, which is just as well, but you could mention hardly any subject, they say, without some Member shyly coming forward and confessing that he knows all about it, whether it is the Battle of Waterloo, the keeping of hens, the geography of Malaya, or the running of a coal-mine. For many years you may have maintained, without much contradiction (in clubs and pubs) that all cows have five legs. But when you rise to make the same assertion in the House of Commons you have to recognize that there are 638 other Members, each of whom may rise, politely or not, to say that he knows more about cows than you do.

The easy answer to all this is that a man should not get up at all unless he is sure of his subject and can speak so well as to command attention. That is a little too easy. The beehive is a tyrant: it has the shifting incalculable moods of a tyrant, and is seldom in the same mood two days running. You may catch it in a sunny mood at tea-time, half asleep at dinner-time, alive but angry an hour or two later. It can be beautifully kind or stupidly cruel. It can make the best man look silly, and the greatest man afraid. Any man, after taking care, can assure himself that he has a good cause, and a pretty good speech. But rare, I swear, is the man who says to himself as the Speaker 'calls' him: 'I am going to be good to-day'—even if he was good last time. Hence those sinking feelings in the pit of the stomach. Mr. Lloyd George, I believe, was nervous to the last.

So are many good actors. But a much heavier strain is on the speaker. He is his own author, actor, producer, and stage-manager. He must provide the material as well as deliver it. He may have to rewrite his part during the performance, and, worst of all, if a back-bencher, he is never quite sure that there will be a performance, and, if so, when. The front-bench fellow, who knows that he is going to open a debate or lead the opposition, can have his oration ready typed, and nowadays, though it is against the rules, is generally

permitted to read the bulk of it. The back-bencher must endure
the agonies of 'bumping.'[1] You wonder sometimes why your Member took no part in the big debate on the Better World. You do
not know how hard he tried. Indeed, he may have played quite a
fine part without your knowing it, for he 'got in' late in the day and
was one of the 'also spokes.' Certainly, for a day or two he worked
hard at an oration, digging up from here and there hard facts and
telling figures and damaging quotations, with, of course, some sting-
ing phrases of his own and a peroration fit to shake the Government
and wake up England.

All this is a great labour, whatever the Member's method. Mr.
Churchill, they say, dictates the first versions of his great speeches,
but what a time even that must take! Some humbler folk, like
myself, are incapable of dictation: that is, being writers first and
speakers afterwards, perhaps, we more surely find the satisfying
phrase and sequence in the act of writing.

At first I used to write out every word of a speech and have it
typed—not for reading but for remembrance. To get good phrasing
and a lucid line—unless you are a Churchill or a King's Counsel—
I still think this is best, though now I much resent the expense of
time and trouble. After that, if I may advise the beginner, it is a
good thing to write the heads of the argument, with any choice
quotations or figures, on the back page, or a blank page, of the
Bill, White Paper, or what-not. It is natural and proper to see a
Member flourishing the Bill which is under discussion, and—who
knows?—he may have jotted down those brilliant arguments during
the debate. I find myself often repelled by the other method—by
the Member who has an evident bundle of notes like a pack of
cards. Sometimes, as each little page is done with, he puts it down
on the bench beside him. Sometimes they are turned over like the
pages of an almanac. Either way, unless the speaker is doing very
well, he may have some of his hearers gazing with morbid interest
at his notes and trying to calculate how much is left. He may even
hear men mutter barbarously: 'Only six pages to go, I *think*.' There
are, of course, some enviable old hands who can get up and make

[1]Jumping up (and sitting down again) in vain attempts to 'catch the Speaker's eye.'

a considerable speech with no notes at all, and, for all one knows, no preparation. But these, naturally, are not so well phrased as they might be; and, more important, they are often longer than they should be. For one thing, the unprepared one has not thought how he is going to end, and tends to wander about in search of the exit. If you prepare nothing else, my boy, be sure that you know how you are going to end.

Well, in goes your Member, ready, though maybe reluctant, for the fray. For my part, on that morning I am in a nervous fret on the Underground; my involuntary wink asserts itself, and young women shrink from me in horror or slay me with virtuous stares. I go out to lunch somewhere and am chatty and gay about something quite different, but at the back of my mind I am wondering about, say, the last bit of this confounded speech. Is it too fanciful? Is it too bold? Is it even right? I thought of it last night after a pretty good dinner, and that is sometimes a mistake. Is it necessary to speak at all? Have I really got anything to say that will not be equally well said by somebody else? At that point, I am glad to say, conceit, or confidence, prevails, and the answer is a fairly resolute yes. Sometimes I sit at the back of a chemist's in the Strand—my old friend Heppell's—take a nerve tonic, and go over the notes again. Yes, it all seems pretty clear; on the other hand, it now seems painfully obvious, and hardly worth saying. At the House, perhaps, I have a fortifying Scotch, at an hour when a Scotch would never enter my mind if I were not about to save the State with a speech. The back-bencher must be in his place when the debate on the Bill begins, but there is small chance of his going into action for two or three hours. The Minister, whose opening is delayed, perhaps, till three forty-five, takes a leisurely forty minutes, and the front-bencher on the other side is nearly as long. When he sits down it is five o'clock and most of the House goes out to tea, which is always hard on the Liberal spokesman, who is next. Your Member, Mr. Smith, wishes very much that he could go out with the other happy Members and have a cup of tea. But that would endanger his chance of being 'called' by the Speaker, so he must sit and listen to this dreary Liberal (all other speakers are dreary when you are waiting to speak yourself). But it will soon be time for Mr. Smith to start 'bumping.' He is, by the way, 'agin' the Government, and he has thought of a rocket of a retort to the Minister. If he listens to the Liberal with any attention, it is only for fear that the Liberal will fire off the rocket first. But he does not, and Mr. Smith writes down the rocket on his notes, carefully choosing his words. The Liberal sits down, and seventeen Members, in all parts of the Chamber, spring to their feet and gaze, like seventeen statues, at the Speaker. Mr. Smith knows well that the next Member called, according to custom, will be on the other side of the House, but there is just a chance that the Speaker, with a corner of that roving eye, will note that he is in the market. The benign eye roves a little and settles. 'Mr. Thompson,' says the Speaker, and sixteen rumps return to their moorings. Mr. Smith must now pay attention to Mr. Thompson and try to find something to say about his speech, however dreary. But who is Mr. Thompson? He remembers the face, dimly, but has never heard him speak. 'What's his constituency?' he whispers. His neighbour finds a *Dod's Parliamentary Companion* and tells him there are four Thompsons. Suddenly Mr. Thompson gives him a clue, by speaking of his father. Of course, this must be the son of old *Charles* Thompson, who sat in the last Parliament! Mr. Smith devises a graceful opening: 'I am sure that the father of the hon. Member, whom many of us remember with respect, would have been delighted by the style and manner of the speech which we have just heard, though he might, I think, have been shocked by some of the substance.' After that, he will turn on the Minister, still sitting there smugly, and discharge the rocket. But, unhappily, when Mr. Smith leaps up again, 'Mr. Robinson' is called behind him. Mr. Robinson makes several of his own points, but not, Mr. Smith thinks, very well. There are interruptions: some of the case does not seem so strong as it did, and Mr. Smith considers how to amend his speech. Mr. Robinson is dull, too, and the House gets thinner still. Even the Minister has gone out, so now the rocket is not much good. But he is still fairly full of fight. The only thing is, he must go to the lavatory. Now is the time, while his own side is speaking, and he scuttles out like a guilty schoolboy. It is now six-fifteen, and in the corridor he meets merry friends who have no intention of speaking, and they invite him to a drink in the Smoking Room. He says no, wondering why, and hurries back to the torture chamber. Robinson sits down at last, and a 'maiden speaker' is called on the other side. Now all the 'bumpers' (and there are still about seventeen, for some late-comers have joined in—curse them!) are thinking very hard; for special compliments must be paid by him who follows a maiden speech, and it may be any one of the seventeen. Who is this fellow? What is his constituency? Was he in the war? And what, exactly, is he trying to say? Mr. Smith composes in his mind a graceful tribute (the tribute to Mr. Thompson and his father is now long out of date; indeed, Mr. Thompson is no longer there). 'I have heard a good many maiden speeches in my time, but I can sincerely say . . . modest and amusing . . . long be with us . . . delight and instruct us.' Ready with all this—and the rocket too, for the Minister has returned from his brief tea—Mr. Smith leaps up with the old agility and new hope. The Speaker has been relieved; the Deputy-Speaker is rather a friend of his, and, though, of course, no friendship could influence the impartial Chair, at the last 'bump,' Mr. Smith fancied, the eye did notice him. Now the Deputy-Speaker looks straight at him, looks straight through him, and calls 'Sir Henry Quantock.' Sir Henry has not, like Mr. Smith, been 'bumping' all the afternoon; but he is a Privy Councillor, and, as such, by an ancient privilege, is called at once. Mr. Smith 'resumes his seat,' for the first time with some sinking of the spirit. It is now six thirty-five. The Privy Councillor is sure to talk till seven. Members will be thinking of dinner and the House will be thinner than ever. At that hour he will have to be good indeed to get any mention in the papers; and now he does not feel so good. He is no longer nervous: he is bored, frustrated, and weary. He has almost ceased to care about the Better World, and he is no longer so sure that a speech from him (which few will read) will help to bring it about. It would be so much simpler to write to *The Times*. His mouth is dry. He would like a drink; he would like to dine. The temptation is to go off to the Smoking Room and let the Better World look after itself. Fortified by a little dinner, says a tempting voice, he can come back, perhaps, and 'get in' before the big guns on the

Front Benches wind up the debate. But he knows very well that the time will be short, and those who go on 'bumping' through the dinner hour will rightly have the better chance. And now the Privy Councillor is saying something supremely absurd. Mr. Smith has thought of a smashing retort, and is hot for battle again. But after the Privy Councillor, who has held a pretty good House, there is an exodus. Mr. Brown is called on the other side, a speaker so dull and halting that, even if it were not the dinner hour, it would be an act of heroism to remain. In fact, as Mr. Smith looks round the scattered audience which he still hopes to address, he can count only sixteen Members. Six of these are on duty on the Front Benches, and the other ten are waiting to speak. It is like the end of a debate at the Oxford Union.

Here, by the way, is one affair in which 'there's a lot to be said for the Lords.' The House of Lords do not pretend that meals do not matter. If it is necessary to work after dinner they quietly adjourn for dinner, and at an agreed hour quietly return again. The Commons do take note of luncheon and dinner by forbidding a 'count' to be taken during meals, but the House inhumanly continues its business, which may seem highly industrious and efficient, but means too often a bore addressing a desert and is hard on both.

Now, the story of Mr. Smith might end in several ways. He may, if the debate closes at ten, sit it out till the end; and when, exhausted, starved, but resigned, he leaves the Chamber at last, the dinner service is over. This is nothing. It has happened a thousand times. Many men, in my short experience, have 'bumped' through a two-day—and even three-day—debate, and never 'got in.' What drives a man so far I cannot tell—is it noble devotion to duty or a kind of conceit? Either way, I cannot imagine myself so keen to make a speech as that. I have been fortunate, and have not often 'bumped' in vain: yet I have seldom persisted much after seven-thirty. But I know how Mr. Smith feels. If he gives up, there will be lingering regret—he has failed himself and the nation —though reason may assure him that it matters nothing if he speaks or not. So let us suppose that he is called at last at eight, after sitting there for four and a half hours. Once on his feet, he is glad that he stuck it out. There is a steady trickle of Members returning from dinner and, if he has a good name or is known as an authority on the Better World, the trickle may become a stream. He has, of course, a smashing retort for Mr. Tomkins, who has just sat down. All previous smashing retorts have been long since abandoned, since the Members for whom they were intended are either eating or correcting their speeches upstairs, and nobody now remembers anything they said. But there is the Minister, who at least has had a hurried dinner, sitting ready for his rocket. Members, having dined, are a little mellower and laugh more easily. Unfortunately, just as the cue for rocket approaches, the Minister is called out for a conference behind the Speaker's Chair, but Mr. Smith fires it off just the same. The speech—though a mere ghost now of the original —goes pretty well: there are a few mild ' 'Ear, 'ear's' (described as 'Cheers' in the papers) at the end, a friend taps Mr. Smith on the shoulder and says 'Jolly good.' He is now exhausted but elated. He has had the baby. He was right, he feels, to suppose that he had something special to say and to insist on saying it. He has already started to remember the things he forgot to say; but he has done his best for the Better World, and he finds it very difficult to pay proper attention to Mr. Rogers, who now has the floor. Indeed, he is in such a state that he missed the graceful compliment (or smashing retort) with which Mr. Rogers began. His one thought now is to get out of the hateful Chamber as soon as he decently can. A rule of etiquette demands that he shall stop in his place during at least the two speeches which follow his own. But hardly has he sat down when someone passes to him a long envelope from the Official Reporter: 'Will Mr. Smith be so good as to come up to the Official Reporter's room and correct his speech, all of which was not clearly audible in the Gallery?' 'Will Mr. Smith send up his notes, and the quotation from Dibdin?' This is very tiresome, for Mr. Smith was under the impression that he had shouted his speech, and should have been audible to all, even in that great barn the House of Lords.[2] His 'notes' are not intelligible to anyone else, and, indeed, he did not stick to them. He will have to go up and do the corrections himself—a long and odious business. But now he is in a dilemma—or rather two. Etiquette demands that

[2]Where the Commons sat after the bombing of their Chamber.

a Member who has spoken be in his place during the winding-up
speeches—or, at least, during the Ministerial reply. Etiquette also
demands that he listen to the dreary Mr. Rogers and the speech
that follows. But after that the first winding-up speech will probably begin. The Official Reporter demands him upstairs, and practical wisdom demands that he go as soon as possible, for by the end
of the debate his sheets may have gone to press. His body demands
a drink and some dinner. It is quite impossible for all these demands to be met. Mr. Rogers is followed by Mr. Rolls: and then,
perhaps, Mr. Smith slips out, holding ostentatiously, as he bows to
the Chair, his long envelope from the Official Reporter. He has
broken the first rule, and there is the risk that Mr. Rolls is now
saying in contemptuous tones: 'I am sorry the honourable Member
is not in his place, as I wished to point out to him that his figures
are wrong and his arguments fallacious.' But it cannot be helped.
Somebody will be saying the same about Mr. Rolls very soon. It is
now nearly nine, and it is clear that Mr. Smith must abandon hope
of dinner. But, after the long ordeal, he must have some refreshment,
and, if he has my bad habits, he probably orders a double Scotch,
and, a slave to duty still, consumes it far too fast. He hurries to the
lift, and up to the Official Reporter's room, high up over the river,
to 'correct his speech.'

This 'returning to our vomit,' as some of us describe it, after all
the strain of the day, is a hideous task, even if there is plenty of
time. We don't hurry to the lift, mark you, to correct our remarks
for the Press. The poor Pressmen will report, if they report us at
all, what they caught in the Gallery, without any further assistance
from us. We rush upstairs to correct the 'Official Reporter,' *alias
Hansard,* the well-printed little record of the Parliamentary proceedings of to-day, which will miraculously appear on my breakfast-
table to-morrow (I live in London). Things are more difficult
now, but before the war I have heard a speech in the House at
11 P.M. or later, and read it in *Hansard* at eight next day, at home.
I do not know whether some fairy prints and binds and delivers it,
but it is one of the wonders of publication. It is still a small volume
of about fifty pages and 75,000 words: it still records every word
of our proceedings from two-thirty to ten-thirty, and the highest

accuracy is demanded in conditions where the Recording Angel himself might well refuse duty. There is a staff of eighteen reporters. Each man takes a 'turn' in the Gallery of ten minutes, and ten minutes must be quite enough. In a speech of nine minutes one quiet day, I see, I said 1,400 words. But that ten minutes may be a wild, riotous ten minutes, full of interruptions or interjections from all corners of the House, and the reporter must do his best to identify each interjector, besides recording what he said. Or it may be ten minutes of complex argument on a 'point of order,' with many quiet rulings and remarks from the Speaker, who is not even visible to the reporter. Mr. Smith, who has not the faintest notion who Mr. Rogers is or what is his constituency, can escape with 'the honourable Member opposite,' or some such phrase. But the reporter far aloft has to read Mr. Smith's thoughts, decide what Member Mr. Smith is talking about, and turn it into 'the hon. Member for Dreary Boroughs (Mr. Rogers).' Some Members speak very fast, some very low; some are near a microphone, some not; some have their backs to the reporter; some fire off a mass of figures and quotations, and they must be precisely right, if nothing else is. What a job! Relieved after ten minutes, he dictates what he has got onto the typewriter. The typescript is revised by two sub-editors. After five-thirty the corrected sheets are sent to the printers in Drury Lane every half-hour. No 'proofs' are seen by the editor or his staff; once the typed sheets leave him he has no further control.

All the time they are sending signals of distress downstairs. What exactly was Mr. Brown's interjection? What was Mr. Thompson's Latin quotation? Could we have the Minister's notes? And, in a desperate case, will Mr. Smith 'come up' himself?

Mr. Smith, not having a Parliamentary private secretary, as Ministers have, does well to go up himself. For, wizards though they be, things are often too much for the reporting staff, and error does creep in, sometimes comes roaring in. In one speech I made several references to the Taxes on Knowledge of the nineteenth century. When I obeyed the summons upstairs I found that in every case they had got 'the Taxes on Norwich.' I blame no one; but I should have blamed myself severely if I had not taken the trouble to go up and correct.

Still, after a day of agitation and 'bumping,' it is a wearisome finale, especially if the speech is a long one and, like Mr. Smith, you are hungry and short of time. In the quiet room over the river, where the assistant editor toils for ever, Mr. Smith finds two or three other Members busy at the grey-green foolscap sheets. Perhaps he has just had an angry interrupting match with one of them, but now there are sympathetic grins; and later they may compare notes about the exact terms of offence they used about each other, in order to get the record right. Mr. Smith is appalled by the pile of sheets they lay before him. Did he really say all that? And, sick of the wretched oration as he is, must he really plough through it again? The report is in a sort of semi-shorthand—'t' for that, 'w' for which, and so on, which makes the finest phrase look pretty silly and the whole affair unreal. Mr. Smith alternately marvels at the brilliance of the reporters and curses their incompetence or inattention. Over wide acres of the speech they have got every word right. Then suddenly—perhaps Mr. Smith has dropped his voice, or there have been interruptions and he has turned his head away—there are two or three sentences which make utter nonsense, and Mr. Smith must wearily reconstruct it. Sometimes the poor reporter has given up and there is a large hiatus which Mr. Smith must fill, recalling sometimes not only his own words but those of the other fellow. This is where the man at the next table comes in: 'Did you say I was a "dismal Jimmie" or a "dismal Willie"?' 'Dismal Jimmie, old chap. Sorry.' All the time, as he scratches and scribbles, Mr. Smith is remembering the fine things he intended to say, but forgot. It is a fierce temptation to pop them in now. But the rules are strict. Mr. Smith may correct his grammar, or the Official Reporter's grammar; he may weld a split infinitive or bring back to earth a *nominativus pendens*. But he may neither insert the brilliant jest which he did not utter, nor expunge the errors of tact and taste which he did. All he can do is to make his *faux pas* fairly grammatical.

And Mr. Smith, remember, is working against time. There is no 'indicator' up there to show who is speaking, but, by the clock, the Minister should be 'up' any minute now. He tries to remember exactly what he said in his peroration, finishes his unhappy duty, and dashes down to the door of the Smoking Room. The indicator shows that the Minister rose three minutes ago. But he is empty and exhausted and surely he deserves at least a quick whisky. He gulps it down, and almost runs to the Chamber. Half-way there, he meets a Member coming away, who says shortly: 'The Minister's up. He was talking about you.' Oh, dear, he has done the wrong thing again!

At last the debate, the division, is over, and Mr. Smith can relax. Others are not relaxing. Another debate has begun and earnest men are arguing about something new—some of them, indeed, may have taken part in the debate on the Better World. But Mr. Smith has had enough. It will be a long time, he feels, before he suffers in the Torture Chamber again. If he is wise, he will now go to the Tea Room and have some tea and a sausage. But he is not wise. His friends will be in the Smoking Room. They congratulate him upon his speech, and stand him a drink; they tell old Parliamentary tales and he stands them a drink. They talk very amusingly, life is fine, and he has too many whiskies. In the morning he wakes with a headache. This, he thinks, is rather hard, for it is directly due to his efforts for the Better World. If he had left the Better World alone he would have had a quiet dinner at the proper time and would now be quite well. But there it is. He opens his *Times,* to see what the world thinks of his effort for the Better World, and he reads 'There also spoke Mr. Rogers, Mr. Thompson, Mr. Smith, Mr. Brown. . . .'

Most Members, you may say, have a stronger nervous system than mine: in which case all that I have said may be of small account. I cannot tell, nor can you. But I strongly suspect that the Mr. Smiths are numerous. At all events, when you say, 'I see our Member made a speech yesterday' (as you would say, 'I see our Member played a round of golf'), I beg you to reflect that your Member may have suffered all the agonies of Mr. Smith, and more. And if you say, 'I wonder our Member did *not* speak yesterday,' remember again the sad story of Mr. Smith, and forgive him. The sweating miner, I am sure, imagines his Member enjoying himself 'jawing away' in Parliament. It would be insincere to say that I would rather work in a mine than speak in the House of Commons. But I am sure that the miner enters the cage with a much lighter heart than I enter the Chamber on a speech-day; and if I have deserved any credit on this earth at all it is because I have driven myself so often to rise up and expose myself in that alarming place.

But it is all 'part of the game,' and I hope I have said nothing to deter any young man from standing or speaking. The ordeal by 'bumping' is suffered only in Second Reading and similar debates. When 'the rule is suspended'—that is, there is no time-limit—as in financial debates, the back-bencher can be sure of having his say in the end. And in Committee he can be sure of speaking over and over again if he likes. For here the Minister has to get his Bill through, clause by clause and amendment by amendment; and he cannot get on to Clause 2 while any Member has anything to say about Clause 1. Moreover, in theory, he can speak on the same amendment any number of times. Here the pertinacious back-bencher can say to the lordly front-benchers: 'We are the masters now.' It is true that recent guillotine arrangements have somewhat curtailed these delightful liberties, but Committee still remains the best opportunity for the beginner to practise the black arts of debate.

7. Private Fridays

On a Private[1] Members' Friday in March 1936 a 'serious' attempt to reform the Licensing Laws was made, but it had no more fortune than mine.

Private Members' Fridays were often good fun, sometimes exciting, and always instructive; and I count it as a major crime of Mr. Herbert Morrison and his obedient followers that they cut these days out of the 1945 Parliament entirely.[2] He and those of his opinion have said that the time was often wasted, because they did not always end in an addition to the Statute Book. I prefer the saying of my dear old friend, the late E. V. Lucas: 'Nothing is wasted.' Though every Bill put down on a Friday was refused a Second Reading, though some were 'talked out' and others 'counted out,' the result was more than an arithmetical zero. New ideas had been planted and perhaps struck root; perhaps, if they were bad ones, were publicly stamped upon and died. As I reminded the new Labour Members in that Parliament, one Samuel Plimsoll began his great career by introducing, *unsuccessfully,* a Private Member's Bill. How often, before I came upon the scene, had the patient Mr. Hol-

[1]'Unofficial Member' was the old expression, and is still the correct one. 'Private Members' are never mentioned in Erskine May.

[2]I apologize. In 1949 they were partially restored.

ford Knight brought in his Matrimonial Causes Bill in vain? I know not. But who shall say the time and toil were wasted? To judge such activities by the successes only is a gross material error. The street-lamp is not considered wasteful because it beams upon a fog.

Then, too, a private Member could boldly grasp such nettlesome topics as all Governments are afraid to touch—though sometimes, privately, they may sympathize when the fools rush in. Divorce—Drink—Betting—are good examples.

Not every private Member was painfully pregnant with Bills, like myself. Many were embarrassed and alarmed when they drew a high place in the ballot, and went round muttering 'What on earth am I to legislate about?' These victims of good fortune would be set upon by eager persons like me and invited to adopt our Bills. If they did not like our Bills, or shrank from such responsibility, or were warned off by their own Whips (as they sometimes were), the Whips as a rule had some small non-contentious measure—concerning taxicabs or ice-cream vendors—up their sleeves. In either case it was an education for the unofficial Member. He must meet and deal with interested parties outside, some of whom will say that he is rashly going too far and others that he is feebly surrendering the battle before he begins. He must get the thing drafted in terms that he can explain and others understand; and, at this task, he will begin to find a warmer feeling for Ministers and Government draftsmen.

Then he must enlist and organize his 'backers.' They must be ready for all the artful and entertaining stratagems of a Private Members' Friday. Generally, there would be three Bills down for Second Reading. Only two of these, as a rule, had any chance of being discussed for sufficient time to justify a vote upon them; and if the first Bill had the seeds of serious contention it would take the whole day (that is, from 11 A.M. to 4 P.M.). But sometimes Bill 1, though through the luck of the ballot it had first place, might be a trivial measure; Bill 2 small and inoffensive also; and Bill 3 more important but unpopular. It was considered 'cranky,' perhaps, or premature; a Government committee might be sitting on the same subject, or the Government had promised to bring in a Bill next year; perhaps the party in power wanted the credit of such a reform. Members, though against the Bill, would not, because of its subject matter, want to incur the odium of voting against it—a natural and proper state of mind, on such a subject, for example, as Holidays with Pay. The enemies of Bill 3, if numerous enough, could halt it, or keep it back, in two or three ways. They could let the inoffensive Bill 1 go through before lunch, and then about lunch-time arrange for the House to be counted out. Everyone except those interested in Bill 2 would leave the Chamber. Someone would rise and say, 'Mr. Speaker, I beg to take notice that there are not forty Members present.' The Speaker turned the two-minute sand-glass, and all over the building the bells rang (a special ring) and the policemen cried down the corridors, 'Count!' If earnest lunchers ran out, still chewing, to 'keep a House,' the plotters confronted them in the Lobby and tried to persuade them not to go into the Chamber. If the Speaker could count forty Members before the sands ran out, the Session continued (and there could be no 'count' for another hour); if not, the House was automatically adjourned, and the day was ended. Bill 3 must try again another day (if any Fridays were left) and Bill 2 as well.

But perhaps the supporters of Bill 2 were numerous and sagacious enough to keep the sitting alive. Perhaps Bill 2 was allowed to go through without disturbance and got a Second Reading at half-past two or three. On came Bill 3. Its enemies then could still hope, quite legitimately, to 'talk it out,' on the ground that the Second Reading of a Bill so important and contentious should not be put to the vote after a mere hour's discussion. As four o'clock approached one of its enemies would be relating, reasonably but not very rapidly, with one eye on the clock, the many objections to the Bill. The aims of the promoters were such as must unite the sympathy of every thinking man, but, etc. Some of the Clauses were unobjectionable, but others deserved the most careful scrutiny, etc. In any case, was it not a Bill too large in scope for a Private Members' Bill? Or (alternatively) was it not a mean and inadequate tinkering with a vast subject upon which no doubt in due course His Majesty's Government, etc. The Chamber filled. Excitement grew. The speaker, unless an old hand, was perhaps running short of ammunition, but he must keep firing somehow till the clock said four. Just before four—not too soon, but not a second too late—the promoter of the Bill must jump up and 'beg to move that the Question be now put.' If the Speaker sat still, 'declining to accept that motion,' as after so short a debate on a Bill of any substance he would, the debate was adjourned without a division, and Bill 3, for that day at least, was 'talked out.'

But only for that day. It was still on the Order Paper, and, with luck and judgment, might be popped in and hustled through during the later stages of another Friday—or two. Meanwhile, it had had an airing. Speeches had been made about it; there would be reports in the papers, and tiresome people might write to protest against the monstrous treatment of this excellent Bill.

So it was sometimes thought best to use another expedient, the most brutal of all. It was quietly arranged to let the little Bill No. 1 (the one about ice-cream vendors, say, or the law of taxicabs) occupy the whole day, so that Bills 2 and 3 never came on at all. Not a hint of mischief would appear on the solemn faces of the interminable speakers, and unless you were waiting, impatient and frustrated, to move the Second Reading of Bill 2 or 3, you could not but admire the ingenuity of those who managed to make so much of so little.

These manœuvres may have a schoolboy sound, and we can all think of some good amendments to the Rules. But often there was some sound political instinct behind them; and, at the worst, they were a good testing ground for the 'unofficial' Member. They could be met, sometimes, by the exercise of wit and diplomacy, by patience or persuasion.

On private Fridays the young man learns much about 'procedure' and practical points of conduct. He begins to think better of Whips and others in authority. For he has to do himself so many bits of drill which he has always seen done by the Whips before—and they seemed so easy then. If he wants to prevent his Bill being 'talked out' he must butt in at the right moment and move 'that the Question be now put.' If there is a division, he can no longer stroll into the Lobby indicated by the Whips, chatting airily with a friend. He is in charge now: he must organize and lead. He must arrange for one of his supporters to be the other 'Teller';[3] he must decide which of them

[3] Two 'Tellers,' one for each side, stand outside each Lobby, and one counts the Members as they come out.

will take the 'Aye' Lobby and which the 'No,' and make sure that the other fellow knows where to go (which, in the excitement, may be very necessary). Then he must remember to give the names of his 'Tellers' to the Speaker, which is easily forgotten, and, if forgotten, ruins all. Even now he dares not scurry off to his 'Telling' post at the Lobby door. He must wait in the Chamber and make sure that a few Members shout 'Aye!' (or 'No!') when the Speaker puts the question for the last time two minutes later. If this is not done the division is 'off'—and the Member is an ass. Then, breathless and excited, he must press through the crowd of Members surging into the Chamber to vote, and take his place for the counting. Then, when the figures have been handed to the Clerk at the Table here is the ritual announcement. The four Tellers line up, bow, and advance one pace. The senior Teller on the winning side announces the figures. The Speaker repeats them, and the Tellers bow again, if possible together. It all sounds simple, and looks simple, when the Whips do it; but, after much experience, one can still make mistakes, and I confess that I have rarely done the bowing to my satisfaction.

If he gets a majority for his Second Reading, the unofficial Member has a long steeplechase before him—Committee upstairs—the Report Stage—Third Reading. His Whips, of course, if he is a party man, are still his guides, philosophers, and friends, and will advise him in the background, but many things he can only do for himself.

He is now a Minister in miniature, and must use the same arts—know when to accept an amendment and when to stick his toes in, how to keep his friends eager and his enemies calm. Many a Minister, I dare say, has been glad of this training.

It is true, too—though they laughed when I said so at the beginning of the 1945 Parliament—that there was on Fridays a charming camaraderie among the parties. Here and there a Bill would come up which had the parties divided as usual. But on the normal Friday affairs—social questions on the fringe of politics—men of all sides worked amicably together; and this, I always thought, was another very good mark for the arrangements. Mr. Aneurin Bevan and two other Labour Members were among the 'backers' of my Divorce Bill, and their party was always helpful. With such topics on the Table all parties could, once a week, forget the party Whips, and be ordinary men with free minds and consciences. As an Independent, I liked to see that, but I am sure that the party fellows enjoyed it too.

And on those days we, the 'unofficial' Members, could create—or try to create. Otherwise we can only criticize and comment. We can move amendments to Government Bills (which will not always be called). We can attack Ministers' policies in general debates: we can criticize their administrative errors in brief debates of half an hour 'on the adjournment.' But the moment we suggest anything that would 'involve legislation,' we are out of order. All initiative, all creative impulse, is reserved for His Majesty's Ministers, who are not quite so wise, I think, as all that.

I do not remember much about the details of the Licensing (Amendment) Bill. It was introduced by Mr. Gledhill, who said:

The main object of the Bill is to put an end to the anomalies that have arisen from the varying hours of sale, to try to institute uniform conditions, and to try to keep off the register the undesirable club which has come to be known as the bogus or one-man club.[4]

I made my second speech, and had the first of many bouts with Lady Astor. In spite of them all, we have remained good friends.

I was earnest but impudent, I see, and said, among other things:

It would be refreshing if, for a change, we could refrain from giving this dog a bad name. It is very easy to throw a cloud of prejudice over things by using such pseudo-scientific terms as 'alcohol,' 'liquor,' 'intoxicating liquors,' 'vested interests,' and so forth. I shall not follow the hon. Member for West Bermondsey (Dr. Salter) in his medical researches, but I would say this to him: 'So far as I know, beer does not have to be boiled before it is fit to drink, and the Minister of Agriculture and Fisheries and the Minister of Health are not racking their brains in order to regulate, certify and pasteurize it in order to make it fit for human consumption.' I might easily go around describing milk as a tuberculous beverage, or motor-cars as homicidal vehicles, but that would be nonsense. Therefore, I ask hon. Members not to use that kind of language. One more word to the hon. Member for West Bermondsey. I believe that certain temperance associations, and perhaps himself, are in the habit, for the purpose of conveying an awful

[4]Done at last in 1949.

warning against the use of beer, of exhibiting in bottles, for instance to the children in the schools, the livers of deceased clubmen, for all I know, past Members of this House. In that case, I would gladly offer my liver to the nation. I suggest that in our great educational scheme, which I believe is to be extended, he should make a further exhibition to the unfortunate children of the lungs of somebody who has perished through tuberculosis contracted from milk.

MR. MURRAY: Would the hon. Member tell the House whether a periodical called *Punch* advertises drink?

MR. HERBERT: That does not appear to be a matter to which I ought to give an answer. The hon. Member for West Bermondsey talks about licensed premises and pubs. What is a pub? We can agree that the pub is, on the whole, a social centre and, I suggest, a very valuable social institution. It is a place to which people can go for political sanity and for temperance purposes, for it is an instrument of control. It is a place where people who do not own rich houses, who have no billiard rooms or gardens of their own, are able to go for social intercourse and the news of the day. I would ask hon. Members, in discussing this question, to remember that the public-house is not a sink of iniquity, and that the publican is not a man who is ruining his fellow countrymen. It is said in the Trade that it is more difficult to become a publican than a parson. He has to give seven years' good character; every minute of his life for seven years is gone into. . . .

My mind goes back to a year ago, when I was naughtily and boldly laying information against the Kitchen Committee of this House. There was not then lighthearted talk about 'intoxicating liquor' and about liberty which nobody wanted. There was indignation, and rightly. This House did not then say, 'Oh well, these things do not really matter: let us have more control, let us obey the law which we have imposed on the people.' This House marched out to battle—horse, foot, and Attorney-General—to defend its rights and privileges, and I congratulate them. I am very glad that they succeeded. The High Court then did not say 'These are trifling matters.' The High Court decided that continued access to refreshment of every kind was essential to the conduct of the business of this House, although the business of this House is the most important business of making laws. I do not say that people demand the same privileges as there are in this House—I think they are glad that this House has special privileges—but they would like to have the same spirit shown in this House when their simple human desires are being considered.

Lady Astor, among other things, said:

I am not going to deal with the hon. Member for Oxford University because we know that he is the playboy of the drink world.

MR. A. HERBERT: May I suggest that a regular course of narcotics would be extremely good for the Noble Lady? She would be less restless.

VISCOUNTESS ASTOR: The Noble Lady will be restless in this House long after the hon. Member for Oxford University. I am not going to deal seriously with him, because we know that he has a picture of the old-fashioned pub where there is music and merriment and good cheer. It is a beautiful picture. I only wish it were true.

That was often my trouble. I would make a serious and reasoned case about matters in which I claimed some knowledge and experience and be told by my opponents that they would not 'deal seriously' with me.

Years afterwards, in 1940, when I transferred from the River Emergency Service to the Royal Naval Auxiliary Patrol, I was proud to be marked A1 at the Admiralty medical examination. I sent a wire to my friend Harry Strauss at the House:

PASSED A1 FOR NAVY FIFTY THIS YEAR PLEASE TELL NANCY.

I liked her reply:

MUST BE SOMETHING WRONG WITH NAVY: NANCY.

The Home Secretary (Sir John Simon) made a discouraging speech, as Ministers generally did on a Friday, but he said 'definitely that it is the intention of the Government next Session to introduce a Bill to deal with bogus clubs.'

The promoter thereupon withdrew his Bill. No Government Bill, I believe, was ever produced.

8. Betting, Frustration, etc.

On 3 April 1936, a Friday, through no fault of mine, the subject of betting came up. Mr. R. J. Russell, the Member for Eddisbury (now dead), presented, brave man!—a Betting (No. 1) Bill to make the football pools illegal. That was all it sought to do.

In my Betting and Bookmakers Bill, the final version of which was ready the following year, I also proposed to abolish the pools. If either of us had been successful the present Government, and some before it, I fancy, would have had a few fewer worries. But in my Bill I gave the people something in exchange for their pools, and I tried to tackle the whole betting affair thoroughly. Now I supported an amendment moved by Mr. Alan Lennox-Boyd for the rejection of the Bill. It was carried by 287 votes to 24.

I am sure it deserved defeat, because it was so limited. But perhaps I was a little unfair to Mr. Russell. At all events, I came down, later, from the high and mighty line I took that day.

Two years later—to take a chronological jump—I contrived an occasion for a discussion of my own Betting and Bookmakers Bill; but, as things turned out, I was the only person who discussed it. I had worked very hard on the Bill, drafting much of it myself, and following, in the main, the very sensible report of the Royal Commission of 1932. But I never got a place in the ballot, and no other Member would touch the prickly thing.

Towards the end of the Fridays set aside for private Members, I observed that there was likely to be an hour or two to spare, for there were only the Third Readings of two or three not very contentious Bills to be completed. My Bill was printed and 'on the Paper'; it was complicated, it had never been explained, and I thought that some might be interested to have it explained, if only in preparation for another Session. I asked the Government Chief Whip, David Margesson, if there was any objection to my putting down the Bill for a 'nominal' Second Reading, with no hope of getting anywhere in that Session. He said 'No,' and there followed one of those comical Friday morning skirmishes which I have described. I sat quietly in my place, listening to the last speeches on the Third Reading of the Baking Industry (Hours of Work) Bill. Labour Members were rightly enthusiastic about this beneficent measure and its originator, Mr. Banfield (Wednesbury). The Bakers' Constitution, somebody called it. 'An important part of his life's work,' said Herbert Williams. 'This must be a happy day for him, because I know that the Bill will go through this House with unanimity. . . .'

I sat waiting for these plaudits to end, wondering why I had wantonly committed myself to making a long speech about betting, with no practical result in view. It was nearly lunch-time, and there would be a jolly crowd in the Smoking Room, sherry and good talk. Mr. (now Sir) Herbert Williams, always ready with kind advice to the young, came and sat beside me. 'The moment you get up,' he said, 'they're going to count you out.'

'Why?' I said.

'They don't like your Bill.'

'But it can't go any farther. I only want to explain the thing.'

'Well, they don't want it.'

'All right,' I said, 'I won't get up. Come and have a drink.' And I began to put my papers together. If no one wished to listen I had no itch to speak, and any good excuse for not making a speech has always attracted me. But Herbert Williams, man of craft, said, 'Wait a bit. I'll tell you what we'll do. The rule is that if a Count is called there cannot be another Count for an hour. Towards the end of this Bill we'll call a Count—and after that you'll have a clear run for an hour at least.'

By this time I was far more inclined for sherry than speaking. But I could hardly refuse such sporting assistance, and it would be amusing to outwit the silencers, whoever they were. So I sat still, and presently someone arose and said: 'On a point of order, Mr. Speaker, I beg to call attention to the fact that there are not forty Members present.'

Mr. Rhys Davies, who was, with reservations, applauding the Bakers' Constitution, sat down; the Speaker turned the two-minute sand-glass, and all over the House the special bells were rung and the policemen cried 'Count!'

In the Chamber there was great indignation among the Labour Members, who thought that a wicked attack was being made upon the Bakers' Bill in its hour of triumph. 'Disgraceful!' they cried. 'Another Tory plot!' and so on. But they had more reason to be anxious than they knew. By this time many Members were having an early lunch. When they heard the bells they naturally supposed that the Bakers' Constitution had duly got its Third Reading without a division, and that the bells were ringing for *me!* 'Ha, ha,' they said, 'silly old "A.P." and his Betting Bill!' and went on eating. So the Bakers' Constitution was in grave danger of foundering within sight of port. But the Whips ran and explained and bullied, and enough Members were hurried to the Chamber, still chewing, in time to save the Bill.

So I had my say after all at one forty-nine, and fired off fourteen columns of *Hansard* in the lunch hour before a very small audience. I discharged for fifty minutes. When I had done, Mr. Liddall said a few words against the Bill, and accused me of 'wobbling,' but almost immediately the House was 'counted out,' and we all went home. I thought I had won. But the law to-day is exactly what the law was then. I shall never apologize for my efforts to get it amended, nor even for making an unnecessary speech—for there has been no other attempt at a thorough handling of the subject in the last two Parliaments. But yet another Royal Commission was appointed in 1949, and something may happen one day.

9. The Marriage Bill

My second Session—1936–7—was the big one.

I have told the story of the Marriage Bill in full elsewhere, and will not tell it all again. But I should like once more to give due praise to Mr. Rupert De la Bère, the spirited Member for Evesham, who made the whole thing possible by bravely giving to my Bill the high place he had won in the Ballot. And you, Young Man, may be interested to hear how I got him. If you mean business, you must be sure to attend the Ballot for Private Members' Bills. This time, again, my number did not emerge from the box among the first thirty-three. At this point of the story I do, if I may, mildly pat myself on the back—or rather, perhaps, I give special thanks to the powers that control us all; for I was faced with a big temptation and overcame it. I was tempted strongly to shrug my shoulders, go down to the Smoking Room and have a beer. I could bewail my fate to the reporters later, complain against the queer machinery of Parliament, and feel myself free to devote my main energy and time to Mr. Cochran, for whom I was writing a revue. That, after all, was part of my profession in life, and might reward me.

But my particular angel, or imp, said: 'No, you have taken this cause upon you and you must do all you can.' So, wondering at my own perversity, I hurried downstairs to the Members' telephone-room, with the list of winners in my hand. On the way, I looked in at the Labour Whips' Office, for Labour had four or five of the first ten numbers; but there, as I expected, I was kindly told that there were plenty of Bills for Labour Members.

So I went into the telephone-box and pursued the Conservatives and Liberals. I tried first the few winners I knew—Mr. Maurice Petherick, for example; but he was already wedded to another Bill in the same line of country. Others had their own Bills, or were not at home, or were entirely dependent on the support of Roman Catholics, or were in conference, or simply spluttered at the word 'divorce.'

A Mr. De la Bère, whom I did not know, had place No. 2. It seemed presumptuous for me even to think of aiming so high, and I was content at first to chase the lower numbers. But the telephone attendant told me that Mr. De la Bère was a new Member, like myself, so he might, I thought, have no Bill in the bag. Someone told me that I might find him at Hay's Wharf: he is a director of that and many other companies. He was 'in conference.' I returned to Mr. ———, who was still out, and Mr. ———, who was 'somewhere in the building but could not be found.' I spoke to an Admiral, who said: 'Divorce? Good God, no! I was in the Navy!' and rushed away. It was vital, I knew, to get my hooks into somebody then—before lunch, for by the time the House met in the afternoon the best places would have been promised to Members with less explosive notions, if not to the Whips. But I had failed to get Mr. De la Bère, my last hope, twice. I had been telephoning for an hour; and that is too much telephoning for me. It was lunch-time, and I felt in need of refreshment. I was about to abandon the quest and seek the Smoking Room, but I thought that I would make *one* more attempt to get Mr. De la Bère—and then give it up.

And here was one more of the happy accidents, for this time he was available. And his first words gave me my first substantial hope. True, he began with the usual password about the Roman Catholics in his constituency, but he did not utter it with the usual conviction. What he did say firmly was that he, too, was of an independent turn of mind, and was afraid of nobody. And this he has abundantly shown.

We agreed to meet that afternoon in the Chamber, after Questions. He sat on the Government benches near the Speaker. Neither of us knew the other by sight. After waiting about ten minutes I edged along the almost empty bench and said to the next Member, 'Do you know De la Bère?' He said, 'I am De la Bère.' We went out and sat in the 'Aye' Lobby.

At once, like eagles, two other Members, with Bills in their beaks, descended on us and tried to carry him off. But I was able to claim priority and bullied them away. He, too, already had a Bill in his hand, an innocent little thing about municipal elections, which the Whips had given him. My heart sank when I saw that, but I did not know Mr. De la Bère.

And let me say here that if the life of any man or woman is changed for the better by the Matrimonial Causes Act, 1937, I hope that they will always remember gratefully the name of Mr. Rupert De la Bère, Member for Evesham.

They should give thanks, too, for the chance that plucked that name from the hat at the second cast. For, apart from the few who already had an active interest in the cause, I do not suppose there was a single other Member on the Government side who could, at that time, have been persuaded to give his place to this Bill. Mr. De la Bère had no special interest in the question; he was not, like myself, an Independent; he took the Whip, though he was never, I believe, one of its most docile recipients. The Government Whips would not, at the best of times, I suppose, have clapped heartily on the back a member of their own flock who said that he proposed to introduce a Divorce Bill on the second Friday of the Session. For such a question, cutting across party, is sure to give the Government trouble, and Governments have enough trouble of their own making. But it was then November 1936. The Abdication crisis had not yet come to a head; and the last thing that anyone wanted then was to provoke discussion of these sad matters in the House.

So it was not an auspicious moment at which to father a Divorce Bill upon a Conservative Member; and when Mr. De la Bère went off to see the Whips again it is not difficult to guess what they said to him, though I do not know. All this, I repeat, is not said in criticism of the Whips, but in applause of Mr. De la Bère's courage. I must add that once the battle was joined we had nothing but friendly (though unofficial) aid from the Whips, though I, as an Independent, had no sort of claim upon them, and two at least were deeply opposed to the Bill.

Well, Mr. De la Bère saw the Whips, and others, and came back to me; and a friend of his, Mr. R. H. Morgan, supported my plea. We said that it was a pity to waste so fine a strategical position upon the Municipal Elections Bill; that this would be the first occasion on which this long-neglected question had had a fair chance at the top of the list; and that, win or lose, this was a big and worthy cause for any private Member to adopt. But I do not think that in fact he needed much persuasion, for he is a fighter. By six o'clock he had made his decision.

But all the afternoon, while I was urging him to say 'Yes,' I was thinking, 'What in the world shall I do if he does?' For rehearsals for *Home and Beauty* were to begin that very week: I had lyrics to write (to music), dialogue to repair, scenes to devise. Supposing by any miracle, I thought, we get a Second Reading and go into Committee, between these two diverse and enormous responsibilities I shall certainly go off my head.

Nobody, however, seemed to think that there was the smallest danger of our getting a Second Reading. Some of the Whips, I was told, thought it was out of the question.

We were highly surprised to get our Second Reading, by 78 votes to 12, with two hours still to go. Sir John Simon, who behind the scenes did much for our cause, came to me in the Chamber with congratulations on the tone of all our speeches, and I believe the impression we made that day gave a fair wind to our fortunes. So here is some of perhaps the most important speech this humble person ever made:

I want to make it plain that I do not espouse this cause because I am a life-long Bohemian who is anxious for sexual licence or as a hard-luck story, but because I believe it will bring new strength to the institution of the family and to the relations between Church and State. Quite apart from the hardships, we have a very shocking state of affairs. It was referred to by the Archdeacon of Coventry at the Diocesan Conference in these words:

The limitation of the grounds of divorce to the one ground of adultery had resulted in a state of affairs which was disastrously prejudicial to public morality. As the law stands at present those who wish to bring an end to the marriage were forced to take one of two alternatives—either one must commit adultery or one must commit perjury. The law as it stands is a distinct incitement to immorality. It was the duty of the Church to press for reform of the existing marriage laws. An extension of the grounds of divorce does not necessarily mean making divorce more easy.

The Archdeacon is right. At the moment the law is mocked not only in words but in deeds. There is collusion and perjury, and it is sufficient to say that the wrong people get what they want and the right people cannot. As for adultery, we are rapidly reaching a situation in which no stigma whatever will attach to a public confession of adultery. I ask my religious friends to consider the matter seriously. Not so long ago a man was ashamed of confessing in court or being condemned by a court of having committed adultery, but now in ever-widening circles there is no man so scrupulous as to bother about it, not because the country is becoming more immoral, but because the country is becoming more rebellious against out-of-date laws. I ask my Roman Catholic friends, are they happy with this state of affairs? Are they content with the present situation and are they really going to oppose any and every proposal for reform? To do the leaders of the Church of England justice, they do recognize the danger and the duty to which the Archdeacon of Coventry referred. The Archbishop of Canterbury a year ago said:

> The time has come when Parliament can no longer resist the growing public demand for some extension of the grounds for divorce.

The Anglo-Catholics and the Church Union emphasize that it is essential to distinguish between the moral standards which the Church of England must impose on its own members and those which a largely secularized State can force upon its citizens as such. Take my own personal position. I represent more Churchmen than any hon. Member of the House. Have I had a single protest? I have made no secret of my intentions—not a single one. There is not the slightest doubt—and I ask the pardon of the House for emphasizing this point— that there has been a great change in the attitude of the Church during the last few years. There is no doubt that most reasonable Churchmen are not only ready but eager for some reasonable reform of the law. A resolution, passed last June by the Bishops of the Upper House of

Convocation of Canterbury, which in plain language means the Bishops of 25 out of 31 dioceses, states:

> The Church should be prepared to give consideration to proposals for such amendment, provided that any proposed amendment does not tend to make marriage a temporary alliance or to undermine the foundations of family life.

It is in that spirit and with that proviso that we approach this problem in this Bill.

I went at length through all the Clauses and concluded:

We have taken, wherever possible, the labours of our industrious predecessors, Lord Buckmaster, Lord Birkenhead, Mr. Holford Knight, the Royal Commissioners, and so forth, but we have endeavoured to add, as I hope and think, those improvements which are more in keeping with the spirit of the present time. My hon. Friend and I are both new and inexperienced Members, and we acknowledge our obvious deficiencies in view of the magnitude of this great task. But we are not afraid, and we do not apologize in bringing forward, as private Members, on a Friday, this great and difficult task.

Let us say that on this day, the 20th November, the private Members of this House rose up and took hold of the great problem which Government after Government had neglected for twenty-four years and said, 'We will lead the way.' To His Majesty's Ministers I would say too, 'We do not come to you hat in hand, asking you to pardon us for bringing up another Friday, tittle-tattle Measure. We bring you, as it were on a charger, this great social reform, which we believe that any Government would be proud to bear upon the records of its achievement.'

These laws of ours are unique in Protestant countries, always excepting the State of South Carolina and New York. They cannot be defended by reference to divine sanction, nor on the grounds of human need, and they are based in the main on historical accidents, on antique prejudices, and upon the strange and almost bestial notion that the one thing which matters in married life is the sexual act, and that the only breach of the marriage obligation which matters is the breach of the sexual relationship. They are like some architectural monstrosity which stands upon a hill and offends the eye of all beholders year after year, and yet, if anybody tries to pull it down, there arises a great outcry. These laws are the cause of great, unnecessary, and unjustifiable unhappiness, and, apart from that, they are a danger to the marriage institution. Twenty-four years ago a Royal Commission worked for three years and condemned them, but nothing has been done. Since then the Press has never ceased to support the demand for reform, and I am sure we have the bulk of the people behind us. It remains for this House at last to rise up and tackle and settle this problem. I have only one more word to say, and that will be addressed to my Roman Catholic friends. I could indulge in a great deal of interesting and, I think, effective verbal play with the Roman Catholics, but I do not propose to do that, because I hope this discussion will be maintained upon a kindly and tolerant level. The House will do me the credit of admitting that I have not bombarded it with letters, but I wish to read one letter, which is a good letter, from a Roman Catholic lady whom I do not know. She writes to me out of the blue:

> Please God, your Bill will pass unmutilated. I am a Roman Catholic, a happy wife and mother, but there are others in this world of ours who most grievously are not. With what anxiety they must be awaiting the result of this truly great reform. We pray for you.

I hope—indeed I pray—that the spirit of that letter may be moving in this House to-day.

We now had the invaluable support and advice of the Treasury Solicitor (and King's Proctor), Sir Thomas Barnes, behind the scenes. One of the Law Officers sat next to me in Committee, for technical advice. But we had to form our policy and fight our battles ourselves.

In those days, I sometimes took our old flat-bottomed canal-boat (the *Ark*) and anchored her for a night or two off the House, or below Charing Cross Bridge. One Friday, after a wearing week in Committee, I was chugging slowly home, thinking: 'Thank goodness! No more divorce till Tuesday!' and enjoying the still Spring evening. Above Hammersmith Bridge I slowly came abreast of a tug (one of Cory's, I expect), towing half a dozen lighters full of coal. There was a head emerging from the engine-room, to which I waved, as usual. I heard a deep voice boom: 'YUS, THERE HE IS!'

Then another head appeared, and a boom much deeper came across the quiet water, penetrating, I felt, into all the homes of my neighbours.

'YOU'RE DOING NO GOOD. BILL WANTS TO GET RID OF HIS OLD WOMAN NOW.'

After a week of the House of Commons, I felt it hard to be expected to take part in a debate of this kind on a Friday evening. So all I could do was to wave again.

While we were in Committee, I was also in rehearsal!

After lunch every day I would rush away across the river to a barn-like building near the Elephant and Castle and endeavour to switch my mind to the manifold problems of Mr. Cochran's *Coronation Revue* (one of which was now, 'Will there be a Coronation?'). Then, with appeals in my ear from a Hungarian composer, an American producer, and an English comedian to write more words or better words, I would hurry to the Treasury Solicitor to get the text of the new amendments and to the House to confer with De la Bère and the team. There I would find an odd assembly of telephone messages. 'From Mr. Kent, insanity amendment on the way'—'From Mr. Collins, please send second verse of *Twilight Serenade*'—'Please ring Treasury Solicitor'—'Please ring Miss Binnie Hale'—'Please ring Mr. Cochran.' Mr. Cochran, who had always been accustomed to get a whole mind from me, nobly forbore to complain of my distraction. Twice I woke up from a fitful sleep and found myself trying to set divorce words to one of M. Brodszky's tunes. A weird and worrying time.

The fight for the Bill went on throughout the Session, and was not finished till the Third Reading in the Lords on 19 July 1937. All through that long and doubtful struggle, my friends assure me, I was a surprisingly 'good boy,' never letting my notorious 'levity' damage the cause. But, on one occasion, through sheer excess of anxiety and keenness, I did let fly. And here is an Awful Warning.

The story springs, once more, from the queer manœuvres of private Fridays. Many people have remarked how lucky we were to get so prickly a measure through. I have always said that we were fortunate but not 'lucky.' Whenever it was possible for the ball to bounce the wrong way it did. I never had any luck in the Ballot. Our first two days in Committee chanced to fall in the week of the Abdication, when no man wished to discuss adultery and divorce, and

Members, not unnaturally, had to be cajoled and persuaded to come in.

Then we had the worst of luck in the matter of time, which, Private Members' Time being strictly limited, was always an agonizing anxiety.

We could not complete our Report Stage and Third Reading in one day, and had to take our place in the queue on the last two private Fridays that remained. On the Thursday before the first of them, by an extraordinary chance, the House had a record all-night sitting. It even sat till after 11 A.M. on the Friday, which, by the rules, meant that the whole of that Friday's sitting was wiped out.

This was a shocking disappointment. But there was one Friday left: and the two Bills before us on the Paper were slight in substance. With goodwill all round we might still get through, and again, after long and studious conning of our amendments, I went hopefully to the House at eleven. The first Bill had to do with the taxicab law: it had occupied only half an hour in Standing Committee. The second Bill concerned ice-cream vendors, and was even less important. But, for some reason which I now forget, many Labour Members disliked it strongly, and, as I soon discovered, they had decided to keep the debate on the Taxicab Bill going all day (that is, till 4 P.M.) so that the Ice Cream Bill would be denied a Third Reading and die (as indeed it did). You can imagine with what impatience and anger this eager law-giver listened to the ingenious speeches on the Taxicab Bill, seeing what he thought was a major reform endangered, and probably destroyed, by such inconsiderable trifles. It was galling, too, to reflect that I might myself be remotely and innocently responsible for that day's proceedings. I had been on the Standing Committee which considered the Ice Cream Bill. It was promoted by Mr. Clement Davies, a good friend of mine. One night, many weeks earlier, one of his supporters had sent me an 'S O S' begging me to attend the Standing Committee the following morning, for the opposition was strong and divisions would be close. I was tired, I was busy, I had no interest in the Ice Cream Bill, and the last thing I wanted to do was to hurry to the House at eleven next morning. Also, the devil whispered to me, 'You will be sorely pressed for time with your own Bill. The fewer Private Members' Bills there are about the better. Why do anything to save this one?' But the Senior Burgess for Oxford University, he is glad to say, replied to the devil: 'That is a practical but unethical suggestion. And besides, how can I expect my friends to help me if I do not help them?' So I went in. On the critical division the Bill was saved by one vote. If I had stayed away it might have died the death in Committee and never come back to the floor of the House.

But here was the blasted thing, imperilling the labours and battles of a Session, and the hopes of twenty-five years. By two o'clock our fate was certain, and I might as well have gone home. After all, it was all in the game, and philosophic resignation was the line. But I hung about the House, fuming as philosophically as I could—and at three forty-five I rose up and spoke explosively, without preparation, as follows:

This is the last quarter of an hour on the last Private Members' Friday in this Session, and although I am a new Member, I attach great importance to the institution of Private Members' Fridays. It seems to me to be the last real expression of the individual in this democratic State. Although my name is on the back of the next Bill, I am not very hot about it, one way or another, but I am full of hot feelings about democracy, and I am hot about Private Members' Fridays. I want to say, with great respect and humility as a private Member, that I regard to-day's proceedings as one of the most disgraceful things I have ever witnessed. This Bill, which was discussed for half an hour in Committee, has taken the whole of the last of the Private Members' Fridays.

I went on, in a fine temper, for about two columns, repeating myself, as one does, Young Man, when angry and unprepared.

In substance, I was right, no doubt; but in practice, probably not. The sad thing was that some of the Labour Members concerned in the ice-cream manœuvres were faithful supporters of my Bill. They may have known, what I did not, that the Government were going to give us a whole day of Government time for the completion of our Bill. They said that they had done no more than the Tories had done many times in the past, and were rather resentful. So I had better have nursed my wounds in silence.

All this made no difference in the end, for the Prime Minister, Mr. Baldwin, did give us a Government day for our concluding stages. And at last I found myself, dazed and incredulous, 'winding up' on the Third Reading.

I must not forget to pay my tribute to the conduct of our opponents in what might have been a bitter controversy, but has not in fact been so, because we are better friends now than when we began. . . .

This was true.

I would say one more word to those who have approached this question from the religious point of view. There are two lines of objection to these proposals. One is the general social line and the other is the religious line. Occasionally they have overlapped, but they do not entirely coincide, and there are doubtless many who could be persuaded to support these proposals on social grounds, but who would find themselves unable to agree with such reforms upon religious grounds. They take the view that we should abide by the words, 'Whom God hath joined let no man put asunder,' and leave it at that. I am most anxious to avoid saying anything which would wound anybody, but I would like to say to those who genuinely feel in the way I have indicated that I wonder whether they can be sure that in taking that attitude they are truly interpreting the message of Christ. For my part, I think Christ was a realist who liked to tear away shams and to get down to the heart of things, and I am very certain that He did not say to the woman taken in adultery that 'hard cases make bad law.' I think we know what He said, and we know what He said to the Pharisees. I do not say this to raise a laugh or to cause a wound, but I wonder what He would have said to the General Council of the Mothers' Union. I wonder what He would have said to any happily married mother and wife who is so confident that her happiness is due to her own virtue, and that the misfortunes of others are due to their own fault, that she will not accede to any alteration in the law even to lessen the unhappiness of those others. I maintain with the utmost reverence that there is not a single word in this Bill of which He would not approve; I say, on the other hand, that there are many deplorable things in the present situation which He would resent. I would like again to thank the House, in every corner of it, for its indulgence, and I would like again to thank His

Majesty's Government for the opportunity which they have given us to-day. This Bill does not do all that we should like, but it does a lot, and it does enough to take away this question for a long time. Even now, humbly conscious though we are of its defects—and I am very grateful for the assistance which we have received—I do not propose to use the language of appeal. No, sir. We feel proud of the fact that we have, by the grace of God and by the goodwill of this House, given to His Majesty's Government and to this country a great opportunity to clear away this tiresome and dangerous question for a very long time. We say that this is a Bill that not only will increase the sum of human happiness, but that will be of great benefit to many valued institutions. Finally, if I may use again that Name which I have already used, we say that above all, in the finest sense of the word, this is a Christian Bill, and I hope the House will give it its Third Reading by a very large majority.

The Third Reading was carried by 190 votes to 37. On the Second Reading it had been 78 to 12.

Mr. Michael Beaumont, though against us, congratulated us as an 'enthusiastic Parliamentarian,' and said that when I introduced the Bill, 'most of us thought the odds were anything up to a thousand to one that it would never obtain the Third Reading.'

There were still more speeches to be made when the Bill came back from the House of Lords. Most difficult of all, for us, was their wise amendment to the famous Clause 1. This originally said that no petition for divorce could be presented within five years of the marriage. The Lords made it 'three' years instead of 'five,' except in cases of exceptional hardship and exceptional depravity, when there could be a divorce at once. I was afraid there might be rather a row about this, involving my personal credit. I had had no hand in procuring the amendment, but some Church folk might protest that I had 'led them up the garden path.' I was tempted to leave the job to Mr. De la Bère. But I thought, 'Keep going,' and went ahead, walking delicately. The Church folk were admirably forbearing. A division was called, but not insisted on. So there was no vote. And that was the last hurdle.

I calculated that, in all, about 340,000 words were spoken about the Bill. I wonder often, with humility and awe, how many lives it has affected.

There are no statistics, remember, of the number of enduring and happy second marriages.

10. The Population (Statistics) Bill[1]

I come now to a speech which caused more talk, perhaps, than any I have made, and got me into some trouble. Heavy folk condemned it for levity; some said it was 'shocking' here and there. It certainly made the House of Commons laugh a lot for a long time; it concluded in verse; and, with some surprise, I have found most of it reprinted in an Everyman Anthology of Humour. But it was most carefully prepared, with serious intent—and serious effect. The Population (Statistics) Bill was a Government measure introduced by Sir Kingsley Wood, then Minister of Health. After the Second Reading debate the Government threw overboard large chunks of the Bill, accepting many of the criticisms which I and others had made, and the Minister sent for me (among others, no doubt) to approve the amendments he proposed—a proud encounter for a humble private Member, and an Independent, at that. Ridicule—or 'levity,' if you will—is a legitimate weapon in politics, and if it wins the day, why despise it? But the scientific folk who had begotten the Bill, and fathered it on poor Sir Kingsley, complained that I had attacked their child in a frivolous *spirit*, that is, without due study of the subject, or due respect for their purpose. That was not correct. I was as anxious as they to see the British race continue, but, rightly

[1]29 November 1937.

or wrongly, I was convinced that they were opening their mouths too wide, and were going to make themselves an unnecessary nuisance to a great many poor people at a most inconvenient time—that is, just after childbirth or just after a death. They said that our arrangements were pitifully behind those of other countries, the enlightened Dominions, for example, and Sir Kingsley Wood had said the same thing in a newspaper article. They proposed, under the Bill, to authorize the registrar to put forty-four questions to any woman who had just had a baby, or anyone who was registering a death. I took the trouble to find out from the Dominions Offices in London just what their arrangements were, and I found that in none of them was such a protracted catechism considered necessary. I challenged the Minister on the point during his speech, but was brushed aside— the poor Minister, I fancy, was speaking to a brief not thoroughly mastered. Nor did I ever get an answer to my constructive suggestion that if a mass of special new information was needed, there should be a special census—a much less objectionable method, for the questions are answered by the householder at his leisure and not by poor women lying in hospital beds.

My main objection to this Bill is the fundamental one that it puts the wrong questions to the wrong people. What is the main question to which we are addressing ourselves? It is 'Why are there not more babies?' To whom is this question going to be addressed? (a) To people who have just had a baby, and (b) to those who have just passed away. (*Laughter.*) This is not a joke. It is the fundamental objection to the whole of this Bill. By every canon of practicality and common sense, this question should be addressed to those who have not had a baby, and are still alive. Somebody the other day—I think it was Father Woodlock: I do not know what was his evidence for it— announced in the public Press that there are now 1,000,000 married couples without children. If that is true, those are the people to whom the right hon. Gentleman should address his questions.

I do not know—it would be indelicate of me to inquire; it is not recorded in the works of Whitaker or Burke, or even Dod or Vacher —whether the right hon. Gentlemen on the Front Bench have, if I may use the expression, ceased to breed. We should all agree, I think, that it would be a deplorable fact if it were so, but one thing that is certain under this Bill is that nobody is going to ask them why, and nobody is going to the Parliamentary Secretary to ask him why he has not even begun. If the right hon. Gentlemen think, as they may well do, that these questions are too personally directed, I am prepared to put them to myself. I am a grandfather. I have four children. I think I have ceased to breed. I am not as young as I was, but I am lusty, and I hope I maintain my powers, and, indeed, I am prepared on certain considerations to increase the population, but nobody is going to ask me about that until I die. That is really a serious point.

I examined at length the statistics already available to us in the Registrar-General's statistical review, and once or twice I used the old word 'bastard,' partly because that was the word in the 'principal Act' which we were amending, partly because I generally stutter over 'illegitimate.' The reporters thought that I said 'parsons,' and on the 'tape,' they tell me, there was later an urgent correction: 'For "parsons" read "bastards."'

One objection which I have to all this business is that the answer to the main question is known to all. I suppose I shall be called facetious if I ask the right hon. Gentleman to look around him at the bountiful processes of Nature. There is the rabbit, that paragon of productivity. There is the cat, a model of maternity. If she is frightened she devours her young. Look even at the prize bull, or even at the racehorse. The hero of a hundred races, when his competitive days are over, and he is placed on the daily and congenial task of populating the paddock, at a fee of £250 for services which most of us would do for nothing—even he does not approach his duties with the same alacrity if you fire off guns all around him and place a heavy load of taxation on his back. . . .

I found the other day, while looking over some old papers, that a year ago I anticipated the anxiety of His Majesty's Government on this question, and wrote a memorandum on the vexed question 'Why are more babies not being born?' If the House will bear with me, I will read the memorandum. I do not know whether it is in order to read a memorandum in verse:

In 1937 was a rumour going round
That Income Tax was soon to be six shillings in the pound;
The cost of education every season seemed to swell;
And to everyone's astonishment the population fell.

They pulled down all the houses where the children used to crowd
And built expensive blocks of flats where children weren't allowed;
So if father got a job there wasn't anywhere to dwell,
And everybody wondered why the population fell.

Five hundred brand-new motor-cars each morning rode the roads,
And flashed about like comets or sat motionless as toads;
Whichever course they took they made the public highway hell,
And everybody wondered why the population fell.

The laws were very comical; to bet was voted lax,
But your betting was the only thing that nobody would tax;
You couldn't have a wine unless you'd sandwiches as well,
And everybody wondered why the population fell.

Great Science nobly laboured to increase the people's joys,
But every new invention seemed to add another noise;
One was always on the telephone or answering the bell,
And everybody wondered why the population fell.

The taverns were controlled by men who didn't want to drink,
The newspapers were run by men who hadn't time to think,
The cinema was managed by a man who couldn't spell,
And everybody wondered why the population fell.

Abroad, to show that everyone was passionate for peace,
All children under seven joined the army or police;
The babies studied musketry while mother filled a shell—
And everybody wondered why the population fell.

The world, in short, which never was extravagantly sane,
Developed all the signs of inflammation of the brain;
The past was not encouraging, the future none could tell,
But the Minister still wondered why the population fell.

11. Munich

Another Awful Warning.

My last speech of that Session was, I believe, what they call a
'Parliamentary success'; but ever since it has been a sadness to me.
I can never remember exactly what the famous 'Sandys Affair' was
about, though it agitated the Commons, and filled the newspapers,
for very many days. I remember only that it had to do with Mr.
Hore-Belisha, Minister for War, and that the young Mr. Sandys,
Mr. Churchill's son-in-law, played a difficult and 'unpopular' part
with dignity and aplomb. Certainly, I cannot recall what made me
burst into the affair in a debate on a report of the Committee of
Privileges. I must have thought that I was right, for I never speak
unless I do. For all I know I was right, but I shall make no researches
into that. For, though I made, they say, a clever and effective
speech, I attacked, and by name, my hero, Mr. Churchill; and he,
with his unique sense of loyalty, was astonished and wounded, as I
learned very soon, by this attack from his old supporter of the Royal
Naval Division, who in the twenties had travelled to the West
Leicester election to defend him about the Dardanelles. You may
say, 'It is surely right to say what you think is true.' But political life
is not quite so simple as that. Impetuous rightness may get the head-
lines but lose your friends.

Mr. Churchill forgave me, as he forgives everyone, and I shall not here repeat the things I said that day. All this may sound not very important, but it had an important effect in my mind in the days of Munich which were a few weeks ahead of us. And, remember, Young Man, that in politics the trifling thing at any moment may become *enormous*.

Having spoken of Mr. Churchill's magnanimity, I feel I must relate a charming example of it which I saw, and heard, him display in 1948. It was in the Smoking Room, and all things said there are confidential. But this saying was to the credit of all, and can do no harm, so I will risk it. Rather late at night Mr. Churchill was leaving the Smoking Room. As he passed a little group of us—all parties —we said, 'Good night, sir!' He stopped and beamed upon us—that wonderful genial beam! There is no face I know that can express so humourously, so grimly, so many emotions. His glance fell on my friend—nay, the friend of most of us—Richard Stokes, the Socialist Member for Ipswich. Dick Stokes never loses his temper (which is a most unfair handicap to those who disagree with him), and says the most frightful things with a smile so youthful and warming that I think of him always as a junior Pickwick. All the war he was attacking Mr. Churchill, fearlessly, continuously, about tanks (among other things). I never knew enough about tanks to know whether he was talking sense or not, but certainly he was a formidable enemy to Mr. Churchill and his Ministers. Now Winston came back and put a hand on his shoulder and said: 'Of course I've forgiven you. Indeed, I agree with very much that you are saying about the Germans. Very good.' He moved away a few paces and said, as if we might be surprised by what he had said: 'Such hatred as I have left in me—and it isn't much—I would rather reserve for the future than the past.' He beamed again and moved off a pace or two, but stopped again, and made that inimitable sound of his own, half grunt, half chuckle, and he said: 'H'm. A thrifty and judicious disposal of bile.'

Foolish people have said that he prepares these sayings in advance, in the bath and so on. It is not so: they bubble out of him like mountain water, eternally fresh and sparkling. It is a sad thing that this great Englishman, such a fount of wisdom and fun and stories, can never have a Boswell. Small fry like myself have a small fund of true stories, which we repeat for ever. His intimate colleagues, who have a mighty store, can never reveal them. General Lord ('Pug') Ismay, who was at his elbow all the war, and is a man of taste and humour as well as loyalty, would perhaps be the man for the task. But he is a soldier in a confidential post: and, as he said when I tried to persuade him, if he 'did a Boswell' how could the next man accept such a post? A pity.

But we are still in the summer of 1938 and Mr. Churchill is still in the wilderness. I am amazed to see how busy a bee I was in those days. In that Session (1937–8) I was on the Standing Committee which considered the Cinematograph Films Bill—an endless, labyrinthine affair—and other Bills. I was preparing my Law of Libel Bill; and in the Chamber I spoke on the Population (Statistics) Bill, the Film Bill, the Administration of Justice (twice), my Betting and Bookmakers Bill, the Finance Bill, and a question of Privilege. Four of these were long, elaborate, prepared orations.

I am amazed because, as I have said, I dislike speaking in that place so much, and cannot think now how I drove myself through so much unpleasantness.

Nineteen thirty-eight was the year of Munich, and all these little Bills and Causes, you may say, seem very small molehills against the black mountains of Foreign Affairs. . . . Maybe—but what will you? Someone must build the bathroom as well as the battlements. Wars come and go, but the theatre remains. The foreigner threatens, but justice is still important at home. 'Some girl,' as the old song said, ' 'as got to darn his socks.' Like most of us, rightly or wrongly, I let the big men deal with the battlements. I listened with awe and admiration to Mr. Churchill, but had neither the itch nor the information to intervene in debates about aeroplanes, tanks, or munitions of war; and if that is a failing I must confess it.

But a private Member, though in speech he may stick to his own small last, cannot, like the private citizen, reject all responsibility at such a time. There is the time of voting. There is the horrid business of making up his mind. An Independent Member has so many advantages that it is right for him, perhaps, to have some special cares. And on the 'big' divisions, of which we had so many in that year and the next, I think he has. A party man may have his doubts, but, unless they are so strong as to amount to a conviction, he does quite right to support his leaders and to sink his doubts in his loyalty. But a fine, free, fearless 'Independent' is naturally supposed to be guided only by his own judgment and conscience. It is not, in fact, so simple as that. Any Independent, however fine, free, and fearless, however ready to assail a Government of any colour which stands in his way in special affairs (divorce, for example), is likely to lean a little to one side or the other in the general battle. If not, it must mean that he has no stable opinions about 'politics' at all. Again, though he may make friends in all parties, he will probably have more friends on one side or another. He will remember how they helped him in his own campaigns, and, human nature being delightfully human, he will listen to their opinions on general affairs. The late Miss Eleanor Rathbone, though Independent, was nearly always in the Labour Lobby. So was Mr. Driberg, before he joined that party. And Mr. Vernon Bartlett, I think, has always leaned to the Left. Mr. W. J. Brown, that very stout and sensible Independent, is, in these days, firmly inclined to the Right; and so, on the whole, I am not ashamed to confess, was I. But, on great or special occasions, I have always felt—it sounds ridiculous—perhaps it is—that I must not 'let the Independents down' by voting without due thought and care. I have even thought that, on great occasions where the parties were furiously raging together, the votes of Independents, cast with, of course, more conscience, might be as straws in the wind and show the party leaders which way the pure air of free opinion blows. Some horrid pride here, no doubt, but at least no 'levity' or lack of conscience.

In those frantic years of 1938 and 1939 there were other complicating factors in the mind of a sensitive Independent as he decided 'Aye' or 'No.' I never liked Mr. Chamberlain (I hardly knew him), but I admired him. For more than twenty years I had adored (that is the right word, I fear) Mr. Churchill. When I enlisted in the Navy in 1914, he turned me and many hundreds of others into soldiers and sent us to the awful Dardanelles in the Royal Naval Division. But ever after he had been a regular guest and beloved hero at our annual Divisional gatherings. I did not think, as so many thought in those days, that he was brilliant, resourceful, brave, but nearly always wrong. I thought that he was nearly always right—right, for example, about the Dardanelles, right about Antwerp, in both of which affairs our Division was involved. But I did think that he rather enjoyed a war: and, after three years in the infantry, in Gallipoli and France, I did not. My soul revolted at the thought of another, and, I was convinced by many expert opinions, a much worse war. (Mr. Churchill himself had painted the possibilities in colours even blacker than we ever saw in the event.) Moreover, since my ordeal in charge of the Divorce Bill, I had been inclined to give any Government the benefit of any doubt, since I knew how easily the man in charge can be misjudged and maligned.

I hated the dictators as much as Mr. Churchill did and often said so in the Press. But, 'wishful thinker,' 'anxious hoper,' 'old soldier,' or 'Christian believer'—what you will—I wanted Mr. Chamberlain to be right, and keep the peace successfully. I would never throw a stone at him then, and I will not now, when we are all so much wiser. Torn this way and that, then, I approached the Lobbies, or stayed outside. It may sound merely like feebleness of mind, but I believe that many Members, if they were frank enough, would confess to the same unhappy state. All this is not important, or interesting maybe, except that it may instruct those citizens who think that Members of Parliament have an easy time. Any man who served through those years, if he did nothing but listen and vote, earned his salary, I swear.

I never did vote, I think, in favour of the various accommodations with Mussolini, for I disliked him even more than Hitler and never believed a word he said. But I could not bring myself to vote with the Socialists, whose position seemed to me to make no sense. They had won the East Fulham election by calling Mr. Baldwin and his men 'war-mongers.' They were still voting against all the Service estimates—on the ground that they disapproved of the Government's foreign policy. But their own foreign policy was to defy the dictators, in Spain, in the Mediterranean, in Manchuria, in the Rhineland, everywhere—not, of course, under the flag of 'war-mongers,' but under the noble name of 'collective security,' and, presumably, without armies. This may be a crude and unjust summary, but I could never follow the reasoning. So I used to abstain. This sounds feeble again, but there are many occasions when in conscience you can do nothing else. Nor, though unsatisfactory to the soul, is it necessarily ineffective. The figures of a big division matter very much to the Whips, and are closely scrutinized. If you abstain, you, at least, influence the figures both ways; and, if you were in the House, the Whips know very well what you have done, even if you do not sit in the Chamber ostentatiously not voting. Let me add, I do not flatter myself that my abstention gave Ministers, or anyone else, many sleepless nights. But does not every sparrow matter?

In the great Munich division one could not abstain. All the vague chords must be resolved at last into a dismal 'Aye' or an outraged 'No.' What agonies of mind were suffered then—and not by feeble-minded Independents only! Those few who followed Mr. Churchill throughout are entitled perhaps to cry 'Men of Munich' (in fact, they seldom do), but not those who had called Mr. Baldwin's Ministry 'war-mongers' in 1937, who listened coldly or not at all to Mr. Churchill's rearmament speeches, who voted till the end against the Services Estimates and hotly opposed the Conscription Bill in the Spring of 1939;[1] certainly not young journalists and elderly Trade Unionists who had never then seen a shot fired in anger (and, air-raids apart, have not seen one now). I stood up, in the end, and cheered, as nearly all the Members did, that melodramatic afternoon when Mr. Chamberlain, pale but determined, announced that he was going to fly to Munich. Any man who stood and cheered that day should think a long time, it seemed to me, before he cast a stone. True, he may say that he did not then foresee the harsh terms of 'Godesberg,' but could he have done better—would he have refused to sign? The behaviour of the House that day has been described as 'hysterical,' but I do not think that is just. The assembled people would have cheered as loudly. We were expressing naturally the Englishman's horror of war and our sympathy with a Christian gentleman who was seeking peace. Far too many of us, I think, forgot how we felt that day.

It is not for me to argue the whole sad sinuous affair. I stand by

[1] Mr. Attlee moved a Vote of Censure for the Labour Party.

what I wrote in my Election Address of 1945, on which I was elected:

I do not think recrimination about *the pre-war years* is profitable or seemly. I have small respect for those young patriots, 'reserved' or unfit (it is sad how many who wanted to 'fight' in 1938 [or earlier] turned out to be C3 in 1939), whose chosen war work was to write remunerative works of abuse under false names against statesmen either dead or bound to silence by the party truce. The Tories can look after themselves, but I am concerned for fair play and the decencies of public life; and, since this stuff is flying about again, perhaps an Independent should say an impartial word.

The main charge is that the Tories caused the war and endangered the country by failing to rearm in time, and failing to rearm with effect. It is conveniently forgotten that in the East Fulham by-election in 1933 the Government now charged with sloth and cowardice were loudly abused as 'war-mongers' (I have the quotations at home) and the Labour candidate rode to victory on a cry which practically was 'Butter before guns.' Further, almost to the end, the Socialist Party voted against all the Service estimates. We know their answer. Their action was a constitutional protest against the foreign policy of the Government, against the 'betrayal of collective security,' and so on. That makes no sense, for even 'collective' security could not be worked without arms. But the main point is that it was quite impossible to rearm *with effect*, to get the hearty backing of the workers, to ask for 'dilution,' or the relaxing of Trade Union rules so long as Labour in Parliament was denouncing the programme as capitalist war-mongering. And the defence breaks down completely when we come to the Spring of 1939. Then, when everyone knew that war was imminent, and arguments about 'collective security' were purely academic, the Government proposed the first instalment of conscription. Both Labour and Liberal parties hotly opposed it, and Mr. Attlee moved a vote of censure. We are now told that it was not till they condescended to enter the Government of 1940 that anything worth doing was done. If that were true it would be nothing much to boast about—they should have come in at the beginning: but it may be observed that the aircraft which won the Battle of Britain, the ships which held the seas, in 1940, were not designed or begun in that summer.

I always refused to support by my vote the accommodations with

Mussolini. I voted for 'Munich,' after great heart-burning, but the more I saw of the war, the more sure I was that the much-maligned Mr. Chamberlain was right. If some of the fiery yellow scribblers had been where I was in mid-1940, and with the same amount of ammunition, they might have agreed.

To-day Abyssinia is free, the Czechs are free, and Britain's name stands high. But these men still think it proper and patriotic to blacken her name again with shouts of 'Men of Munich,' and miscellaneous mud from the past. There are some deplorable Britons who see an element of 'Munich' in Russia's action of August 1939, and in the present plight of the Poles. But they do not rush about shouting those opinions. It may well be that everything Russia does is an act of immaculate statesmanship, but let us have fair play for our own people, even if they are 'politicians.'

If I had chosen to spend the war writing yellow books of abuse about the 'Prog, M.P.,' I could have made a good and lucrative job of it. I am glad I did not. Every party, the whole people, as Mr. Bevin frankly said, share the responsibility for the years before the war, and it profits nothing to dig them up again. After all, the aim of 'appeasement' was to preserve the peace by Christian dealing; and it is possible to be proud that we suffered so much provocation so long, and tried, in Christian fashion, not to believe the worst of others. But, pride or shame, we are all in it. Now we have got together, let us go on together.

But I was very unhappy, like many others, during that long four days' debate of September 1938. Earlier, in August, I had seen a good deal of General Louis Spears and a stalwart group of Conservatives expert in foreign affairs. They had no doubts. But though I hated Hitler more and more, I became less sure. I heard Mr. Runciman give an account of his mission to Czechoslovakia, and that thickened the fog. There was something to be said for the Sudeten Germans—our favourite motto 'self-determination.' I attended one meeting at which Mr. Churchill was present, but after our fracas over the Privilege affair, I felt that he could not be very glad to see me there and was uncomfortable. So after that I kept away. The one gleam of humour that I remember in those dark days was the young Fascists selling their paper *Action* at Piccadilly Circus, and crying, '*Action!* Twopence! We don't want a war!' '*Action!* Twopence!

We don't want to fight for the Jews.' I prepared a small speech for the debate, urging the immediate inclusion of Mr. Churchill in the Government—'Churchill the conqueror and Chamberlain the cool' together. Later, I believe, they did go well in harness; for Mr. Chamberlain was an admirable chairman, and more tough, at the end, than he was considered then. But it seemed too obvious and I kept quiet. I voted sadly for 'Munich': and the whole thing made me ill.

12. 1939

But now I had no more doubts. There would be war. On 5 November 1938, the day they sent me to bed, I enrolled myself and my small boat in the River Emergency Service, for war duty in London River, where we were to spend five years together. During the Spring and Summer of 1939, under Admiral Oldham and the Port of London Authority, the R.E.S. did training and 'exercises' up and down the river. Patrol boats steamed perilously (and pointlessly) alongside moving ambulance steamers, made fast, lost most of their paint, and transferred 'casualties' to the admirable nursing ladies. Elderly gentlemen fished dummies out of the river and gave themselves lumbago or intercostal neuritis. We hauled up long-suffering volunteers from the bottom of deep lighters, or carried them from barge to barge, brave men, on stretchers. We mugged up and practised our Morse and semaphore again, studied the International Code, and learned a great many flag signals that we never had to use in war. But I never felt that we were 'having fun' or wasting our time. We were preparing seriously for a real war. And nothing was wasted.

So I did less in Parliament that year. I woke up one day, like the Duke of Devonshire, and found myself making an extempore speech on the Naval Estimates, and supporting a demand for more destroyers, for I had served in the Convoy Section of the Admiralty at the end of the first war and accompanied the Commodore of a thrilling convoy to Alexandria. When Lord Hugh Cecil retired from the House Sir Arthur Salter was elected in his place, and I very proudly became 'Senior Burgess.' Sir Arthur is a member of the famous Oxford family whose steamers have given so much joy to so many on the upper Thames. I was much amused, a little later, to hear that a certain dignitary of the Church had said, with not much accuracy—or Christianity: 'Oxford University to-day is represented by a boat-builder and a buffoon.'

I see that I began my little speech about destroyers with this story, adding that I assumed I was 'the boat-builder.'

What I said next, as things turned out, was not wildly unsound. But it would not be difficult to persuade me that the Government, without our advice, were already conscious of the need for multiplying our escort vessels (which, indeed, with glorious effect, later Governments, and, for all I know, that Government did). That was always the difficulty I felt about 'butting in' on such general and technical debates. If one was silent one might be betraying the country; but, more likely, if one spoke, one was merely reiterating the obvious, which I, at least, am never keen to do. One doesn't know.

When one does know—or thinks one does—one may still be talking well-meant nonsense, or one may simply meet a brick wall. That year, for example, I vainly spent much time and trouble in badgering the Minister of Transport about canals—and about the Thames. Here, I thought, I did know what I was talking about—with the coming war in mind. I do not claim prophetic powers, but I did imagine a war in which we should have much less control of the Channel than we had had for a long time, in which it would be much more difficult to bring oil, or coal, or anything else from the west coast to London River by sea. So, indeed, it turned out. Now, on the map there is a good inland waterway from the Severn to London, but the section from Severn to Thames was useless through neglect—weeds rampant, channel shallow, locks out of order. I wanted the Government to put that waterway in order, in readiness for the war. Nothing was done. For oil, we had to lay a great pipe from the Severn to Walton-on-Thames, and fine work it did. It may be that that pipe was planned already (far more was planned ahead than the Government got credit for) and the Minister could not reveal it. But oil was not the only thing. Coal and timber and metals travel well by canal. I may have been wrong, but I do not think I was raving. The Germans would have done it.

They would also, I swear, have built more piers in the Thames, another matter on which I badgered poor Mr. Burgin. Lack of piers had long been a major obstacle to the London water-bus scheme, or dream—in the old days there were, I think, twenty-five piers between Tower Bridge and Hammersmith; in 1938 there were four. But now I was thinking of the war, of the patrol boats, the ambulances, the tugs and fire-floats, the small Fleet vessels which would be built up-river. Also, suppose that other means of communication were blocked, and we had to use the Thames. Again, I was not raving. There was often, in the war, a difficult and dangerous congestion at the piers, many valuable eggs in one basket at Westminster, for example, M.L.s and Air Fleet Rescue boats. On the night of 7 September 1940, I saw four piers burning or battered within a quarter of a mile in Limehouse Reach—the Surrey Commercial, the West India Dock, the old Metropolitan Asylums Board, and the Limehouse Pier. The last was damaged; the others were destroyed. North Woolwich Pier was hit on the same night. In May 1941, the night they hit the House of Commons, the big Tower Pier was bombed and sunk. From then till the end of the war there was only one pier (Limehouse) between Greenwich and Westminster (seven miles), and if the Admiral-in-charge, London, wanted to go afloat, as he often did, he had to motor from Tower Hill to Westminster. But in 1938 they thought that I was talking nonsense.

After these experiences, I did not regret that I had not spent more time assisting Ministers to prepare for the war. They knew so much. Let them get on with it.

13. 'Say It in *Punch!*'

Once more the Londoner's a right to ride,
Like Pepys, a passenger on London's tide.
—Festival of Britain Programme

Nothing is wasted. I hope, Young Man, you will never be cast down by Parliamentary rebuffs, however cranky you are thought to be, however soundly you are smacked on the nose. So often the battle-cry of to-day becomes the commonplace of to-morrow: and your unsuccessful shouts may have had more effect than you knew.

In 1837, on the accession of Queen Victoria, Crown patronage was severely cut down by the Civil List Act of that year. The sum available for Civil List pensions (for distressed authors, artists, scientists, etc.) was limited to an annual increase of £1200. The Duke of Wellington, then Chancellor of Oxford University, denounced this figure as mean and niggardly.

I did not know this in 1936 when King Edward VIII came to the Throne, and I proposed that the figure should be increased to £2400 a year. My advocacy, I expect, was a little clumsy, and I had a bitter battle with Mr. Neville Chamberlain, Chancellor of the Exchequer. 'Say it in *Punch!*' he hissed at me when I was being (I thought) most eloquent and earnest. I was defeated by 185 votes to

110: and I thought, 'Well, that is that, for twenty or thirty years.' For the subject can only be raised at the beginning of a new reign: so if Edward VIII had reigned as long as we hoped, the Civil List Pensions would still be what they were. But in 1937 there was a new Civil List Bill: and in it, without a word, Mr. Chamberlain (bless him!) increased the annual addition to the pensions to £2500, £100 more than my original figure. In the debates the matter was not mentioned: I never liked getting up simply to say 'I told you so.' But just one hundred years after the Duke of Wellington made his protest, a humbler representative of Oxford University was proud to write and say 'thank you' to the Chancellor.

I started 'saying it in *Punch*' and elsewhere about the London water-bus far back in the twenties. In 1932, with Mr. W. H. O. Bunge, I wrote a book about it (*No Boats on the River*).

The London Thames is, I hope, rather more than a local affair. So many Britons, so many men from over the seas, have looked at it, and loved it, and wished, in vain, that they could use it. Now that they can, I do not regret the time and trouble—and treasure—we spent, though we never got anywhere.

On 29 March 1939, in a roundabout fashion, I contrived a skirmish in the Chamber about the general neglect of the London Thames. It could only be a demonstration, but there was vigour in it, you will agree—and perhaps a touch of temper. I was disappointed in the Minister for Transport, Mr. Burgin (he sounded such a go-ahead fellow), and deeply disappointed in the London Passenger Transport Board. Before I entered the House in 1934, while the Bill creating the Board was being debated, I had drafted an amendment transferring to the Board the London County Council's powers to run a passenger service on the river, which was adopted. This seemed the sensible thing. But London Passenger Transport Board would not consider providing such a service.

Meanwhile, Mr. Herbert Morrison and his merry men had come into power at Council House. They had been turned out by the Municipal Reformers in 1904, very largely because of the 'Penny Steamers.' They might well be willing to bring them back. But now, through my own act, they no longer had the powers. No wonder so many citizens prefer to leave things alone.

So now, in despair, I drafted a little Bill and asked leave to introduce it under the 'Ten Minutes Rule.' The Ten Minutes Rule is a very good institution.

If you wish to introduce a Bill you can hand it in at the Table and have leave to introduce it without a word said. It is then printed (which is something) and formally deemed to be 'read a first time.' You have then the ordinary chance of getting a Second Reading debate, but if you have no luck, you may never be able to speak about it.

Under the Ten Minutes Rule, if you choose, you can 'ask leave' to introduce your Bill, and make a brief speech explaining it. Someone else can make a brief speech in opposition, and then there is a division (or not). You may or may not get your 'leave,' but at least you have given your theme an airing; and, since all this happens just after Questions, you may have a very big audience.

That day, I heard later, her present Majesty the Queen was in the Speaker's Gallery, making her first visit to the House of Commons.

THAMES RIVER STEAMBOAT SERVICE

MR. ALAN HERBERT: I beg to move,

That leave be given to bring in a Bill to restore to the London County Council power to provide a service of passenger vessels on the River Thames and for purposes connected therewith.

This is a matter of more importance than it seems to be on the surface, for it touches the efficiency and equipment of the Port of London not merely in times of peace, but in time of war. . . . There is the highly important question of piers and landing-stages. The position at the moment is that the London County Council may build a pier, but may not build or run a boat. Private persons, on the other hand, may run boats but not build piers, I understand. The Port of London Authority may build piers, but not run boats; and there we are—a very typical situation in this great country. Section 19 also laid upon the London Passenger Transport Board the general duty

to consider and take such steps as they may think fit, by virtue of the powers transferred to them, to utilize the River Thames for the purpose of passenger transport, whether by steamboats motor-boats or other vessels.

For one reason or another, good or bad, the Board has taken no such steps whatever—they have no money; they have a great many things to do, and anyhow they are a landlubberly lot.

ROYAL ASSENT

Message to attend the Lords Commissioners.
The House went; and, having returned,
Mr. Speaker reported the Royal Assent to—
1. Consolidated Fund (No. 1) Act, 1939.
2. Cancer Act, 1939.
3. China (Currency Stabilization) Act, 1939.

But here the stranger to our proceedings deserves some explanation. The 'last preceding' bit, as we say in Acts of Parliament, means that that confounded fellow 'Black Rod' came in and interrupted my eloquent remarks. Ever since the intrusion of Charles I the Commons have been jealously severe about the admission of Strangers, however distinguished, to the Floor of the House. All Acts, in theory, are the work of the King—in Parliament; and, spiritually, he is always there, as he is in his Courts of Justice. He could still, I believe, if he wished, attend our proceedings as a spectator in the Gallery. Queen Anne came from time to time, and afterwards 'warmed herself at the fire.' But he must not set foot on the Floor of the Chamber. The same rule applies to our honoured colleagues the Peers, though we reserve a Gallery for their use upstairs. Not even our own fine Messengers, with the golden Mercury on their breasts, may step beyond the Bar to hand us a message. They must beckon and whisper from the Bar. The Sergeant-at-Arms, and the Clerks at the Table, are the only unelected persons whom we admit without question to the sacred Floor.

But, from time to time, the King, or the Lords, send a message to the faithful Commons. It may be merely a personal message from His Majesty—thanks, for example, for a Loyal Address, a birthday greeting, or a vote of money for the Royal Purse. Such a message is then brought by a Member of the Royal Household, who is also a Member of the House of Commons. He is in Court dress. He appears at the Bar and bows. He advances five paces towards the Speaker and bows. Another five paces, and another bow. That brings him to the Table, where he delivers his message, and then retires—still five paces at a time, still bowing—and backward.

But when the King (or the Lords Commissioners who represent him) desires the attendance of the Commons in the Lords to hear the signification of the Royal Assent to 'certain Bills which have been passed by both Houses,' the thing is different. The message is brought by the Gentleman Usher to the Black Rod, an official of the House of Lords (as a rule, an Admiral or General). He is not a Member of the House of Commons (or even the House of Lords). What is more, he represents, at the moment, the King, whose approaches, officially, we still distrust. So we shut the door in his face. He knocks on the door with his rod of office (in the old House, destroyed by the Germans, they used to show you the great hole he had made in the door). Our attendant cries, 'Who's there?' and he answers, 'Black Rod.' The attendant, cleverly interpreting our wishes, opens the door and admits him, and in funereal tones announces, 'Black Rod.' Till then, the Member who is speaking, intent upon his argument, may not perceive what is up. All he has heard is someone saying 'Order—order,' and he wonders what he has said or done wrong now. But now he sits down, with, perhaps, a secret swear. Black Rod comes to the Bar and bows. He is in knee-breeches and stockings, with silver buckles on his shoes. With great dignity he advances to the Table, with the same precise drill of pacing and bowing, and, at the Table, when he speaks of 'this honourable House,' he bows ceremoniously both to Government and Opposition. The Speaker, obeying the summons, rises then and goes to the Lords, followed by Ministers and ex-Ministers in pairs, with any other Member who cares to go. They return in ten minutes or so. The Speaker reads out the Acts to which he has heard the Royal Assent, and the debate begins again.

All this is fine. It is history, and I like it. It is wholesome to know that you are doing this and that because Charles I did this and that centuries ago. But it is no end of a nuisance to the wretched Member who is speaking. He has just settled down to his argument, has just begun to capture his audience, when he has to break off. Some Members who go out with the Speaker do not come back. The spell is broken, and he feels he should start all over again. I used to feel that I was a sort of magnet for Black Rod. Once he interrupted while I was fumbling for my peroration. Since we do not mind banging the door in his face, you may ask why we should not ask him to wait till the end of a speech. But, in theory, His Majesty is waiting in the House of Lords, though, in fact, it is only three of the Lords in cocked hats. On this occasion, I dare say, his visit was timed so that the Queen should see the ancient ceremony, in which case I have no complaints.

On a division my Water-Bus Bill was defeated by 174 votes to 132, which did not surprise me.

That was my last shot in the long campaign. I gave up. But nothing is wasted. Mr. Tom Macpherson, I am glad to say, the cheery Labour Member for Romford in the 1945 Parliament, has picked up the sticky torch which I took over from Sir Samuel Instone. He is[1] Chairman of the Thames Passenger Services Committee set up by the Minister of Transport, representing various bodies and interests.

With some swift and admirable vessels built by Mr. Odell, the Lambeth tug-owner, a limited service was started in July 1948. In the fine summer of 1949 there were nearly a million passengers: and everyone, except the faithful, was much surprised. New piers and vessels are to be part of the official plans for the Festival of Britain, and visitors at last will be able to travel through London by water from Hammersmith to Gravesend—fifteen miles. The State, though all our transport is nationalized, leaves all the risk in this affair to private enterprise; which makes me laugh. But one day His Majesty's water-bus may ride the river. May I be there to see!

[1]1948.

14. War

We were quite right, I fancy—the private Members—to keep going at our small works and wrangles. For if everybody drops his tools the moment the foreign bully threatens, the bully has won before he begins. But all that year the war was crowding in upon us, and the King's Government was making ready for war, more evidently there perhaps than elsewhere. Ordinary folk might go about their business, but the Order Paper was always reminding us of reality. We learned with incredulity, but satisfaction, that we had guaranteed the security of Rumania and Poland. There was the National Training (Conscription) Bill, with special interest for University Members. There were debates and Bills, about Civil Defence and War Risks (insurance), about Gas and Conscientious Objectors. There was the White Paper on the Schedule of Reserved Occupations (concerning which I wrote an Ode).

We adjourned on 4 August, without much hope, and scuttled back from the seaside on the 24th with none. I had had the *Water Gipsy* newly painted, white and Oxford blue, for a family trip from Hammersmith to Oxford. But this was no more than a defiant gesture. Parliament met on the 24th and the 29th. On one day— the 24th—it passed through all stages in both Houses the terrific Emergency Powers (Defence) Act which surrendered most of the rights of everybody to the Government. The old machine can work swiftly enough, at need.

After the last debate, when almost all had gone, a few of us sat round Mr. Churchill. And one said, 'Do you think there will be war, sir?' 'Yes,' he said, without a moment's hesitation. Then he said surprisingly, out of the blue (for no one had mentioned the river): 'But I think we shall have to abandon the Thames.' I remember piping up proudly: 'I belong to a Service which means to see that we don't, sir.' Bold words, and foolish; but, after all, we never did.

I had a queer, modest, but exciting, and, I hope, useful part in the war, divided, a little unfairly, between the House of Commons and the tidal Thames. 'Unfairly'—because, I confess, I spent much more time in my ship than in my seat, especially after the Spring of 1940 when some of our Service joined the Navy and so were on duty all the time. Yet I made about twenty-five speeches besides some skirmishes in Committee, and now and then was very active.

I managed, as well, to write for *Punch* most weeks, and from February 1940 I never failed to send to the *Sunday Graphic,* somehow, a piece of verse or two designed to cheer, comfort, or chide my fellow-citizens. Being fortunately able to say my say in two papers, I felt the less regretful or guilty about saying less in the House.

Every Member, I suppose, did something else as well during the war (we met, for the most part, only three days in the week). But I admired, though I did not envy, those who still made the House their main place of duty, and attended regularly. It was a grim, frustrating, difficult duty. You could seldom say all that you meant or knew, because of the 'public interest.' If you applauded you were probably a 'yes-man,' or 'hero-worshipper'; and if you criticized you might be labelled ignorant, indiscreet, unpatriotic, or merely a 'nagger.' If, in spite of all, you felt impelled by conscience to say this or ask that, there were always the demons 'Security' and 'National Interest' eager to stop your mouth. The Speaker, through the Clerks at the Table, might refuse to accept your question—or the Minister to answer it. I do not think I ever suffered in this way myself. I am trying to speak fairly of some whose activities I seldom applauded at the time. They thought it right to go on being Members of Parliament, war or no war. I always, at least, admired their industry and courage, and now and then they had 'something to show' at the end. Even if they had not, our ancient democratic system had something to show. For, in spite of Security and National Interest, many hard things could be said, and were. Mr. Churchill himself, at the height of his power and popularity, had to stand up and answer them. Hitler did not have to do that. But Hitler did not win.

Without the freedom to nag ('Security' and 'National Interest' always excepted) the true solidity of Parliament and people would not have been so unanimously displayed. The few could chide, and so the many had a chance to cheer. Mr. Churchill and the Government Whips were always delighted when the Independent Labour Party (three or four Members only) insisted on 'forcing a division' after some big debate, and the Prime Minister would laughingly thank Mr. Maxton for his opposition afterwards. For 'a majority of 497 to 4' will catch the eye of the world when 'carried unanimously' does not. How foolish—but how human!

The war Parliament—Lords and Commons—deserved all the sincere compliments that Mr. Churchill used to pay it. It never surrendered all its rights; but it was content, on the whole, to nudge rather than nag, and was more of a help than a hindrance. Coming and going between their constituencies, their regiments, their ships, their battlefields or offices, and Westminster, the Members carried to the heart of things the feelings of the people and the Forces, and when some strong tide of opinion flowed in the country it surged up those channels to the Whips and the War Cabinet. Mr. Churchill did not have to summon the Gauleiters or the Gestapo to find out what the people were thinking.

Moreover, that Parliament was always there—a feat of fortitude for which it has not perhaps received enough praise. Just before the war there were great plans for the 'evacuation' of the House, and I remember receiving a mysterious packet of secret instructions and labels. No destination was named, and I have no notion where we were to go. I did not ask, for, wherever Parliament met, I was determined to stick to my old river, which, I rather felt, could not survive a war without me.

The plan, after all, was reasonable enough. It would have been no joke if, on a big day, a sudden raid had caused three or four hun-

dred by-elections, and perhaps got half the Cabinet as well. And, it
may be, I should not have seen so many bombs fall on poor St.
Thomas's Hospital and the County Hall if Parliament had departed.
But it never did—by the firm desire, I believe, of Members themselves, strongly supported, I am sure, by Mr. Churchill. We did
move, for a few months, a few hundred yards, to Church House in
Dean's Yard, Westminster. But, grateful though we were to our
episcopal hosts, nobody was happy there. The building, we thought,
was cold and uncomfortable. We missed our warm panelling and
spacious lobbies, our Library and Smoking Room. When we went
back to our own place all were agreed, I think, that the risk of
bombs was better than the home of bishops. At Westminster, through
everything, the Mother of Parliaments remained, a prime target,
easily distinguishable beside the river. The House of Commons
Chamber was destroyed: a bomb fell the same night (10 May 1941)
through the roof of the Lords, not far from their Chamber. The
Palace of Westminster and precincts were hit by ten high-explosive
bombs, one oil bomb, and many hundreds of incendiaries. St.
Thomas's Hospital, across the river, was hit many times. Almost
every building in sight beside the river was wounded. One morning
I left Westminster Pier and saw large holes in the eastern face of
Big Ben. But the Speaker was still in his fine house by the bridge. For
the most part, true, they sat during the hours of daylight only; but
the doodle-bugs were not afraid of daylight. The old lady sat there
still, speaking for Liberty.

It was a pretty grim place to work in, too, during the war. The
black-out, in such a building, was an almost impossible problem.
A few hurricane-lamps on the floor were the only lighting of the
great Central Hall, and they made it a lofty tomb of gloom. All the
windows went in the early blitzes: the east side was all cardboard
and sandbags, and you could not see the river from the Smoking
Room. On the terrace was a Guards machine-gun post (of which
I went in fear many nights on patrol, in the early days, when E-boats
were expected in the Strand). Our favourite pictures and tapestries
were taken away, and left depressing gaps. The Harcourt Room
was full of beds for the A.R.P.; the lower corridors were anti-
gas refuges. The Smoking Room closed earlier—very rightly—to let

the staff get home before the blitz. And all the time there was the feeling that the things that mattered were happening elsewhere—a strange sad feeling for the proud M.P. and law-giver. It was pleasant enough for me, after a long voyage up the river from Canvey Island, to pop into the Smoking Room in the evening, hear the gossip and have a drink (if there was anyone left), to dart in now and then, with special leave from the Navy, and make a speech about this or that. But I could not have endured to be there all the time, and I honoured those who were.

My queer division of duty between Westminster and the water led me into some comical situations, especially in the first two days. Early in the morning of Saturday, 2 September 1939, all members of the River Emergency Service received a telegram which said simply, but excitingly, 'Stanhope.' This meant, 'Proceed with your vessel to your appointed station.' My mate (a neighbor, Dr. Magnus Pyke) and I carried our box of iron rations over the mud, got up anchor, and steamed down the river to battle—feeling much better for the great crop of captive balloons which had sprung up during the night. My first 'appointed station' was Lambeth Pier. As I turned into the tide below the bridge I remembered sadly that almost exactly twenty-five years earlier (I think it was 5 September 1914) I had enlisted in the R.N.V.R. near Lambeth Pier, for the war to end wars. But here, in every sense, we were again.

But there was no time for sad reflection. The Grand Fleet, assembling in the North Sea, could not have taken itself more seriously than we did, and there was much to do. The mobilization was fine. Up and down the tideway, from Southend to Hammersmith, all the sixty small ships turned up at their stations, and, as soon as they could escape from their offices, their crews. Parliament was meeting across the river that afternoon. But I was far too busy to be bothered with Parliament. I had two crews to muster (for we were 'Civil Defence' then—forty-eight hours on and off) and instruct and report and ration. We had to draw supplies, prepare the black-out, tend the engines, test respirators, and all the rest of it. They might be arguing about war over there at Westminster, but at Lambeth we were at war already. Some of the Service were billeted behind us at Lambeth Palace, the Archbishop of Canterbury's residence. About sundown I saw the old Archbishop (Dr. Lang) walking slowly home across the bridge. I darted up and accosted him about some difficulty the men had had with his butler about the black-out. He said he would do what he could. Almost as an afterthought, I remember, I asked him what was happening in the House. He seemed to think that everything was rather vague.

But we were not vague in the *Water Gipsy*. That was the first night of the black-out, and how conscientious we were! The wicked Germans were sure to jump the gun. I had to telephone that evening from a public box which had no black-out, and I remember how guiltily I struck a match—just one—to see the dial. But over the other side nobody knew where we were, and Mr. Amery was crying 'Speak for England!'

It was a very hot night. There was thunder and lightning and tropical rain. How it rained! In the little cabin it was stifling, but we would not show a chink of light. We sat there stewing, read the Standing Orders, and practised our Morse with electric torches. (One can laugh at all this now, but 'nothing is wasted,' and later, in the North Sea, my Morse, I believe, may have saved five men's lives, my own included.)

Later, William Mabane and Peter Thornycroft arrived from the House, stumbling about the black pier in the violent rain. It was so dark you could only see Lambeth Bridge by the lightning. The legislators were soaking wet and in some distress of mind. They babbled about Mr. Chamberlain and Mr. Greenwood and Mr. Amery and the French, and we could not make head or tail of it. Bill Mabane kept saying, 'It's too hot. Open the window!' I said: 'We can't. Don't you realize there's a war on?' (It was the first time, perhaps, that that famous phrase was used.) But one of them said: 'There's no war! The French aren't in yet.' 'Then where are we?' we said. They didn't know. But still I would not open the ports. When they had gone we went to sleep, under the roaring rain, with the cloudy impression that there was to be no war, or, if there were, our country would be alone. It sounds comic, but it was a nightmare night.

But next morning, Sunday, 3 September, the sun shone benignly, and we felt that there must be a nice definite war on such a day. France might be out, but the *Water Gipsy* was ready. The House was to meet at twelve, and I thought that I must not miss this day's proceedings. But I was also sure, as so many others were, that the war, once begun, would fall with full force on London at once, and I could not risk being absent from my post for a moment when it fell. So I arranged for my crew to anchor the ship near the Speaker's Steps, and be ready to take me off in the dinghy. I went up to Heppell's, the chemist, in the Strand, and heard Mr. Chamberlain broadcast there. I did some shopping and had a chat with the sunny Mr. Somerset (of Heppell's), who was never short of a smile from that day till the end of the war. I strolled down to the House, carrying a book he had given me called *Hitler's Last Year of Power,* which I exhibited confidently to the crowds outside New Palace Yard. I was crossing the Yard when the sirens sounded the alarm. Was it the alarm—or was it a practice? I asked one of the policemen what he thought. He shook his head and looked at the skies. But I thought it was the real thing. 'It would be just like them,' I said— as we all said. I ran at once to the Speaker's Steps, congratulating myself on my foresight and my insight into the German mind. The dinghy was already on the way when I reached the stairs; the anchor was coming up. The moment I clambered aboard the ship was under way. Few naval evolutions can have gone with such precision. As we chugged past the terrace a group of Members leaning over the wall—Sir Peter Macdonald, I remember, was among them—gave me a hearty cheer (though the Press Gallery, I fear, might have described it as 'ironical'). I plucked the flagstaff from its place and waved the Blue Ensign aloft. A minute later we were back on station. London was saved, we felt.

During the first few months of the war, we had, like others, not much to do except to train and practise and patrol a little. We put on our gas-masks and did exhausting exercises in them, started the engines, heaved up the anchor, steered by compass, sent away the dinghy for drowning men, and made fast to lighters. All this might have been very useful if the Germans had ever obliged by using gas. My crew, for example, at the fore end of the ship could not hear the orders I boomed into my respirator at the wheel, and we arranged an elaborate code of manual signals—'Make fast—anchor,' and later, 'Cease Fire,' etc. My very good friend Richard Collett, the director of the D'Oyly Carte Company, but now, alas, dead, joined us enthusiastically on a gun-drill day. In his unaccustomed respirator he at once got a ghastly wound in the shin from one of the unaccustomed anchor-flukes, developed phlebitis, and could never serve again. I instructed my crews in Morse and semaphore, and my wife, an ambulance driver, gave us some first aid. I learned by heart the compass courses through all the bridges, which was useful on many a murky night throughout the war. We kept a cold watch all night on Westminster Pier, and shovelled away the snow in the morning. The I.R.A., it was supposed, I remember, might toss a bomb onto the pier from the Embankment. I never knew what we could do if they did, except report the matter or register a protest; but they never did that, or, as far as I know, any other mischief, for which, I think, they never received the nation's thanks.

I was often used, and proudly, as a go-between between the river authorities and Whitehall, and did all I could to show the world how ready the river was. Mr. Herbert Morrison sometimes would come across from the County Hall and have a sausage. One night I took him down to Tower Bridge, where our Headquarters vessel lay. Below Waterloo Bridge it turned foggy, and below Blackfriars Bridge we were nearly sunk by a tug. I had a high official from Scotland Yard to lunch, at anchor off the House. It was a gusty day, the wind against the tide. After the first sausage the high official was sea-sick and had to be landed. No slight is intended upon this gentleman. The Thames can be very rough, even there; and down below, on the long run to Canvey Island, I have had many a sea-sick passenger aboard—Wrens and ratings as well.

Sir John Anderson was then Minister for Home Security, and one dark night I gave him, and his cheery Parliamentary Secretary, Mr. Allan Chapman, a laborious demonstration of our powers. We made fast to a lighter just above Cannon Street Bridge, where the ebb-tide is savage and the eddies dangerous. Mr. Allan Chapman, in the public interest, consented to be a waterman unfortunately wounded during an air-and-gas raid on the farther side of this particular barge-road. Two of us, panting in our gas-masks, carried him across two wide lighters and along the perilously narrow deck at the side of a third. Mr. Chapman, though a hero, was by no means a feather, and he was lucky indeed not to be dropped in the rushing waters for his country's good. But the Minister for Home Security, we hoped, was duly impressed.

I hate to have to admit it, but it might almost be said that this part of our training and practice was wasted. When the real war began we never had to rescue a wounded waterman from a lighter; nor did we ever have to go alongside a moving ambulance as dashingly as we did in 1938, though that practice was often useful when closing steamers in Sea Reach later. There were numerous casualties in the river, but not so many as were expected—for the simple reason that anyone who could got off the river and went belowground. Even the ambulance steamers had less work than we thought they would. The excellent doctors and nurses had a tough, trying, and sometimes terrifying time, tied up, quite without protection, to remote piers at Rotherhithe, Woolwich, and Erith. But in 1943 the Service was disbanded. What will you? No man can foresee everything, but here, as elsewhere, the Thames was ready for everything.

During this, the 'phony' period, there was a great purge of the little patrol boats; and, it was decided, not for the last time, that the *Water Gipsy* was not fit for war work in the tideway. She was too slow, and too slight, would be banged to pieces, and never do the work. But she was reprieved. She is a queer, comical, uncommon craft, I must confess, and was not built for war, but she is tougher than she looks. She is 39 feet long, beam 9 feet, and draws 2 feet 6 inches only. She has a cockpit forward (which is all wrong) and the wheel right aft, with no sort of protection for the helmsman from weather or war. She weighs 6½ tons, with nothing in her, but has only two small 9-horse-power petrol engines (by Messrs. Thornycroft of Reading). She is high out of the water, with very little under it, and so is difficult to steer in a high wind; and sometimes at the windy corners we have gone round in circles two or three times before I could get her to go ahead. It was a wonder many a day that she did not roll over, or fatally plunge her open nose into the big waves of Sea Reach—and they can be big. I had a movable 'weather-board' made for the big seas forward, and the crew used to stand by with buckets forward, but always, I think, she had about three inches to spare at the stem-head. She was well built, by the brothers Cole of Hammersmith, of seasoned oak and pine. Twice in the dark, on tricky night exercises, we rammed a barge-road. Once we hit the unlighted Ovens Buoy, and broke a rib or two, on the starboard bow. A steamer rammed her at anchor in about the same spot. A small bomb fell a few feet from her on the starboard bow and filled her with splinters (I was in the House and my mate, at the wheel, was wounded). She was squeezed between lighters, buffeted and banged against steamers and mine-sweepers, battered against the piers by the wash of fast tugs. One day, in Limehouse Reach, her rudder fell off. She should have died a thousand deaths, but her timbers are tough, and she is still alive. She was slow indeed, and her engines were small, but they were lovingly tended, and she kept going. With her eighteen horses she steamed 20,000 miles in the war, with the tide against her or under her. The lightermen laughed at her—but not for long. For five years she wore the *White Ensign* and carried two machine-guns. She was a queer, comical, uncommon craft, but she served the King sturdily, and I was proud of her.

When Parliament met again I was not too busy saving London, I am glad to see, to strike another blow for Private Members' Time. It was doomed, no doubt, to perish in the war, for war is the best excuse of all. But the war was still so 'phony' that there was just a chance of saving something, if it was only the Ten Minutes Rule procedure and the right to get our Bills printed. If we had, the final story might have been different, for the smallest remnant would have kept the memory and the tradition alive. But the fort fell, finally, that day. So I record without shame that even on that day— 29 November 1939—I made my usual protest.

This power of initiative is based upon the assumption, agreeable, I think, to private Members and not, I hope, offensive to others, that the stock of creative legislative wisdom does not cease at the southern end of the Treasury Bench. I see no reason, however grave the war may be, why that assumption should be abrogated.

On a division the Government won by 213 to 115.

My next utterance was about the kindly Sir Kingsley Wood's wicked proposal to put a tax on books, in July 1940. But many more important things had happened before that. Everything had happened. Hitler had sprung; the 'phony war' was finished; Mr. Chamberlain had fallen. In the confused division which put him out, I suppose it may be said that I was on the wrong side again, for I voted for the Government. I did this—and it was over-logical, maybe—not from loyalty to Mr. Chamberlain but from love of Mr. Churchill. For the debate was about the naval expedition to Norway. Mr. Churchill, as First Lord of the Admiralty, was responsible for that expedition and made the concluding speech for the Government. I did not feel like voting against him the first time he was in trouble, even if that vote could be interpreted as an oblique vote against the Prime Minister. I wanted to see Mr. Churchill at the top, but I thought this was a dubious way of getting him there. But here I was probably wrong, and I should raise my hat, as I do, to those patriotic experts who contrived to get him there, by any way at all.

At all events, there he was. And I have never been so proud and glad to be a Member as I was when I listened to those first tremendous orations. I never could get a seat on the thronged Floor of the House; but in the old Chamber there were overflow galleries on either side, two benches deep. It was better to be up there than below, for one saw the whole scene—the Members squashed on the benches like so many prawns, sitting on knees, squatting in gangways, standing in rows at the Bar, the Ambassadors with grave, dumb faces bending over the rail, a few uniforms below. On such great occasions there is an electric charge in the House which sparks and crackles everywhere long before the big thing happens. Small jokes receive enormous laughter. Every 'cheer' is a roar. Members are good-humoured and kind with each other and do not complain however many late-comers slip in and thrust their sterns into a space that is not there. Only the Speaker in his wig seems to be the same, as if he would show the world that wars may come, and new Prime Ministers, but the British Parliament flows on for ever. At last Questions are over and every ear is itching. But the curtain-raiser is not yet done. Some Ministers have a statement to make, and dutiful Members put questions about it, but now they are heard with some impatience. A new Member, fresh from a by-election, is trembling at the Bar. Confined and elbowed like a prisoner between two Whips, he performs his paces, and his bows, to the Table. Few know, or care, who he is, but he gets an encouraging cheer, and lucky he is to come to the Commons on such a day. Then the Chief Whips and the Clerks do some ritual mumbling together. For some reason—known to few—the House is going into Committee of Supply. The Speaker leaves the Chair and the House (poor man, it is one of the few days, maybe, on which he is eager to hear speeches). The Sergeant-at-Arms advances and puts the Mace in its bracket under the Table (because the Speaker, the King's representative, has gone). The Chairman of Ways and Means sits at the Table beside the Clerks in their wigs and gowns, and at last he says: 'The Prime Minister.'

All heads are turned one way, and there is heard the sound which, on paper, is written, 'Hear, hear'—or 'Cheers.' It is not, in fact, a cheer—that, I fancy, would be out of order, nor is it 'Hear, hear,' but ' 'Ear, 'ear' always. These two diminished syllables can express an astonishing range of emotion and meaning. There is the ' 'Ear, 'ear,' mild and encouraging, polite and patronizing. The ' 'Ear, 'ear' ironical, which says, 'Oh, really?' or 'Just what we expected!' and the ' 'Ear, 'ear' accusing, which says, 'We told you so,' and the murmured ' 'Ear, 'ear' of respect for royalty or the dead. There is the good-humoured ' 'Ear, 'ear' of surprise and delight at an unexpected jest or a new point admirably made. Then there are the concerted, the almost choral ' 'Ear, 'ear's', the raging, the bitter, sometimes the almost animal ' 'Ear, 'ear's' of party resentment or triumph, and these, now and then, are ugly to hear. But best of all—and different from all the others—is the deep bass booming ' 'Ear, 'ear' of a united House, growling defiance at a common foe, whether it be a London newspaper or a foreign land, and swearing support to him who speaks for them—and for the people. No statesman, I suppose, not even Mr. Pitt, has provoked the thrilling sound so often as Mr. Churchill. Perhaps on that first day, the day 'of blood and toil and tears and sweat,' the cheers were not so loud as they were later, for there was still some rumbling about Mr. Chamberlain's treatment, and besides, the time was almost too tremendous for cheers. Hitler had Norway and was roaring to the Channel. Poor France was rolling down the hill—though then, I think, we still had hopes about 'The Bulge.' We were likely to be left alone, as we had not been for centuries, with a powerful enemy at Calais and Cherbourg. But then, at the Table, stood this one man, with the pale round bulldog face, grim but undaunted, precise and strong in speech and intention, ready to lead us 'if necessary, alone.' 'You ask me my policy. My policy is Victory.' Short words, but shattering, explosive, electric. I have been moved in theatres and churches, but never so deeply as those early speeches stirred me, up there in the Gallery, the famous phrases which passed into history as soon as they were spoken. All knew at once that they were history. Some have said—Mr. Churchill has modestly said—that he did no more than express what was already in the hearts of the people. I think there was rather more to it than that. The trumpet does not blow for nothing. It was one great difference between Mr. Churchill and Mr. Chamberlain. He, after all, was tough enough and, since the war began, had been heart and soul with Mr. Churchill. But when he said the fine true thing it was like a faint air played on a pipe and lost on the wind at once. When Mr. Churchill said it, it was like an organ filling the church, and we all went out refreshed and resolute to do or die.

HOLEHAVEN

Some time before these great events my ship, to my delight, had been transferred to our lowest station on the river, at Holehaven, in Canvey Island, five miles above Southend. (Our beat ran to Sea Reach Buoy No. 4, just above Southend, where the Commander-in-Chief, Nore, took over from the Flag Officer-in-charge, London.) The river war was to become real enough at Westminster, but in Sea Reach it was real already, all the time.

One of the *Water Gipsy's* first jobs was to take out fuel to a mined steamer which was being towed up Sea Reach and needed petrol to keep the pumps going. How proud we were! And she was moving at a fair speed, so that our 1938 practice in closing the ambulances assisted us. Now, too, we had real messages in Morse from the Central Tower at night and flag signals in the International Code by day; we could laugh at those who had laughed at us at Westminster. I became quite an expert in the International Code,[1] and in quiet mornings the signalling officer and I would have conversations by the flags, for practice. That black day when we heard that France had fallen, I remembered, as I rowed out to my ship, a queer signal I had noticed in the book—'ATI.' 'There is no need for alarm.' It was not exactly what we had felt in the 'Lobster Smack,' but I hoisted the three flags now. The officer replied, 'BDV' ('Approved'), and made it a general signal to the little fleet, and I think we all felt better.

Sea Reach in those days, even above Southend where the convoys gathered, was a very war-like place. At Shellhaven, just above us, torpedo tubes were ready for an invading Fleet. One day a mine layer laid a string of shiny great eggs across the river just below Holehaven, and it was one of our many tasks to see that no ship dropped an anchor among them. Just below that, opposite the fort on Canvey Island, they drove thousands of piles into the Blyth Sands on the other side to complete the line of the anti-submarine boom. The fort used its searchlight a lot and from time to time fired a shot across the bows of a foreign steamer: then a patrol boat would have to go out and explain to a harassed Greek captain why the British were shelling him.

Three 'hoppers' full of soldiers with Bofors guns were moored on the north side of the reach, and there were many trips to be made to them, difficult work in the rough weather. The wounded ships were always coming in, to be repaired or beached, and we proudly did what we could for them. Some of us patrolled the reach all night and lectured the ships at anchor about their blackout if a chink showed anywhere. Chinese seamen gave trouble at

---

[1]Was Goebbels good? At least he missed a great opportunity when the British began their 'V'-sign campaign. 'V' may stand for Victory; but in the fine and famous International Code—begun by our own Captain Marryat—it means 'I require assistance.' If Goebbels and his staff were really good, they would have said: 'Listen to those poor Allies—tapping away their three-dots-and-a-dash, crying to the world: "I require assistance." Of course they do! And where are they going to get it?' 'Lord Haw-Haw' could have put this over very well.

first, for they would tear down the black-out to let the evil spirits out.

Then they shifted the East Blyth Buoy, and the little boats, flying a little L-flag,[2] had to direct the mighty steamers to steam north of the buoy. What a chap I felt one early morning when one of His Majesty's destroyers obediently altered course at my command! Sometimes a motor-barge from the Medway would try to slip up on the south side: then the *Water Gipsy* would roll and waddle across to intercept her, flying the K-flag now—'You should stop your vessel instantly'—and with a rifle ready to fire across her bows! Yes, we had a rifle now, for, though 'Civil Defence' still, we were part of a 'striking force' against invasion. One rifle a boat, fifty rounds of ammunition, and no notion when any more was to be had. The more I saw of our resources then, the less I doubted my vote about 'Munich.'

All this was exciting enough for the owner of a small boat built for family parties at Hammersmith, and 'unsuitable for war work.' It was a rough, tough life. But the little fleet was manned by jolly fellows, we were much in earnest, and ready for anything, and in off-hours the little 'Lobster Smack' was a haven indeed. Church parade was held on the gravel outside the pub. I used to sit at the cracked piano by the window in the bar, and play the hymns, while Mrs. Went made ready for opening-time. In the evenings I played for many a hearty sing-song. Like millions of others, I was happy in a humble part. But Holehaven was a long way from London for professional men on voluntary duty, and already I had lost some of my admirable crew.

At this time, by the way, I believe that many of us modestly regarded ourselves as doomed and heroic men. For a mile or so above us were the multitudinous oil-tanks of Shellhaven and Thameshaven; there was another group close behind our anchorage on Canvey Island. They still wore their bright coats of aluminum, and in the moonlight they shone like a range of snow-peaks. It was a common opinion that when the Germans hit one—as, one day, they must—all the rest would go off with a bang and level everything for miles around. This did not happen, though many were bombed and burned. They burned for a long time with a thick

_____
[2] "You should stop. I have something to communicate.'

black smoke, like a lamp turned too high. The firemen did heroic work protecting the others. We did not envy the soldiers stationed there—Captain Bill O'Bryen, for example, of theatrical fame, with three M.C.s.

I loved Holehaven in that electric Spring and Summer, when we served the ships and waited for the enemy. Much as I love her, I should never pretend that London River is truly beautiful. She does not compare, for example, with the lower Seine. From the Nore to Woolwich, let us confess, she has nothing to show but flat land adorned with a few factories, and, far behind, a few little hills. Yet, like a good woman, she acquires beauty by force of character, and, the longer the acquaintance, the more you love her. The comedians may laugh at Southend-'on-Sea,' but there is real sea in Sea Reach. Barnacles grew richly on our bottom, and some nights there was a fine show of phosphorus. There were cockles to be had in the sand when the tide swept out of the haven. The bawley-boats caught more than shrimps, and, now and then, we pulled up a plaice in a hoop-net. On bright days the reach is blue. At low water the haven is all flat sand, shining amber in the sun, and the creek is a ribbon, difficult to enter. Festoons of sea-weed on the high Dutch dyke gave a brave smell of the sea. From the haven narrow creeks wind inland through the meadows to Benfleet and Pitsea, the home of many water-birds. At low water they are but oozing culverts, rising at every corner to high banks of mud. These high brown banks are curved and shaped like the bosoms and buttocks of giant blacks. They lie hidden at high water and every turn is a trap. Only at half tide can you learn your way between them. As we drew so little water, it was one of our jobs to study and remember the channels, in case of an invasion across the flats. We should not, I think, have long delayed the enemy; but we took the task very seriously and I knew the secrets of many muddy miles. The quiet cows looked down upon our cruises: the water-birds (whose names I never knew) slipped in and out of the reeds and rushes. We imagined they were Germans and out-witted or destroyed them all.

On a dark night, patrolling the reach, which here is 1½ miles wide, we felt at sea indeed. With not a light to be seen, the flat

lands on either side might be the ocean itself, and our small craft
was an impertinence, a duck defying the Atlantic. Then, far off,
the sirens wailed at Southend and Benfleet. The sky began to groan
and growl, and the searchlights pointed their protesting fingers. The
pale petrol-tanks emerged like clumps of mushrooms from the night.
There were the small steamers at anchor, and the great tanker
(God help her!) full of oil.

Due south at Chatham, seven miles away, began one of those
terrible, brilliant bombardments, a concentration of flash and
fireworks, the more frightful because, unless the wind was right,
it made no noise. It was like seeing the silhouette of a murder
behind a suburban blind. Which flash was bomb—and which was
gun? We knew not. But many a night we wondered if anything
could be left of Chatham. Still, far off, let us confess, it was exciting, almost enjoyable. In later days, when the bombers began to
roar over us for London, we were in the front row of the stalls.
Tall tents of light were erected all about us. The wide reach was
like a street; the petrol-tanks were giant pearls; even the little
Water Gipsy must be evident to God and the enemy. The din
was outrageous. The 'shrapnel' clattered on the deck, or hissed as
it hit the water; and we felt like a small child who has strayed
by chance into a lighted stage before an audience of malignant
grown-ups. Yet we were in the audience too. From Sea Reach we
could see the whole vile show. We saw the procession of searchlights march up to London, and, far off, over London, the flicker of
the shells. Then the lights, and the noise, came back: and there
would be that one bomber they had caught in the lights, wriggling
and twisting like something at the end of a monstrous toasting-
fork, a brilliant bird on a luminous spit. Then—*then* we manned the
little gun again and 'stood by.' For surely, surely, one night some
weary Hun-bird would be forced so low that even the *Water
Gipsy* could shoot him down. We should send the dinghy away
and save the crew—or steam alongside with revolvers ready—and
we should carry our prisoners in triumph to the haven (and probably buy them a drink at the 'Lobster Smack').

It never happened. The last beast droned over; the lights went out; the 'All Clear' came, a thin, reedy, pipe far off, across the water. All was over: and again we were alone in the dark. Something shining and beautiful and stimulating had gone away. That is, perhaps, the worst of war: it can be beautiful—and, far enough away, you can enjoy it.

High folk in London did not take my duties as seriously as I did. The Ministry of Information were always badgering me to lecture. I did compose a lecture on 'Liberty,' and delivered it at Bath. It bored me, but they seemed to like it, and I believe that in it I used for the first time the phrase 'a sense of urgency' which has since become such a statesman's favourite.

That same lecture nearly did me a mischief at the time of Dunkirk. It was a pity, and a mistake, we thought, that they did not send the River Emergency Service Fleet across, as a fleet in formation, with Captain Coleman, R.N., our fine Commodore, Harbour-Master of the Port, in the van. Our engines were fuelled and tuned and working; we had our own discipline and drill and signallers and flags and rations. The ships were small, but they could have gone the farther inshore; and many just as small did go, or start at least, ill equipped and unready. In that weather even the *Water Gipsy* could have got across, I think, though she might have had to go in a convoy of one. The thing was considered, I believe, and earnestly, but the Admiralty thought that the river must not be left quite defenceless and unattended. A compliment, no doubt. So the boats had to stay on station, but individuals, in their forty-eight hours off, might go if they could be back in time for duty.

I cannot complain of the decision, for, if the fleet had gone, I should have been left behind. He who leads a double life is always finding himself in the wrong place with the best of intentions. That wretched lecture on Liberty had done the citizens of Bath so much good—or so the Ministry of Information said—that they, the Ministry, urged me to deliver it again. Very reluctantly I had consented to do it again at Portsmouth (only because it was Portsmouth, the home of the Navy) on a Wednesday in May. As the day approached, and the war warmed up, I tried hard to get out of it. But the Ministry seemed to think that, unless I delivered my lecture on Liberty, the 'morale' of Portsmouth might as well be written off, and so I said, 'Oh, very well.' And it turned out to be the Wednesday in Dunkirk Week! On the Monday evening, knowing nothing about 'Operation Dynamo,' I went off on my forty-eight hours to rub up my lecture and go to Portsmouth. At Portsmouth, dining with the Mayor on a hot summer's evening, in Dunkirk Week, I was not surprised to hear that he did not expect a very large audience. His Clerk kept popping out to peep at the hall and coming back with a gloomy face. I told them that the last thing I should want to do that night would be to listen to me delivering a lecture on Liberty, and, if the audience was small, I would much rather get them round the piano, make them sing, and cheer them up, perhaps; for almost everyone in that town had relatives in peril. But the Mayor did not think that that would be quite the thing. So I blew off the lecture on Liberty to an unexcited company of about two hundred—and what a wonder it was to see so many!

When I got back to Holehaven next day the two stout fellows I had left in charge told me what had happened—or not happened—and rushed off at once to go to Dunkirk as 'individuals.' They never got beyond Sheerness, for it was too late, but there they joined the Navy, and never came back to us. I cannot blame them now, though I did then. Another stalwart of mine, Grinling, an old soldier, had decided that he must go back to the Guards. So now we were very shorthanded, and two or three nights I was left quite alone. That night, I think, there were two of us, and we went about our humble duties cursing the Ministry of Information, the Principles of Liberty, and everything else. Three of our Service did manage to get across as 'individuals,' and did good work. The small boats, and the small sailors, who had been doing nothing all the war were rightly applauded for that week's exploit. But we, who had been training for twelve months and serving for eight, were asked, rather queerly, 'Why didn't you go to Dunkirk?' The signal for us was 'General Frustration.'

But this is a common circumstance of war, and at least we knew that their Lordships of the Admiralty thought well of our work.

On 18 June I left the ship at 07.00 and went to Westminster to hear Mr. Churchill. It was the speech in which he said:

For all of us at this time, whatever our sphere, our station, our occupation, our duties, it will be a help to remember the famous line:

He nothing common did, or mean,
Upon that memorable scene.

It was the speech which ended with the famous passage:

Let us therefore brace ourselves to our duty and so bear ourselves that if the British Commonwealth and Empire lasts for a thousand years men will still say: 'This was their finest hour.'

With what a glow of the soul we heard those words!

But, alas, that very night the *Water Gipsy* was having one of her finest hours, and 'the master' missed it.

The Battle of the Thames began long before the Battle of Britain, and continued long after it. It might be said to have begun far back on 22 November 1939, when the enemy attacked the pier and anchorage at Southend and dropped fourteen magnetic mines between the Chapman Light and the Boom. I find 'Air Raid Warnings Red' in the log in late April and early May. But the first real attack of 1940 fell upon Holehaven on 18 June, when the unsuitable *Water Gipsy* had a front place and a miraculous escape. Alas, I missed the affair, for it was my 'day off' and I was in the House. A bomb fired an oil-pipe running from the tanks to the jetty. The *Water Gipsy* was sent out into the river to stand by the jetty, in case any 'personnel' were cut off by the fire. The Germans came back, bombed the blaze, as they did in those days, and a bomb (it must have been a small one, but still) fell close to her starboard bow. An officer on the dyke thought it was a direct hit, but when the splash had cleared away there was the little unsuitable ship still bobbing about. My mate, at the wheel, Mr. Udale, was hit in the helmet and hurt. I am a foot taller and should have got it 'in the neck,' they said. So Oxford, perhaps, was spared a by-election. But the unsuitable *Water Gipsy* and her deputy-captain were the first casualties in the Service, and, I believe, in the river.

The next thing, two days later, was naval officers arriving, at dead of night (0135, by the log), to ask if we would join the Navy for whole-time service; the commanders of vessels to be Second

Hands. This was a very different affair from Civil Defence (two, or three, days on, and off) and none of my old crew could give so much time, even if they were fit—not even my old faithful, D'Arcy Braddell, the architect, who had come back to help us when he could (he was building a hospital). But I thought that I must say 'Yes,' though I could not imagine how things would work out: for how could London River flow on without me? Twenty-six years earlier Mr. Churchill had prevented me from going afloat with the Navy, and now Mr. Churchill's Government were giving me another chance. In a small ship, certainly, but it is no small thing to wear the White Ensign. So I said 'Yes,' and passed the doctors A1. (The three stalwart men, by the way, who had done good work at Dunkirk were all ploughed by the doctors, a strange thing.) One could wear one's ordinary glasses for the eyesight test, but it was just as well that the doctors did not ask me what would happen if it rained, and how, without glasses, I should read the compass then. No doubt they did not imagine one of the King's vessels having no cover over wheel or compass. I did have some anxious times steering by compass in the rain, but I managed, and the doctors were right. Later, when I was constrained reluctantly to go before an Officers' Medical Board, I was classed as C3, fit only for office-work, because of my eyes. Yet for four years I had been navigating at night, in a narrow river full of unlighted dangers, which I declare, without doubt or hesitation, is much more difficult than sailing the sea—and I have had some of that. 'No, thank you,' I said, 'I will remain a Petty Officer—A1.' I always resent and resist the arrogant airs of the 'deep-sea sailor' towards the mere coastal or river mariner. It must evidently be easier to avoid collision or shipwreck in a large space than a small one. This question came up in very practical form in the House much later, when they denied the men of the river, even the mine-sweepers, their medals. I fought for the river, but was defeated. To be fair to the Navy, it is only some of the high-and-mighty who talk after this manner. Many a naval officer has told me that he moved in terror on the Thames and thanked God when he got to sea again.

But now, for the second time, I was enlisted in the Navy; and we went to Chatham Naval Barracks to be 'kitted up,' an exhausting

affair, though they were very kind to the queer fresh-water fellows.
No one realizes how much time the sailor ashore spends carrying
heavy weights—great stuffed hammocks and monstrous kitbags.
I had been on patrol all night without sleep in the reach, and kept
dropping off in the gas-mask lecture. The considerate lecturer, a
Paymaster-Commander, dropped a book whenever I slept.

But we were proud in our 'Number Twos' at the 'Lobster Smack'
next evening, with the fine red Crown and Crossed Anchors on our
arms. In the first war I had started as an Ordinary Seaman, was
married in bell-bottomed trousers, and rose to Lieutenant and
Adjutant, mounted on a fierce black mare who frightened me more
than the Germans. Now I had gone back to non-commissioned
officer, but I was still proud. After all, I had a 'command' in the
Navy. When we hoisted our first White Ensign (an enormous flag
it was) I might have been Admiral Jellicoe himself. The first patrol
orders we received were addressed to H.M.S. *Water Gipsy,* and
I have the staggering document still. That, you may imagine, did
not last long. We came down to 'H.M. Patrol Vessel,' and in the
end we were reduced to a 'Naval Auxiliary Boat' (the mean fellows). They reduced us grudgingly from Second Hand to Petty
Officer, and from Petty Officer to Petty Officer (Small Craft Only).
Having cajoled us into the Navy with fair words at midnight, they
did not always treat us very generously. But the fine flag flapping
aft of us was always the same. They could not modify that.

We got our first issue of battle-ship grey within a week, and
slapped it on in patches when we could.

But we were more interested in our armament. Soon we had
two rifles (with plenty of .303), two revolvers, and (strangest of
all) two cutlasses. The cutlasses (in the use of which we were never
drilled) made them laugh in the Smoking Room, but down at
Holehaven we felt we were very much in the 'invasion area,' and
we kept the weapons very seriously handy, over two of the bunks.

We were also to carry a Hotchkiss machine-gun, like the other
patrol boats, but ours was a long time coming. Little as I like loud
noises and explosive weapons, I was very keen to be a terror to the
Huns as soon as possible. A fellow Member at the House said he
could easily get me a machine-gun (as if they grew on trees) at the

Ministry where he was working. So I went to the Ministry of ———, an amused General received the Petty Officer, and I marched proudly out of the front door with a Browning machine-gun under my arm. But this was an Air Force weapon, and our .303 ammunition was no use to it: so we were no nearer to killing Hitler than before. On whose advice I forget, I went to a famous aircraft factory at Kingston. The sergeant in charge of the defences on the roof was delighted to acquire the Browning (which fires, I believe, some fabulous number of rounds a minute), and to give us an air-Lewis which would take our ammunition but, having no water-jacket, got very hot very soon. Not long after, we 'drew' our official Hotchkiss, and the *Water Gipsy,* for her size, must have been the most heavily armed vessel in His Majesty's naval forces.

15. A Tax on Books

I pass to the Battle of the Books.

This story, at least, has a happy ending: and it has much more than a local interest—for any English-speaker.

There was, originally, to be a purchase tax on newspapers and periodicals as well. The estimated revenue, from newspapers and periodicals, was between £3,250,000 and £3,500,000, and from books between £1,000,000 and £1,750,000. The newspaper-tax, not surprisingly, was soon abandoned. But Sir Kingsley Wood, the chubby, cheerful Chancellor of the Exchequer, was obdurate about books. After receiving a deputation of the highest authority, led by the Archbishop of Canterbury and including men of the greatest light and learning, he dismissed the whole thing as if it were merely a question of the 'publishing trade' having to suffer the same as other trades.

Others, Mr. Kenneth Lindsay, for example, another University Member, did more and better work in this affair: but I believe I made the first speech against it, in the General Budget debate, on 25 July, the *Water Gipsy* being in dock. I let myself go.

I hope that the relations of Oxford and the City of London will always continue to be friendly, but when I hear the representative of the City of London referring to a tax on books, the 'machine-tools of education,' as someone has said, of the great craft of literature, the great profession of learning, as a tax upon a mere 'hobby,' to be compared with golf, then that is a mind with which I can make no contact, and I do not propose to try. . . . Does the right hon. Gentleman desire, or does he not desire, in his extraordinary language, to '*limit the civilian consumption*' of domestic hollow-ware, brushes, brooms, and, as he said finally, with that charming smile, books. Does he really desire to '*limit the consumption*' of Bibles and Prayer Books? I suppose I cannot get an answer to that. If he does, there is still a niche in that Lobby, and he may go down in history as the first Chancellor of the Exchequer to put a tax on the Word of God. . . . I was reminding the right hon. Gentleman just now of a book I have here, *The History of the Taxes on Knowledge,* with which I hope the Treasury officials will try to become acquainted, because they seem to have forgotten, if they ever knew, that it is only seventy or eighty years since the great fight against the Taxes on Knowledge was fought and won in this House. They were taxes on the free communication of minds, on the movement of thought, and on the free expression of opinion. These taxes were finally wiped out between 1850 and 1870, and the principle was then established that we would not put any taxes upon the things of the mind. That principle has stood firmly against every attack since then and has survived two major wars. It has remained for the right hon. Gentleman the Member for West Woolwich (Sir K. Wood) to break it down.

It is a sad and shocking thing that at this time, in this titanic conflict, when we are saying, and saying truly, that there are arrayed, on one side, the spirit of force and, on the other, the forces of the Spirit, we should have sunk so low as to be seeking to put a tax upon, and to treat all learning and enlightened literature in the same way as we should treat brooms, or something which is kept under the bed. The right hon. Gentleman had a great opportunity. He might have said, 'However many Hitlers are at the door, however many dangers and difficulties confront us, we are not so down and out and so poor in resources that for the sake of £500,000, which is my estimate of the yield of this miserable tax, we are going to do this barbarous thing.' . . . Well may the shades of Milton, of Caxton, of Sheridan, and of Charles Dickens, and of those brave men, who in the last century fought and won the principle of free enlightenment, groan in their honoured graves to-day to think that that lamp which they hung on the walls of Westminster has been clumsily torn down at last by a Chancellor of the Exchequer, who, at this hour of civilization, sees no important distinction between boots and books.

The tax on books (and 'domestic hollow-ware') was to be at the rate of 33½ per cent. The story is that as the Chancellor sat down on the Treasury Bench before one of the debates he turned and said to someone: 'I'll show them! I'm going to tell them they're lucky I didn't put books at the higher rate.'

But great is the House of Commons (now and then), and it prevailed.

I was not in at the death. In Committee, on 13 August, Mr. Isaacs (Labour), a printer, later Minister of Labour, moved to 'leave out lines 38 to 53,' and made a good speech he had cut short because the Chancellor had already 'dropped a hint.' Sir Kingsley had seen the red light and he rose at once. He was a little grudging and for once seemed wounded: 'I must say that I feel that a good deal of the sound and fury has been unjustifiable.' But 'while there is much to be said to the contrary, in view of the considerations to which I have referred, which do not apply to other articles in the Schedule, I think that, on the whole, I should agree that books as well as newspapers should be exempt from the tax—at least for the present.'

'*At least for the present.*' But we heard no more of it. No mean victory was won that day. And not for Englishmen alone, I hope.

16. In the Navy

Now we were in the Navy there was no more question of choosing a crew of friends from Hammersmith or Chelsea. The *Water Gipsy* was fed with men from the Patrol Service Headquarters at Lowestoft—and very well fed she was. Nothing could have been more 'democratic' than that little vessel. The one main 'cabin,' in which two of us slept and, sometimes, four of us ate and cooked and washed up and washed and argued and cleaned the weapons, studied our flags, practised our knots and splices, and wrote our letters, or prepared our speeches, was only 11 feet long by 7 feet wide. But there, for five long years, we lived together, nearly always very happily, whether we were a butcher, a greengrocer, a plumber, a chauffeur, an insurance agent, a stoker, a Yorkshire fisherman, or Lancashire pitman, or a University Member. One engineman fired off a Lewis gun in the little cabin, and missed the stomach of my mate by an inch or two, but that was an accident—cleaning arms. There was only one fight in the little ship, and hardly ever any trouble or temper. And yet we lived in irksomely and dangerously close quarters; and there was the Captain eating and sleeping and sharing everything with his crew, which is supposed, in the Navy, to be an impossible condition of things. They say, I believe, that you cannot have Christian names and good discipline:

but somehow we managed it. I count myself a pretty good 'mixer';
we were all keen on a great cause, and in the dark times, of course,
we were united by discomfort and danger. But there was more to it
than that. They were fine, forbearing fellows, those simple, humble
men from many corners of England. We got along well in the drab
times and the dull duties too, and I shall always remember all of
them with gratitude, affection, and pride. They came and went.
Not all of them were born for the water, and some went back unfit.
Some went to sea, and some got commissions. But always there was
the same fine friendly spirit.

In the early days of the Battle of Britain our unsuitable ship
was assigned to a new and strenuous but splendid duty. 'Mail and
store-boat' has a menial sound, maybe, but who sees more of life
than the postman? And we were a postman armed to the teeth.
Now we were no more confined to a single station, but covered the
length of the river every day. One night we would lie at Westminster, Chelsea, or the Tower, and hear the news of London; the
next we would be at Holehaven, among the seaweed and the
sailors and the 'shrapnel.' It was a tough job, for men and engines.
We picked up mails and messages, miscellaneous gear and reinforcements at the Tower Hill Headquarters, and stores at Bruns-
wick Wharf, Blackwall, the place from which the Pilgrim Fathers
sailed. Sometimes the little ship looked like a 'moving' van as she
rolled on down the river, and I could hardly see to steer, for the
miscellaneous mountain of stuff on her flat top-deck: great cans of
oil and petrol, office furniture, ammunition, revolvers, toilet paper,
cutlasses, buoys, soap, flags, bread, tinned foods, rum, cleaning
cloths, medical stores, and coils of rope and wire.

We called at seven or eight stations on the way down and got
rid of some of our load at each—always a great business of counting and checking and receipt-signing, and we felt pretty small
counting our toilet-rolls or ammunition at Tilbury Landing Stage,
with big steamers coming and going, tugs banging us against the
stage, officers 'moving us on,' and watermen crying, 'You can't lay
there!' With these delays, we could hardly ever carry the same
tide all the way, so most days the voyage took seven or eight hours.
At Holehaven we stood by for blitzes with the others at night, and

started back at daybreak or before. Twice, I see, we kept this up for thirty consecutive days, Sundays and all, forty-six miles a day. Hard work, but we loved it. We were proud of our eighteen horses, and we learned more of the river every day. We became adept at 'cheating the tide,' creeping up inshore against the strong ebb, but not so close as to go aground. That gave us about five knots 'over the tide,' but without our artful 'cheating' we were lucky to make four. Soon we could boast that we knew every buoy and barge-road, every wharf and dolphin, every useful eddy or stretch of slack water, all the short cuts inside the lighters and every wreck that made them dangerous. We became so confident that we steamed on, sometimes, in thick fog when all the tugs and their tows had to tie up, and every steamer lay at anchor, ringing her bell. From Holehaven to Tilbury I had compass courses from buoy to buoy, and two or three times we steamed successfully for an hour and a half without seeing the shore, a thing you would not think could be done in the River Thames. That was fun—though cold work in the winter.

In peace-time, I should not, however, recommend the practice to any yachtsman in the upper reaches, or even in the lower reaches, unless the tide is adverse and he can stop quickly.

At the end of the war I had a personal boast that, sitting in the cabin and catching a glimpse of the skyline through a port, a chimney, some cranes, a warehouse roof, I could say at once exactly where we were in our sixty miles of river. After the war I was asked to open an exhibition of London River pictures at the Port of London Authority. I went round the show, testing my vaunted knowledge. Only one picture baffled me. They sent for the artist. I said: 'Now, where did you do that? I can't make it out.' He said: 'As a matter of fact, I made the background up.' That pleased me.

So the mail-boat job was a great education. And day by day, as the blitz roared on, we saw the wounds of London River from top to bottom—the wreck of a tug in Northfleet Hope, a big hole in Tilbury Landing Stage, a big bite out of the jetty at Barking Power Station, oil-tanks blazing at Purfleet, the shattered 'skid' astern of a mine-sweeper that meant a mine gone up, a collier sunk off Beckton Gasworks, another pub gone west at Blackwall, two new

green 'wreck' flags opposite Greenwich, suspicious smoke from
Ford's works at Dagenham, a train hit on Cannon Street Bridge,
the Tower Bridge not working to-day. One night (25 September),
lying by the old *Seven Seas* schooner at Charing Cross, we woke
up and saw Hungerford Bridge (the signal-box) on fire just above
us. We looked down the river and saw a fire on Waterloo Bridge
too. That bridge was then encased in scaffolding and I thought,
'This will be a blaze indeed!' In the early days of our training, I
remember a puzzled friend saying: 'But what exactly will you *do?*'
and myself replying, 'Well, for example, if they hit Waterloo
Bridge, I should have to report it.' He said: 'But wouldn't they
know?' And I said: 'Not necessarily.' And now here I was solemnly
steaming up to Westminster Bridge to inform my officers and the
Port of London Authority that both Waterloo Bridge and Charing
Cross Bridge were on fire—a thing that not many men have seen.
Not much use, perhaps, but my officers were interested to hear the
information. Then we went back to the bridges, to see if there
was anything we could do. But already there was a N.F.S. squad
on Waterloo Bridge and a fire-float pumping the river on to it
from down below: and by the time we got there, both the fires were
out. Smart work.

Few Londoners realize how far up their river the marine war
came. One day we reached Tower Bridge and found all traffic
stopped and the Pool of London a congestion of tugs, barges,
colliers, and tankers tied up and impatiently waiting permission
to proceed. A highly credible officer had reported the fall of two
parachute-mines off the Tower in the blitz of the night before, and
the sweepers were at work, with difficulty, in the narrow space.
Those mines, I believe, were never confirmed, nor were the ones
reported at Hammersmith. But at Bellamy's Wharf, almost within
sight of Tower Bridge, a ship had her nose blown off by a mine. A
tug, with her tow of barges, disappeared off Deptford. Many mines
fell, and were blown up, in Blackwall Reach, and some in Gallions
Reach. A collier was sunk off Beckton Gasworks (a little below
Woolwich). Farther down, in Sea Reach, a great tanker burned for
three days at Thameshaven. She had brought her precious cargo
safely across the ocean, had safely run the gauntlet of the Channel.

She was almost secured—the tugs had not left her—when a mine, dropped from the air and not reported, sent her up in flames. Every man aboard was lost, I believe, and the tugs as well.

Sometimes, when we reported in the morning at Tower Hill, the order was 'Port closed.' All ships and tugs were forbidden to move, and the *Water Gipsy,* feeling a little like Lady Godiva, though not so stately, clattered down the river alone, meeting nobody but mine-sweepers and an occasional patrol craft. (The largest hold-up at Southend, which controlled the convoys, was three days; and at the end of that there were 140 ships in the anchorage.) Other mornings there were reports, not wholly believed in, from everywhere. 'Reported mines in Gallions Reach—keep to the southward.' 'Something under Vauxhall Bridge—keep to the Surrey side.' One morning, not having heard the latest, I shyly asked the Commander, Mine-sweeping, if there were any special instructions for us: *'You!'* he said, breezily. 'They won't bother about the *Water Gipsy.'* So, fortified by this assurance, the *Water Gipsy* rattled along.

On this job we covered 6,000 miles during the six months of the blitz. In the four weeks ending 23 November, I see, we did 1,037.

All this grim nonsense began, as all men know, on 7 September 1940, and that Saturday night the *Water Gipsy* had a grandstand view of the burning Surrey Commercial Docks. We had been given a night's rest at Hammersmith and were celebrating my wife's birthday. But I saw the great blaze in the east, reported by telephone, was summoned to the headquarters barge at Tower Pier, and set off at once with Seaman Longstaff on my most fantastic journey through London. There was a strong ebb under us and no lights on the bridges, which, as a rule, was a worry; but to-night, from Lambeth, at least, every reach was bright from the conflagrations; and no craft were moving. The Houses of Parliament looked as if the flood-lighting was ready but not yet fully on. Bombers were still roaring and bumbling overhead, and, as we passed, a bomb whistled over Parliament into Westminster. I am easily alarmed, and, alone on my unprotected little 'bridge,' with the real war in London at last and God knows what before us, I kept thinking, 'I ought to be frightened. I don't seem to be. Why is this?'

The answer was, I suppose, that, whatever happened, I knew I should not be buried by a mass of masonry or perish slowly pinned by an iron girder. Also, there was the hope that there would be something important to do. Nevertheless, one felt a little naked and presumptuous, alone with a tin hat in the middle of the lighted river. At headquarters all was calm, though the din was terrible. Commander Coleman sent us down to the Pool to find and fetch a tug near the Hermitage Entrance to the London Docks. How many nights have I gone through the Tower Bridge on the ebb when it was so dark—not a light anywhere—that I was almost afraid to go on (for there are tiers of moored barges on either hand of the narrow fairway, and the tide is fierce). But that night the Pool was like Piccadilly in the good old days. Apart from the great glow of the Surrey Docks, there were two or three blazes by the Pool itself—I think that was the night they got St. Catherine's Dock and the wool warehouse at Wapping. We could read the name of our tug—the *Hero*, I think it was—a long way off, but there was no man aboard. So we slowly 'punched the tide' back to Tower, thanking God for our brave little engines, as every small craft ought to do in a narrow tideway.

Now we were given a grander mission—to find a P.L.A. wreck lighter somewhere in the Lower Pool, pick up some wire, and take it to Woolwich, ten miles away. The wire was wanted for towing burning barges. Very proud, we went down through the great bridge again. We had an important task; we should save London yet, and cared nothing for bombs. We found the wreck lighter at last, moored off Rotherhithe. The friendly crew, who were placidly sitting there, watching the fires and listening to the bombs, told us that nobody could get to Woolwich, because no one could get past the Surrey Docks: two or three craft had turned back and told them so. But we were full of our mission and demanded the wire. While the wire was coming aboard and I was signing receipts, a bomb whistled over us into unhappy Rotherhithe and the two crews fell into a heap of humanity and coils of wire on the lighter's decks, cursing a lot but laughing heartily. We set off at once. At the bottom of the Pool I thought sadly that this was the end of the 'Prospect of Whitby,' the little Wapping pub I had so often visited.

There was a blaze each side of it, and I was glad Jim Bean had 'gone in private' before the war. We rounded Limehouse Corner and saw an astounding picture. Half a mile of the Surrey shore, ending before the Greenland Entrance of the Surrey Commercial Docks, was ablaze—warehouses, wharves, piers, dolphins, barges. The wind was westerly, and there was a wall of smoke and sparks across the river. Burning barges were drifting everywhere, and I thought, 'Well, this is surely where they want our wire.' But there was not a soul in sight—the small police-boat ahead of us had turned back to report—and we had been ordered to Woolwich. A wooden ship, and petrol-driven, we did not like the look of it much, but we put wet towels round our faces and steamed at half speed into the torrid cloud. Inside, the scene was like a lake in Hell. We could hear the hiss and roar of the conflagration ashore, but could not see it, only the burning barges and the crimson water which reflected them. It was not so alarming as it had looked outside, for the main whirl of sparks and smoke went over us. We took off our towels and felt quite happy. It was something to be the only boat in Hell. We steamed on slowly, using the compass and dodging the barges, and at last the *Water Gipsy* came out safe, but sooty, the White Ensign nearly black, the other side. After that, all the other fires we passed seemed no more than night-lights, though there were some brave ones. I now had a feeling that nothing could touch us—a thing I never felt in a house. At the top of Blackwall Reach a bomb fell fifty yards ahead of us. I ducked down behind the wheel, I know, but truly I felt no fear, and this astonished and delighted me. We delivered our wire at Woolwich—I hope it was some use—and came back through the smoke again to Westminster.

Next day, Sunday, Captain Coleman sent us down again to investigate this and that and report. The 'Prospect of Whitby' was still standing, a smoking hiatus on either side, and two barges upside down on the foreshore below. In Blackwall Reach a barge had been blown ashore and stood leaning, end-up, against a house. The Greenwich Tunnel had been hit and filled. At Blackwall we went ashore and wandered in the battered streets, marvelling at the brave, worn people.

The police, though it was only nine in the morning, had wisely ordered the pubs to open, a noble tribute to the pub—and there they soberly told each other the tales of that black night, the first of the many. The next morning, 9 September, the Fishmongers' Hall, by London Bridge, was burning. It was the first fine old building I had seen in flames, and I remember my useless rage. We carried on with the mails to Holehaven. In forty-four hours the little ship had done 104 miles.

17. The Battle of Lambeth Bridge

On September 11, 1940, was the tiresome affair which I call the Battle of Lambeth Bridge. We had come up from Holehaven, Seaman Longstaff and I, and were lying at Charing Cross Bridge for the night. The sirens went, and Longstaff mounted the new Lewis gun which he was itching to use upon the enemy. Soon after the blitz began we saw a fire above Lambeth Bridge, on the Surrey side. We cast off and 'proceeded' through the bridges, to see if there was anything we could do (I still had hopes of dramatically rescuing somebody from something). But the fire turned out to be inland a little, and we heard the fire-engines approach as we did. I was for returning to our berth—and bunks. But Longstaff, the tiger, said: 'Why don't we stay round here and fire on the ———s when they come back and bomb the firemen?' I could see no objection to this—except the noise he would make, which I knew I should not like. But noise was just what the citizens of London wanted. On the previous nights, as all complained, London seemed to have no 'reply,' and, as we had a weapon, it seemed right to use it. It was a moony night, with occasional cloud. We could clearly see our nearest balloons, and Longstaff kept saying that he could see the Germans. I saw no reason to doubt him. They had had so little resistance that they might well be coming in low. Sometimes he said that he could see his 'tracer' bullets going past them, and though I did not think he was likely to bring a bomber down, I supposed that red bullets going past would be discouraging to the foe. Anyhow, there stood my tiger most of the night in the moonlight, with his beard and monocle, blazing away at the enemy whenever he saw good reason. It was, I claim, the most westerly action fought in the Thames under the White Ensign: but, though responsible for it, I found it rather a bore and retired to the cabin. Not to sleep. That happened to be the first night of the London barrage, and my mate was not the only one making a noise. During the night a dud anti-aircraft shell passed through the window of the House of Commons Library, not far below us, and penetrated the roof of the Members' 'refuge,' where nobody was. In the morning, when I went ashore for newspapers, I was struck by the new expression of the people hurrying to work. They looked short of sleep, but perky. There was no evidence that any German bomber had been brought down, but London had 'answered back' at last, the noise had pleased them, and I felt rather proud that my mate had made some contribution to the noise.

I left an 'Ammunition Expended' report at Headquarters (it was about 200 rounds), and we started down the river for Holehaven, as usual.

But if the Battle of Lambeth Bridge had bored me, it had greatly excited others. At our first port of call I was summoned to the telephone for a friendly rebuke from Captain Coleman, Harbour Master and leader of the Patrol. Complaints about the battle, it seemed, were crowding in. The big Fire Service Headquarters on the Surrey side said that we had drawn dangerous attention to the neighbourhood. One of the captive balloons had been shot down and we were suspected. There was even an improbable report that the Guards detachment on the Terrace of the Palace of Westminster had complained that we kept them awake. 'Don't you know,' said my harassed Commander, 'that there's no war above Dagenham?' I answered respectfully that Hitler did not seem to have heard of this rule—nor had I. 'Well, that's the rule for patrol boats,' I was told. I said, 'Aye, aye, sir,' and steamed along, a little discouraged, but thinking the matter closed. But evidently the storm grew about my Commander, for at every station at which I called I received a peremptory order to submit a special report in writing explaining why the *Water Gipsy* had fired her Lewis gun at the enemy. This began to weary me, and I determined to let them have a very special report. We did patrol duty in Sea Reach that night, and I had no time for prose composition till the following night, when we lay at Cadogan Pier, Chelsea. Meanwhile, the Flag Officer-in-Charge, London, had issued an order (the first I had seen) concerning the use of patrol vessels' weapons. They were not to be fired unless (a) the height of the aircraft was not less than 1,000 feet, (b) the enemy markings were clearly visible, (c) the patrol vessel was being attacked. I sat up till 0200 writing my report, and, this time, ignoring the behaviour of the enemy.

I rejected at length and with dignity the suggestion that we had shot down a balloon. I mentioned that my gunner had been able to see all the nearest balloons and had taken particular care not to fire in their direction. I reminded my superiors of the weight of metal that was flung into the air by the A.A. forces that night, including the unexploded shell which had passed through the window of the House of Commons Library not far from our mooring, and many large fragments of exploded shells. I submitted respectfully that about 200 rounds of .303 ammunition could not have added substantially to the peril of the balloons or the inhabitants of London. I forget the rest, except the end, to which I gave much thought. I said that I was unable to understand the new order and asked for guidance.

Strictly interpreted [I said] it seems to mean that I am only to use my weapons when my own vessel and crew are in danger. I ask, with respect, for guidance, for such a limitation does not seem to me to be in accordance with the traditions of His Majesty's Navy, and will be accepted with reluctance by the crew of this vessel.

I have, sir, the honour to be

A. P. HERBERT
P.O. i/c *Water Gipsy*

My mate, and others to whom I showed the epistle, said that if I wanted to be flung out of the Navy or into the cells at Chatham

Barracks, I had probably taken the best and quickest course. But I sent it in.

A day or two later, having to call at Dagenham, I saw my Commander coming down the narrow gangway. 'Now for it!' I thought, and halted with a smart salute.

'Good morning, Herbert,' he said as genially as usual. I said, 'I hope my report was what you wanted, sir?'

'Oh, that,' he said. 'You don't want to go on with that, do you?'

Till the end of the war my question remained unanswered.

18. Navigation As a Vice

Alas, I have forgotten her name, and I have lost her address.

'She' is the dear lady who wrote to me in the second or third year of the war and asked if I would like to have the sextant of her husband, a sea-captain, who had died. I gratefully said Yes, for I had never seen a sextant. She sent it, saying, 'I shall be glad to know that it is in the hands of a real sailor.'

I blushed at that; for, though I had done much tideway and coastal sailing, I had never found my way about the open seas, except in a liner: and I hardly knew a sextant from a slide-rule.

I thought the least I could do was to learn something and try to live up to the gracious lady's words.

I bought many books and began. At school I had been weaned from mathematics just before logarithms. (What a mistake!) I now found them fascinating, and passed on bravely to trigonometry and the spherical triangle. I used chiefly Norie's *Epitome,* that excellent little work, C. A. Lund's *Navigation for Yachtsmen,* and Reed's *Nautical Almanack.* I knew the stars pretty well already, but I bought great charts and mugged them up again.

So there I was, with a ship, a sextant, and a good deal of self-taught paper-knowledge. I was still a little vague about the nature of a cosine or a cosecant (I am still), but I knew where to look the little fellows up and how to use them in a Marcq St. Hilaire or chronometer working. I was all ready to navigate the seas and do my lady credit. The only thing was, I had no sea. I was confined to the tidal Thames, and except in Sea Reach (the last reach) could hardly ever get a 'horizon' more than a mile away. In Sea Reach, of course, when the heavenly body was in the right direction, there was often a 'sea-horizon,' but Sea Reach can be pretty rough for taking sights in a small boat.

Most unhappily, I read somewhere that it was possible to use a 'shore-horizon,' with a special allowance for 'dip.'[1] I had no book then which told me how to find the 'dip,' but blow me if I didn't invent a formula of my own! And though my purpose here is not to boast, but to warn the world against navigation, I am rather proud of that. My formula may not be strictly accurate. It gives a result about 9 'seconds' different from the tables I later discovered in Mr. Burton's work. But it takes immensely less time than the formidable formula in the Admiralty Manual, Vol. III. That, as of course all my readers will remember, is:

$$\theta = 0\cdot565\,\frac{h}{d} + 0\cdot423d$$

(h = height of eye in feet and d = horizon in nautical miles)

That takes days to work out; and I am always put off by θ.

My own formula is: Log h (height of eye in feet) — log distance of horizon (in feet) = log Tan Λ = Dip.

There you are: H.E. 20 feet — horizon; half a mile.

Log   20 $1\cdot30103$
Log 3040 $3\cdot48287$
Tan $7\cdot81816 = 22'\ 38''$ Dip

Burton, using another Admiralty formula, gives $22'\ 48''$. The Admiralty formula (above) gives $22'\ 48\cdot6''$ (after hours of toil) and I dare say they are right: but mine seems near enough to me, for

[1] '"*Dip*" or *Depression of the Horizon* is the angle of *depression* of the visible sea-horizon below the true horizon, arising from the elevation of the eye of the observer above the level of the sea.' (Norie's *Epitome*.)

amateur practical purposes, especially in a small boat. How, a mere tyro brought up on the classics, I ever arrived at it I cannot now remember. Nor do I wish to get into an argument about it. I merely record that it ruined my life.

For that really started me on my unprofitable navigational career. Armed with this fatal formula, I began taking sights of the sun, moon, stars, and planets in every reach and corner of the tideway. (For duty purposes I had charts of every reach and could measure my d pretty accurately.) If I was at Westminster Pier I would bring the sun down to Lambeth Bridge for my 'noon position.' Waiting for doodle-bugs, I did some queer experiments with the planets, I remember, bringing Jupiter or Venus down to the end of a pier (with a 'dip' of 6 degrees or so). On week-end leave I sometimes stood at my front door and brought the North Star down to the front door across the road (I think the 'dip' was 9 degrees!). I towed a life-buoy (on a measured line) away from the sun, and brought him down to that. Considering the impossible things I attempted, I got a few surprisingly good results. Twice, in Sea Reach (with a 'sea-horizon'), in rough weather and a rolling boat, I got my longitude right to within 300 yards, using my wrist-watch, and having no Tankey.[2] But even the wildest experiments and wrongest results were instructive, taught me something about the use of the sextant, and the way about the books, and made the formulae familiar. If His Majesty ever sent me to sea, I thought, I should be that much to the good, and I commend my methods to the amateur student who has to study at home.

But of course far better leave navigation alone. Do crosswords, play chess, or choose some exercise for the brain which will not be such a strain on eyes and patience. Peering at the vernier or the Pole Star, ranging up and down those endless columns of haversines and cosecs, I wonder I did not ruin my sight. One of my crew caught the craze—not a seaman, but an engineman, the son of a butcher; and soon he was never happy unless he was working out the latitude of Limehouse or Tilbury or Canvey Island. Up and down the river they marvelled and laughed at us. But sometimes the laugh was with

[2]The navigator's assistant in the Navy—from the fact that the navigating department was responsible for the fresh water.

us. One of our naughty—and indeed illegal—habits, in the winter
when crowds of water-fowl came into the river, was to 'supplement
the meat ration' with an occasional duck and a .22 rifle. Once or
twice, while my crew were retrieving the bird in the dinghy, a police-
boat came along. There was His Majesty's Naval Auxiliary Boat
Water Gipsy drifting aimlessly on the tide. But why not? For there
was her old fool of a skipper on his little bridge, solemnly 'shooting
the sun.' And this was such a wondrous spectacle that the shooting
of the duck escaped notice.

'What,' said the mockers, when we boasted of some good result, 'is
the good of proving that you are where you know you are—especially
if you don't get it quite right?' We pointed out in vain that it is not
everyone who can prove he is where he is by looking at the sun and
doing some sums. We said in vain that we were practising for a day
when we might not know where we were. They understood us only
when we said it was no more crazy than doing the crossword puzzle
every day.

Fate gave me the chance to laugh at that school of thought in 1943
when Mr. Attlee sent me, with two other M.P.s, on a mission to Newfoundland. In a small sailing-vessel of about sixty tons we went 300
miles up the coast of Labrador, among the icebergs and the whales.
My colleagues flew back from Goose Bay. I stayed with the Newfoundlanders in the boat. On the voyage back to Newfoundland we
were driven by storm and fog into a tiny cove in one of the innumerable small islands, all exactly alike, which fringe that formidable
coast. There we lay, fogbound, for nine solid days, eating salt cod
and seagulls (of which, I must say, I preferred the seagulls). The
Newfoundland skipper, a very fine seaman, thought we were in a certain cove in the Seal Islands. His brother, the mate, thought we were
further north, in the Partridge Islands. On the seventh day, for
about five minutes, the sun showed wetly through a hole in the mist.
It was over the land and would have been no use to the normal navigator. But there was I, equipped with my Thames technique and my
formula for 'dip.' I dashed below for the sextant, much to the amusement of the Newfoundlanders, and slightly to their alarm, for there
were some who said superstitiously that I had 'shot the sun' out of
the sky. I took a sight, bringing down the sun to the shore of the cove,

400 yards away (as I judged). Assuming that we were in the place the captain thought, I worked a Marcq St. Hilaire, and got an intercept of 15″. As a check I worked the sight for latitude and longitude and was 30″ and 10″ away. Experts, of course, have told me loftily that I proved nothing, that you cannot establish your position with a single sight. In all the circumstances, I maintain that I did. At all events, I confidently told the captain that he was in the Punch Bowl, Seal Islands, as he supposed. And so he was. They then sent the small boat through the fog to another island for stores. So—as they say—there!

And of course my vice has been some help on yachting trips. But, on the whole, O Lord, the time and toil I have wasted on the heavenly bodies! After the war, instead of putting the fat books away like a sensible man, I worked out the distance to various points on the opposite bank of the Thames at Hammersmith, and began taking unnecessary sights from my garden wall. Many a day, when normal men are having the first beer at the Black Lion, I am getting my noon position. I tell myself—and it is quite true—that without constant practice one forgets the formulae and the way about the books, and if you keep going you are ready for the next invitation to yacht. But it is no good: I know it is a vice.

Then—worse and worse—some grateful theatrical folk who knew about my vice, presented me with a super-marine averaging bubble sextant. This was the end, for now, without horizon trouble, at any hour of the day or night, I can be up to my mischief.

In 1949 I went to Buenos Aires—four weeks out and three weeks back in two very fine ships. Always before I have managed to do a good bit of writing on ocean voyages, and now I intended to work hard and finish a book. But, damn it, I didn't write a word. I took both the old lady's sextant and the 'bubble' affair (never, they said, had a passenger come aboard with two sextants), and I spent the whole of both voyages taking sights and doing sums. The captains and their navigating officers were very kind to me; and it was wonderful, after all my amateur study, to see the professionals at work every day. It was thrilling to be one of the battery of sextants on the bridge at noon, and more thrilling still when my 'noon position' was not so far from the bridge's as usual. Sometimes it was pretty near;

but though at first I thought it would be unfair for a man with two sextants to go in for the sweep on the 'ship's run,' I soon found that my scruples were exaggerated. The passengers, of course, thought I was mad, especially when, the other side of the Equator, I roamed the deck admiring Sirius and Canopus and Orion (upside down) instead of seeing a film. But one of them got me a nice compliment from the Captain.[3] 'Do you often,' he asked the Captain, 'have a passenger who dabbles in navigation?' 'It's not "dabbling," ' said the Captain seriously. And on prize-giving night I was hauled forward and presented with a cross-staff constructed by the ship's carpenter to the Captain's orders. It is a wonderful piece of work, and the Captain, once or twice, got within 5' of the sextant. But what tickled me was that it was inscribed A. P. HERBERT—NAVIGATOR. It hangs proudly on my study wall, and I wish my old lady could see it.

But it is not, I fear, much comfort to my wife—or my publisher.

And a base love of logarithms was not the only trouble the old lady brought upon me. During the war (all because of that confounded sextant) I invented a device for teaching navigation, and another for helping castaways in open boats to find their longitude, which, after long labour and some expense, were duly turned down by the Admiralty and Ministry of Transport. Also, when sick, I went mad and re-named the stars, wrote a book about it, and addressed the Royal Astronomical Society. And in 1949 I began hunting low-flying aeroplanes with my bubble sextant and proving by trigonometry that they were too low!

All this may do no harm, but the love of logarithms remains. It is, I suppose, like chess. Nothing takes my mind off everything so well. I begin the working of each new sight like a child with a new toy. I am thrilled if a Marcq St. Hilaire ends up with a nice small 'intercept.' And if it does not, I am downcast, but I work through the whole thing again, hunting hopefully for a nice mistake. Old lady, you have much to answer for.

[3]Captain Hooper, then in command of the *Highland Brigade* (Royal Mail).

19. Mind Against Mines

'The worst attack [of 1941] was the last,' says Mr. Churchill. That was the blitz of Saturday, 10 May 1941, the night the House of Commons was destroyed. 'He lit more than 2,000 fires, and by the smashing of nearly 150 water-mains, coupled with the low tide in the Thames, he stopped us putting them out.' Thereafter, they built pumping-stations against the central arch of every bridge, and it is a thousand pities it was not done before. It might have saved the City. But, as usual, we had forgotten, or neglected, the Thames and its tiresome tides. The Germans, I am sure, did not forget them.

The same night Tower Pier was destroyed, and our head-quarters vessel (H.M.S. *Tower*) was sunk, with some loss of life. The next afternoon—Sunday—I went down by water (almost the only way) to the Tower, to report, and walked back to Chelsea. This took me five hours, picking a way through the firemen and the hoses, the policemen and the rubbish. On the way I went to see the ruins of the House, and found the firemen still at work in the great hiatus. It was strange to stand there under the sky among the smoking stones, which had seen so much and heard so much of history. On the Wednesday (7 May) there had been a Vote of Confidence, and I had been one of the majority—'Ayes 447, Noes 3.' Mr. Churchill had finished the debate thus:

It is a year almost to a day since, in the crash of the disastrous Battle of France, His Majesty's present Administration was formed. . . . When I look back on the perils which have been overcome, upon the great mountain waves in which the gallant ship has driven, when I remember all that has gone wrong, and remember also all that has gone right, I feel sure we have no need to fear the tempest. Let it roar, and let it rage. We shall come through.

That was the last division. Those were the last words most of us heard in that old Chamber, and a fitting epitaph they were.

You will not find any reference to the destruction of the House of Commons on 10 May in *Hansard*. You will find this only:

8 May 1941
Adjournment.
Resolved 'That this House do now adjourn.' (Mr. Munro.)

Tuesday, 13 May 1941
(Mr. Speaker in the Chair.)

'Let it roar!' The House sat on, at the other end of the building.

That same 10 May my little diary says: 'Turned over to C.M.S.' (Commander, Mine-sweeping.) The Navy had taken on a tremendous new task in London River and a vast feat of improvisation: and the *Water Gipsy* got a new job. Almost from the beginning the miscellaneous mine-sweepers had been at work, from top to bottom of the tideway. But the sweepers, with their long tows, could not move inside the barge-roads or close into the wharves, and the enemy were not always obliging enough to drop their mischief in mid-stream. Two or three ships had been blown up by mines which had fallen, unobserved, close inshore. The urgent need was that anything falling in the river, or the docks, should be observed and reported, so that the mine-sweepers (or mine-disposal boys) could be directed to the danger spot without delay, instead of vaguely sweeping where danger was not.

But the Navy, clearly, could not find the men to keep such a watch over sixty miles of tideway and 676 acres of dock-water. So the civilians, and, indeed, the rest of the river population, afloat and ashore, were called in and fortified, charted, instructed, and trained by 'night-exercises.' Commander Lord Teynham, R.N., a grand organizer, and, later, Captain, Mine-sweeping, British Assault Area, France, was the first head of the Mine-watching and Mine-clearance Section at the Admiral's Headquarters on Tower Hill. It would take too long to relate the ingenious and elaborate details of this quiet, unique operation. But, at the peak, there were close to one thousand numbered posts on the chart: and, when the whole thing was in train, there was an unpaid army of thousands, having nothing to do with the Navy, but working with the Navy, eagerly and often skilfully, over sixty miles of tideway, from west of London nearly to the sea.

The *Water Gipsy*, because of her name for knowledge of the river, and, I hope, good seamanship, was appointed a sort of staff-boat to the Mine-watching Section. Our job was to know almost everybody and everything beside and upon the river, to distribute our officers' information or instructions, to warn, encourage, or cajole the civilian watchers—the lonely watermen, for example, in charge of barge-roads—and, once a fortnight, to steam about, without lights, and give the watchers practice with a night-exercise, in which, with the aid of an illuminable balloon, we pretended to be about fifteen parachute-mines over a ten-mile stretch of the river. Lieutenant-Commander Bates, who ran the show for more than two years, says in his good book,[1] I see: 'It was done every fortnight, and the success of this work is reflected in the fact that the enemy soon ceased his minelaying raids within the Port limits when he realized that a combination of highly trained Mine-watchers and Mine-sweepers was defeating his efforts.' Well, I hope there was something in that. I like to think of the Luftwaffe baffled by the unsuitable *Water Gipsy!*

All this was very healthy exercise for a middle-aged Member, tramping and leaping, in sea-boots, over rows of barges, and climbing up oily ladders. After calling at twenty barge-roads or jetties in a morning, one knew one had done something. And then, there was always the artistic delight of handling the ship as well as one could. I do not drive a car, but I suppose the motorist will understand me. Often we would 'go alongside' something or other thirty times in a day, a pier or a wharf, a steamer or a barge, a ladder or

[1] *The Londoners' River* (Frederick Muller).

companionway or a set of stairs. Every time the problem would be a little different—this barge was high and overhanging, that one loaded and low, another lying athwart the tide. Here you had to nose into a small space between two moored craft, with an oblique tide 'setting' you in, so that, if you were careless and unaware, you were swept onto the lower craft and scraped her bows. Here there were wild eddies from the bridge above, which might send you any way. Here you had to creep in under a big ship's mooring-warps. Here, the tide falling, you were not quite sure if you had enough water. Here you had to make a tiny circle, perfectly judged, or drop in stern first, with a high wind trying to blow you athwart the tide. Here there were tugs or pilot-boats about, and the big problem was to get alongside without being in the way. Every time we came in neatly and gently, without a fumble or a heavy bump, without tearing the gears with 'full astern' stuff, without touching or offending anyone, it was a pleasure. One of my officers delighted me once by saying that he could see I had been 'brought up in sail' by the way in which I brought my ship alongside. And then I was always meeting good, simple men, who loved the water too, and, though they were no 'respecters of persons,' respected any who used the water well. It may seem a queer way for a Member of Parliament to spend his days and nights, but I do not think I was ever bored.

Even the 'quiet' nights could be exciting enough. Once we nearly wrecked a Cabinet Minister. About midnight, I embarked at Westminster my old friend the Right Honourable Arthur Greenwood, then a member of the War Cabinet, who had often asked curious questions about our work on the river. We reached Woolwich, twelve miles from Westminster, about 0200. To approach the first of the Arsenal posts we had to move in through a small gap in a barbed-wire boom, not easy at night-time, with a strong tide running; but we got in and out safely, the watchers responded promptly to our challenge, nobody opened fire (which I always half expected when approaching the Arsenal), and I hoped that the Minister was prop-erly impressed. We worked down Gallions Reach, found the other three Arsenal posts awake, and about 0300 our duty was done. I 'secured' (as the sailors say hopefully) for the night to a coal-barge on the Arsenal side of Cory's barge-roads. I forget how many great buoys there are, but for half a mile there is a floating island of coal, many 'bottoms' wide. There must, I suppose, on an average day be more than 100 lighters there, some empty—but mostly full, and when loaded they carry from 100 to 150 tons of coal. We had spent many a night there in reasonable peace, for there was no traffic inside the roads and the barges broke the wash of hurrying tugs. The Minister undressed to his under-clothes, and I tucked him up in his blankets. He was to be at a Cabinet meeting fairly early in the morning, and I promised to get under way in good time. I had only one 'crew' aboard, Engineer Elsbury, a fine young man. He had turned in, and I was sipping my rum after a 'last look round.' It was a still night, cloudy, with a moon, but no enemy about. I was glad that my distinguished guest had struck a quiet night. Then there was a heavy thump on the port side. I went out forward and looked astern. I saw a great coal-barge drifting away on the ebb, silent, like a black ghost in the murky midnight. It was empty, and when they are empty they stand much higher from the water than my little ship, and their protruding 'swims' at each end, like an exaggerated yacht-counter, are alarming. I wondered what had happened; but chiefly I thought how fortunate it was she had not hit us head-on, for then her overhanging head would have overlaid the top of our cabin, and, with the tide pressing her on, we should have been in a nice mess. Then I turned my head forward, and I saw something more frightening than bombs. Not one, but about twenty barges—a whole road of barges—probably through the overloading of a buoy, had broken adrift and were bearing down upon us—hundreds of tons of coal. I never saw anything like it before or since, and it was a fantastic chance that it should happen, at the buoy just above us, fifteen minutes after we had made fast, with a Cabinet Minister aboard. In the dim light they looked like a herd of elephants advancing, and their iron hulls grunted and clanged, not loudly, as they do when a fast tug tosses them about, but softly, stealthily, as if the elephants were muttering, 'Quick—we'll get 'em!' I thought they would. The devil of it was that the tier astern of us was wider than ours, and ours wider than the one above, so the runaways were dead ahead, and even if we got clear we might be carried on to the tier below and crushed. But there was still a chance. I yelled to Eddy, and we got the engines going and cast off our lines and 'springs' as swiftly as the villain in a detective story. But by that time they were on us and, it seemed, all round us. I went full speed ahead with our two little engines and tried to fight a way out through the black malignant beasts. But they carried us down, sideways, and suddenly we were caught on the tier below, with a great black fellow squeezing us on the starboard quarter and towering over my small 'bridge,' for it was an 'empty'—and just as well. Our ship heeled over under the pressure, and I thought she would be cracked like a walnut; but we shoved like madmen, our eighteen horses roared, and somehow we scraped out of the squeeze, thanking God. But astern I heard the unmistakable walnut sound: my beloved little sailing dinghy was a wreck, and under water. And then, of course, a spare line floated out of the dinghy and fouled one of the propellers. About this point a tousled head emerged from the engine-room onto the 'bridge,' and the Cabinet Minister said mildly, 'What's going on?' I think, in our extremity, we had forgotten his existence. We confessed that we were thirteen miles from Westminster, with a propeller fouled, and no dinghy. But Eddy Elsbury stripped, went overboard with a knife, and, after long cold labours, cleared the propeller. So the Right Hon. Gentleman attended the War Cabinet in time, after all.

20. Some Naval Occasions

We all know about the skill and courage of the Navy, but I should like now to celebrate its tact and manners. Having determined to serve as a non-commissioned officer, I was eager not to 'have it both ways'—that is, not to trade upon being a Member of Parliament, a writer, and so on. In the way of duty, work, leave, I do not think I ever did—'well, hardly ever.' But, outside that, every officer I had to do with was so considerate and kind that I was often afraid of trespassing beyond the bounds of good order and discipline. I felt that, for their sake, I should try to do nothing which would not be permitted to a regular Petty Officer. But then, a regular Petty Officer would not meet Captain Fitzroy, R.N., the Speaker's son, at Pratt's Club and have a high old argument about the conduct of the war in the Thames. He was Director of Mine-sweeping at the Admiralty, and the *Water Gipsy* was remotely in his ken and command. Indeed, he came aboard for one of our 'exercises' and ragged me merrily, as he always did. But the next time I met him he would listen seriously to some earnest theory with which the Petty Officer was bursting. I do not know how the Army would have dealt with the nuisance of a Sergeant M.P., but the Navy faced it with a charming ease and grace. They were not so jealous of good order that they feared to show goodwill.

I was always punctilious with my salutes; my friendly young officers complained that I saluted them too much. But then, I liked saluting them. I prefer the neat salute of the Navy to the elaborate antics of the Army, but I have never understood those crotchety folk who maintain that all saluting is somehow degrading and ridiculous. I have always had an almost mystical feeling for the Navy, and salutes are like songs, or flags, or flowers—a way of saying things you would not like to speak. They are, I think, more blessed to give than to receive. In Piccadilly I would salute small midshipmen with sincerity and pleasure—why not? They would soon be on a bridge somewhere, bound into danger. Their mothers liked it, but the poor boys blushed. Later, I was delighted to salute my own son. Sometimes the embarrassment was mine. I would meet some strange young Lieutenant or Sub-Lieutenant in the docks, salute smartly as we passed, and hear him reply brightly, 'Good morning, sir.'

One day, in Half-Way Reach, we saw ahead of us a damaged destroyer working slowly up to the docks. She was moving so slowly that it was clear that even the *Water Gipsy* would be compelled to pass her at last. I told my crew (of two) to take their mugs of tea below, smarten up a bit, and stand by to do honour to the wounded ship-of-war. We crept slowly up to her bridge. I saluted earnestly and my crew stood to attention. But the officers on the bridge were looking ahead or to port, and no one saw our little tribute. We steamed on, disappointed, and relaxed. When we had gone about 200 yards Tom Cheesman said, 'Skipper, they're waving.' I looked astern and saw the officers on the destroyer's bridge waving cheerily to the Petty Officer 1/c *Water Gipsy*. Most improper. It could not happen, I feel, in the Army.

One sunny day in Jermyn Street I gave a Captain (R.N.) a 'smashing salute.' He stopped and said, 'You're Herbert, aren't you?'

'Yes, sir.'

'You wrote those verses about ———, didn't you?'

'Yes, sir.'

These were some verses of a mildly 'smoking-room' character which I had written a long time back. Many such works have been put down to me with which I had nothing to do—indeed, with some distress I have seen typewritten copies with my initials at the bottom. This was the only one to which I confess.

'Before the war,' said the Captain, 'I was on the China Station. We wrote a reply. Care to hear it?'

'Yes, sir,' I said, delighted.

So there I stood at attention on the narrow pavement, with taxis hooting about us and cross pedestrians thrusting past, while the Captain in his big bass voice recited the China Station's reply—four verses, in exactly the same metre as mine. And very good and amusing it was. At the end I gave him a *very* smashing salute.

How proud I was one day in 1941 to carry down to Greenwich Captain Sidney Jasper Herbert, R.N., my one surviving brother! (Owen, the youngest, was 'missing' at Mons.) We three had sailed boats together on the Round Pond, and ever since Sidney went to Osborne and became 'R.N.' I had envied him. In August 1914 I had bicycled from Bethnal Green to Lambeth and enlisted in the R.N.V.R., with a wild idea of 'joining' him; but Mr. Churchill made a soldier of me, and Sidney was in submarines. Now here we were together in the Navy at last. Here he was, a Captain, on *my* bridge, and the patrol boats, even the mine-sweepers, were saluting him. We were bound for Greenwich with a very serious purpose. My brother was full of some tremendous plan for making British ships unsinkable—or, at least, less sinkable. He had worked long upon it, and I felt there was 'something there,' though I understood little of what he told me. Now he was going to consult some Professor at the Naval College, with a mass of papers and figures. I put him ashore at Greenwich Pier and saluted. I never saw him again. With all his plans for unsinkable ships, he went down in the *Hood*.

21. The Main Brace

1825 (11) Extra Issues of Spirit—Extra issues of spirit are not to be made, except in very exceptional circumstances, and with the approval of the senior officer present. An officer authorizing an extra issue of spirit is to make a full report of the circumstances to the Commander-in-Chief or officer commanding the squadron, who is to transmit it to the Admiralty with an expression of his opinion thereon.

The order 'Splice the Main Brace' is to be regarded as authorizing the special issue of a ration of one-eighth pint of rum to each officer or man of over 20 years of age who desires it. . . .

(The King's Regulations and Admiralty Instructions for the Government of His Majesty's Naval Service.)

The spirit issue—or 'tot of rum'—is a big thing in the Navy, and is rightly surrounded by a monkish fence of rules and regulations. In quantity it is generous—one-eighth pint a day, which corresponds to a 'treble' at the pubs. 'No person is to receive a spirit ration in kind, or grog money in lieu until he is 20 years of age' (1827—1). 'No officers are entitled to the issue of a spirit ration (except in special circumstances such as "Splicing the Main Brace"). The allowance of spirit for the ship's company is to be mixed with three parts of water to one of spirit and issued every day on deck in the presence of such officer as the Captain may appoint. It is, as a rule, to be issued at dinner time . . .' (1827—2). And 'No raw spirit is ever to be issued except to officers, chief petty officers and petty officers' (1827—3).

I never exercised my Petty Officer's privilege of taking my tot 'raw'; I 'issued' as much water to myself as I did to my crew—sometimes more. But I found my tot very comforting on many a cold alarming night as I wriggled into my blankets and wondered why I was spending yet one more night in the 'unsuitable' and tossing *Water Gipsy*. And I always thought gratefully of the Admiralty for allowing our little boats, commanded by Petty Officers only, to enjoy the ancient customs of the Navy instead of giving us 'grog money in lieu.' They might well have been governed by the obvious temptations and opportunities—the seaman not so keen on rum as others, able, in a river, to go ashore nearly every day, to save up the 'unconsumed spirit' in a little bottle and profitably dispose of it ashore. But, instead, according to the fine and ancient tradition, they trusted their Petty Officers; and I know of no case in which that trust was abused, though I think a smuggling seaman was caught and punished in one of the mine-sweepers. Certainly, it was through ignorance, not insolence, that I am able to make this boastful claim, that, though a mere Petty Officer, I 'authorized an extra issue of spirit,' and boasted, wrongly, it seems, that I had 'spliced the main brace.'

The practical meaning of the order, 'Splice the Main Brace,' has been explained to you already by King's Regulations. The reason why those words have that meaning is not so plain. I prefer the explanation some sailor gave me long ago. To 'splice the main brace,' he said, is a thing you would hardly ever do (you would rig, I suppose, a new main brace instead), so it fits the very rare event of a *special* issue of rum to all hands (including officers, who as a rule are rumless). So rare is it that, in practice, His Majesty is almost the only officer who gives the order, generally after a review of victory. The King's signal to H.M.S. *Amethyst* ended, you may remember, 'Splice the Main Brace.'

We were down at Holehaven, preparing for one of our big night exercises between Southend and Tilbury. There was a strong northwesterly gale, and Holehaven in a nor'-wester can be the very devil, for the pier and anchorage are on the east side of the spacious bay, and a real sea roars across and breaks on the high Dutch wall. It was the sort of weather in which the *Water Gipsy,* with her high top-hamper, refuses to steer and luffs up into the wind, as she did that afternoon. We had anchored in the creek and gone ashore for a bite at the Lobster Smack, thankful we had no job to do on such a night. At low water another patrol boat went aground on the bar, where the creek runs into the main river. When the tide rose they were blown at once to the foot of the sea-wall, at the top of which was a mass of barbed wire, against the German invasion, so that no one could get at them from the shore. They had laid no anchor out, I know not why, and were quite helpless, pounded against the wall. The officer in charge, Lieutenant-Commander Needham, tele-phoned to Tilbury for a tug, but all the tugs were busy chasing barges blown adrift, or otherwise. Mr. Needham, I think, had no more faith than I in the *Water Gipsy's* capacity to act as a tug in a fierce gale; but you never know, and he was willing for us to try. We got the anchor up and rolled sideways down the creek. By luck or judgment we dropped the anchor in just the right place, so that, the wind blowing us across the flood-tide, our stern pointed directly at the wreck. Then I sent my sturdy crew, Conoley and Elsbury, away in the dinghy, at the end of a long line. They got a line to the other boat, and hauled themselves back. We started heaving up the anchor and at the same time went ahead with all our eighteen horses. To everyone's astonishment the distressed boat came slowly away. This was highly exciting, though I still feared that when the anchor was up we too might be blown on to the wall. But all went well, and we proudly towed our prize into the creek. My crew were wet and cold, and I said, 'Boys, I think that calls for another tot.' We 'made it so,' and thought no more about it.

But when we got back to London, I was asked for a report upon the salvage episode. At the end I wrote, not knowing, poor innocent, the terms of 1825 (11) : 'In the circumstances I took it upon myself to issue an extra tot of rum: I hope that this may be approved and the necessary adjustments made to our spirit account.'

A few days later, in a corridor at Headquarters, I met a Pay-master, who said, 'Oh, Herbert, I've sent your rum request in. It may be all right. But, of course, it has to go to the Admiralty. The Admiral can't deal with that.' I went back to the ship and studied King's Regulations in real alarm. 'The Senior Officer present . . .' The only officer for miles had been Mr. Needham on the bank, and he had done no 'authorizing.' Three tots of rum sent up to their Lordships for approval! 'Goodness,' I thought, 'this will be the end of rum in London River!' And I should be held responsible for evermore.

But, in a week or two, there came a nice pat on the back from Admiral Dunbar-Nasmith, F.O. i/c London, and at the end:

'The issue of spirits referred to in paragraph 3 of the report is approved under K.R. and A.I. 1825 (11).'

'God save their Lordships,' said the *Water Gipsy*. But it was, I gather, an 'extra,' not a 'special' issue.

22. The Horse's Navel

In 1942 I was sick for a week or two, and, convalescing, I sat up in bed and renamed the stars. I still maintain that this is a good notion. What is wrong, you say, with the old romantic names which have served the stars so long? They are for the most part inept, unfitting, unworthy of the stars and the human race—and therefore do not excite our interest as they should. They are unrelated, meaningless, difficult to distinguish, pronounce and remember—and therefore do not assist the student. 'But,' you say, 'Orion—the Great Bear —Andromeda—Perseus—how beautiful!' (Such things, by the way, are always said by literary people who do not, in fact, know one star from another!) But these are the names of constellations, not stars; and it is stars the navigator uses. Puffed up, no doubt, by my own studies, I used to teach my crew the principal stars; and, indeed, they were often practically useful on short courses in Sea Reach. But the Arabic names were always a trouble. Take 'Betelgeuse,' one of the big stars in Orion. It means, they say, 'Armpit of the Central One,' and God knows how it should be pronounced. The sailors call it 'Beetle-juice.' How romantic! Take 'Benetnasch' (Chief of the mourners'), the tail-star of the Bear (Plough, or Dipper), or 'Dubhe,' at the other end—and how do you pronounce that? An old salt quarreled with me harshly in a nautical journal: how dare

I try to meddle with such 'old romantic' names as 'Alpheratz' (in Andromeda), bestowed by the Arabs before the Greeks knew one star from another—and so on. Well, according to one of the big books I studied, the meaning of Alpheratz is 'Horse's Navel,' though some have offered other meanings. Whatever it means, it was just Arabic to my crew. 'Fomalhaut,' one of the finest stars, means 'The Fish's Mouth,' and 'Diphda,' 'The Second Frog,' they say. The airmen, at least, are on my side, for in the *Air Almanac* they have already cut down some of the larger names—'Benetnasch' is 'Benet,' and 'Arcturus,' 'Arctus'—and since the 'old, romantic' names have no meaning for them they mutilate them without shame. Take a child onto the lawn and tell him: 'That is "Betelgeuse"—and that is "Alnilam" '; and he will yawn. But tell him, 'That is "Nelson"—and that is "Columbus," ' and he may be interested and look again. That is the general line of my 'reform': have done with 'Hen's Beaks' and 'Fish's Mouths' and 'Horse's Navels,' and relate the fine stars to the human race and the best things in human history. I gave a constellation to almost every nation—a little rash, that, I agree, and not essential to the general scheme. The Great Bear went to Britain, and Leo to Russia (for Leo is much more like a Hammer and Sickle than it is like a lion). Then I divided the Heavens into two main sections—Men of Action and Men of Mind. Orion, for example, became 'The Sailor,' as follows:

Betelgeuse	Nelson
(Armpit of the Central One)	
Rigel	Drake
(Left Leg of the Jauzah)	
Bellatrix	Hawkins
(Amazon)	
Saiph	Magellan
(Sword)	
Mintaka	Cook
(Belt)	
Alnilam	Columbus ⎱ The
(String of Pearls)	⎰ Belt
Alnitak	Cabot
(Girdle)	
Nair al Saif	Da Gama

Close to the Sailor, in my Better Sky, are the Soldier, the Airman, and the Traveller, which should help the student. At present, he is told that Hercules, which 'resembles a lily,' is next to Ophiuchus (Snake-holder), which 'resembles a wishbone'; and he can only wonder why.

I did my best to be internationally fair in selecting heroes fit for the Heavens, and no doubt Unesco, or some committee of astronomers, would do even better. Among the constellations of the Men of Mind—the Poet, the Painter, the Music-maker, Science, etc.—the British names, I am sorry to say, were very few.

But I have set forth the scheme in full elsewhere,[1] and must not do it again. My own proposals may be nonsense, but if the great men of the world would accept the principle, it should not be difficult to reach agreement—international agreement—at all events for the sixty-four main 'navigational' stars.

Our own astronomers, certainly, are not hot in opposition. I boldly sent my suggestions to the Royal Astronomical Society, and received the following nice reply:

The President of the Society yesterday brought your letter of the 25th October, together with the enclosed article and chart 'A Better Sky,' before the Council. The chart was examined with great interest, and your whole suggestion of changing the nomenclature of the stars was received with appreciation. At the same time it was felt that as far as Astronomy was concerned the adoption of such a change would require international agreement, which is clearly impracticable at the present time.

And, since we were still at war, I could hardly quarrel with that.

There was also an invitation to dine and discuss, which I gratefully accepted. It was, for me, a memorable meal. We met at some restaurant in Soho, at a long, narrow table set diagonally across the room, I suppose to represent the ecliptic. There were about thirty astronomers, and one other guest in naval uniform, Vice-Admiral Sir John Edgell, K.B.E., C.B., F.R.S., the Admiralty Hydrographer. I had the honour to sit next to the President, the great Eddington. Opposite to him was the Astronomer Royal, Sir Harold Spencer-

[1] *A Better Sky* (Methuen, 1944).

Jones. Across the table, on my starboard bow, was Sir James Jeans. The astronomer on my right, as we sat down, made a very surprising remark. Looking round the company, most of whom were well advanced in years, he said: 'We generally have a Quiet End—and a Noisy End. To-night, I rather feel, we're at the Noisy End.' I had visions of the astronomers pelting each other with tomatoes or singing rude songs, but they behaved very well.

You can imagine with what trepidation this amateur person rose to address that eminent audience about the stars. But I harangued them for twenty minutes. Sir James Jeans then rose up and went out without a word. After a short speech from the Hydrographer of the Navy, we had a general chat, which, I thought, was surprisingly friendly. There was no cry of 'Hands off our Sky!' Indeed, I concluded that astronomers do not much care what names we give to the stars. For in their official work they do not use names but the Greek-letter labels. 'Betelgeuse' is α Orionis, and 'Benetnasch' is η Ursæ Majoris, so 'Nelson' or 'Milton' would suit them just as well —though to change the names of constellations would be another thing.

Encouraged by the evening, I wrote to Sir James Jeans and asked if he would write an introduction to *A Better Sky*, which was asking for trouble, no doubt. Sir James took the view that there was quite enough international ill feeling already, and seemed to think that my proposals might start another war. Major Walter Elliot, M.P., nobly did the job instead.

The most favourable review of the book—and I have no shame in rubbing this in—was written by the Astronomer Royal in the *Sunday Times*. He said, rightly:

He is fighting for a principle, not for his particular naming or grouping. . . . Every reader will be tempted to try his hand at improving the scheme. He will find it entertaining and instructive, and in the attempt he will learn a great deal about the stars and the constellations. And perhaps eventually a better sky will be the outcome.

So there!

I should like to add that I am not the first wild fellow to play this game. The Venerable Bede began it. He wanted to name the Signs of the Zodiac after the eleven Apostles and St. John the Baptist. Why not? We could start that way, as well as any other, and the Apostles are surely more suitable to the sky than the Ram, the Scorpion, and the rest of the pagan zoo.

There, then, I leave the torch for some younger runner to carry along. And I must remark once more that all the trouble was directly due to the dear old lady who gave me that wretched sextant.

23. The Thames Prepares

London had 'taken it.' London had defended herself and won.
The river traffic was down to about 25 per cent of the normal, I
think, but the ships came and went, the convoys sailed,[1] though the
enemy were only seventy miles from Southend Pier, where the convoys gathered. And at length, from Teddington to Southend, one
began to smell the spirit of attack. Strange craft, amazing monsters,
were stirring in the ancient womb of the Thames. The first monsters
were the floating twin towers, like something in the works of H. G.
Wells, which we saw at Gravesend or in the tidal basin at Tilbury.
These, like the Maunsell Forts, which had four legs, were towed
slowly down the river and sunk outside in the estuary. Now they were
like a man, or a row of men, standing up to the shoulders in the sea.
Their tops, above water, were equipped like a ship and heavily
armed, and carried crews of many officers and men—a trouble to
E-boats, U-boats, and mining aircraft. What ingenuity and skill
were here! Soon, too, there were men hammering away at L.C.T.s
(Landing Craft Tank) on the west side of Blackwall Reach. In
every reach there were men doing odd things to old London River
'lighters,' 'dumb barges,' never meant to go to sea, cutting out the

[1] In all, between September 1939 and June 1945, 3,367 convoys sailed out of
the Thames—84,297 ships.

ends of them and putting in collapsible 'ramps,' fitting them with bridges and wheels, and, wonder of wonders, with engines and propellers! (And, indeed, in the end, those old dumb barges of London River made the coast of France.) Soldiers in khaki began to appear in tugs and lighters, learning how to handle the craft. One heard of lightermen who had signed on to join the Navy (for a time) and steer the lighters. The smaller landing-craft began to be seen, and whizzed about noisily, making a great wash. Then between Barking and Erith one saw queer doings on the empty flats. Crowds of men working where there was no factory—nothing; forests of iron poles, and odd cuts in the high banks—filled in with corrugated iron—odd because the land there is below the level of a big tide, and the Port of London Authority is 'particular' about its river wall. What was all this? 'All this' was the first beginnings of a 'Phoenix,' one of the vast blocks of concrete that made part of the Mulberry. The method had the simplicity of genius. They took an empty part of the bank behind the river wall, dug down, made the concrete bottom of the Phoenix, cut away the river wall, towed the Phoenix out at high water, and finished it off in dock. Seventy-five per cent of the concrete work for the Mulberry Harbour was made in London River, and 135 'Phoenix units' were sailed out of the Thames.

Watching these things as we went about our duties, knowing what was being done and half guessing what was still to be done—we laughed a little at the zealous folk who were yelling everywhere, 'Aid Russia!' In 1942! We had a long way to go in 1942.

Still, things were moving.

24. 'Wait Till Tuesday'

Nineteen forty-two was an unhappy year in the House. Outside, young men and women were chalking on the walls 'Second Front Now.' Inside, there were such long faces that I was always glad to get back to the river, where at least one could see the 'Second Front' stirring. The favourite word was 'frustration.' · 'The country as a whole is suffering under a huge edifice of frustration built upon a foundation of disappointed hopes,' said one Member. On 19–20 May there was a two-day debate on the war in which criticism of Mr. Churchill was severe and loud, and six weeks later we gave two days to a Vote of Censure, moved by Sir John Wardlaw-Milne (a Conservative), and seconded by Mr. A. Bevan (Labour), in these terms:

CENTRAL DIRECTION OF THE WAR

That this House, while paying tribute to the heroism and endurance of the Armed Forces of the Crown in circumstances of exceptional difficulty *has no confidence in the central direction of the war.*

Certainly there had been a grim procession of misfortunes—and everyone could rattle off a long list of ill-omened names: France— Norway—Greece—Crete—Hong Kong—*Repulse—Prince of Wales* —Singapore—Rangoon—*Scharnhorst* and *Gneisenau*—Tobruk.

Certainly the critics, who were patriotic, powerful, courageous, and well informed, were entitled to say that they were doing their duty as Members of a still free Parliament, and Mr. Churchill never said otherwise.[1] Certainly those debates were a wonderful exhibition of democratic method, inconceivable in any Hitlerland. But now, knowing how the war did end, it is interesting to read some of the things that were said in those debates about its central direction. The hero of 1945 has a hard time in the *Hansard* of 1942. He was trying to do too much and not doing it well.

It is an amazing state of affairs [said Sir John Wardlaw-Milne] that instead of leading the country they [the Government] are always be-hind. Leadership? Apart from the personal leadership to which I have already paid tribute, where is the leadership in this Government? What are the Government? One man. . . . It is such a responsibility that I do not believe any one man can carry it.

I say quite frankly that it is the Prime Minister I am criticizing. . . . As Prime Minister and Minister of Defence he is trying to carry too heavy a burden, and the country, with all its belief in him, which many of us share, with all its trust, with all its gratitude, is beginning to feel that it would be well if he were to share that burden with some-body else.

Mr. McGovern, who followed, said:

I had a letter the other day from a man who listened to the last speech of the Prime Minister dealing with the war. He said in his letter:

I listened to it in the very same pub that I listened to his speeches twelve months ago. Twelve months ago you could have heard a pin drop-ping on the floor, everybody anxious to listen, but there was talk, laughter and jokes being expressed, and the proprietor had to turn off the wireless because no one seemed interested in the speech.

The letter said that all sorts of disrespectful remarks were being made about the Prime Minister. I do not know whether the Government and the Prime Minister realize it or not, but that is the feeling in the coun-try. *Everybody is asking when this Government is to come to an end.*

[1]'No one need be mealy-mouthed in debate, and none should be chicken-hearted in voting. . . . Everyone in these rough times must do what he thinks is his duty.'

Mr. Richard Stokes (Ipswich) was nearly always a severe critic of Mr. Churchill, which distressed me sometimes, for Dick Stokes has always been a good friend of mine. Besides, about tanks, for example, his pet subject then, for all I knew, he was right. But he could say things without raising resentment, which, if they came from Aneurin Bevan, for example, with venom in his voice and manner, could cause a storm. Now he said:

I said eighteen months ago that the Prime Minister is a great leader, but that strategically nobody ought to follow him. I hold to that opinion, and everything that has happened since bears it out. I hold the view sincerely that unless we can get a change on the question of the strategic control, we not only will not win the war, but will lose it. We shall not even avoid defeat.

I have given already the charming picture of Mr. Churchill forgiving this fierce critic.

I wish I had a similar story about that other critic, Aneurin Bevan. He too was a friend of mine in the early days; and though, I suppose, I am now 'near-vermin,' I hope, still is: for a very charming companion he can be. His criticisms, I am sure, were as sincere as they were courageous, but he did give many of us a disturbing sense that his formidable fires were fed by a personal animosity towards Mr. Churchill. Aneurin always denied that he had any such personal feelings, and one day, an amateur bridge-builder, I told Mr. Churchill what his enemy had said. 'H'm,' he said. 'Well, all I can say is that when I look across the Chamber I see in those eyes the fires of implacable hatred.'

Mr. Hore-Belisha, who opened the second day of the May debate, said:

I do not think you can divorce the almost unending and unbroken sequence of strategic disasters from this mixture of the political and military elements in your war-machine. . . . Who decided to send an Army to Greece without adequate air-support—an impossible operation? . . . When a man of great political experience and dialectical skill sits with Service men who are not accustomed to the careful use of language and the deployment of argument, you do not know whether the substance that comes out of these discussions is diluted or undiluted.

Who decided to defend Crete? Who decided that Crete was defensible when the mainland had gone? Who decided that Singapore should be defended? . . .

After Mr. Hore-Belisha, I see, Petty Officer Alan Herbert made one of his rare interventions in a general debate. I have never, I think, deserved the name of 'yes-man,' but I confess that Mr. Churchill has always afflicted me with something like hero-worship. There were many of us: and perhaps sometimes we deserved the rebukes of Lord Winterton, who, fearless and forthright, as always, said in the Censure debate:

If, whenever we have disasters—because they are disasters—whenever we have defeats, we get the same answer from many Members of this House, and from the Press outside, that whatever happens you must not blame the Prime Minister, we are getting very close to the intellectual and moral position of the German people 'The Fuehrer is always right.'

The speeches from which I have made unfairly small extracts contained a mass of informed and conscientious criticisms: and, for all I know, they may have borne fruit later. But the general air of the first day had been so gloomy; we seemed to be so near to a 'Churchill Must Go' Movement, that I thought that a mere hero-worshipper might not be out of place. At all events, I piped up as follows:

Although many speeches have dealt with the question whether or not it would be right to alter the staff machinery, I do not believe that is the real subject of the debate. The real subject of the debate is, have we faith in the Prime Minister, or have we not? We have now come to the stage where some hon. Members say plainly that they have not. If they feel that, it is right they should say it. But what is the charge against the Prime Minister? It is that a political Minister, as the right hon. Member for Devonport (Mr. Hore-Belisha) described him, 'butts into' strategic affairs? But if the Prime Minister butts into strategic affairs, it is not very surprising. He has been a fighting soldier. He has been First Lord of the Admiralty, he was the first Air Secretary, he has been Secretary of State for War, and Minister of Munitions. If he 'butts into' strategical affairs, it is not very surprising. By the way, I think I may say to the right hon. Gentleman the Member for Carnarvon Boroughs (Mr. Lloyd George) that we were very glad in the last encounter that the political leader butted into strategic affairs; if he had not done so, we should not have had the convoy system, and many other things. But with the present Prime Minister, being the man he is and having had the experience he has, if he does 'butt in,' I am sure you will not stop him butting into strategic affairs by juggling with Generals and committees, putting a new General here, a new committee there. This is a question of personality. You have to face that; either you have faith in him and let him have the machinery he can work with, or you must say frankly that you do not want him any more. I hope that will not be the answer. Certainly, it will not be mine.

I say with great respect and with perturbation that I see some signs of Spring fever in this House, especially in some of the speeches which have been made in this debate. I take, for example, the speech of my hon. Friend the Member for Kidderminster (Sir J. Wardlaw-Milne), who has spent so many hours of patient and devoted labour in his post as Chairman of the Select Committee that he seems almost unable to get out of the Chair—the Chair seems to be glued to him. He speaks now with such a weight of authority as, I suppose, has not been seen in any legislative assembly since Moses brought the Tablets down from the mountain. As a learned and wise statesman, and as a financier, I think he gave a most unbalanced picture. He spoke of a 'steady series of defeats,' and he was not talking of the last few months only, but of the whole course of the war since the fall of France—Norway and so on.

But is that really a true and favourable picture of the last two and a half years? If one is attacked by a tiger, to say nothing of two, and remains erect at all, that, in my opinion, is a major victory. In the long catalogue of British misfortunes, for which the Prime Minister is said to be responsible, I do not think that the hon. Member omitted a single episode, except the Battle of Hastings and the wreck of the schooner *Hesperus*. He might, I felt, have dealt a little longer on the Battle of Crécy; and I think, if he reflects, he will find that the fall of Khartoum was owing to the bad influence of the Prime Minister—who was certainly about on that day. Anybody can say Singapore, Hong Kong, Rangoon, and all the rest of it, but is it fair unless you also say Abyssinia, Somaliland, Libya—Abyssinia was mentioned yesterday only in parenthesis, yet it was one of the greatest feats of arms in our history; let me continue the list—Egypt, Syria, Iran, Iraq, and Madagascar? He gave not a word of credit for any of these things. My right hon. Friend the Member for Devonport (Mr. Hore-Belisha) spoke about territory lost. I do not think it matters much, but, as a matter of fact, I think if you did have a territorial stocktaking of the British possessions at the moment, you would find that we are in an immeasurably better position compared with twelve months ago.

MR. HORE-BELISHA: We have lost all the rubber and tin.

PETTY-OFFICER HERBERT: I know, but my right hon. Friend spoke of 'territory.'

MR. SHINWELL: Where are the new territories?

PETTY-OFFICER HERBERT: I have just given the list. But what is far more important than territory is that our strategic position in that part of the world is immensely stronger than it was. For heaven's sake do not take only one side of the picture. The man who was responsible for Hong Kong and Singapore is entitled also to say that he was responsible for Tobruk, Malta, and the sinking of half of the Italian fleet. The man who sank the *Prince of Wales* and *Repulse,* if he did, can also say, 'I sank the *Bismarck* and the *Graf Spee.*' He is entitled to say, if we are going to have this stocktaking, 'I am responsible for the fact that in the last twelve months the people of England have been able to sleep quietly in their beds, and that the wheels of industry have been able to revolve uninterruptedly while very much the reverse has been happening in Germany.'

Another unfair critic, I thought, was the hon. Member for Ipswich (Mr. Stokes). It was said that in Napoleon's time every soldier had a field-marshal's baton in his knapsack. How much more fortunate we are in this House, where almost every Member has the flag of an Admiral of the Fleet in his pocket as well. One of those is, I fancy, my hon. Friend. He talked a lot about Singapore. Few of the critics, I notice, ever say anything about Pearl Harbour, for which disaster, I suppose, the Prime Minister is responsible as for everything else. The hon. Member did mention it, but he quoted from a statement of President Roosevelt to the effect that the American Fleet would not have been able to help in any case. If that is correct, it is a queer thing that the Japanese came so far and took so much trouble to knock the American Fleet out. The suggestion now apparently is that we ought to have evacuated Singapore. I have heard it whispered—and we may as well have these whispers out—that some General announced, I do not know how long before the disaster, that we ought to evacuate Singapore and that the political influences at home went against him. If I had been Prime Minister—I do not see any immediate danger of it—and a General had said to me as the Japs approached this great place on which we have spent so much time, money, and blood, 'We have 70,000 British, Dominion,

and Indian troops at this base, and my advice to you is to evacuate it,'
I would have said, 'By God, sir, no! It is too late to talk like that. We
will fight. We have 70,000 troops there. They will give a good account
of themselves. At all events, we are not going to surrender without a
fight.' If that is the sort of political influence which is complained of,
I am bound to say that I should have found myself in the same error.

In the last war I was in the Naval Division which was designed and
invented by the Prime Minister and sent by him to Antwerp, an expedition which was at the time derided but was undoubtedly sound. It
was then sent to the Dardanelles, another terrible place, and there we
certainly did not have the full equipment that is demanded now before
anything is done. Our bombs were jam tins, and we did not have any
modern devices—but we won in the end. What I want to say is that
every year since that war finished that Division has gathered together
the remnants of the officers and men, and we have sent an invitation to
the Prime Minister to come to our gathering. He has always been our
most honoured guest and he always will be. I am sure that same thing
will be said about the units who come back from the Middle East, and
even from Singapore. For that is the real mind of the soldier. They do
not expect a victory every day. I believe that is true of the whole people
at this moment. This is not a vote of confidence, but I am sure it is a
question of faith. I do not see, going about the river, and the shipyards,
and dockyards, in the East End people going about with long faces and
'a sense of frustration,' wondering what is going to happen after the war.
I do not agree with the hon. Member for Kidderminster that the
people as a whole have a sense of frustration, a sense that nothing is happening. On the contrary, I find them cheerful, eager, and optimistic
—one right hon. Gentleman rather complains about that—and bel-
ligerent. They complain and grumble, of course, as is the right and
duty of every Briton, but their hearts are sound and they are eager,
and I believe it is because they have faith in their leadership. G. K.
Chesterton said—and I give this to the critics—that faith is the capacity
to believe that which is demonstrably not true. It may be that kind of
faith, but it is worth having in a leader of men and a leader of forces.
It is a great defect of democracy, a great dilemma, that while on the
one hand we are always saying 'Give us a leader! Where are the giants
of the past?' whenever a head shows itself well above the others, the
instinct of so many is to knock it down again. Let us resist that tendency, unless we are very sure that we have another head to put in its
place. I believe the people know that they have a great man; they are

determined to keep him, and determined to deserve him—and so am I.

Later, Mr. Beverley Baxter (Wood Green) in a spirited speech, took much the same line:

No one, not even his most loyal supporters, would say that the Prime Minister has not made mistakes. They are clear to the eyes of us all, but he has never wavered in his broad conception of aid to Russia and the development of the alliance of the English-speaking peoples. He never allowed events in the forefront to rob him of the vast horizon of his own conception. We are reaping to-day the harvest of the Prime Minister's faith, and that harvest spells victory.

He also said:

It is difficult for any Member of this House to make a speech such as I am doing without incurring some charge of sycophancy.

'Sycophancy'—to stand by Mr. Winston Churchill! But he was quite right. It was, as I have said, an unhappy House in 1942.

The critics were not satisfied, and on 1 July Sir John Wardlaw-Milne moved his Vote of Censure. Tobruk had fallen the week before. Sir John was patriotic as well as able, and he said at once that he had 'tabled this Motion with the one object, and the one object only, of assisting us to win this war in the shortest possible time.' He dealt with Mr. Churchill's dual rôle—Prime Minister and Minister of Defence—'the first vital mistake that we made in the war,' and the Far East; with Libya; with tanks and guns and dive-bombers. And he somewhat surprised the House by a suggestion that 'it would be a very desirable move . . . if His Royal Highness the Duke of Gloucester were to be appointed Commander-in-Chief of the British Army—without, of course, administrative duties.' Admiral of the Fleet Sir Roger Keyes seconded the Motion—though he had no desire to lose Mr. Churchill. Sir Herbert Williams said: 'The public are angry, disquieted—above all, bewildered.' Lord Winterton said he could not vote for the Motion, but had some stern things to say.

Assuming that we suffer—as I hope we shall not, but it looks as if we may—from a major disaster in Egypt and we lose the Suez Canal, and there is another debate, are we to be told: 'Whoever is responsible, the Prime Minister cannot be held to be responsible'? We all agree [he said, in a fine phrase] that the Prime Minister was the captain-guard of our courage and constancy in 1940. I think that not even to the right hon. Gentleman the Member for Carnarvon Borough (Mr. Lloyd George) does this country, both the present generation and posterity, owe more than it does to the Prime Minister. But a lot has happened since 1940. If this series of disasters goes on, the right hon. Gentleman, by one of the greatest acts of self-abnegation which any man could carry out, should go to his colleagues—and there is more than one suitable man for Prime Minister on the Treasury Bench now—and suggest that one of them should form a Government, and that the right hon. Gentleman himself would take office under him. He might do so, perhaps, as Foreign Secretary, because his management of our relations with Russia and with the United States has been perfect.

Mr. Clement Davies, the Liberal Leader, concluded grimly:

Every man must judge for himself, or his own conscience, but if there is one man in this country who, on a two years' record of that kind, can say 'I have complete confidence in that Government' I am sorry for that man.

Mr. McGovern said:

It is a fact that the Prime Minister is exercising a tremendous dictatorship. . . . From my own experience he is the most arrogant and intolerant Member of this House. He walked out when the Noble Lord (Lord Winterton) was speaking. The Noble Lord said he hoped that he was not going out, as he had one or two things to say. He never even turned his head; he marched off. I say that that is the attitude of a man with a dictatorial mind, and so far as I am concerned, if I had to choose between Hitler and the Prime Minister I should not know exactly on which the choice had to fall.

Oh, dear!

The debate, which began at 12 noon, went on till 2:40 A.M. next morning, and came to a queer end.

A BRAWL

I wish that kind instincts and actions did not so often lead us into trouble. That night I fell into my only Parliamentary brawl, in defence of a friend and the principles of free speech and fair play. Mr. Churchill was to speak on the second day, and so many Members wished to explain how the war should be directed that on the first day it was arranged to 'suspend the rule,' which meant that the House could sit as long and as late as it liked. My energetic young friend, Major Charles Taylor (Eastbourne), was charged with some urgent message about the use of aircraft in infantry warfare. He showed me his speech, which, so far as I understood the matter, seemed very sound, and I wished him luck. The ship, I think, was at Westminster Pier, and the enemy were quiet. I went out to dinner somewhere, I think at Pratt's Club, and was going back to the ship when a Member came in and said that the House was still sitting. I asked if Charles Taylor had 'got in' yet, and he said No, so I thought I would go back to the House. There was poor Charles, on the front bench below the gangway, still grimly waiting to save the country. I do not know whether he had had anything to eat, but the debate had begun at 12 noon—it was now eleven at night—and he had been 'bumping' doggedly all day. 'I'm going to make this speech,' he said, 'if I have to sit here all night.' I marvelled at such resolution, and said I would stay and support him. I sat and listened to two speeches, one of them by Mr. X (I will not mention his name, for there is no malice between us, and never was). He was a good and courageous speaker, but seldom spoke for less than fifty minutes, and always gave the impression that he liked himself a little. Now, late though it was, he took his usual ration, and filled twelve columns of *Hansard*. After him several Members stood up, and Charles once more failed to catch 'the eye.' My speech-resistance, which is very strong, then asserted itself, and I went out, promising to return. I went to the Library and looked up some point or other, and so to the Smoking Room, where some of us talked for, it seemed, a long time, and I dare say had a drink or two. At last the indicator rattled again, and the legend was: Major C. Taylor. 'Come on,' I said to somebody. 'Let's give the lad a House. He's been bumping for fourteen solid hours.' And three or four good fellows went in with me.

It was now after half-past two in the morning, but the Member next to me told me that there were still four Members who wanted to speak after Charles Taylor, and I marvelled again. When we had heard two or three sentences from Taylor, Mr. X sidled along the second bench on the Ministerial side, the bench, that is, immediately behind the Treasury, or Government bench—and halted just above the Prime Minister's place (then occupied by Sir Stafford Cripps, who was leading the House). I was sitting, for once, on the other side, below the gangway, just about where Mr. X had recently made his protracted speech. So I had a good view, and have a vivid memory, of the satisfied smirk on Mr. X's face as he, of all people, pronounced the old formula: 'Mr. Deputy-Speaker, sir, I beg to take notice that there are not forty Members present in the house.' In other words, he was 'calling a count.' What he said was evidently true, and the ancient wheels at once began to revolve. The two-minute sand-glass was turned over. Somebody pressed a button, and the special bells for a 'count' rang all through the building. I was shocked and enraged by Mr. X's behaviour, and if you like to add that the hour was late and I had had one or two drinks, I shall not quarrel with you. My rage will still be seen to have had some sound and respectable foundations; and if I had not had a drink, I might have made no protest, which would have been a pity. There were three 'counts' in the case against Mr. X: (1) having made a long speech at a late hour himself, he was trying to silence a young Member who had only just begun, not to mention four others who had been waiting all day, and were still waiting to speak; (2) by calling a 'count' from the second Ministerial bench, he seemed to be suggesting that he was acting unofficially for the Government; and (3) if he succeeded—that is, if forty Members did not appear—the whole debate would collapse and be at an end. And Mr. Churchill was to speak to-morrow. No one could say all that in an extempore exclamation, but I did say, I remember, very loudly, 'What a bastard's trick! We listened to you for fifty minutes!' And I believe I expressed a few more similar opinions while the two minutes ran, and the Deputy-Speaker counted the very few Members who trickled in to 'make a House.' They were not enough. At the end of the two minutes, at 2:40 A.M., the House was adjourned—and, what is more, the debate was over.

Mr. X, contented man, went out behind the Speaker's Chair. I said to myself 'He can't get away with *that!*' I sprang up and gave chase. I remember darting across the floor, and I remember the startled face of Sir Stafford Cripps, who was standing, as I swept, like an angry tiger, between him and the Table. (In all this unusual scene, by the way, no voice, so far as I know, said 'Order, order!' and not a word was heard from the Chair.) Outside the Chamber, the picture was like something in a film. I saw before me the Members' Lobby, with the shining circle of brass in the centre of the floor, quite empty. Beyond was the short corridor which leads to the Central Hall. Here was part of a famous line of sight. In the old days, they tell me, at the opening of Parliament, there was a fine symbolical moment when all the doors were flung open and the King sitting on the throne in the House of Lords could see far off the Speaker of the House of Commons, over the heads of the two great Houses. That night the Senior Burgess for Oxford University could see only a small man with a little black bag scuttling happily homewards. No one else was about. If you can imagine a long lean greyhound pursuing a rather squat and slow-paced hare carrying a small black bag, you have the picture. I caught him in the Lobby. I offered no violence, I did not touch him; but I did head him off from the Central Hall, which was the way to the world outside. And then, I confess, I addressed him in grossly un-Parliamentary language. 'You so-and-so so-and-so,' I said. 'We listened to you making one of your so-and-so speeches for fifty so-and-so minutes. Why the so-and-so do you stop the debate when there are four or five Members waiting to speak? And did you realize that Winston is to speak to-morrow? What a so-and-so you are!' The honourable Member, during this address, was glancing rather anxiously over his shoulder, as well he might, for other Members were coming from the Chamber, as angry as I. I shall never know which 'so-and-so' he meant, but suddenly he said: 'Say that again, and I'll knock your block off!' I remember solemnly putting my spectacles in my pocket, and saying (I expect rather pompously): 'You're a so-and-so.' Perhaps I selected the wrong 'so-and-so,' for he made no attempt to knock my block off. I was, I confess, surprised and a little relieved; for Mr. X was said to be a very tough representative of a very tough part of a certain tough city. And I have always thought, therefore, that, morally, I won my only Parliamentary brawl. But I can make no confident claim to brawl-money, for, before I could utter another 'so-and-so' and put the matter to the test, two officials of the House tore us asunder.

VOTE OF CENSURE

Next day there were some pointed questions about the exploit of Mr. X. Mr. Bellenger spoke of 'a misuse of the rules of the House which will only bring Parliament into contempt.' Sir Stafford Cripps, Leader of the House, replied: 'Every hon. Member has a right to make use of the rules of the House in what way he thinks fit, but I hope that not many hon. Members will think fit to use them as they were used last night.'

Technically, the debate was dead, but 'with the leave of the House' Sir John formally moved his Motion again, and Aneurin Bevan seconded it. Walter Elliot said of his effort: 'We have at last heard the authentic voice of a Vote of Censure.' 'It was,' he said, 'a powerful speech, a well-informed speech, and, especially at the end, a cogently argued speech.' It was also a fearless and eloquent speech. But Mr. Churchill spoke, not surprisingly, of 'the bitter animosity of the diatribe of the hon. Member for Ebbw Vale, with all its carefully aimed and calculated hostility.' Much of it reads strangely now, especially if you have just heard our present (1949) Minister of Health complain of a 'campaign of denigration' by the Opposition. He began with some admirable doctrines: 'It is the duty, as I understand it, of Members of Parliament to try and reproduce in the House of Commons the psychology which exists in the country, and there can be no doubt that the country is deeply disturbed by the movement of events at the present time.' But that, after all. is the basis of all Parliamentary 'denigration.'

He said:

It seems to me that there are three things wrong. First, the main strategy of the war has been wrong; second, the wrong weapons have been produced; and third, those weapons are being managed by men who are not trained in the use of them and who have not studied the use of modern weapons.

Why is the strategy wrong? I say, first, that it is because the Prime Minister, although possessing many other qualities, sometimes conceives of the war, it seems to me, in medieval terms, because he talks of it as if it was a tourney. But the strategy is wrong because the Prime Minister has a wrong instrument of Government. . . .

The Prime Minister has qualities of greatness—everybody knows that —but the trouble is that he has too much to do. He has not around him colleagues to whom he can delegate any of this matter concerning the central direction of the war. The result is that all these defects which he possesses are made dangerous, because the Prime Minister, among all his other qualities, has a gift of expression which is exceedingly danger- ous. He very often mistakes verbal felicities for verbal inspiration. The Prime Minister will, in the course of an evening, produce a whole series of brilliant improvisations, but has not the machinery to carry them through. . . .

I seriously suggest to the House that whatever they may do about this motion, they should for Heaven's sake insist, at this grave hour, that the Prime Minister be kept under the charge of strong men who have no departmental interest. . . .

This, of course, was but another variation of a theme common to all the critics. They wanted Winston, but they did not want him to do the work he was doing or to do any work in his own way.

Later, he said:

We have in this country five or six Generals, members of other na- tions, Czechs, Poles and French, all of them trained in the use of these German weapons and this German technique. I know it is hurtful to our pride, but would it not be possible to put some of those men temporarily in charge in the field, until we can produce trained men of our own? . . . Why should we not put them in the field in charge of our troops? They know how to fight this war; our people do not. . . .

There should be a new Secretary of State for War.

I say that the Prime Minister has great qualities, but obviously pick- ing men is not one of them. . . .

He finished with an earnest call for a 'Second Front Now.'

No such extracts do justice to the quality of any speech, but they show how hot was feeling, how fallible is man, and how free was the Mother of Parliaments in that terrible time.

At the end of the two unhappy, snappy, yet dignified days Mr. Churchill rose to reply. I know no other face in public life which so faithfully reflects so many moods. If I think of Stanley Baldwin or

Neville Chamberlain, I see the same face always—though, Heaven knows, I saw them in every sort of scene of every sort of drama, including Munich and the Abdication. But the Churchill face—if I may say so without offence—has the range, the variety, of one of those indiarubber faces we used to play with in our youth. You pressed them, this way or that, and they looked all sorts of things, in turn. Mr. Churchill, being more of an artist than those other two, I suppose, is sensitive as well as tough, and the pressure of events and people adjusts and changes the face amazingly. There is that glorious happy beam, when it is the face of the sun or the face of a laughing baby, a rosy dimpled face; there is the face of the imp, the face of Puck in action, not so happy but alert and vital. There is the face of the Statesman, calm but brooding, a curtain drawn before tremendous things. There is the pugnacious damn-you-all face, with the chin well out, the face of 'blood and sweat and toil and tears.' There is the rather bored face in the Smoking Room, which makes the young Member think 'What the Hell shall I say? Or would it be better to say nothing?' Then—lest I should be thought to suggest bad manners, which I certainly do not intend—there is the sudden smile, and twinkle, which make the young man glad to be alive, and doubly glad that he was elected—for here he is, a mortal, on intimate terms with a god, in good humour. I have no doubt there are many other faces, and someone who knows about faces should study and describe them all. But, last, there is what I think of as the grey face of the black times—times made black, not by foreign enemies but by his own people; times when, still defiant and full of faith, he deeply felt the stabs of injustice or disloyalty, or lack of understanding. I cannot describe it—I hope I shall never see it again —but the whole face changed, almost collapsed. You would not have said, if you did not know, that it was the same assembly of flesh and blood and bone as the beaming, shining, grown-up baby-face we all have seen and loved. How often I have peeped along the benches over the noses of twenty Members and seen that face, and it has wrung my heart—the bowed head, the scowl, the lips and chin thrust out, the eyes aimed angrily below the Table—as it might be a great bull baited by cunning little men. I will not pretend that I remember how he looked as he spoke that day. But the grey grim face was certainly there during the debate. Imagine what he must have felt! Tobruk had fallen the week before. The very morning the censure debate began Rommel had opened his assault on the South Africans, at the gates of Alexandria. Behind was a long catalogue of discomfiture and disappointment; ahead there might be worse to come. He could not say all that he knew—whether of the past or the future. For example, when they asked why stronger forces were not available to sink the *Scharnhorst* and the *Gneisenau,* he could not tell them about the Italian 'frog-men' who had successfully stuck their little bombs on the bottoms of our ships in Alexandria Harbour. We heard that later in Secret Session—and a hair-raising story it was. For a period we had no big ship that could move in the Mediterranean, and what should have sunk the *Scharnhorst* had been sent out there (I forget the details, but that was the gist of it). They clamoured for a 'Second Front'—and no one had a stronger itch to be at Hitler's throat than he: but he could not tell them what was cooking or how long it would take to cook. He must, by now, have had the sense of his own destiny strong in him. Surely he had not emerged from all those years 'in the wilderness' for nothing. Yet here were men of all parties, important men, serious men, men who had clamoured for him in 1940, joining in the hunt—not only the malignant whippersnapper from Wales, but Wardlaw-Milne, strong Tory, Roger Keyes, his old companion, Clem Davies, leader of the Liberals, Winterton and Shinwell ('Arsenic,' as the funny men had it, 'and Old Lace'). Either he had done too much or had done too little: they were against him. It was by forces no stronger than these that Neville Chamberlain had been cast down, and Chamberlain had had only one defeat to his account—he had a dozen. He may well have thought: After all that I have done—is this the beginning of the end? And all the time, as he said in his speech, while they were yattering away about things that he did or should have done eight months ago, while he was listening to Bevan's 'diatribe,' he found it very difficult 'to withdraw my thoughts from the tremendous and most critical battle now raging in Egypt.' What was happening there, at the door to the Suez Canal? I know nothing that you do not know, but I should not wonder if those days were reckoned among his worst.

Yet when the old lion rose at last, with his first roar he proclaimed and defended the right of all comers to bait and attack him:

This long debate has now reached its final stage. What a remarkable example it has been of the unbridled freedom of our Parliamentary constitution in time of war! Everything that could be thought of or raked up has been used to weaken confidence in the Government, has been used to prove that the Ministers are incompetent and to weaken their confidence in themselves, to make the Army distrust the backing it is getting from the civil power, to make the workmen lose confidence in the weapons they are striving so hard to make, to represent the Government as a set of nonentities, over whom the Prime Minister towers, and then to undermine him in his own heart, and, if possible, before the eyes of the nation. All this poured out by cables and radio to all parts of the world, to the distress of all our friends and to the delight of all our foes. I am in favour of this freedom, which no other country would use, or dare to use, in times of mortal peril, such as those through which we are passing. But the story must not end there, and I make now my appeal to the House of Commons to make sure that it does not end there.

Then he filled twenty-six columns of *Hansard*—about ninety minutes.

You can read the great man's speeches in full elsewhere, but here are a few 'character' chips from that great chunk of history:

When on the morning of Sunday, the 21st, I went into the President's (Roosevelt's) room I was greatly shocked to be confronted with a report that Tobruk had fallen. I found it difficult to believe, but a few minutes later my own telegram, forwarded from London, arrived. I hope the House will realize what a bitter pang this was to me. What made it worse was being on an important mission in the country of one of our great Allies. Some people assume too readily that, because a Government keeps cool and has steady nerves under reverses, its members do not feel the public misfortunes as keenly as do independent critics. On the contrary, I doubt whether anyone feels greater sorrow or pain than those who are responsible for the general conduct of our affairs. It was an aggravation in the days that followed to read distorted accounts of the feeling in Britain and in the House of Commons.

At one point Mr. Hore-Belisha interjected:

What about the Churchill tank?

THE PRIME MINISTER: At the present moment I have not got there.

But he did.

This tank, the A.22, was ordered off the drawing-board, and large numbers went into production very quickly. As might be expected, it had many defects and teething troubles, and when these became apparent the tank was appropriately re-christened the 'Churchill.' These defects have now been largely overcome. I am sure that this tank will prove, in the end, a powerful, massive, and serviceable weapon of war.

I remember how we laughed at that. I have often said that if Mr. Churchill had done nothing else he could still, at least, be England's greatest humourist. For, on any subject, before any audience, with no fault of taste or tact, he can make laughter when he will. Who can say more? Time and again, in those immense war-speeches, full of detail, defiance, and dignity, there came the sudden and perfect jest that made the whole House happy. And here, in (to my mind) the most difficult speech of all, he had the time, and the nerve, to pop in a little joke that was against himself, and yet, obliquely, was an answer to the whole debate.

Of the struggle in Egypt, he said:

General Auchinleck is now in direct command of the battle. It is raging with great intensity. . . . I cannot tell the House—and the enemy—what reinforcements are at hand, or are approaching, or when they will arrive. I have never made any predictions except things like saying that Singapore would hold out. What a fool and a knave I should have been to say that it would fall! I have not made any arrogant, confident, boasting predictions at all. *On the contrary, I have stuck hard to my blood, toil, tears, and sweat, to which I have added muddle and mismanagement, and that, to some extent, I must admit, is what you have got out of it.*

And he went on:

I do not know what my critics would like me to say now. If I predict success and speak in buoyant terms and misfortune continues, their tongues and pens will be able to dilate on my words. On the other hand, if I predict failure and paint the picture in the darkest hues—I have painted it in pretty dark hues—I might safeguard myself against one danger, but only at the expense of a struggling Army. Also I might be wrong. So I will say nothing about the future except to invite the House and the nation to face with courage whatever it may unfold.

That is the sort of stuff to rally the dubious vote: and I must say I admired the faith and fortitude of those who, after such a speech, could vote against him. He finished as strongly as ever. It would be foolish to recommend the new young Member to finish his speeches in the same manner, even if he had the same command of words and wisdom. Certainly, he should have his ending ready in his mind; but everyone is waiting for the back-bencher to sit down, and his ending, however strong, should be sharp and short. But a statesman, a leader, in a tight corner, at a crisis in his country's fortunes, at the end of two days of 'denigration,' could hardly do better than this:

The setting down of the Vote of Censure by Members of all parties is a considerable event. Do not, I beg you, let the House underrate the gravity of what has been done. It has been trumpeted all round the world to our disparagement, and when every nation, friend and foe, is waiting to see what is the true resolve and conviction of the House of Commons, it must go forward to the end. All over the world, throughout the United States, as I can testify, in Russia, far away in China and throughout every subjugated country all our friends are waiting to know whether there is a strong, solid Government in Britain and whether its national leadership is to be challenged or not. Every vote counts. If those who have assailed us are reduced to contemptible proportions and their Vote of Censure on the National Government is converted to a vote of censure upon its authors, make no mistake, a cheer will go up from every friend of Britain and every faithful servant of our cause, and the knell of disappointment will ring in the ears of the tyrants we are striving to overthrow.

Question put:

That this House, while paying tribute to the heroism and endurance of the Armed Forces of the Crown in circumstances of exceptional difficulty, has no confidence in the central direction of the war.

The House divided: Ayes, 25; Noes, 475.
Mr. Bevan had said at one point:

The fact of the matter is that the British Army is ridden by class prejudice. You have got to change it, and you will have to change it. If the House of Commons has not the guts to make the Government change it, events will. Although the House may not take any notice of me to-day, you will be doing it next week. *Remember my words next Tuesday and Wednesday. . . .* Therefore, you have to change that business: you have to purge the Army at the top.

The words recorded, I remember, had a grim effect on many of us. Cassandra might be right, after all; and it sounded a little as if the prophet hoped he would be right. But while the Commons yapped at the Minister of Defence and the Secretary of State for War, the Army, under Auchinleck, were pushing Rommel back. In Tuesday's *Times* there was a dispatch from Egypt which said: 'The position here is growing steadily more healthy'; and the headline was 'Allies Retain the Initiative.' Cassandra, I suppose, would feel entitled to reply, 'Ah, but next month General Montgomery (though chosen by the bad chooser of men, and not a Pole) was sent to Egypt.' But, so far as I know, the general 'setup' which had been so much attacked remained unaltered, and Mr. Churchill retained his 'impossible' dual position, as Prime Minister and Minister of Defence, to the end. At all events, three months later, the Battle of El Alamein took place, and there were no more votes of no confidence.

25. Mr. Churchill Recites

Here, I think, is a pleasing picture of the lighter side of Mr. Churchill, in the later days, when things were better.

Early in the war, it was decided that the church bells should be rung as a warning of invasion. So they had to be silent on other occasions. I never thought that this was a very sensible arrangement; and how, while it lasted, could we blame the enemy for bombing church towers? On 7 November 1941 I wrote some verses about it in the *Sunday Graphic:*

BRING BACK THE BELLS

Bring back the bells. The bells are dumb
Until the parachuters come;
And even Huns may be excused
For bombing belfries so abused.
Let there be steel in Aaron's rod,
And fighters in the ranks of God;
But leave the little church in peace
While we have soldiers and police.
If we can not inform the town
That parachutes are coming down
Without inviting Huns to search
For targets in the parish church,

The old inventive British brain
Had better, surely, think again.
Bring back the bells; and use a drum
To let us know that Hitler's come.

Sixteen months later, on 20 April 1943, they were published in a little book of verse called *Bring Back the Bells*. I sent Mr. Churchill a copy next day, and it must have reached him, by a happy chance, on the very morning when, in answer to a question by Sir Thomas Moore, he announced that the bells were coming back.

We have come to the conclusion that this particular method of warning was redundant, and not in itself well adapted to the present condition of the war.

SIR T. MOORE: Will my right hon. Friend say what alternative arrangements have been made?

THE PRIME MINISTER: Replacement does not arise. *For myself, I cannot help thinking that anything like a serious invasion would be bound to leak out.*

MR. AUSTIN HOPKINSON: How can the news possibly leak out, when it is an offence to spread alarm and despondency?

THE PRIME MINISTER: Factual statements of that kind, especially if well intentioned, would not fall into that category.

Three pages later in the book were some simple verses I had written for his sixty-seventh birthday:

TO W. S. C.

Many happy returns of the day
To the father of purpose and plan,
To the one who was first in the fray,
Never doubted, or rested, or ran,
To the Voice of old Britain at bay,
To the Voice of young men in the van,
To the Voice of new worlds on the way—
To 'We must—and we will—and we can!'
May he live to hear History say,
'This was their finest man.'

He went to Washington and addressed the assembled legislators of the United States. Then 'I thought it well to go to North Africa,' and he flew to Gibraltar and Algiers with General Marshall. He came home and on 8 June made a long speech (or 'statement') about all this. At the end we all trooped out for lunch. In the Smoking Room, when Mr. Churchill came in, the only seat vacant, by chance, was next to mine, and he sat down. We stood the great man a sherry, and he talked about Roosevelt, and de Gaulle, and Africa, and this and that. Then, suddenly, he said to me, 'Those verses you were kind enough to write for my birthday—where did you get the metre?'

I said, 'I don't know. It started "Many happy returns of the day," and then it seemed to go on.'

'I thought I recognized it,' he said. 'I went to a shelf—and found it.'

Then he began to recite. I do not now know what the piece was. It was some kind of a *ballade,* with some French in it. There were three or four stanzas. He began a little haltingly, but the last verses flowed as smoothly as a Head Boy's recitation on Speech Day. We listened in astonishment, wondering how in the midst of his mighty cares he had been able to get all that verse into his mind, and keep it there.

We offered him another sherry. But he said: 'No. I am going to lunch at Buckingham Palace, and it would not look well if I were to slither under the Royal table.'

26. Less Nonsense

On 23 March 1943 my slender Muse (through no fault of mine) was hauled before the Commons. In October 1942 I had written some verses called 'Less Nonsense,' which appeared in *Truth* (editor my bold and brilliant friend Mr. Collin Brooks). They were intended as an answer to the excessive adulators of Russia and 'Second-Front-Now-Boys.' Here they are:

> *Let's have less nonsense from the friends of Joe;*
> *We laud, we love him, but the nonsense—NO!*
> *In 1940, when we bore the brunt,*
> *WE could have done, boys, with a second front.*
> *A continent went down a cataract,*
> *But Russia did not think it right to act.*
> *Not ready? No. And who shall call her wrong?*
> *Far better not to strike till you are strong.*
> *Better, perhaps (tho' this was not our fate),*
> *To make new treaties with the man you hate.*
> *Alas! these shy manœuvres had to end*
> *When Hitler leaped upon his largest friend;*
> *(And if he'd not, I wonder, by the way,*
> *If Russia would be in the war to-day?)*
> *But who rushed out to aid the giant then?—*
> *A giant rich in corn, and oil, and men,*

> *Long, long prepared, and having, so they say,*
> *The most enlightened leader of the day.*
> THIS *tiny island, antiquated, tired,*
> *Effete, capitalist, and uninspired!*
> THIS *tiny island, wounded in the war*
> *Through taking tyrants on two years before!*
> THIS *tiny isle of muddles and mistakes*
> *Having a front on every wave that breaks.*
> *We might have said 'our shipping's on the stretch—*
> *You shall have all the tanks that you can fetch.'*
> *But that is not the way* WE *fight this war;*
> *We give them tanks, and take them to the door.*
> *And now, we will not hear from anyone*
> *That it's for us to show we hate the Hun.*
> *It does not profit much to sing this tune,*
> *But those who prod, cannot be quite immune,*
> *And those who itch to conquer and to kill*
> *Should waste less breath on tubs on Tower Hill.*
> *Honour the Kremlin, boys, but now and then*
> *Admit some signs of grace at Number Ten.*

Whatever their merits, they seemed to 'fill a need,' and had a wide private circulation. Indeed, they quietly went round the world. In Newfoundland I met a Canadian who showed me a copy which had just been sent to him by a friend in Australia. Unfortunately, some keen poetry-lovers, who were also leaders of men, distributed copies of the work among their men, for the purpose of 'ameliorating morale.' At Short's works at Rochester, I was told, the shop-stewards threatened a strike and sent an angry telegram to Sir Stafford Cripps, the Minister for Aircraft Production. On 23 March 1943, Mr. D. N. Pritt (another Wykehamist) put down a solemn question and produced a comical column of *Hansard:*

VERSES, 'LESS NONSENSE'

MR. PRITT asked the Secretary of State for War whether he is aware that Lieut.-Colonel Parkinson ordered to be distributed, on 24 February 1943, to units under his command over 200 copies of a piece of verse entitled 'Less Nonsense,' which is offensive to the Soviet Union and calculated to injure our friendship towards that country; that these copies were to be distributed on the scale of three copies for every unit down to batteries and companies, one copy for the officers' mess, one for the sergeants' mess, and one where it could be seen by the men; and whether he will take immediate steps to put a stop to this political activity and arrange that lectures on the Soviet Union be given to the units involved to counteract the effects of this propaganda?

SIR J. GRIGG: I am making inquiries into this matter. On the facts as stated, I do not think the action of the Divisional Commander was at all suitable. The troops in the area in question are already getting lectures on Soviet Russia from both military and non-military sources besides a good deal of other material on the subject, and I doubt if any special steps are necessary.

MAJOR-GENERAL SIR ALFRED KNOX: Is it not true that this poem contains nothing offensive to Soviet Russia, and is it not British patriotism from a British point of view?

SIR J. GRIGG: I have been careful to express no opinion on the merits of the verses.

COMMANDER LOCKER-LAMPSON: Can they be circulated as a White Paper?

PETTY-OFFICER HERBERT: Is the right hon. Gentleman aware that these verses, whatever their merits, were not directed against Russia at all, but against certain British citizens who are never happy unless they are running down their own country and the efforts of their own countrymen in the war?

Mr. Pritt did not say a word.

27. Flying the Atlantic

In the summer of 1943 Mr. Attlee, not only Deputy Prime Minister, but Secretary of State for the Dominions, invited me to be one of a Parliamentary mission to Newfoundland. I felt myself highly honoured and accepted at once. It was an instructive, strenuous, and exciting venture, but it led me into the most unhappy problem, and the most severe defeat, of all my Parliamentary time. The other two members of the mission were Mr. Charles (now Lord) Ammon (North Camberwell) and Sir Derrick Gunston, Bart. (Thornbury). We began with a trip to Scotland, to see the Newfoundland Woodsmen contingent, who were methodically and magically stripping the Highlands of trees in the cause of victory. We were to fly to Scotland. It was my first flight. I need hardly say that we had to come down at Doncaster, because of bad weather, and finish the journey by train. I was not so much alarmed as I expected to be, but I was far more bored. I was more than bored: I was ashamed. Once we were up, and I had survived my first lifting from the earth, I expected to feel, in a humble way, some part of the triumph of Man, who had conquered the elements and could now behave like a bird. But I did not feel like a bird. I did not even feel like a masterful man. As we rattled and rolled, for a long time, low over the suburbs of London in our tin-pot machine, I felt more

and more like a drunk man reeling home in a clattering milk-cart
and insulting the quiet citizens who looked up at the noise and
saw us. Even in the open country the bird's-eye view is not a good
view, except perhaps of mountain ranges. Neither houses, cows,
nor trees look best from above; and I am nearly always over the
wing, and see nothing but a ramshackle, rattling expanse of brown
metal. The one point in flight I positively enjoy is the point at
which they told me I should be alarmed—when the thing begins
circling before landing, with a heavy list to port. Then I do feel
some sense of the mastery of Man. For the rest, I feel as Dr. John-
son felt in a ship,[1] a prisoner. In the smallest ship you can walk
about and be at ease; the humblest passenger can ask any member
of the crew, from the Captain down, 'Where are we?' and even
the Captain will eagerly inform him. In the air you sit huddled
in your allotted seat, half afraid to stand, for fear of upsetting the
machine. Those in charge are remote, invisible, and god-like beings,
whom you will never meet for a cheery chat or a stroll upon the
deck. You hardly dare to ask the steward where you are, and he is
most unlikely to know. Long before you start, the airport procedure
has cowed and confined your spirit—the incessant admonitions
by loud-speakers, which always seem to me to have a tone of hostility
and menace seldom heard in the loud-speakers of the sea, the little
columns of fellow-prisoners being marched this way or that, the
long waits, the sudden scurries from cell to cell, and the cool announcement that the flight is off. The Sea, I feel, is glad to see
you; the Air, the superior Air, is always saying: 'Who are you?
How nice of us to have you! Behave yourself.' All this, no doubt,
betrays a sad old-fashioned soul; and to say that you are bored
in the air, is, I am well aware, a high tribute to the great brains
and gallant men who have made flying a bore. It is much better
to be bored than frightened. But there it is: I am nearly always
sorry to leave a ship—I am always glad to escape from the Air.

Still, I deigned to fly the Atlantic—once. And this, I thought,
because of my friend Derrick Gunston, was rather brave of both of
us. Derrick Gunston is a fearless adventurous fellow, a soldier and

[1]'No man will be a sailor who has contrivance enough to get himself into a
jail; for being in a ship is being in a jail, with the chance of being drowned.'

a yachtsman; but he had recently, it seemed, become a kind of Jonah of the Air. In two years he had had four or five misfortunes. Once he had crawled out from under a burning aircraft; once the pilot had lost his way in fog over Portsmouth; and, of course, when he went up on a Parliamentary glider, he was in the glider that crashed. But none of this disturbed Derrick; and as the great sea-plane rumbled out into the dusk of the Atlantic I heard him happily telling an Australian M.P., in his deep, husky voice, 'The plane turned right over and caught fire.'

The Boeing was far more like a ship, though there were too many passengers to move very much. When she heeled over and circled slowly in the sunset above the Shannon River, when she touched the water at last with no more fuss than a swan, I almost enjoyed flying.

'Completely destroyed,' said Derrick. 'I lost my luggage.'

It had been fun to spend an evening and a day in Limerick. It was my first night in my native land, and there I was, by chance, in my father's own part of Ireland. For he came from Muckross, in Killarney, and there used to be many Herberts in Limerick.

'I said to him,' said Derrick, 'but why didn't you *bring* any charts?'

I had resented my native land being a neutral. But—a town where you could have two eggs and bacon when you wished— 'three, if you like, sorr!' And, after all these crawling years, to be in a town with no black-out! After supper I went out to admire and enjoy the lights. Up the street came a bicycle with a great searchlight hanging on it. Instinct was too strong, and I yelled, 'PUT THAT LIGHT OUT!' A little man rode up and said politely, 'An' why would I do the like of that? Sure, there's no moon at all.'

Derrick said, 'The next time, we came down in a tree.'

The Atlantic looked very large and very lonely. We were pretty low, but all the way over we never saw a ship.

But it was a fine night, and I was looking forward to the darkness, for then I could try my gadget for finding longitude by the stars. It was one of the thoughts that had reconciled me to flying the Atlantic.

'Ellen Wilkinson broke a leg,' said Derrick.

Now I could see a planet. But at once, of course, the steward went round and 'did the black-out.' That was the end of my experiment.

'I suppose,' said Derrick, 'a U-boat might take a pop at us.'

For the rest of the Atlantic I read my book. Fourteen hours—one cup of tea. What a bore—thank God!

28. Newfoundland

It is not fair to Newfoundland to arrive by air. Early in the morning we flew out of the great wall of fog over the Banks and, sleepy-eyed, saw a sunlit sea at last. But I looked back at the fog, an awesome spectacle. It was indeed a great wall, blue-grey, nearly black, as clear-cut as a cliff. It was as if God had taken a great knife and made a clean slash from north to south. The fog is caused, they say, by the meeting of the Gulf Stream and the Labrador North Polar current. Most days you can see the wall far out to sea from the heights above St. John's; or even from the harbour. And most days it stays out there, for the prevailing winds are westerly. Easterly winds bring some of it to the eastern coast, but I saw less fog in Newfoundland than I should have seen in London, and the Newfoundlanders rightly resent their foggy reputation. On the western coasts we had nothing but sun and blue sky. Later, it is true, off Labrador, I was fogbound for nine days; but my Newfoundland companions firmly agreed that that was an exceptional freak: and they are supported by that great Englishman Sir Wilfred Grenfell.[1]

But now the sunlit sea ahead was sprinkled with ice and dotted

[1]"There has somehow got about the idea that Labrador is continually wrapped in fog. This is an entirely erroneous idea. . . . As a matter of fact fog is almost left behind at the Straits of Belle Isle. . . . On the average a more or less foggy day once a fortnight may be expected.'

with icebergs, or, as they are called more pleasantly in these parts, ice-islands. All this dangerous sea litter comes from Greenland's icy mountains and drifts southward (below Newfoundland, sometimes) in the Labrador current, till it melts or goes aground. It is decorative, but it is not an Englishman's notion of a sea coast on 21 June in latitude 50°N., well south of London's, which is 51° 30′N.

Then, I must say, my heart sank as we flew in from the north over an area of ponds and swamps, cringeing little fir trees and barren rocky spaces with not a sign of human habitation. But, again, the bird's-eye view is deceptive. This is the view familiar to travellers between Britain and America who stop for a day or an hour or two at Gander and say, 'What a country!' But if you come in from the sea to any of the innumerable fishing villages (or 'out-ports') on a sunny day, you would say you were in Norway, or Cornwall, or (except for the whale rolling and blowing in the bay) a Swiss or an Italian lake. Every house is of wood, and every church; and, since you can paint wood in any colour you like, the distant view is varied and gay. The coloured wooden churches, with their brave wooden spires, always dominate the picture, partly because of their greens and reds and purples and blacks, and partly because in nearly every community, however small, there are three of them—Catholic, Anglican, and 'United Church.' Below the churches and the white wood houses, the fish-plants and ware-houses stand on legs in the water, which is as clear as your bath. The grand old schooners lie at the wharves, and somewhere, you may be sure, are a few acres of split cod drying in the sun. Many of the coves and water-villages are enchantingly pretty, and the Bay of Islands, on the west coast, is an estuary with a gracious beauty of which any country might be proud. The high coast is fringed by innumerable islands and split by innumerable arms and inlets. Newfoundland has only 42,750 square miles, but a coast-line of 6,000 miles. There are endless, enviable square miles of land-locked fiord-like water, very deep, and almost anywhere you could safely tie the *Queen Elizabeth* to a tree and go ashore for a beer. But the northern half, for about five months of the year, is covered with snow, cut off by ice, and unapproachable by land or sea (ex-cept by dog-sleigh). There are those swamps and barren rocky hills, and, of course, more profitable, the immeasurable forests of fir, much denser than the jungles of Ceylon. So, though the island is half as large again as Ireland, it has the population of Bradford;[2] though it was 'our oldest colony' it had the communications of a 'new' country; and though it was a 'dominion' it was—or had been —desperately poor.

All these parts, they say, were once covered by a gigantic ice-cap, which after a very long time broke up and dispersed itself in all directions. The glaciers which crunched their way south deposited their moraine, their crushed debris and collected soil on the North American continent which has been fertile ever since. The glaciers which ground across Newfoundland and Labrador swept all the goodness into the Atlantic. And that is why agriculture is not the leading industry on the ocean coasts. In the rest of Newfoundland there are good soils, fine farms, and gardens, luscious vegetables and innumerable potatoes. But this is not enough. The fish in the sea, and the fir in the forest, are the island's bread and butter.

As for the people, I wrote these notes about them after seven days of fog in that cold boat off Labrador:

What charming folk these Newfoundlanders are! In all these dreary days I have not heard a word of wrath or seen a sign of wear. And though we are not in an open boat or a Berlin bomber, continual fog and rain and coldness *are* wearing. They are the best-tempered, best-mannered people walking. I do not believe I ever heard a Newfoundlander swear. . . . They are gay, good-humoured and generous; tolerant, temperate, tough, God-fearing, sabbath-keeping and law-abiding. Fond of holidays, but fine workers: politically maddening but personally the salt of the earth. They will give you all they have got, or put you up for the winter, in a bad year, but cannot bear the thought of 'rates.' They will subscribe the earth for a man who has fallen through the rickety bridge, but do nothing at all about mending the bridge. Every man can build his own house, his own boat, but he won't build a parish council. They have all the crafts except the political. They are devoted to the 'Old Country' (however much they may reproach her). I have heard moving accounts of the black days when France fell, and most people over here thought that we were done too. The Newfoundlander—never. They would not hear of it.

[2]In 1943, 335,000.

And, though this may sound like an Englishman's conceit—I say that they are intensely English. Their names are English, their ancestors were English, and after all these generations their accents are English still. The great go-getting, twanging continent next door has not got the Newfoundlander yet.

If you fell 'blindfolded' by parachute on to any part of Newfoundland and you listened to the talk, you might say you were in Devonshire, in Dorset, Cornwall, or Somerset, or Yorkshire: you might say you were in Ireland or Scotland (not often in Wales). But you would never say you were in Canada or the United States.

And when you think that all day long they are bombarded by the 'Voice of America' on the wireless, and even by American announcers on the B.B.C.; when you think that the island is full of Americans and Canadian Service men (bless them all); when you think that they use and talk dollars all day, and never see an English coin, an English paper or magazine, it is amazing how little that mighty continent has touched them. Indeed, I think they talk less American than our young people at home. Certainly, they talk much more good English—and old English. They use many words and tricks of phrase that we have forgotten.

All this is highly important politically. For when men discuss, as so many discuss, the future of Newfoundland, one of the possibilities mentioned is Confederation with Canada—or even the United States. There are many things to be said about that which had better not be said now. But some easy thinkers, and anything-for-a-quiet-lifers will tell you that Newfoundland is 'naturally' and 'logically' so much a part of the continent that it would be sensible to accept and make it so.

It depends what you mean by 'naturally.' Geography is not everything, or Northern Ireland and Southern Ireland would be one big brother, and Southern Ireland would not have a German Embassy in Dublin at this moment. (And what about Malta—and Gibraltar?) All I will say now—for the foul hag Discretion is coldly plucking at my elbow —is this. The Newfoundlanders no more 'belong' to the American continent, in any sense, than I do.

Nor, with great respect to everyone, do they wish to.[3]

I was not alone in that opinion. Our leader, Mr. Charles Ammon, who favoured confederation, wrote about the same time:

It is apparent that the people of Newfoundland would at this juncture be profoundly out of sympathy with any such proposal. . . . But

[3] *Punch,* 17 November 1943.

[he went on] I feel that the possibilities should be kept continuously in mind, in the event of public opinion in Newfoundland showing any marked change in sympathy towards Canada in the near future.

It is my sad charge against my own country that we deliberately bullied them—or rather a little more than half of them—into a change of mind; that we turned our own child into the snow.

In 1583, on 5 August, Sir Humphrey Gilbert went ashore in St. John's Harbour, planted Queen Elizabeth's flag, and annexed the island to England on behalf of his sovereign as the first colonial possession of the Crown.

He set up his tent on the 'beach,' where the Newfoundland War Memorial now stands. On 5 August 1943 we three were present at the same spot for the moving ceremonies of Commemoration Day. There were the White Ensign, the top-hats, the medals, the Scouts, the Church Lads' Brigade, the English hymns. We might have been anywhere in the West Country. And, though long before I had made up my mind, I swore to myself again, as I stood at the salute in that historic spot, that I would do whatever I could to keep this English island free and independent.

In 1670 it was proposed and discussed 'that the Plantation be discontinued'; and what with tidal waves, hurricanes, forest fires, city fires,[4] bank failures, and political crises, poor Newfoundland has suffered enough shocks in the last hundred years to sink an ordinary island. But she struggled on, ever begrudged and belaboured by a niggardly and hostile Nature, but ever growing in political stature. In 1832, for the first time, she elected members to a representative assembly, and in 1855 her Prime Minister and Government became responsible to the Legislature—which, like ours, had two chambers—the Legislative Council and the House of Assembly. In 1931, by the Statute of Westminster, she was declared a Dominion, the equal of Canada. But, in 1933, at the request of her own Ministers and Legislature, we 'put the receivers in'; and her self-governing powers were suspended 'until such time as she should become self-supporting again.'

Meanwhile, she was to be governed by six Commissioners ap-

[4]St. John's, the capital, suffered terrible fires in 1816, 1846, and 1892; in the last, 11,000 people were made homeless.

pointed by the Crown, three Newfoundlanders and three from the United Kingdom (as a rule, civil servants). The Chairman of this executive body was the Governor, the genial Admiral Sir Humphrey Walwyn, K.C.S.I., C.B., D.S.O. This was an evidently undesirable arrangement. We all three, separately, deplored it in our reports and recommended—without effect—the appointment of an independent Chairman. The Commission of Government had, on the whole, done a difficult and thankless job pretty well. But, as I wrote then:

If the three British Commissioners were men as able as Mr. Churchill, Mr. Roosevelt, and Mr. Stalin, they would still be foreigners. If the three Newfoundlanders were men like Sir Robert Bond [a great Newfoundland statesman] they would still hold office by appointment from the Dominions Office and not by the Newfoundlanders' choice. . . . The fact remains that Government by Commission is an alien and anomalous régime, repugnant to the instincts and traditions of a freedom-loving British people accustomed for 110 years to the apparatus of Parliament.

War made poor Newfoundland self-supporting almost at once. The American and Canadian bases helped very much, of course, but there it was—not only did she pay her way, but the bankrupt island lent much money to the mighty United Kingdom (the 'Official Receiver'), besides sending many good men to fight for the Allied cause by land or sea.

So when three deaf, weary Members of Parliament touched earth for the third time (since Poole) outside St. John's, they found themselves at the capital of 'our oldest colony,' still a Dominion (in suspense), financially self-supporting, lending money (free of interest) to the mother country, but governed by an oligarchy. And the oligarchy was not even an independent oligarchy, but one severely controlled and directed, in finance and policy, by Whitehall. Our job was to find out, informally, the facts of the situation, and the mind of the people. Was the island likely to go on paying its way after the war? And, either way, what did the people want? A pretty—simple—delightful kettle of fish!

We found at once some sad but natural resentment against our country. Going the rounds of St. John's, we naturally asked to see the Parliament building, and were taken to Colonial House, which contained both chambers of the Newfoundland Legislature. As Members of the House of Commons, still free and vocal, we approached the place with proper reverence. I thought we should see these chambers unpeopled but respected: the Speaker's Chair empty, but in good order, waiting to be filled again. I thought to see, perhaps, a Newfoundlander at the door of the House of Assembly with his children, saying: 'That is where your ancestors used to make the laws of Newfoundland; and that, please God, is where the Newfoundlanders will make their laws again.'

I saw no such thing. The Speaker's Chair was not empty—it was not there. The Bar was not there. All the furniture of a Parliament more than a hundred years old had been stripped and put away in a loft—nobody seemed to know where. The place was occupied by civil servants. Excellent civil servants, no doubt, doing good work for the Department of National Resources, which was run by one of the best of our Commissioners, Mr. Dunn. But I thought: How should I feel if I went back to England and found the House of Commons full of civil servants, however good, doing work, however worthy, by the order of another Power, however friendly?

We were shocked. But I thought: Perhaps all this is fanciful and foolish. Newfoundland is very short of Government buildings, and, after all, we are at war. But when I talked to some sensible citizens I found that the rape of their little Parliament had been resented heavily and rankled still. This unimaginative act was done in peacetime in cold blood, by the first Commissioners, civil servants themselves. It fortified the good old rule that no man is fit for absolute power.

We had done another extraordinary thing. When France fell and it was feared by most of the American continent (not the Newfoundlanders) that England was out on her feet, some prompt and energetic moves were made to defend the Western Hemisphere against the Huns let loose. The United States, you remember, let us have fifty destroyers, and we let her have bases—on ninety-nine-year leases—in the West Indies and elsewhere. No part of Newfoundland was concerned in that transaction, but the island was a first-class strategic corner, and both America and Canada, at vast expense, built great stations and bases there—sea, land, and air—

and sent many thousands of fine troops to man them. And we, though only temporary trustees for a self-governing Dominion (in suspense), gave ninety-nine-year leases! The bases were not built purely for love of little Newfoundland or purely for the defence of the American continent, but for the defence of the things the English-speaking peoples were fighting for everywhere; and there is not the smallest reason to suppose that Newfoundland (if she had been self-governing still) would have done anything but welcome the friendly (and remunerative) invaders, as she did. Indeed, it was a fine thing to see the four governments (including ours) in happy harness in that one small island. But it is highly unlikely that she would have granted ninety-nine-year leases of important sections of her territory. And she was not like a West Indian island, the whole of which, in theory, the Crown could give away to-morrow if it thought fit. We gave away what was not ours to give. So those loyal and good-tempered people did raise a wondering eyebrow or two.

Mr. Attlee, if I may say so without impertinence, did very sensibly in sending out a small patrol of back-benchers ('of a goodwill character') instead of a portentous Royal Commission. Lord Amulree's Royal Commission of 1933 had left behind them deep tracks of resentment. Moreover, a Royal Commission, a necessarily heavy body, could not go everywhere, see everything and everybody as we few and unpretentious persons could—and did. It could not sit on the fish-wharves and argue with fishermen and merchants, magistrates and Rangers and ministers of religion; and get so near as I think we did to the minds of a rather shy and reticent people. It could not embark on a small boat and travel round the island to places inaccessible by land. I broke away, now and then—for I dislike going about in a gang, however friendly—but in three months, between landing and leaving, I covered 3,400 miles—only 100 of them by air, 1,200 in small boats at about 7 to 8 knots, and the rest by slow train or bumpy car (some of the roads were like a heavy sea). The boat was the best, though we had some rough passages. I think the fishermen liked to see the Members of Parliament coming in from sea; Derrick and I could both talk sea-stuff with them, and Charles Ammon had been a junior Minister at the Admiralty.

The names on the map are a continual joy to the traveller. Admiral's Bald Head Cape, and Seldom Come By, and Come by Chance, and Heart's Delight, and Heart's Content and the Annieopsquotch Mountains. Topsail and Gaff Topsail and Maintopsail, the names of heights. Bay of Exploits, Bonavista Bay, Trinity Bay, Notre Dame, Conception Bay. Rarely a name that is not English until you are half-way up Labrador. Then the Eskimo begins to dominate the chart with such mouthfuls as Ticoralak, Ukalluktok, Napakataktalik, Anniowaktook, Ukasiksalik, Tunungayualuk, Kikkutaksoak, and Nanuaklok. The Eskimo is fond of 'Ks.'

In the little wooden outports the proud legislators from Westminster found much to be 'superior' about, but much that made them feel humble and admiring. Never a Mayor[5] or council; never an acknowledged leader of the community. Seldom the beginnings of any organization against fire, though fire was the principal peril of those most inflammable hamlets, swept by high winds and without a 'water-supply'; and, wherever we went, we seemed to hear of a recent fire. Everything neat and shipshape by the water, and everything neat and tidy in the houses—a harmonium, a radio, old paintings of England, Lodge certificates, the King's picture, a fine well-kept stove. Ship pride, craft pride, house pride, but seldom a sign of town or settlement pride.

No State school—but plenty of schools. For education is the monopoly of the churches. The Education Act speaks of 'the principle of denominational education which is by law established in this colony'; and you can get no money for education except through one of the denominations. The population is about equally divided between Church of England, Catholic, and 'United Churches' (Nonconformist); and the Salvation Army, here and there, is strong as well. So in each little hamlet—with, perhaps, 300 inhabitants, or less—we saw from the sea three coloured churches, and we found three different schools beside them. How inefficient! we said. What a dispersal and waste of resources! But then we noticed another queer thing missing. We saw—*no policeman*. We were met by the Magistrates, and we were met by the Rangers—a fine force in khaki, akin to the Royal Canadian Mounted Police. But

[5]There were then only two Mayors in the whole Dominion.

they had come to meet *us*. They had, perhaps, thirty similar settlements in their 'beat,' a wide area of country, and would not be
there that night. So every night, all round the island, perhaps
200,000 citizens sleep without an officer of the law for many miles,
without anyone near whose duty it is to take cognizance of robbery
or murder.

I put the question once or twice: 'Suppose in this little place
there were robbery or murder to-night, what would happen—
whose job would it be to do something?' The Newfoundlanders
opened their eyes wide and gave this simple answer: 'But we don't
have robbery or murder.' And that is the extraordinary fact. A murder in Newfoundland is as rare as a suicide in church. It is perfectly
true that they do *not* seem to need policemen as other mortals do.
And from that, I think, they tend to argue that they do not need
Mayors and councils, firemen and scavengers.

But how is it that they do not need policemen? Well, then they
point to the three painted spires up the hill, and the three denominational schools beside them. And the English legislator has to think
again about that wasteful inefficient system.

The mystified but polite Press of St. John's called us the 'Goodwill
Mission,' and this embarrassing label stuck to us firmly for 3,000
miles. We sometimes wished that we had been a Royal Commission
after all.

The members of a Royal Commission [I wrote home, later] may look
a little solemn sometimes, may select their witnesses and company. They
may even withdraw from the public view for meditation. But a mere
Goodwill Mission must wear a grin all the time. They must see everybody and always be on tap. A Royal Commission, too, can be reasonably
static: it sits in the centre like a great spider, and summons the evidence.
A mere Goodwill Mission has to go scrambling about the world, snatch-
ing up what it can. We have travelled endlessly—1,000 miles a month.
We have travelled, deliberately, with the people, by the same slow and
uncomfortable (though friendly) means of locomotion that they have
to use, by trains that vibrate like destroyers, by roads like unfinished
switchbacks, by small boats in large seas, by plate-layers' trolleys on the
line. By land or water, we never move without pitching or rolling. We
arrive at last and tumble out like jellied eels, but the guns of goodwill

must be in action at once. There is not one parson but three parsons to visit—and sometimes the Salvation Army Leader as well. Then there are the schoolmasters, and the principal merchant, and the store, and the fish-meal plant, and the seal-plant, which is not now working, and the salmon-canning plant, which is now being built, and some pleasant talk on the wharves with the fishermen. There is also, as a rule, a meeting with representative Labour men and the Great War veterans, besides a few individual interviews with citizens who have particular points of view or troubles to mention. Sometimes there is a regular public meeting, and the three of us sit round a Union Jack and make or listen to speeches. Everybody is very friendly and charming at these encounters, but at each one we have to ask the same questions and discuss the same answers. The Grin of Goodwill, the alert interest, the eager ear, must never falter or fail.

We live, not in trunks, but in handbags: the horrors of packing confront us every morning.

Charles Ammon, who is seventy, stands up to the strenuous life magnificently. But he is a teetotaller (a tolerant one). Derrick and I find Goodwill exhausting, and we do not get so much refreshing fire-water as we are accustomed to at the House of Commons. The Liquor Laws are queer—Government Stores (but only two in the whole island), individual permits (for so much a month), etc. No pubs or bars, but nothing against the bottle in the bedroom. We generally contrive to have an iron ration in a little flask or bottle, leaking, as a rule, on to the last clean collar. But one is never quite sure that one's host for the night is not a strict teetotaller (the farther north you are the more likely that he is), and we must not give offence or jeopardize Goodwill. So, after the long labours of the day, there is a good deal of guilty whispering in the bedroom. And, Derrick being rather deaf, not even whispering is easy. Then there is the glass problem. Derrick thinks he saw a glass in the bathroom, but there is Someone there. When Someone comes out one of us nips across and stealthily abstracts the only tooth-glass, which we share. We forget to take the glass back, and no one in the house can wash his teeth properly next morning. It is all very difficult.

Then there was the laughable but testing episode of the Dry Islands. These were on the north-eastern coast. The main denomination was United Church, and the population, we were warned, were nearly all teetotal. We had been travelling for many days through the forests of the west, and our supplies of fire-water had run out;

I had two or three tots of rum in a flask, and Derrick had nothing. We were to stay, for once, for three or four nights, for Charles Ammon was to preach on Sunday. Worst of all (though this we did not know), the legend had gone ahead of us that Derrick and I were, like our worthy leader, severe teetotallers.

We were billeted in different houses. I was with a charming American doctor and his wife. Evidently they took nothing but water, and I hid my wicked flask deep in a drawer. Moreover, I did not use it, thinking the last drops should wait till Derrick and I were together again. I never quite know why I was knighted; but it should have been for this.

On the second day, while we were all inspecting the lighthouse, Derrick and I had a furtive conference, as guilty lovers snatch a few words at a party. Derrick said his hosts were utterly dry, and he was tired and suffering too. 'I asked that nice driver,' he whispered, 'and he says there's not a drop in the whole island. HOW FAR CAN THE LIGHT BE SEEN?' he added loudly, to the lighthouse-keeper.

'I know,' I whispered, while Ammon and Chadwick[6] received the proud reply, 'My people are the same. I SEE THAT YOU ARE A RADIO-DIRECTION-FINDING STATION AS WELL. But I tell you what. I have still a little rum in my flask. If you can get hold of a bottle I will let you have a tot.'

Derrick said to the lighthouse-keeper, 'I EXPECT YOU HAVE SOME PRETTY GOOD STORMS HERE? My dear fellow, I can't be seen taking *bottles* into my place. My hosts are charming, but strict T.T. But I'll call at your place and come up to your bedroom.'

I said, 'No, you don't. My host is not only T.T., but a *doctor*. We can't have secret drinking-parties in his house. What about Goodwill? THANK YOU, MR. LIGHTHOUSE-KEEPER. GOOD-BYE.' Derrick agreed, and we sadly parted.

Our last day in the Dry Islands was a lovely day, the kind of day that makes you wonder how frost and fog and Newfoundland were ever mentioned together. It was Sunday. Charles Ammon preached. We all met somewhere for a watery lunch; and in the afternoon I lay on a cliff and composed some new words for the Newfoundlanders' favourite song, which goes to the tune of 'Fair Spanish Ladies'

[6] G. W. St. J. Chadwick, of the Dominions Office, our able secretary.

and has the refrain, 'We'll rant and we'll roar like true Newfound-landers.' I lay sunning in a bathing-dress in sight of three large and beautiful ice-islands. They are by no means incompatible with a warm summer's day, and would look lovely off the Cornish Coast. Derrick went out in his host's motor-boat and had a solitary swim, not half a mile from an iceberg (I have done the same).

I came back to the house about six, still admiring beauty and glad of the sun, but thinking basely that it would be nice to end the day with a golden wine, as they would be doing at home in wicked old England.

As I passed the living-room I saw my nice hostess and another lady sitting there. I could have sworn that they both held a small brown-coloured glass, and I was reminded of the bad old days of cocktail-parties. Some sort of medicine, no doubt, the doctor had ordered for the ladies. But my hostess called out the news, 'Musso-lini has fallen,' as I passed. I said, 'Hooray!' and passed upstairs to change with a lighter heart. And now, for a moment, I wondered about the brown-coloured little glasses.

When I came down, it was clear that I had been very wrong. There were the same two ladies—but no small brown-coloured glasses. I thought, 'It only shows what grim mistakes the closest observer can make.' We discussed the fall of Mussolini, and other palatable topics for about half an hour. Then, to my great surprise, Mrs. B—— said shyly, fearfully, almost stammeringly: "I wonder, Mr. Herbert, if you have ever tried our Newfoundland rum?'

I admitted, rather shy too, that I had tried it, and I consented to try it again. I did. We toasted the downfall of Mussolini and the Triumph of Right. Then the doctor came home from the hospital, and we celebrated the downfall of Mussolini again. I still, in my secret mind, attributed the strange scene to the downfall of Musso-lini. This triumph of the Allies had, for an evening only, com-pelled even the rigid abstainers of the Dry Islands into unwonted celebrations. We all went for a beautiful drive along the Atlantic cliffs—singing songs and rolling heavily among the rocks and ruts. In the blue dusk the coast reminded me of Cornwall more than ever —except for the icebergs looking like enormous ghosts.

On the way home, we called on Mr. A——, Derrick Gunston's

host. I at least was astonished to find Mr. A—— and Derrick happily celebrating the fall of Mussolini in the wine of the country. (What a blessing Mussolini was!) We joined them. There began a general discussion on the fall of Mussolini, the chances of war, the future of Newfoundland, and Anglo-American brotherhood. There was no excessive speaking or consumption, but all things were easier in all directions. Many important topics were discussed with freedom, freshness, and profit which before had been avoided or played with. The British, the Newfoundlanders, said just what they thought about each other; and then we joined and tore our American friend to pieces. He, with equal spirit and goodwill, blew us both out of the water, and all was well.

Wine, I know very well, can be the father of bad blood and belligerence. But so often, too, it can be the mother of light and understanding: and this was one of the best exhibitions of its best powers I can remember.

But I still thought that our virtuous friends had been driven from their cloisters by the fall of Mussolini, and would return there in the morning. Then Derrick Gunston, toasting his host, said, 'Well, cheer-o! Jolly good rum! My goodness, I could have done with a tot of this when I came out of that cold sea this afternoon!'

Mr. A—— then made a singular remark. He said: 'Cheer-o! As a matter of fact, while you were swimming about among the ice my wife and I popped down to the cabin and had a secret nip, *thinking you would be shocked!*'

Then, at last, the truth emerged. Each had thought that the other was a teetotaller, and had nobly respected the other's way of life. Is there anything finer in our Empire history? And is there anything funnier than the picture of those two good Newfoundlanders secretly swallowing a rapid rum in the cabin for fear of shocking my good friend Derrick, the grim teetotaller, swimming happily in the icy sea?

But we worked. How we worked! We studied Nature as well as man, and dug deep into the mysteries of fish and forest.

'Fish,' for the Newfoundlander, means còd and cod alone—cod, the great founder, and future, maybe, of the island's fortunes. An old legal judgment, I read, decided that salmon was not 'fish.' It is no wonder that the cod is a kind of tribal idol in Newfoundland, for cod, historically, was the cause of the Newfoundlander. It was the quantity of great cod about his vessel that impressed John Cabot— and the merchants of Bristol—with the possibilities of the 'new-found isle.' Sebastian Cabot said that the shoals of codfish were so numerous that 'they sumtymes stayed his shippe.'

Sir Wilfred Grenfell, in one of his books on Labrador, tells surprising tales of the voracity of the fish, which I, at least, had always thought of as a temperate and modest creature.

A book in three volumes [he says] was taken from the stomach of a codfish off Lynn, England, and presented to the Chancellor of Cambridge University. Scissors, oil-cans, old boots, testify to the catholicity of the cod's appetite. Captain Hall, who lost his keys over the side in the North Sea, had them returned to him from the inside of a codfish. Two full-grown ducks have been found in a cod's stomach: the birds were quite fresh and had apparently been swallowed alive. An entire partridge, a whole hare, six (small) dogfish, an entire turnip, a guillemot (beak, claws and all), a tallow candle, have all betrayed the omnivorous leanings of our friends.

'The record cod on the American coast,' Sir Wilfred writes, 'weighed one hundred and sixty pounds'—about the same as myself.

To Britons, who do not put the cod very high, and even use the name as a synonym for the bogus, the veneration of the fish seems odd. But fresh cod in Newfoundland, I confess, has a very different flavour from the fellow we meet at home. And he has other claims.

He may be called [says Sir Wilfred] the bread and butter of the sea, for more surely than any other marine species does he supply a food of which the white man's palate does not tire. The flesh is rich and gelatinous, without being fatty. Every particle of the body is useful to man. The skin and bones make excellent glue. The tongue and swim-bladder are rare delicacies when well cooked, and have also been used as raw material in the manufacture of isinglass. The refined cod-liver oil is among the most sterling remedies yet devised for man's bodily weaknesses, which so often lead to deadly phthisis. The refuse oil may be used for tanning purposes: the offal is very valuable manure. In Norway the dried heads have been largely used as food for cattle. The roe is an excellent bait and forms a notable part of the Norwegian annual export.

On Arctic shores the well-dried bones, for lack of other material, have been used for fuel. For curing purposes the cod is unsurpassed. Compared with fresh beef, the nutritive value of the dried cod is as nine to ten.

And, 'Each female lays from three to nine million eggs each year. . . .'

So, housewife, pause before you sneer again at this paragon of the sea.

Nor did we neglect the fir. We learned to tell a black spruce from a white spruce, and a fir from both. We saw, I suppose, ten million billion trees.

We saw the fir (*Abies balsamea*) through all its adventurous career from the hill-side forest to the leading article; and no writer, no newsprint-user, perhaps I should say, can view this process without excitement. We saw the mighty and industrious Newfoundlander fell in thirty-five seconds a great tree on which Nature had been at work for seventy years. Far out in the forest, tormented by black-fly, gnats and (believe it or not) heat, he 'notches' his tree—a few taps with the axe to make it fall the right way. Then he kneels with his box-saw, and saws, both arms, kneeling, on the other side. And, in thirty-five seconds from the first notch, I have seen the big thing crash, precisely as planned, to the cry of 'Timber!' if anyone is about. I do not say it is always so swift.

It looks easy, but it is lusty labour. And he has scarcely begun. He saws the tree into the appointed lengths and hacks off the branches and the untidy bits. And when the snow comes, it is hauled across the snow by horses, and tumbled down shoots into lakes and ponds, and driven down streams and rivers, or piled by roadsides till the trucks come for it, and carted over bumpy little switchback roads, and penned afloat behind great booms till the machine is ready for it, the machine that obeys in turn the great dams and dynamos, thirty miles away. Then the innumerable logs are grabbed with deft irons from the water, and rolled aloft, and carved up like cheeses by singing saws, and flung into fat, round revolving 'barkers' to be stripped of bark (the bark slips away to be used for fuel), and whirled down long water-chutes to the mill, and given to the savage grinders to be ground into pulp, or hurled into towering, simmering 'digesters' to be ill used with acids and become sulphite instead. (The sulphite pulp, with the longer fibres, makes a more delicate leading article than the 'ground' pulp. Ground for the masses—sulphite for the poet.) You pursue the romantic pulp, the noble bones and blood of the trees, from floor to floor and from vat to vat; you clutch at hot banisters and shrink back from bubbling pools; till suddenly you are in the great room of rollers, the room of roaring, where the flat wet plains of tree roar over roller after roller, losing water every roll, gaining body every roll, growing at every roll and squeeze like something you remember, something you *know*, and, marching beside the long regiment of roaring rollers, you come to the uttermost machine and the miracle happens—a vast, white, cylindrical egg of PAPER is laid at your feet, paper the people's food, the poet's pride!

And who caused these wonders in a distant wilderness of wood and rock? Who dammed up the waters, before the war of 1914, to make the path easy from tree to table, that, peace or war, there might always be fine work for the Newfoundlander and fine leading articles for London? Who are the wizards of the woods?

The names that made the two great paper-citadels are English—Northcliffe at Grand Falls and Bowater at Cornerbrook. And the enterprise, the brains, the money were English, and are English now.

It is well that this be proclaimed at a time when some seem to think that only America and Canada can do things in style for the smaller corners of the British Empire.

And there is yet more cause for pride. Around these vast and busy works, that are never idle by day or night, they have built up two cities of light and leading in a land which, with all due deference, requires them. The paper-company towns are 'model' towns, models of housing and sanitation and local planning and pride in a land which is not so hot in these affairs. The contrast is severe when you pass from the orderly paper domains into a free-and-easy place no smaller, where there is no local government at all, no Mayor, no scavenger, no fire-patrol, and any man may build a shack or a privy of any kind, where he will.

The paper-rule is on the autocratic side, maybe—but what will you—if Newfoundlanders will not govern themselves? It is a singularly enlightened autocracy, blazing a trail for democracy all the time. They are teaching the people the blessings of local government and order; and they have even taught the people to pay unofficial rates for their light and water—*et tout ça.*

'If only,' I wrote, 'more British capital were here!'

29. Labrador

From the Dry Islands we worked north to St. Anthony, at the top of the island, the main base of the Grenfell Mission, where Dr. Curtis, a charming and able American, was in charge.

Then we went to Labrador. The Labrador Peninsula lies to the north-west of Newfoundland. The island owns 'all the coast of Labrador'—about 700 miles—and an area of 103,000 square miles, nearly three times as large as her own (42,000 square miles). It is a 'coastal strip,' of varying depth, but it extends, at its greatest depth inland, about 400 miles westward from the Atlantic coast. West of it is the Canadian province of Quebec, and a dispute about the boundary was finally determined in 1927 by the Privy Council—much assisted, I believe, by the advocacy of Sir John Simon.

Labrador, I believe, is the answer to many things, and might have been the answer to the future of Newfoundland as a prosperous independent Dominion.

In the House, I see, on 2 March 1949, I said:

Labrador may become another Alaska, because it has the largest iron ore deposits in the world waiting to be exploited. . . . Whoever runs them, Labrador will be an old-age pension for Newfoundland for a very long time. That is what I suggest.

In my report, six years earlier, I had written, though then I did not know so much:

His Majesty's Government should make it clear that they are not blind to the possibilities of Labrador and their responsibilities there; that they intend in due course, with Newfoundland, to assist the development of the one and the discharge of the other more adequately than has been possible hitherto. A special economic survey of prospects in Labrador should be undertaken (if this has not already been done). . . .

I never heard that any such thing was done. His Majesty's Government were either blind or bored.

But others had their eyes open. A little before we left London I asked a high Canadian official, 'Do you want Newfoundland?' He said, 'No.' 'Do you want Labrador?' He said, 'Yes.' When we got back I met him by chance outside the Dominions Office and put the same questions. This time he firmly answered 'Yes' to both. In other words, if I am right, it now seemed so important to get Labrador that the difficult little island must be taken in, if possible. I do not blame Canada in the least: she was naturally keen to get on with a job—and a job on her own doorstep—in which Imperial Britain had shown no interest. As far back as 1935 the Commission of Government had granted a mineral concession of some 20,000 square miles to a Canadian mining and exploration company. A Frenchman said that Labrador was the country that God gave to Cain. History may say that it was the country that Britain gave to Canada.

See what the Canadian papers are saying to-day (1950):

Few Canadians yet seem to realize that the possession of vast iron resources is going to have a profound effect on the whole Canadian economy.

With great expansion planned for Ontario iron mines and *the tremendous deposits along the Labrador–Quebec boundary*[1] just waiting to be developed, Canada is due to become one of the world's major producers and exporters of the heavy metal on which our industrial civilization is based. . . . In a few years' time, Canada's iron ore

[1] They straddle the boundary, I understood. What proportion is on either side? I have seen numerous contradictory assertions, and cannot say.

would be an important means of earning U.S. dollars and improving our balance of trade. Eventually it will provide the firm foundation on which Canada can expand her whole industrial economy. And if the *Labrador iron ore* should be the deciding factor in getting the St. Lawrence Seaway completed at long last . . . the *Labrador–Quebec iron ore* deposits in the heart of the *Ungava Peninsula,* where reserves of some 400,000,000 tons of high-grade haematite ore have already been proven, and an initial output of 10,000,000 tons a year is already planned. . . .

The U.S. need of iron ore resources to replace or spin out the dwindling Mesaba reserves . . .

Excellent. Good luck to these bold projects! But, to my mind, they make nonsense of the suggestion that Newfoundland was so poor and resourceless that she could never hope to stand alone again.

We set sail in a small vessel—a sort of 'floating clinic' belonging to the Grenfell Mission. Her name, I think, was *Marabel.* She was about sixty tons, schooner-rigged, with a Diesel engine. As a rule she carried a nurse, or doctor, if available, along the God-forsaken coast on which, for 700 miles, there was only one resident doctor. She had a crew of four, and a local minister came along for a holiday. He was to miss two sermons, but he missed four or five. Our main cabin was the dispensary, full of sulfathiazole, acetylsalicylic acid, sodium salicylate, sulfanilamide, Blaud pills, Brown's mixture, and many alarming instruments. When the ship rolled heavily for the first time a large bottle of oil of wintergreen broke adrift and descended into my soup. We felt guilty about taking her from her beneficent duties, but she was the only vessel that could be found for us. At many little harbours our embarrassment returned, for eager fishermen would row across from the schooners to have aching teeth 'hauled' or stomach troubles relieved; and they were politely disappointed to find four Englishmen with nothing to offer but good-will. I did prescribe for a stomach case or two, and hope the fishermen survived.

Also, there were supposed to be U-boats in the Straits of Belle Isle. There had been a sinking on the east coast very recently, an iron-ore ship. Sometimes, while the Captain ate, I took the wheel, and while looking for suspicious objects (and seeing a great many) I gave some thought to my juridical position. If a U-boat popped up ahead, one would yell for the Captain and ram, of course. But should one? The Red Cross was painted on the dispensary sides. Though a proud member of His Majesty's Navy, I was not in uniform. In ramming a submarine, therefore, I should be doubly out of order, and might cause justifiable annoyance to the enemy. And there might well be some special international rule against Members of Parliament behaving in this way. I did not think that my juridical position would be very strong, but the problem never arose.

Once alongside the Labrador coast (though the latitude was about the same as Hull's) we met a great ice-island every mile or so, much loose ice, many whales, sometimes a merry school of seals. They were a pleasant diversion from the dismal scene to port, which made us think often of the Frenchman's saying about the land God gave to Cain. For the instruction of His Majesty's Government I described it thus:

The Labrador coast is one endless fence of grey cliff, grey rocks, and grey or black hills, growing to mountains as you go north. And this fence is fringed with uncountable islands of every size and shape, from the small submerged reef to the island seven miles long. It is as if the Titans had celebrated some great wedding all along the coast, and sprinkled rocks like confetti in the water at their doors. Between the islands and the mainland there are many avenues of quiet water, called 'runs,' where the small boat can gratefully move for miles in comfort when the swell is heavy outside. Behind these islands the schooner can find shelter or wait for the fog to lift: so the fishermen, at least, are well served, and indeed, about one-third of Newfoundland's total catch of fish comes from 'the Labrador.' . . . Only the biggest islands can boast a tree or two, and for the first three hundred miles we saw not many on the mainland. The last scrape of the ice-cap shaved the whole coast pretty closely.

But inland the picture is different. After two hundred miles we turned into the celebrated Hamilton Inlet, the greatest of all the passages into the interior. This leads into Lake Melville, a huge fiord, sixty miles long and ten to twenty in width. The tide runs to the top of it, 90 miles from the sea: there are depths of 117 fathoms half-way up and 60 near the top. Here there is beauty. The hills for the most part are thickly wooded—virgin forest, so far as we could judge from mid-lake, and, I presume, 'commercial.' The Bowater Paper Company roughly surveyed the land and reported there were 10,000,000 cords of standing timber[2] (about one quarter as much as the Newfoundland resources). It is also said that the Grand Falls, 300 miles inland, are much grander than Niagara, and if they were harnessed could provide enough power for half the continent (if the power was wanted). We know that the Indians catch fur-bearing animals and the Eskimos catch seals. What else is there? Did God indeed put nothing worth having in this mighty space but fish, fur-bearing animals, and trees. . . . There seems to be good hope that, in the interior, He did. There is iron ore (magnetite?),[3] perhaps more, near the Canadian border. A Canadian company of good standing has a concession. . . . Canada, it is clear, thinks that 'there is something there.' They are buying back some shares given long ago to Sir Wilfred Grenfell and by him to the Grenfell Association.

Canada prospects the minerals. America finances (largely) the Grenfell Mission. What is Great Britain, now in charge of all this area, doing?

You are entitled to smile at this poor scribe, this very amateur economist, stumbling about in boots far too big for him, and trying to stir Imperial Whitehall with vague Alaskan visions. I knew very little. I had never heard then of the dwindling Mesaba resources of iron-ore in the United States. I had no notion that within five years people would be boasting of 400,000,000 proven tons of haematite ore (whatever that may be) on the Quebec-Labrador boundary. I simply smelt a rat or two, and I think my untrained nose was pretty good. There is no more doubt about the minerals; but one day, as well, those great Falls will be harnessed. One day, I dare say, that timber will be cut, a railway will run from the mines to the St. Lawrence, and Labrador will laugh at the frozen sea.

We sailed along happily enough. Gunston and Chadwick tapped away in turn at the only typewriter, and I played with my sextant or studied the charts. It is due, I suppose, to the nearness of the magnetic pole, but the compass in those parts appears to be crazy. That year, in latitude 56°N. the magnetic variation was 38°W. In 55°N., 60 miles south, it was 37°W. At the north point of New-

---

[2]That is, in convenient situations: there might be another 10,000,000 besides.
[3]Where on earth did I get that?

foundland (in 51° 38′N.)⁴ it was 35°W. This makes chart-work a little confusing. It means that if you are standing, say, in Parliament Square looking due north up Parliament Street, your compass-needle will be pointing over St. James's Park, very nearly into the lake. The local mariners do not bother about 'true' bearings or courses, but describe every direction according to the compass, which is trying for a well-bred English seaman, accustomed to seeking and using the truth. They will insist that the wind is S.S.W. (by the compass) when the superior Briton (after some frantic calculations) knows very well that it is more like S. by E. They don't bother very much about charts either, knowing the neighbourhood as they do.

We had heard disturbing tales of the discomforts and terrors we should have to face ashore in Labrador—including black-fly, mosquitoes, deer-fly, and dogs. Black-fly and mosquitoes we had met already in Newfoundland. If you have to work in the swamps or forest, or insist on fishing in woody places, they can be a torment, I believe; but they do not much molest the ordinary visitor. The deer-fly is, indeed, a formidable winged thing—a cross between a horse-fly and a hornet. It 'bites terribly,' says the book, 'making a wound which does not heal for days.' They pursued me in the *Marabel* all the way down Hamilton Inlet and even out to sea. I killed a great many, but they never touched me, though I was vulnerable in a bathing-dress. In the interior of Labrador, I read, 'the black-fly and the mosquito make some districts practically uninhabitable by man'; so hats off to the pioneer surveyors and miners! The mosquito breeds in stagnant water and the black-fly in running streams; the deer-fly in swamps and streams; and much of the interior is one or the other. So I do not know what is to be done. But Canada, no doubt, will find a way, as Panama, and Brazil, and other places have done. For the ordinary purposes of travel or recreation in Newfoundland, no Briton who is accustomed to British wasps, flies, and gnats should be deterred for a moment from visiting that pleasant land.

The dogs are the Labrador 'huskies,' the real Labrador dog, which according to Sir Wilfred Grenfell is

⁴Tower Bridge is in 51° 30′N. The variation there was about 9° W.

a very slightly modified wolf. . . . A good specimen stands two feet six inches, measures over six feet six inches from the tip of the nose to the tip of the tail and will scale a hundred pounds. The ears are pointed and stand directly up. The appearance generally is of a magnificent Pomeranian. The eyes are Japanese and give the animal a foxy look about the face. The large bushy tail curves completely over the back and is always carried erect. . . .

In the summer, in the bigger settlements, most of the dogs are penned up. They set up a fiendish howling at night, which, when it begins, is exactly like an air-raid warning (red). When one howls they all howl. In winter they are needed to draw the sledges or *komatiks* (the only form of transport in a frozen world), and could not, in any case, be penned up, because of the snow-drifts. They then, I gather, roam at large in groups and are a terror to the stranger. If you fall down, they eat you—or try to. I met an English-woman in St. John's who had seen a child very nearly eaten. She warned me to carry a stick. A Newfoundland girl, who had worked for years in Labrador as a nurse, said that she was still scared of the dogs. I met many of them prowling about the solitary shacks I visited, but they did not attempt any modified wolfery. I did not carry a stick, but I was very careful not to fall down.

In the winter they do wonderful work. They are the train, the steamer, and the car. They draw the mails, the doctor, the parson, over the frozen roads and bays of the sea, over the hills and through the forest.

There can be no question [says Sir Wilfred] that the dogs love to be driven. They go perfectly wild with excitement when they are in harness. The *komatik* must be lashed to a stump or stone and the line cut only when the driver is ready to go . . . the ideal team is a clever mother followed by a dozen of her own pups.

Nevertheless, the driver always has his gun ready, for at any moment a modified wolf may turn and attack his driver—or his mates. Each dog has his own 'trace,' so has much freedom of move-ment. Dr. Forsyth, however, late of Southend, and then doing fine work at Cartwright ('the only doctor for 700 miles') told me that he found dog-team travel a bore, and read a book all the time.

The dogs have great endurance and speed. One team is said to have covered 180 miles in two and a half days, and showed no signs of slackening at the end.

The dog mail-service, I understand, comes under the Government: so these animals can claim to be the only modified wolves in the Civil Service. Or perhaps not.

After five days we came to the top of Lake Melville, where is a station of the former Hudson's Bay Company. Farther on is Goose Bay, a pocket lake four miles by two, where the Canadians had made one of the wonders of the war—if not of the world—the Goose Bay Airport.

At the top of the bay [I wrote] when you are beginning to think that you are alone with virgin Nature at last—and very warm and lovely she is there after the shrewish coast—you come upon a large jetty with ocean steamers unloading. One hundred feet or so above that is a vast plateau designed by God, and discovered by a man called Guy, to be an airfield, in a wilderness of rocks and trees. It is stupendous. The runways are as smooth as a billiard-table and the central way is, I think, a mile long. But two years ago there was nothing here but the small pine and spruce, the sand, the white reindeer moss, like rubber sponge, the rocks and the pink flowers.

Now there are two citadels—the American Air Force on one side, the Royal Canadian Air Force on the other. All, of course, is wood and in the Aldershot school of architecture. But these buildings of tasteful green have an air of style and grandeur seldom achieved by (or for) the British soldier. All is done lavishly. The new officers' mess, not yet ready, with a superb view across the lake to the blue Mealy Mountains, has the proportions (and the floor) of a ballroom, and would house the Brigade of Guards (though there are only fifty officers, all told). The model laundry is larger than the House of Commons, and could deal, I should say, with all the washing in Newfoundland. Water is pumped up from the Hamilton River. Hot water circulates through overhead pipes. Electric light blazes in the wilderness. Millions of gallons of gasoline. Films three times a week. A great hospital, which now does most of the work the Grenfell Mission used to do. The soil is all sand; but the fragments of the original forest left untouched between the buildings, with their carpets of reindeer moss and wild flowers, are very pretty—and show imagination as well as efficiency at work.

This is the way to do things—if you have the money. Our dear

Treasury would faint if they saw the place. . . . Our poor Dominions
Office may well inquire how they are to teach the virtues of economy
and the philosophy of 'go slow' to the simple Newfoundlander if these
younger countries will fling their money about in this way. The contrast, to a Newfoundlander, whose Government seems to be able to
spend so little money on him and cannot give him the local road, the
post office, and the hospital he needs, must be glaring. *He could not be
blamed, and we should not be surprised, if he began to shift his affec-
tions to the westward.*

This is a great wonder of willpower and organization in the wilderness: the work of one of our young nations. And, if it gives us a provok-
ing example of how to do things in style, perhaps it is as well.

We were most hospitably and kindly used by the young and lively
tribe of Goose.

After supper one evening (superb trout) I was taken for a ride in a
jeep, and the young officer driving was explaining proudly how varied
were their uses—'As good as a tank,' he said. 'You should see them deal
with a tree.' I said idly that an elephant once pulled up a large tree for
me at Kandy in Ceylon. Without a word of warning, without slackening speed, the officer shot off the road into the forest, drove straight at
a tall young tree, flattened and went over it. I have seldom been so
surprised. I remember one of the officers crying 'Mind your glasses, Mr.
Herbert!' but by that time we were bound for the second tree. Down
went that. We darted to starboard and felled a third. To port again,
and straight at a much taller and tougher tree. This went over also, but
we were perched on top. No one seemed to be surprised or disconcerted. They got out axes and jacks and planks and spent twenty minutes unravelling the jeep. At the end it was none the worse. The trees
were real tough spruces, but in the sandy soil their roots have little
hold. I do not recommend 'tree-jeeping' in England. And, if trees must
be uprooted for my entertainment, I still prefer the elephant.

The rest of the party flew off to Newfoundland, according to
plan, for further travels and inspections in the island. But I mu-
tinied, went back in the *Marabel,* and incurred displeasure. They
were back in 'civilization' in a day. It took me sixteen days. But I
was happy. I am always glad, as I have said, to get out of any gang
when I can. I had my sextant; and, besides, I wanted to see more
of 'the real Labrador,' to which, I thought, no one was giving
enough attention, neither the British Government, nor even our

mission. I wanted to see more of the human side of life in this remote, extraordinary part of the British Commonwealth and Empire; and I wanted to pick up some more information, if it was only guess or gossip, about the economic side. 'I got,' as the Americans would say, 'a load of both.'

I talked to the Hudson's Bay folk and the Grenfell people at North-West River, working amicably side by side. All, here, in its modest way, was orderly and civilized. There were the hospital, the school and the church, and the comely Eskimo or Indian half-caste dancing old English dances with the doctor's wife. Everybody, even then, was beginning to prepare for the long winter in prison— collecting piles of fire-wood, canned food, and cured fish of every kind. In November the last mail steamer calls, and that is a big event. Thereafter, if you have failed to order what you want from Newfoundland—canned food, vegetables, tobacco, razor-blades, batteries, books, rum—or the shop has forgotten, or the goods are lost, you must do without till next June at least, when the first mail steamer may (or may not) get through the ice. Yet that place is no farther north than Yorkshire. How thankful we should be about the Gulf Stream! But we should never make the mistake of supposing that what we do not like is not likeable. Neither here, nor in northern Newfoundland, where the winter is similar but shorter, did I hear anyone pity himself because of the long isolation. Many told me that they preferred the winter. 'We have fun in the winter,' said one grand old islander. 'We get round that stove and we have fun.'

They have fun, too, I gathered, on the mainland of Labrador, in the cosy settled corners at the head of rivers and inlets. There are two or three dog-mails a winter. There is football in the snow, ice-boat sailing, skiing, and deer-hunting. March is the best month —bright, cold, and bracing. 'The skin gets so tanned that the whites begin to resemble Indians in colour. . . . This constant sun-bath, in spite of the low temperature, has an excellent tonic effect on weakly people.' There is the radio; and in 'May-month,' perhaps, the mail-boat calls again.

But they complained very much of the neglect of Man. They were the Forgotten Country. They had no votes (the population was about 5,000). It was no one's special job to look after them, and they did not know to whom they should complain. All this seemed fair enough. I met no one in St. John's (except the fishermen) who seemed to have much interest in that enormous property or its tiny population, and very few Newfoundlanders (always excepting the fishermen) had travelled as far as we had.

Away from the settlements, and out on the islands, human life can reach a low level indeed. There is much to be said against 'being away from it all.' On one island out to sea, at which we called, there were three inhabited shacks—mere huts. One was occupied by a fine fisherman, with a boy of fourteen, who smoked a pipe, and a daughter. He had no wireless, but he had seven guns with which to shoot the polar bear and other animals. There was a wireless in one of the shacks, but the boy said he did not listen to the news and could not tell me anything about the war. He had not heard of Mussolini, but he had heard of Hitler, 'the man who caused the war.' He could not read or write, but did not seem to mind.

The father had a similar shack in Partridge Bay, on the mainland, and might go back there for the winter. But he might stay on the island, which would not suit me. In October the last of the schooners will have gone south with their loads of 'green fish.' In November the last steamer calls. Then, when the ice begins to form round your island, there is an uneasy period when boats can move with increasing difficulty. In December they cannot move at all. But you cannot walk or drive your dogs to the mainland till January. Then you will net seals and shoot the white bear, and 'any game killed in December will remain good till June, being hard frozen as soon as killed.'

But suppose you have violent toothache, as the father had now. He had had it 'off and on, all the summer.' He was very cheerful about it, but I had a threatening tooth too, and I went back to the ship with the padre to find the forceps. On the way back to the waterside I saw a motor-boat come alongside the ship and leave again. Our Captain told us that she had had half a dozen men all looking for a doctor to 'haul' a tooth (they talk of 'hauling' a tooth as they do of 'hauling' a trawl). I was just nerving myself to go ashore and attempt my first extraction when the skipper said he must shift his berth as the wind was rising and the water was deep. So we steamed away, and I never saw the poor fisherman again.

I hope that no one will tell me again that life is 'too civilized' nowadays, or sigh to 'get away from everything.' Permanent toothache must be bad enough. But the fisherman might have had a broken leg or a lethal appendix. He would be fairly lucky, for he is only seventy miles from Dr. Forsyth at Cartwright, and could go there in a motor-boat, weather permitting. But the doctor is no good at teeth—he told me so. I suppose he could 'haul' a tooth, but he could not stop one. The nearest dentist, within the meaning of the Act, is at St. Anthony, in Newfoundland, 300 miles away by sea. Think of that, all you who yearn to 'get away from everything.'

All honour, therefore, to the work of the Grenfell and Moravian missions, of doctor and nurse going forth in motor-boats at night or plodding over the ice behind a dog-team.

You may say that the fisherman was a fool to be there with his two children. But I could not get his tooth out of my mind. I often thought about it. It was not my fault, but I felt I should have 'hauled' it. It may be there still.

I spent another night with Dr. Forsyth and his wife at Cartwright, and had a good gossip about the affairs of Labrador. Then the wind went easterly and rose. We rolled along in heavy beam seas on a lee shore, and a rocky shore. Fog joined the wind and, at last, we crept into a small cove called the *Punch Bowl* in the Seal Islands. There we stayed, fogbound, for nine solid days.

It blew from the south-east. It rained as well. It hardly ever stopped raining. The fog thinned, now and then, in the cove, but never lifted off the sea outside. The crew all said they had never seen anything like it. I kept telling myself, 'Be thankful. You are not in an open boat.' But it was not much fun. I was cold. My tooth was a worry. I had only a few drops of rum. And I was always hungry. The *Marabel* had been equipped for three weeks only and supplies ran short. There was hardly anything but salt cod, which I could not endure. But the padre was a great man with a gun and shot seagulls and 'kittiwakes.' In Hamilton Inlet a jolly troop of seals had gambolled up to meet the Members of Parliament, sticking their little heads out and roaring with laughter. The man of God shot the leader through the head. It sank at once and the others disappeared. I was very angry about this, but now I was glad of his powers. One day he shot an eider-duck—delicious. But even the small seagulls were better than salt cod.

I sat in my great-coat in the dispensary among the medicine bottles and wrote and wrote. In those nine days I must have written 30,000 words, most for His Majesty, but some for *Punch*. One ironical thing was that in that great centre of the fish world we had no means of catching fish. The *Marabel* was not accustomed to lying fogbound, and the fishermen whose teeth she 'hauled' readily supplied her. Now at the end of my essay on the place of fish in the Newfoundland economy, I sadly wrote:

The whole island—and Labrador as well—thinks fish, knows fish. You can hardly meet a lumberman who cannot handle a fish as well as he handles a fir. The children fish almost as soon as they can walk. They stand in impish rows under the outfall of the great power station at Deer Lake angling for trout. If you leave oxen standing near a heap of herring the oxen have a go at the fish. The very dogs eat fish, bones and all. I always understood that fish-bones were bad for dogs, but this, it seems, was an old English wives' tale. The Eskimo dogs stand on rocks watching for fish, or prowl about in the shallow water till they tread on a flat-fish which they dig out and devour. All those wild waters were made for fish. The very icebergs moored along the coast in summer-time, they say, are good for the fishing, because they keep the water cold. I should not be surprised if the rocks were somehow designed for the service of the fish and their pursuers. North, south, east and west, for hundreds of miles, the sea, the bays, the inlets, the rivers, the lakes, the ponds are teeming with fine fresh cod, all ready for the pan, with delicious salmon and succulent trout, with seal's flappers and whale's steaks, with tuna and halibut, with flat-fish and smelt.

But there is no fish in this ship.

I read one night a learned article about the flora of the Arctic *tundra*. The author said that there are certain growths which, while not ordinarily attractive as foods, may yet serve in emergency to sustain life for 'an indefinite period.' He mentioned especially the *Cladonia* (or reindeer-moss) and the *Umbilicaria* (or rock-tripe). Next day—beginning to think that we might be in the *Punch Bowl* for 'an indefinite period'—I took the padre for a foraging expedition on the island. We found enough plants to furnish many rock-gardens—delightful plants with little red berries; and pink flowers, and queer thick leaves, huddled defensively against the ocean gales: saxifrages and lichens, and carpets of the white moss; and frightened little dwarf willow, spruce, and larch trees that lie quite flat on the ground. Except for the rocks and stagnant pools, every inch was covered; every inch was a brave pathetic effort to decorate that harsh and iron scene, soon to be covered with snow. But except for the bake-apples (little ground-fruit the size of raspberries—*Rubus chamaemorus*) we could not find anything to eat. I made a parcel of roots and dwarf trees and mosses for Kew (but they all died), and a parcel of *Cladonia* for the cook (but he would not cook it).

On the seventh day the sun peered through the mist for three or four minutes. I took my 'sight,' as I have related, and told the Captain where we were. He was impressed, I think, but not surprised.

On the ninth day I woke and heard no pitter-patter of rain on the deck, no rattling of the throat-halyard against the main-mast, no roar of wind and surf. The wind was westerly at last. There was sunlight and blue sky, and out to sea I could see the islands, with wisps of mist stealing away like scene-shifters caught by the rise of the curtain.

What a relief! 'We are away,' I wrote hilariously:

The end of a long fog is like the end of long pain—one sharply perceives the blessings of the normal. In the sun I see that the coast of Labrador is more admirable than I thought. I enjoy the naked humps and spikes of the sky-line, and the bare brown fringe along the shore where the winter ice has stripped and ground the rocks. And all those vague grey-green slopes between I now know to be carpeted with interest and charm, with bake-apples and dwarf trees, and curlew berries and edible moose-moss. The seagulls, of whose relations I have eaten so many, are mere seagulls no more. Even the rolling of the ship—and, my hat, she is rolling!—is at first a pleasure after nine days' immobility.

We called at Frenchman's Island and found there quite a well-stocked store, not more than two miles from our fog-bound fortress. We bought tinned milk and tea, and—for the wonders of this region are inexhaustible—I bought a pair of *silk stockings* for the home.

Fantastic waters! I stood on deck with my silk stockings as we cleared the islands, and beheld, at different points not far away, three great icebergs. A few minutes later the biggest whale I have seen thrust his black back out of the water a hundred yards from us. I waved the stockings at him, and thanked God.

We called at Hawke's Harbour, where there is a whaling station, run by a Scottish firm, with a Norwegian manager. Their ship, like ours, had been lost in the fog for nine days.

I asked the Norwegian if they ever saw a white whale. He said that they catch many white whales. Which seems to suggest a weakness in the story of Moby Dick.

He gave us eight whales' teeth and two whales' ears, and we sailed away. A whale's ear is like a very large conch. It is hard and looks like ivory.

I never saw a white whale; but, soon after we left, a great black fellow showed his back about 200 yards on the starboard bow. I wished him luck, poor whale. I wish we did not have to kill them. One seldom sees them again when they emerge so near, and I cannot imagine how the whalers ever get within range. But a good captain, they say, can guess which way the whale will head under water, and how soon he will come up for another 'blow,' and steers his ship accordingly. A good whale, I should have thought, could keep him guessing.

At St. Anthony they were glad to see their lost padre, the *Marabel,* and her fine sailors again; and the air of Newfoundland was humming with Morse about the lost Member of Parliament. Both the Commissioners and my colleagues seemed to think that I had got myself fogbound on purpose. But I was not an Independent Member for nothing; I had seen, I thought, the sort of thing I had been sent out to see; and I rode the storm without regret, and as gracefully as I could.

That is the worst, Young Man, of going about in gangs. You do not wish to be discourteous to those who have made plans, but you may miss so much if you stick to the plans.

In 1925 I represented *Punch* at the Third Imperial Press Conference in Australia. One evening we landed at the famed Honolulu. The ship was to leave after lunch next day. The official programme for the morning was: '(1) Inspect Naval Base. (2) Visit Pineapple Cannery and (3) Visit Industrial District of Pali.' In all the six months of that expedition I was, I think, a pretty good boy. I went where I was told and made speeches when required. But now I said, 'This will probably be the only morning of my life that I shall spend in storied Honolulu. Am I going to spend it looking at a pineapple cannery, an industrial district, or even a naval base?' 'No,' I answered quickly. 'I am not Lord Burnham, our great leader; I am not John Astor, proprietor of *The Times;* I am not Anthony Eden or Sir Francis Newnes. They, of course, must follow the plan and see the pineapple cannery. But I am only a humble young contributor to *Punch,* who matters little. And, if they execute me afterwards, I am going to spend this one unrepeatable morning trying to surf-ride on Waikiki Beach!' So, in the morning, after breakfast, I hid in the lavatory. I heard them calling for me as the fleet of cars assembled and departed. And, when all was silent, I crept quietly down to the beach. A Hawaiian 'boy' said, 'Yes. I teach you surf-ride,' and away to sea (300 yards or so) we went. There are no motor-boats, no ropes or harness here. All you have is a heavy board, about eight feet long, and the ocean. But with the gorgeous luck of the beginner, I stood—*stood!*—on my first wave—at about the speed of a Derby winner—all the way to the shore. I never did it so well again. But all the morning I tried, and it was one of the luminous, unforgettable mornings of my life. I behaved like a toad, no doubt. But was I wrong?

Now I sadly said good-bye to my old friends of the *Marabel,* and went on down the west coast to the lovely Humber River. The crew of my little vessel was Canadian—with one Newfoundlander. I was not looking for 'politics': I was happy to be on the water, going home. But I could not help noticing (and hearing) what a lonely fellow was the Newfoundlander. A good fellow, I thought, but he stood apart; and the Canadian sailors thought very little of him. They said so.

At Cornerbrook, the sunny citadel of paper, as a guest of Mr. H. M. S. Lewin, manager to Bowater's, an Englishman, I studied the paper industry, and many things more, and finished my pompous and enormous report to Mr. Attlee. It was 30,000 words long, and was never published—a shocking blow to a professional writer.

It was a queer document, maybe, for a humourist, but, I think, not bad. My summary of recommendations began thus:

His Majesty's Government should make an early announcement of policy.

(1) The first purpose of this should be to restore the confidence of Newfoundland in this country and her own future. It should make it clear that we intend to use her with firmness but affection, to educate and to assist her, to free but foster her; to work out with her a positive policy of construction and development, and not, by neglect or parsimony, to drive her into the arms of any other Power.[5]

I attached a rough estimate of the cost of a Ten Years' Plan—or, to be precise, 'of additional requirements, beyond provisions in present Budgets, to meet further Reconstruction Schemes and improvement in Communications, Education, Health and Social Services during the next ten years.' Early in our tour I had asked one of the Commissioners to do such a rough (and purely personal) reckoning for me, which he kindly did. The figures he gave for ten years' capital expenditure (non-recurring) was $44,500,000, with Annual Maintenance (recurring, after three years) $5,100,000. 'The total additional expenditure would be about $80,000,000.'

Each of the three merchants of goodwill wrote his own independent report. Those long days in the *Punch Bowl* had given me an advantage, I dare say. But when I saw Derrick Gunston again I found that, in odd corners and moments, he had nearly finished tapping out his version of Newfoundland. And John Chadwick, at the more stately speed of the Civil Service, was drafting a most able report for our leader. This, I think, was a good arrangement. I do not believe very much in the modern technique of artificial

[5]But this, I fear, was just what we did.

unanimity. Unless it is a jury case, let all opinions be heard. And the remarkable, valuable thing was that, scribbling away in separate corners, we agreed about so many things.[6] I had, I think, a little more faith than the others in the desire, and the capacity, of Newfoundland to return to self-government soon. I wrote: 'After many weeks of travel and talk in the island my faith in its future is rather stronger than it was'; and, in spite of many proper criticisms, I believe the others would have agreed with that—subject, that is, to wise and generous behaviour by the Mother Country. Certainly, not one of us recommended that Newfoundland should cease to be a Dominion and be absorbed by any other country, and we all agreed about the Ten Years' Plan.

So, after a happy week-end with the Governor and his Lady, and far too many farewell parties, with Newfoundlanders, Canadians, and Americans, we turned our faces to old England again. Or, rather, alas, to Whitehall.

[6]'On fundamental matters we are in accord.' (Mr. Ammon, *Hansard*, 16 December 1943, col. 1744.)

30. Mary's First Attempt

Derrick Gunston and I came home from Newfoundland in a destroyer. We had both been bored by our first Atlantic flight, and had long ago determined to return by sea if we could get a passage. Charles Ammon, our leader, thought he should be back in Whitehall with his report as soon as possible, so he and Chadwick, the secretary, were to fly, fondly supposing that flight would be quicker. Derrick and I had noticed two British destroyers lying in St. John's Harbour and wondered what they were up to; but our hospitable friends of the Canadian Navy had nothing to say. Nor had the kind and charming Captain Hope, R.N. But we could hardly help noticing that Mr. Churchill was in Quebec, and there might be something in that. So, when we were told that we might go home in one of them, the *Orwell*, we asked no questions but were privately and properly excited. The *Orwell* was a fine new ship, still on the secret list. Her commander, Lieutenant-Commander J. M. Hodges, D.S.O., R.N., like so many naval officers, was no mean poet. So, by the way, was Captain Hope. Just before we left, Captain Hope shyly showed me a parody of Gray's *Elegy* and other verses: and we had not been long at sea when the Commander shyly showed me his parody of Gray's *Elegy*. They were both very good, if I am any judge. The sailor—I have noticed it in bargemen too—seems to have a finer feeling for words than his brother in arms; and in the long lone watches he finds time to think and things he wants to say. So the slower sailor runs to poetry and the speeding airman to slang.

The farewell hospitalities of Newfoundland, the British Navy, the Canadian Navy, and the American Consul had done me no noticeable good; and Derrick Gunston had lost his voice. This was serious, for the Commander wanted one of us to give a lecture to 'the troops,' and I was far from keen on the job. I had the Commander's spacious cabin (he slept, at sea, if he slept at all, near the bridge); but it was right aft, over the propellers, and the vibration, the roar, and rattle, the thudding and creaking and banging, were too violent for sleep. A destroyer steaming at high speed in the rude Atlantic is not a very comfortable place. We rolled all the time. But I am a pretty 'good sailor' and felt better in the morning. Derrick was still croaking, though, so I was detailed for lecture duty. That was the strangest address I ever delivered. The Petty Officers led us to some bowel below and set us on two chairs among a mass of sailors, not all of whom were visible, because of bunks and garments. The ship was rolling more heavily than before; oilskins and wet clothes swung backwards and forwards; now and then my chair rolled right over and I fell upon the Petty Officer presiding. The sailors, I expect, were surprised not to see the Member of Parliament sick. I was much more surprised to hear myself, in these conditions, yelling at them for a good hour about the importance and the procedure of the British Parliament. They stood it very well.

One way and another, a busy day. For that afternoon had seen the big event, our rendezvous with the *Renown,* in which great ship was Mr. Winston Churchill, his wife, and his daughter Mary. It was a dark and ugly afternoon, low, purple clouds, not a gleam of sun, driving rain, and a dirty sea. Our sister destroyer looked small and lonely, plunging along in a flurry of spray. Suddenly, converging through the rain, we saw a small fleet, two cruisers, whose names I forget, and the *Renown,* with four destroyers about her. All were steaming at twenty-six knots; all were winking Morse at a fantastic speed through the murk. Perhaps I am a sentimental old jingo, but I must say it stirred my soul to see that punctual meeting of the ships, the British Fleet defying the enemy in mid-Atlantic and carrying the great man safely home. The speed of the evolution was astonishing. Almost immediately, it seemed, we were on the starboard bow of the *Renown,* and the destroyer we relieved had gone.

Then Derrick Gunston and I went into committee. We felt it our duty to salute the great man, and to let him know that he had a House of Commons as well as a naval escort. Our Commander was all in favour. Moreover, being a poet, he agreed that the salute should be in verse. But 'security,' in that high moment, I am glad to say, controlled the Muse. I thought, 'Who knows what periscope may read our salute? I must not use the name of Churchill. But what about Ulysses, returning to his island after many toils and dangers?' Trouble at once. We did not know if Mrs. Churchill and her daughter Mary were aboard. I could not remember if Ulysses had a daughter. I could not even, at first, remember the name of his son; and their Lordships had failed to provide H.M.S. *Orwell* with a classical dictionary. But at last I composed, and the Commander passed, the following signal:

(Sta. 121/33) 22213 Wt. 9241/D 5028 25,000M 6/40—McC & Co—51-7024

NAVAL MESSAGE

To: RENOWN   From: ORWELL
CORRECTION (2)

From Derrick Gunston and A. P. Herbert. Respectful salutes and greetings. Return Ulysses soon to show the secrets of your splendid bow. Return and make all riddles plain to anxious ITHACA again. And you PENELOPE the true who have begun to wander too we're glad to meet you on the foam and hope to see you safely home.

1520.

Light.   P/L.   T.O.R.   1526.   K.   Dist.   Cdr. Thompson.   N.O.
                                                   Cdr. Dawnaw.

The final couplet was to have been:

RESIST THE TENDENCY TO ROAM
AND KEEP YOUR MIGHTY MAN AT HOME.

But, in committee, we rightly rejected that, and finished with the more tactful, but perhaps inferior, lines:

WE'RE GLAD TO MEET YOU ON THE FOAM
AND HOPE TO SEE YOU SAFELY HOME.

I remember vividly how that unusual signal was dispatched. Morse signals, by day, are sent by a sort of searchlight, with shutters, which make a great clatter, rather like a milk-cart. The little ship was rolling largely, and, the wind being on the starboard bow, our own smoke kept hiding the *Renown*. But nothing, not even verse about Ulysses, disturbed the Yeoman of Signals, a regular, and very keen upon sending any message to Mr. Churchill. He stood behind the bewildered young signaller and dictated the message: 'Uncle (clatter-clatter-*clat*)—Lizzie—(clatter-*clat*-clatter-clatter) —Yellow—Sugar—Sugar—Easter—Sugar (clatter, clatter-clatter).'

Then we all peered eagerly through the smoke and, looking for the long light ('T') which means 'Word understood,' I peered with especial eagerness, feeling responsible, in a kind of way, both for literature and the Navy. I imagined the Yeoman in the *Renown* muttering angrily, 'What the so-and-so is U-L-Y-S-S-E-S?' But after a slight pause, a light glowed steadily in the big dark shape astern, and how excited I was! The *Renown*, of *course*, was equal to 'Ulysses.' The Yeoman went merrily ahead; and in all that message only one word—I think it was 'Ithaca'—had to be repeated.

All next day there was no reply from the great ship. Derrick Gunston and I said anxiously, 'Perhaps we have done the wrong thing. Perhaps Mr. Churchill does not think it seemly for Members of Parliament to send the Prime Minister signals in bad verse, in mid-Atlantic, in time of war. Or, if not the Prime Minister, perhaps the Admiral has frowned?' Even our Commander, I think, was worried. But a little before dark a sailor came to us and said, 'A signal's coming through to you from *Renown*.' I rushed up to the signal bridge and enjoyed the flashing and clattering again. Alas, I cannot find the whole signal. It was six or eight lines longer than ours, and it ended with the charming couplet:

TO CHIDE THESE SIMPLE RHYMES BE CHARY:
THEY ARE THE FIRST ATTEMPT OF MARY.

(Some months later I happened to meet Mrs. Churchill and her daughter getting out of a car. I congratulated the young poetess again upon her 'first attempt,' and asked, ungallantly perhaps, 'Did you do it all yourself?' 'Yes,' she said, 'all except the last two lines. Those were Daddy's.')

By now the whole ship's company were interested parties to the correspondence, and two or three sailors said, 'Send Miss Mary a message for us.' Rolling about in the Captain's bunk, the night before, I had at last remembered the name of Telemachus; and, very rapidly, I did my best. We began, I remember:

TELEMACHA, THE SAILORS SEND
THEIR GREETINGS TO A FIGHTING FRIEND.

and ended:

WHY NOT, WHEN MISTER MASEFIELD'S PASSED,
A LADY LAUREATE AT LAST?

All very childish, no doubt, and not, I suppose, the kind of thing that would happen during an Atlantic passage of serious men like Adolf Hitler or Joseph Stalin.

But, meanwhile, the important business of preserving Mr. Churchill was not being neglected. About midnight I climbed up many ladders to the bridge. We had had, as usual, a rather embarrassing dinner, for the officers, all the way over, drank nothing and did not seem to eat very much. They rushed into the mess, uttered a monosyllable or two, bolted their food, and hurried back to their duties. Derrick and I were almost ashamed to have a gin; but, worn out by our long travels and diplomacy, I think we did have one or two; always, I am sure, with our glasses lifted most respectfully to the Navy. A destroyer's bridge—I have been privileged to stand on four or five—is an extraordinary place. A small square space, completely unprotected, packed with power, full of telephones and contraptions, and almost insanitarily overcrowded with persons. On either side was a young 'Hostilities Only' seaman, in his duffel-coat, with power-glasses and bearing-board, ready to report 'Red—50—aircraft' or 'Green—20—smoke, sir.' Telephones were always buzzing, speaking tubes in action. Besides the Captain, there would be a junior officer who was always at one telephone or the other, when he was not diving into a canvas dug-out to study charts, or discussing the course with the unseen quartermaster at the wheel below. The Yeoman of Signals was never far away, and there would be other important chief ratings about. There were steps here, and obstructions there, and the visitor, naturally, was always in the way; though this was never admitted and nobody seemed to mind. He felt that he was intruding in a small busy office in the open air; and though all seemed calm and efficient on a peaceful day, it was difficult to imagine what happened in action in the dark.

To-night the sea had abated, and we rolled more gently. But there was thick fog now. Nothing was to be seen of the *Renown*, or any other ship. Instead, we could hardly see the fore part of our own. Yet, by the magic of 'radar,' the officers knew exactly where, and how far distant, were the big ship and the other destroyers. Aft of the bridge the Azdic creaked and clicked continuously. But it was very quiet up there in the fog, on the small square of power. The Commander wore a white hunting-stock at sea. He was wide-awake and cheery but pale; he looked like a ghost against the fog, and we all talked low, as if afraid to provoke the enemy or wake Mr. Churchill. Presently there was a stir, as we altered course on to a new leg of the 'zigzag.' 'Twenty-six knots and thick fog,' said an officer. 'I should have thought the Old Man might have done without the zigzag.' But the Old Man, meaning, I supposed, the Admiral, thought otherwise. All night they zigzagged through the fog, at twenty-six knots, with the great invisible ship astern of us. But I climbed and clung my way to bed. From right aft, where the depth-charges lay ready in their racks, our boiling, roaring wake was a formidable sight, rising high above the deck, as we pitched, like a cataract. In the dark entrance to the companion-way lay huddled on the deck, in their duffel-coats, the depth-charge crew. I trod on most of them and turned in, saluting in my soul, once more, the Royal Navy.

Next morning there was nearly a by-election. After a good breakfast I started forward, lighting my pipe and thinking rather boastfully what a 'good sailor' I was. When I was half-way, the ship chose to make a big turn on to the new 'leg' of the zigzag. I saw green water lap over the deck right forward. It did not look alarming, and I think a mere landsman would have sauntered on. But, knowing a little about the sea's behaviour, I grabbed the nearest fixed object, a torpedo-tube, and hung on. Just as well, for half the Atlantic swept over me. Some sailors, relieved but amused to see the burgess dripping but still aboard, collected my pipe and spectacles, undamaged. All very well in September, in the Gulf Stream. But how did they run these little ships—what must they have suffered, I thought, in the Russian convoys, in the snow and ice?

That night, I think, we lost our job. The pace was too hot for our fuel supplies, and the *Renown* went ahead without us. We made Lough Foyle at 0800 on 19 September, having left St. John's at 1115 on 15 September. We should have liked to travel on to Scapa in the *Orwell*, and the Commander was very willing; but the Dominions Office had been doing some busy staff-work, and orders were orders. We were sent across to Glasgow in a frigate, a fine ship whose name I forget. On the way my eye caught the name of a young seaman stencilled large on the back of his duffel-coat: 'A. HADDOCK.' For many years I had been writing in *Punch* about an imaginary character called 'Albert Haddock.' I said to the young man, 'Is your name, by any chance, Albert?' 'Yes, sir,' he said.

At Glasgow we were bundled into the night train and reached Euston at 1630 on the 20th. So by the old-fashioned ship and train we travelled from St. John's to London in four days and nineteen and a half hours.

The other two, who had relied on flight, did not reach England till ten days later. And then they had to land in Gloucestershire, because of fog.

31. 'Goodwill' at Westminster

I should have kept a proper diary. (How I envy and admire that great fellow Harold Nicholson, who keeps a proper diary all the time! And how much I should like to read it!) We all went to see Mr. Attlee, I know; and later we all went to see Lord Cranborne, who succeeded him as Dominions Secretary on 28 September 1943. Charles Ammon, a valiant fighter, as you will know now, refused to have Newfoundland treated as a subsidiary subject in a general Dominions debate; and the island had a whole debate to herself on 16 December 1943.

Charles Ammon moved, very well:

That this House welcomes the statement made on behalf of His Majesty's Government *of the acceptance in principle of the right of Newfoundland to self-government* and urges His Majesty's Government to give effect to such approval by taking the necessary preliminary action as soon as possible.

Note the words of the Motion. Note also that the Motion was 'welcomed and accepted' by the Government (*per* Mr. Emrys Evans, Under-Secretary of State for Dominions Affairs) and carried unanimously by the House of Commons.

Mr. Ammon said, among many other things: 'Then there is

the question of linking up with Canada. There is a large number
of people who want that, but *an overwhelming number who are
against it.*' I am sure he was right. (Yet, in 1949, it fell to Lord
Ammon to pilot through the House of Lords the British North
America Act which made Newfoundland part of Canada.)

But now he also said:

This House, the Government, and the country *will fail in their duty
to Newfoundland*, if while admitting and recognizing the right to
restore full self-government as soon as possible, they did not take steps
to see that when they do so Newfoundland would be in a position to
develop and maintain her country economically to the fullest possible
extent. . . . We cannot expect that Newfoundland can stand on her feet
alone economically, so we have ventured to put proposals to the Dominions Office whereby they must be helped. If we want a British
Empire we must be expected to shoulder the responsibilities as well as
the glory.

Derrick Gunston, in an excellent speech, said, as I had written,
'I left Newfoundland much more hopeful than when I went there.'
He said also, about confederation with Canada, 'I am sure if it
was put to the vote it would be overwhelmingly defeated.' So, on
that, we were unanimous.

Jimmy Maxton and Beverley Baxter, old friends of Newfoundland, were very hot, hotter than we were, about her wrongs, and
wanted self-government restored at once. Jimmy Maxton was kind
about my report, which he had read. He said, 'Hoping for light
entertainment, as I go to the other literary efforts, I was disappointed. I pay a tribute to the hon. Member and say that it was
not a bit of humourous writing but a first-class study of both the
geographical and the psychological problems involved.'

He joined with many others in protesting against the Government's refusal to publish our report—even 'edited' versions. It was
hard, indeed, after all our travels and researches, to be expected to
make this tangled problem plain in three fairly short speeches.

But Mr. Attlee, when he spoke, thanked us all for 'an extremely
valuable service.' He remarked that 'The unfortunate—as I think—
Act, which was passed against the views of some of us in the House,
provided for the setting-up of a Commission, but did not provide

any way for bringing it to an end nor for setting up a new Constitution.' Maxton's answer was, 'Give them what they had before!' But we had reported that they did not seem to be sure that they wanted that. Many of them were afraid of their own breed of politician. Baxter answered boldly: 'We do not give self-government as a prize, as a lollipop. We give it as a command.' He wanted an election in Newfoundland at once.

We should say to Newfoundland: 'Now call your leaders together, arrange to govern yourselves, and we will stand by you through bad times and good times, not rating less high your democratic rights than your financial solvency. Govern yourselves, come side by side with us into the future and let us end our own shame here for having closed a Parliament that had governed for 100 years.'

I shared the spirit of that, and now I am not going to say that, practically, that might not have been the best course. But Mr. Attlee defended our more cautious approach, and had already, I believe, accepted the machinery I had myself proposed, the National Convention, followed by a plebiscite.

The National Convention (my 'Council of Citizens') was to discuss other possible forms of government if the island did not want to return to full self-government and Dominion status.

Before we left London I had been attracted, as I said in my speech, by a suggestion made by Sir Edward Grigg:

It was that it may be possible to consider the inclusion of Newfoundland in the United Kingdom on lines roughly, but not exactly, similar to Northern Ireland. That again, I believe, has been rather turned aside in high quarters, but I hope that high quarters will consider it, because it meets the dilemma, as some call it, of my two main propositions that (1) Newfoundland must govern herself and (2) we must help her financially.

That seems to be a constitutional dilemma; but, after all, it is happening all the time in Northern Ireland, and no one notices it at all.

The idea was that Newfoundland should have two or three Members in the Imperial Parliament which would mitigate the sense of isolation, the sad and well-justified feeling that 'no one at home knows anything about us.' They could be at Westminster on

Friday and fly home for the week-end. Their affairs would not often arise in the House: neither do the affairs of Northern Ireland. In the island I had found some interest in the proposal, but I could never get anyone to consider it in Whitehall. I wanted, one way or another, to keep this loyal, British, and strategically valuable corner in our own orbit. Whitehall, I fear, was longing to be rid of it.

I told the House my

unofficial estimate of the cost of a ten years' plan. . . . It came to 80,000,000 dollars—£16,000,000. Over ten years that is a very big figure to Newfoundland but a very small figure to us. I know that there are a lot of 'flea-bites' about. The Empire is asking for 'flea-bites' everywhere, but, if that figure is correct, it is a remarkably small one, and it would make very little difference to us.

I know that it is asking a lot of this House, and of British tax-payers, of whom I count myself no small part, to be generous not only with freedom but with finance. I never quite know what is meant by Imperialist. . . . But I am glad that England did not stay at home, does not stay at home, and, please God, never will stay at home. I am glad that we sent our sons from Bristol and from Poole to catch the cod and plant the flag of England and settle by the frozen seas.

But I recognize that, when they did so, they laid upon us an inescapable charge. There they are still. . . .

I am sure that as long as we stand by them the last thing they want to do is to leave us.

I had not been long, but I thought I ought to stop; so I said a few words about Labrador, and began to fumble for my peroration. But, as so often—in came that confounded Black Rod! It seemed hard, after a voyage of 7,000 miles and a report (unpublished) of 30,000 words, to be interrupted by that august official just before one's peroration. And thereafter I got into a rude and crazy little row with Lord Winterton. It arose from a complete misunderstanding, and we were immediately the best of friends again. That is the best of that queer place. But it is no wonder that speechmaking drives some of us to drink.

When Lord Cranborne had settled down he sent for us, and was most refreshing. He was all for our Ten Years' Plan, and for nursing Newfoundland back to freedom. Indeed, from first to last, he was the one man I met in Whitehall who seemed to have some faith and fire in this affair; and did not regard the island as a tiresome baby. But, some time later, we were summoned again. The Dollar had reared its formidable head; and the Treasury, I understood (Sir John Anderson was Chancellor then), would not hear of a Ten Years' Plan which would have to be paid for in dollars. But they were going ahead with my proposals for the National Convention and Plebiscite, and that, I thought, was something to be proud of. At least, I do not know of any other important recommendation we made that had the least effect. And that, perhaps, was wrong.

32. The Ovens Alight

Meanwhile, I was back in the *Water Gipsy,* and found it strange, at first, to see no whales or icebergs ahead. But London River was exciting enough.

One cannot now remember the dates. When did we see the first Thames-built L.C.T. go down the river completed? When did we see that astonishing 'thing,' the first completed Phoenix, sixty feet high, alongside Tilbury Stage? And the Dutch M.L., which suddenly secured to Westminster Pier? The first ships flying the Stars and Stripes in Gravesend Reach? It does not matter. One remembers the general picture. It is the picture of this old river— still wary of attack and readier than ever—poising herself for a mighty spring, boiling and bubbling with offensive fire in every corner of every dock, in every little yard and factory—pregnant with revenge and victory. The odour of D-Day hung over every reach. We knew nothing, we asked no questions; but we could smell it. I swear we asked no questions that sunny afternoon when we lay at the Terrace Pier, and suddenly saw the great Drum come slowly down the tide between Gravesend and Tilbury. A vast steel, shining bobbin in the water it looked, towed by a fine American ocean tug. It passed down the river towards Southend. We gazed and we wondered and gave it up. That was the 'conundrum'—the

secret of Pluto—the thing that took the oil across the floor of the
Channel. Perhaps the most bold, fantastic invention of them all.
Later, I saw a similar drum sitting pretty in the belly of a ship,
and someone told me what it was for. I never said a word about
it—not till the news was disclosed. That is not remarkable; for
I was not merely a non-commissioned officer in the Navy, but
a Member of Parliament, and reticence was very much my duty.
What was remarkable was the reticence of so many riverside
citizens, so many people at Gravesend and Tilbury who had no such
formal obligations. In the roads off Southend Pier, these mysteries
and monsters were always a mile or more from the shore. All
Southend people, lovers of the River Thames, were strictly forbidden to use their field-glasses; and loyally, I know, they observed
the order. But in the narrow reach between Gravesend and Tilbury,
through which all the mysteries and monsters had to pass, no mag-
nifying glasses were necessary. The public ferry-boats passed close
to them. Thousands could see them from the shore; thousands knew
the secrets of them—or enough to be dangerous; and yet the secrets
never seemed to get about. I used to go back to the Smoking Room
of the House of Commons, where all men know everything, where
all is confidential and nothing is held back. I never heard a word of
all these secret things in that room. It may be that my colleagues
were being as careful as I was. I do not think so. I do not think
they knew. All honour to the people of London River.

So it went on—this gradual, secret, relentless manufacture and
assembly of new and wonderful things. One day, by the old red
Chapman Light, we saw a thing at anchor that looked, in the distance, like a great table afloat upside down. When we were nearer
we were not much wiser; it might be a bridge or a new sort of ferry.
That, too, like the other mysteries, went past Southend Pier and
out to sea. It was, in fact, one of the ingenious 'Spud Piers' for
the harbour at Arromanches. The concrete blocks—the Phoenixes
—became common sights, 'deguassing' at Tilbury or slowly passing
out to sea. One went aground and broke her back. One day at
Greenwich we saw men busy on the queerest craft yet—a London
River lighter in bright new grey with a great many tall chimneys
protruding. That one we guessed—it was a landing barge, *Kitchen*.

A few days later there she was, rolling in the roads off Southend Pier. The more we saw the more we wondered at the brains behind this fabulous affair—and at the work that London River had done —and the less we thought of the 'Second Front Now' school of 1942.

An important point in the preparations was the lighting of the river. For the first year of the war (and more) there were no lights at all, afloat or ashore. There were no lights on the bridges even; and hitting the bridge-holes of Waterloo Bridge, for example, with a strong tide under you, was no great fun. Then the lights on the bridges, well shaded, were allowed, and later certain shore-lights on dock-heads and jetties, and dimmed navigation lights as far down as Tilbury. But below Tilbury, till the end of 1943, there were no lights at all. Then, in preparation for the coming event, some of the buoys were lit, and the old Ovens blinked again.

33. A Critic in the Blitz

During one of the 'Little Blitzes,' on a snowy night in March 1944, we were lying at Westminster Pier. Someone thought they saw something fall on the barge-roads below Waterloo Bridge, where one of the roadsmen on our mine-watching roll was alone in his little hut. So we cast off and steamed down over the flood. One of the engines gave trouble, and as we came slowly through the bridge the All Clear sounded. Nothing was amiss at the barge-roads, but there was a fire towards Fleet Street, a little way up the hill. I said, 'I bet that's my publishers!' (Methuen's, in Essex Street). It was no part of our duties to extinguish fires ashore, but I felt that in this case a reconnaissance was justified. We made fast alongside the *Discovery* (Captain Scott's ship), left the *Water Gipsy* in charge of the Sea Scouts (rather naughtily, I fear), and crunched through the snow in our sea-boots. My crew then were Leading Seaman Tom Cheesman, a Yorkshire fisherman, and Stoker Stan Atkins, a Lancashire lad. It was the night 'they' damaged the fine Middle Temple Hall, which I had viewed so often from dear old E. V. Lucas's room at the back of Methuen's. As we came up the steps into Essex Street, I said, 'My God, it *is* my publishers!' and we did the rest 'at the double.' The building on fire was in fact two doors off, but an incendiary bomb was burning on the leads outside 'E.V.'s' window, and water from the hoses next door was pouring into Methuen's basement, which was full of books. There was one fire-watcher, and nobody else about. So we offered ourselves as a working-party, and hurried down into the pitch-dark basement, where the water was already some inches deep. My eager crew were in no mood to discriminate between one author and another. This was the skipper's publisher, and a book was a book. Their torches fell first on a great pile of girls' books, of the *Head Girl at St. Hilda's* kind, and with great armfuls of these they splashed upstairs. But, since it seemed likely that the whole stock would be destroyed, I thought I would be more choosy in my salvage. There were miles of books, in shelves from floor to ceiling, with narrow alleys between. Glad of the sea-boots, I paddled here and there, flashing my torch. What should I save? Suddenly I realized, for the first time in my life, I was a literary critic. And, in the circumstances, my standards were very severe. I had become highbrow too. I will not reveal what well-known names I left on the shelves to perish, for all I knew, in flame or flood. I did not see any of my own books; but, indeed, I was not looking for them.

The boys clattered back down the wooden steps, and Stan Atkins yelled, 'Skip, where are you? It's all right, Skip. Fire-watcher says it's all insured.' I took a poor view of that, though the fire-watcher, I am sure, had offered information, not advice. 'You carry on,' I said, and they saved, I suppose, more bundles of *St. Hilda's*. I splashed on a little, and came across a book of my own, *Uncommon Law*, which had long been 'out of print.' Since it was insured, I felt justified in slipping it into the pocket of my duffel coat. Then, at last, my search was over. I found a large colony of Mr. Hilaire Belloc's books. Some of that great man should be saved, if it was insured twice over. I collected a great bundle of Belloc and started back for the stairs. But just then, clutching the books with both hands, I dropped my torch in the water, and it went out. It was pitch-dark; I had come some way from the stairs, and the place was like a maze. I took a step forward and charged into the end of some shelves. I could, of course, have dropped Mr. Belloc and used my hands, but I am glad to say I decided against that, and I stood still and yelled. One of the boys yelled back: 'Come up,

Skip! Fireman says to come up!' I yelled to them to come down. The water was rising, and, during the short wait, I confess I was conscious of slight unease.

Though I did not know it, the incendiary had come through into the ground-floor, and Methuen's was in fact, though mildly, on fire. It would, at least, have been a good literary end—an author dead in his publisher's basement, embracing the books of a master. But Stan came with his torch and we handed Mr. Belloc over to the fire-watcher. At the top of the stairs a very formidable fireman was in suspicious talk with Cheesman. He may well have wondered what three sailors, in tin-hats, duffel-coats, and sea-boots were doing at a literary fire; and I took over the telling of our highly improbable tale. On such occasions I always, if I could, refused to say, 'I am A. P. Herbert, a Member of Parliament, etc.,' preferring to sail under my proper flag as P.O. i/c *Water Gipsy*. I had succeeded, I thought, in persuading him that this sort of thing was all in the day's work for the crew of a patrol vessel, when I saw his eye wandering to the book, *Uncommon Law*, which protruded from my open pocket. 'Heavens!' I thought, 'I am now going to be charged with "looting" one of my own books.' But the fireman, bless him, said nothing and let us go. He and his men did very good work, and the damage was not so bad.

Back in the ship, Stan Atkins said: 'Skipper, I saw a letter with your name on it and brought it along. Thought you might like it for a souvenir.' How right he was! By the queerest chance it was a letter to Methuen's from a gentleman in the United States who wanted a copy of *Uncommon Law*. He had tried everywhere: could Methuen's help him? And on the letter was an office note showing that Methuen's had answered, 'Sorry. Out of print. Unobtainable.' But they were wrong. I made up my mind to send the American the book, the letter, and the story. But I fear I forgot.

34. The Thames Attacks

May 1944—a bustling, bracing month on the river. The United States had invaded the Thames. The Stars and Stripes was almost as frequent as the Blue Ensign; powerful tugs—harbour craft—landing craft, and the Liberty ships, the M.T.s, steaming up to the docks to get their load of vehicles and troops. It was a thrilling thing, one misty afternoon, to meet the first flotilla of L.S.T.s—Landing Ship 'Tank.' These grand ingenious vessels, designed, I believe, in England, but built in America, did wonders in the fight, and were perhaps the most fruitful new vessel of the lot. Their great jaws opened like prehistoric monsters and disgorged thirty tanks.

There was a lift to the upper deck, and that was crowded too, with smaller vehicles. Some of them flew the White Ensign, but most were manned by the Americans. Now they steamed into the Tilbury Docks, the West India Dock, or to the special ramps that had been built for loading here and there, and to the Limehouse Reach. There the Americans had a special base for these ships at Convoys Wharf, above Deptford, where later they suffered severely from the V.1s. There they lay, three 'bottoms' deep, a mile or two from the heart of London—American ships of war loading British tanks to drive the Germans out of France. And the heart of London knew nothing about it.

Coming up Limehouse Reach next morning, seeing these ships at their business on either side a few hundred yards from the ruins of Deptford Victualling Yard and the scarred shores of the Surrey Docks, my mind went back to that night of 7 September 1940, when London River took its worst. It had needed the best part of four years' work, but London River was ready to strike back. The Battle of the Thames was still to finish.

When we saw these things and the M.T. steamers massing in the docks, we knew that the Day was near. There were other signs. All down the river, at the wharves, and on the buoys, our own small steamers blossomed suddenly with name-boards and numbers —little coasters that seemed too innocent for this affair, but they were at it too, stuffed with oil or ammunition. The big transports came out of the docks, crowded with vehicles and khaki, and made way for others. All the time the ships were pouring into the river. Those that were ready must, somewhere, wait for the rest, and so the Great Congestion began. Look at the figures:

	Ships Arrived	Ships Sailed	Total
1944—January–March	3,256	3,370	6,626
April–June	4,950	5,659	10,609
July–September	5,186	5,838	11,024

That was an unforgettable scene. There have never been so many ships in London River before; there will never be so many ships in London River again. There were not enough berths in the river for all the ships. They anchored them in long lines down the middle of the lower reaches, in the Northfleet Hope, in Gravesend Reach, in Sea Reach—all the way. Looking down Sea Reach from Hole-haven, one saw an endless forest of ships—transports, hospital ships, landing ships, tankers, and barges.

They lay quiet with their distinguishing flags and the pilot flag flying, waiting to go. It was a weary time for the soldiers and the crews. No one was allowed ashore. Between Holehaven and the Mucking Light lay thirty small coasters carrying oil. I called on some of them that were signalling for water or supplies, or needed a boat.

They had been lying there ready for eleven days. This could not be avoided: the troops must be loaded last. Indeed, it is a wonder how all this movement and marshalling of ships in the narrow waters was done so smoothly and well. I heard few complaints. I know of no blunders. But the pilots were too few and had a hard time. They were worked to death, and fell asleep on the small craft taking them to the next ship.

By degrees the ships were worked down-river towards the mouth —to the domain of Southend Pier. One evening we took 'last letters' from the coasters at Mucking, and they got their anchors and slipped down the river to another anchorage below Southend. One morning there would be seven packed transports in Long Reach—in the afternoon they were gone. They went very quietly, these shipfuls of fine troops; there was no cheering, no singing, no waving. I never heard a song from all those ships. They went past without a sound. They looked down at us without a word, the soldiers trying their lifebelts on, or in conference with their officers. All the time, as we watched this moving of the ships, we wondered why the enemy had nothing to say. There were alarms. High-flying spies came over. But they dropped nothing. He had new terrors by then—the 'oyster' or pressure mine, for example. A few of these in Gravesend Reach, in Sea Reach, could have wrought fearful damage and delay. We went up and down the river, urging the patient watchers not to relax. Nothing happened.

At Southend, the Commodore and his men had a problem, such as Southend will not see again. All this time the convoy work went on as usual. London must be fed, though Europe be invaded. But, for the D-Day affair, the commercial traffic was handled in the Warp, below the Boom. In other words, the convoy orders must be conveyed to ships four or five miles away.

Inside the Boom everything was 'operational.' And on the night before D-Day there were 203 ships in the Southend area inside the Boom. The water was marked off on the chart like a chessboard or 'grid.' Every square was a berth and every square was numbered. The pilot coming down the river had one of these 'grids' and somehow had to get his ship to the appointed berth in the crowd. To relieve the pressure, the Commodore used Nelson's old anchorage on the other side. Imagine, if you can, the coming and going of the small craft that had to serve this huge and scattered fleet—moving the captains and the pilots and the army commanders and meeting innumerable emergency demands. Over fifty small craft were fully employed in this work.

The weather worsened and the river shook its head. It was rough enough in Sea Reach for the small craft going alongside the ships. What of the smaller craft that were to land the soldiers on a hostile beach? But how much longer could the troops be kept on the crowded ships—with small accommodation and supplies? If the thing could not happen soon they would all have to be taken ashore again, the great spring released and painfully coiled again. For some days the naval crews in the river had been forbidden to go ashore, and we knew that the thing was due; but on the morning before the Day, in the rude scowling weather, we made sure that the thing was off. Indeed, on that morning, I saw one of our naval tugs collect a party of seamen from the small coasters anchored by the Mucking Light.

But on that day, as all the world knows, General Eisenhower, his admirals and generals, made the great decision. On D-Day—1, Monday 5 June 1944, at Southend, in the Solarium (or 'Suntrap') at the end of the pier, Commodore Champion summoned eighty-nine masters together with twenty of their escort commanders, and four long conferences were held for each of their respective convoys at 1100, 1400, 1800, and 2000. There, among the cardboard pictures, the banana-trees and tropical blossoms, before those cool but glowing mariners, the Commodore unrolled the map so many longed to see— the map that showed the beaches of Normandy and the way the ships would go from Southend to the Norman shore, the map that meant the liberation of a Continent, and London River's revenge. At H-Hour on D-Day there were to be six different convoys—three of Landing Ships 'Tank'—on their way to France, that had come out of London River and spent the last night in the waters of Southend. They sailed, the first of them, at 0200 on the morning of 6 June, and Southend woke up to find that the main part of the vast fleet had gone, though many ships remained, waiting to go in their turn, when the great 'build-up' began. Farther up the river, that day and the next, there was a sense of desolation and emptiness after all the bustle we had seen and shared. The river seemed lonely and dead without those silent shipfuls of soldiers in the fairway. How were they faring and how many would return? And we wondered still what the Luftwaffe were about. Perhaps there was a 'trap.' The first contingents of the Army having landed, the enemy would mine the ports and their approaches, prevent the 'build-up' and cut off our men's supplies. We talked almost hopefully of 'counter-invasion' by parachute troops. Nothing fell—not a mine, not a parachute. We went about our duties sadly, wishing they had sent us too.

But on the third morning the first ships came back—led by a long line of the Landing Ships 'Tank.' As they passed the pier they signalled the number of German prisoners they had on board, and thrilled the weary staff who had done so much to get them to France, and needed no more comfort or encouragement than that. That morning, early, I came out of Holehaven, bound up for London, and saw the noble procession go by. It was a fine sunny morning, with a fresh wind from the west whipping the flood-tide into small white horses. All Sea Reach was a-dancing and a-glancing to see the first ships home from Normandy. They came up at a strong speed, with an air of urgency, their pendants streaming bravely in the sun, their bow waves foaming across the reach, their sides black with exhaust—or explosion—prisoners below, bedding and wounded on their decks. It was a warming thing to see them pass. They had crossed the Channel, those queer vessels; they had grounded on the coast of France, where the Germans used to rule; they had opened their elaborate jaws and flung defiance and death at the enemy; they had come back safely and impudently to England, escaping guns and mines and bombs, E-boats, midget submarines, and all the rest; and here they were in London River again, bound for Tilbury or Limehouse, for Woolwich or Blackwall, to load their decks with fire and slaughter, and cross the Channel again. But still there was no cheering, no waving, no show. The job was but begun. But we, rolling and tossing in the great wash they made, did humbly and happily salute them.

Next came back the first of the motor transports, the Liberty ships, the beginning of an endless stream. At Southend Pier, I fancy, none could relax for a very long time. From D-Day onward the drill was eight or nine outward convoys a day. The 'build-up' was the thing, the incessant flow of reinforcements and supplies. It may surprise you—it surprised me—but, by their graphs and statistics, the movements were greater after D-Day than before. Between D-Day and 31 May 1945, the volume of military stores, ammunition, petrol, and the rest handled in the port was 2,760,000 tons, including 202,000 tanks and other vehicles. More than 40,000 ships passed in and out. The peak quarter of the whole war was January to March 1945—11,924 ships, and I make that more than 130 a day.

London River, which for two days had felt herself out of the picture, was very much in it for a very long time. The work done after D-Day, when the first excitement was past, and dogged duty and dull efficiency were the order of the day, was highly meritorious.

It is not for me, in this modest account, to salute or glorify the fine administrative deeds of the Admiralty or the Ministry of War Transport in this affair. No doubt the Admiralty will do that one day. I can speak only of the men I know and the things I saw on the river. I can testify, for example, to the good work of the Royal Naval Auxiliary Patrol, at Cliffe Fort and Tilbury and Greenhithe, whose officers and patrol craft were an ever-ready link between the river and the Ministries, passing orders, reporting arrivals, carrying pilots, flashing and flagging, directing or assisting the shipping—a skilled and willing handmaid in the whole affair.

35. The Time of 'Doodle-Bugs'

I have often thought: How angry Hitler must have been when his famous 'secret weapon'—the V.1—the flying bomb—was named by us, or, rather, I believe, by the Americans, after a flying insect with a tiresome noise—the 'doodle-bug'! And how right he was to be angry! For the 'doodle-bug' was surely by far the worst thing he did to London, and we should have treated it with much greater respect. Indeed, in our secret hearts, I think we did.

The first night of the doodle-bug[1] was the most colourful and crazy scene I remember in the river war. A day or two earlier the enemy had sent over a few experimental monsters, one of which fell not far from Gravesend. This, for good reasons, no doubt, was kept from the people, and even from the commanders of patrol boats. But one of my former officers, then stationed at Tilbury, gave me a confidential whisper about what we had to expect. Dutiful but wondering, I said no word to my crew.

We were at Tilbury, acting as temporary handmaid to Commander Chapple and his three North Sea trawlers. These were a kind of bomb-and-mine disposal flotilla, ready to fish up anything from anywhere with all the arts of the fishing fleet. He and his three skippers, all from Grimsby, I think, gathered round a little rum,

[1] 15 June.

were about the best company in the river. The gallant bomb-fishers were very fond of cockles; we fetched them sackfuls from the Hole-haven sands—or wire or warps, whatever they wanted. Now they were after a Mosquito, which had plunged with all her bombs into the river below Tilbury. They never found her, but they caught all manner of things. Time and again we watched while the winches rattled and puffed, and the tough trawler heeled over heavily, and some great thing came slowly up to her side. Sometimes it was a vast anchor; twice, as it broke surface, it looked like a bomb—a round and shining section of a huge and ancient tree-trunk, as black as coal, and nearly coal itself.

That night, when the sirens sounded, we were anchored below the landing-stage, just above the 'World's End' tavern and Queen Elizabeth's Fort. It was a perfect spot for that obscene spectacle. We could see the little lights appearing, far off, like fireflies, over the Kentish Hills; and the unprecedented monsters roared in procession over our heads, for London. Everything in the river (except the *Water Gipsy*) let off everything it had—steamers, mine-sweepers, patrol boats—all. Sailing bargemen fired their rifles. The river seemed to go mad in the face of this new madness. The Bofors Battery, on the north shore near to us, made a noise like a destroyer in action, and the men were yelling. The red 'tracer' bullets, chasing the pale green speeding lights from every part of the wide reach, made a fantastic picture. Brock's have never done anything better. But as the guns on the south side lowered their trajectory in pursuit of the fleeing targets they seemed to be shooting just over our heads, and I feared for our lives. But nothing of that sort mattered. Tom Cheesman was itching to blaze away with his Hotchkiss like the rest, and could not understand why I restrained him, till I began to disclose my suspicions about the beastly things. Even then, as they roared over, I felt guiltily that I might be betraying a confidence, and, perhaps, ruining the cunning plans of the High Command. One of the things came down in, or near, the Tilbury Docks, and all the sailors cheered like mad. I said, 'I'm afraid that's what they want,' and felt like a killjoy. I wished, indeed, that I had never heard that 'confidential whisper,' for everyone else was having fun. It was like a rat hunt. And we were the only dog on the chain.

I wonder how much ammunition was vainly spent that night. And what fools all those eager gunners must have felt next day, when they were told that it was futile and forbidden to fire at the monsters! I assume, respectfully and politely, that the Authorities knew best in this affair; and one day I hope to hear exactly what was in their minds.

The next day we were summoned up to London, very sad to leave our trawler friends, and for the following weary weeks we continued to have good views of doodle-bugs. All London's citizens think that they saw the one which was different from all the others; but that very night I really believe that we met, and avoided, the unique V.1. We went up by night, and about 0200, the flood finished, we tied up to some barge-roads a little upstream from Ford's factory at Dagenham, but on the other side of the river. Before the 'watch below' could turn in, one of the Things came roaring and glowing up from Tilbury towards us, and we all waited on the bridge to see it go over. But, some way short of us, the monster's light went out and the engine stopped. 'Boys!' I remember yelling, 'it's a by-election!' We all scrambled below and lay flat on our stomachs, expecting the worst. Nothing happened, and presently, incredulous, I heard the noise of an engine again. I clambered out onto the bridge, and there, astern of us now, was the Thing in full flight again, light and all, as if it had taken a good look at the *Water Gipsy* and decided to go for bigger game. It roared away and came down about two miles off in the Barking area. I have heard no other tale as tall as this, but I swear that it is true.

After that, 'By-election!' was always the operative word for our stomach drill on the cabin deck. This was, no doubt, in our little wooden ship a fairly futile rejoinder to all that explosive power. But the cabin deck was a few inches below water-level, and I thought that the outward and upward blast from a Thing bursting on the water, not too near, might go over our bodies, whatever mess it made of the ship.

'By-election' drills were frequent in the next few weeks. Once or twice a week we used to patrol down the river at night and lie at Blackwall or Woolwich, chiefly, I think, to let our roadsmen see that we were still about, and the great warship was in action, though there was nothing she could do. These voyages were quite exciting, but made one feel not futile only but foolish. Every Londoner, I suppose, had a special hatred for those fiendish contrivances, for two reasons, apart from fear, that nothing could be done about them—and they went on for ever. When the sirens sounded and the bombers came over, our guns—even our fighters—could be heard; and that noise was heartening, though nothing resulted. Now the poor Londoner heard tales enough of fighter-planes in the country diving daringly onto the monsters and blowing them up, of wonderful work by A.A. gunners. We told them ourselves, when we came back from a trip below, of the great barrage of balloons that was shooting up and spreading like a row of runner-beans over Tilbury and Gravesend and the adjacent counties. But all they saw were the triumphant beasts which got through and sailed over the city, like royal eagles, with none to say them nay; and the only noise was the noise of the enemy. Moreover, when the All Clear 'went' the citizens could relax. Somebody, they knew, was on guard, and would sound the alarm again if danger returned. But early in the days of doodle-bugs we ceased, sensibly enough, to sound the sirens for them. So every man became his own sentry. Every man, in the worst times, had half an ear cocked for the distant beginning of a buzz. And it was astonishing how many common sounds of the city set the mind alert—a car being started in the street below, a lorry ticking over, a vacuum-cleaner next door; even, I am told, the sound of certain refrigerators. Conversation, work, continued; but each man knew what the other was thinking. When you were in a building and the noise was heard strongly overhead, the assumption was that the Thing would roar on safely and hit someone else.[2] But when the whine ceased suddenly and the silent glide began, none could tell in what direction, all this un-Christian calm was shaken. Now came the time to be under tables, to get away from windows, or dive into cellars. Many legends

[2]No one ever hoped that a fellow citizen of his would be bombed. But these devilish devices compelled him, almost, to wish injury to others: unless he were strong enough to recite my *Model Prayer for Model Citizen*
Stop, Noise, immediately, that I,
And not some other chap may die!
Sunday Graphic, 23 July 1944

grew up. It was said that to escape the worst consequences of 'blast' you must lie in the gutter with your stomach just clear of the street, the rump a little raised. I remember solemnly instructing some women friends in this drill at a cocktail-party. Women who refused to lie down in the gutter, because of their clothes, were said to have escaped without a scratch, but stripped stark naked by the blast. Everyone seemed to know all about them. One in every six, I heard, had a radio attachment which went 'pip-pip' as it fell so that the Germans could measure the length of the flight. Everyone had seen one quite different from any other. I saw two of the 'deviationists' which turned in a half-circle at the end and returned a short way almost in their tracks. (These were a great discouragement to office roof-guards who sounded the 'Danger passed' too soon and saw it returning.) At Hammersmith one night we saw two chasing each other up the University Boat-Race course and made bets about them.

But let not posterity—let no northerner or neutral—suppose that these Things were a kind of tiresome joke, or even a minor form of bombing. They were, I think, London's most terrible trial, and what a mercy it was they did not begin a year or two earlier! Portsmouth had some, I believe; but apart from London and the south-eastern counties, England was at peace. Business men who came down from the North for a night were very glad to go home; and we, after all our experience, were highly relieved when an occasional job down the river kept us for a night at Tilbury or Holehaven. Some of them did frightful slaughter in busy markets and shopping centres, schools, chapels. They seemed to me to increase in explosive power. The worst to see, and I suppose the most deadly in effect, were those whose engine never 'cut out' at all. These descended vertically at last and hit the earth still roaring. They would plunge from top to bottom of a tall building and reduce it all to rubble, as one did a tenement near my home at Hammersmith that sickening Sunday morning. Another, only 200 yards away, destroyed four small fac-tories. And another fell on the same line, only 600 yards from that, and, though it was in the river, did great damage ashore. One came through the Tower Bridge one sunny morning slap into the Tower Bridge Tug. One crew was relieving the other, and both were lost.

Another put half Charing Cross Bridge out of action, which was more than years of bombing had done.

It was wonderful how the work went on. Imagine the crews of trams and buses, entirely surrounded by glass! The drivers could not hear the things, the girl conductors could not always be looking out for them. No warning sirens, no All Clear. They just drove on, in peril always. Imagine too an actor on the stage, playing a tense or tender scene, when he hears the approaching drone—and, worse, the stopping of it, which may mean that the Thing is at that moment swooping without a sound on to the theatre! Yet they kept on. The most heroic stage story I know was told me of that gallant lady Dame Lilian Braithwaite by Miss Gertrude Lawrence. You must know that in the theatre, if on Wednesday this week the takings are £300, and last Wednesday they were £290, then 'we are ten pounds up' and all is well. But if it is the other way round, 'we are ten pounds down,' and nobody can understand it. When the doodle-bugs began, the Dame had had a long run in a certain play, and it was suggested, after a week or two, that she must be tired and might think the moment suitable to go on tour. 'Go on tour?' said the stout heart. 'Where shall we go? Let us go to Dover.' The play went on in London. At night, according to the story, the Dame, who lived alone on a top floor, used to wrap herself in a dressing-gown, sit in her little bathroom, and hope for the best. After one of the worst nights, a household help, or someone, found the Dame fitfully asleep, cold and drooping in her dressing-gown. 'Oh, Dame,' she said, as she woke her, 'did you have a terrible night?' 'No, indeed,' said the old lady proudly, 'we were thirty pounds up!'

Under way on the river, we were unable, because of our eighteen clattering horses, to hear the Things coming; so unless you kept your head circulating like a hen's, you looked round suddenly and saw one coming straight at you from abeam or chasing you astern. I must say, we felt very silly on those occasions, alone on our bridge in the middle of the Pool or Woolwich Reach. There was no basement to dive into, and no nice gutter to lie in. But at first, at night especially, the illusion was that they were not approaching very fast, and that 'evasive action' was still possible. One night in Greenwich Reach we were persuaded that three of the wandering lights were converging on us with devilish intent, and I remember cunningly calculating that if I worked across to the Surrey side and inside the barges I might thwart them all. What a hope! We were doing about five knots against the tide and they—was it 350? We were not half-way across the river when the first went over us. One fell ahead at Greenwich, and another astern on two American Landing Ships loading more tanks for France. We did two by-election drills and came up cursing after each. It was a shame, to make you feel foolish as well as afraid.

But how much more foolish, frustrated, futile, and furious we felt lying at Westminster or Chelsea Pier! We kept a watch all night, of course, and counted and logged every monster we saw—whence? whither? etc. I do not quite know why. There we were, a naval vessel —and the most heavily armed vessel in the Royal Navy for a long way!—and all we could do was to watch and record an unimpeded procession of enemy missiles over our country's capital, knowing that nearly all of them were bound to kill or injure innocent people somewhere, hearing very often the crash and rumble as they hit a building. This enemy was bound to win. All we could do was to 'put him in the report'—and, now and then, cry 'By-election!'

During my own turns on watch, having, like so many, a special anxiety, I found it easy enough to keep awake. My daughter Jocelyn, who was expecting twins, had been brought to our house at Hammersmith a week before D-Day. The twins (like all babies, in my experience) were 'behind schedule,' and the four weeks before their birth were four weeks of doodle-bugs. There was a regular 'lane' of them just north of us and another to the southward; and, later, there was a new lane (from Dieppe, I think) that came suddenly over the houses on the other side of the river and right over ours. Jocelyn and my wife, who anxiously looked after her when not on ambulance duty, refused to use the 'strutted basement' I had had prepared at the beginning of the war. They sat always in a ground-floor room, with wide windows opening on the river. Jocelyn never turned a hair; but I turned many, and fussed, I expect, outrageously. I had worked out, on the map, the bearing of Hammersmith Terrace from Westminster and Chelsea, and whenever a Thing was evidently bound for West London I rushed to the compass and judged

its course. (You will tell me that alongside the iron of the pier my
compass would be in sad error. Yes, but I had worked out the error
and allowed for it. Or so I thought.) Also, I started the stop-watch,
and by complex calculations, the basis of which I have now quite forgotten, tried to estimate how far away the damned Thing burst. The
result of all this scientific work, as a rule, was that Hammersmith
Terrace was certainly destroyed three or four times a night. Yet it
survived. The twins, 8½ lb. and 6 lb., respectively—boy and girl—
were successfully born in Hammersmith (Ducane Road) Hospital.
They had another ten days of doodle-bugs there (and I had to work
out new sets of compass bearings). But few children, thank God, can
show fewer signs of 'war psychosis' than Miss Olivia and Master
Julian Lousada.

When I was not saving twins I studied the doodle-bugs in the
light of all we had seen. (I suppose we saw as much of them as any,
but I have had no access to official records.)

There was much indignant talk about this 'indiscriminate' bom-
bardment; and, no doubt, the Things were flung about in all directions to frighten the people. But it seemed to me that they could be
pretty accurate when they liked. I was struck by the many 'groups
of three.' We saw, from Westminster Pier, the one that disabled
Charing Cross Bridge. Not long after, another just missed the bridge
and fell in the water against the Embankment; another fell under
the Embankment about fifty yards nearer to Cleopatra's Needle. A
very small group indeed. Two at least just missed the central arch of
Tower Bridge. There were three or four more on the banks between
Tower and London Bridge—that much-belaboured reach. I have
told of the one that hit the American L.S.T.s at Convoys Wharf.
Another fell on the water opposite, and another, I believe, hit the
base ashore. Our three at Hammersmith 'straddled' the bridge. Then
there were the power stations. Three, heading straight for Fulham
Power Station, fell in almost the same spot on the opposite bank,
300 yards away. I saw two fall in the water near Lots Road Power
Station and one on the land behind it. Many fell near the Battersea
Station, but not, I think, so near. They were all round Deptford
Power Station and hit it once, at least. I do not know if there were
similar 'bunches of three' ashore; and it may be that mine were

merely coincidences born of indiscriminacy. But it seemed to me that they did have a habit of hitting the same spot, more or less, three times; and if there was anything in the story of the 'wireless attachments' from which the enemy could calculate, more or less, where they fell, then it would seem he had only to 'repeat the mixture' and do it again. If that is nonsense, we may say, at least, that it was fortunate he had no time to develop such refinements. And how foolish he was to waste so many of his precious monsters on the citizens of London when he might have bombarded continuously the convoy roads off Southend or the vital funnel for shipping between Tilbury and Gravesend. Or suppose that he had used doodle-bugs which, falling in the water, acted as mines. That, I imagine, would be child's play to the author of this kind of devilry; and a nice mess he might have made in the river during the days before and after D-Day.

At one time we used to laugh at Hitler's 'secret weapons.' But this one, at least, was not very funny. And the V.2 was still to come.

36. Monty in Action

At the end of July 1944 I was highly astonished and delighted to receive a letter from General Montgomery, beginning:

Dear Alan,
Thank you very much for your latest book. . . . Two copies arrived; I think you must have sent me a copy before I asked for one!
Would you care to come over to Normandy and stay a night with me—or two? If you can arrange it I will send my aeroplane for you. . . .

Then followed, in his own neat writing, a page of 'staff-work,' about the details of the proposed visit, as precise and thoughtful as if I had been an Army Corps, moving to the attack. These private letters, in his deliberate long-hand, written from 'Tac. H.Q.—21 Army Group, B.L.A.,' often at the beginning or the peak of a battle, have been a wonder to many. Though private, they should, I think, be mentioned publicly, for they are a sure sign of the man and his methods. He trains his troops, he instructs his generals, he inspires them both, and sends them into action. Then, because he trusts his own work and theirs, he sits down, 'stops fussing,' and writes long letters home.

My wife and the Field-Marshal's, the gay Betty, who died tragically from a seaside scratch a few years before the war, had been great friends. We stayed with them when he commanded a battalion of the Royal Warwickshire Regiment at Alexandria. But I had not seen him for some time, and this invitation was like a fairy-tale. Cinderella could not have been more surprised. Fortunately, I had some leave due to me; my officers were forbearing, and let me go.

I met the Fairy Godmother—the charming Colonel Dawnay (Personal Assistant)—at the Savoy, and away we flew from Northolt for Normandy, in the Chief's *Dakota,* on a lovely afternoon. But we came down somewhere near Portsmouth, for a delightful reason. The American crew of the *Dakota* unloaded a motor-bicycle and one of them rode away. I wondered a little, but it was then explained that before D-Day the Field-Marshal had been sending his washing to a convent near Portsmouth, and we had come down for that. The motor-bicycle returned with a bundle, and with this happy cargo we flew out over the sparkling Channel to the seat of war.

Tac. H.Q. (or Tactical Headquarters) was then in the Bois de Cérisy, a delightful place. If Sir James Barric had ever set a scene in a battle headquarters, I thought, it would have been like this. It would have been perfect for *A Midsummer Night's Dream.* Tall thick trees reached up to the sun. In the luxurious fern a tame rabbit wandered about at a batman's heels. The absurd dogs, Rommel, Hitler, Keitel, and company romped on the camouflage netting; and in the General's caravan a canary sang its head off. There were the General's three caravans in the centre—two captured from the Germans—and a few more dotted about the wood, for staff officers and guests, a small marquee, which was the 'mess,' and a small tent or two. The wireless sets and the inter-communication arrangements were all out of sight in the forest. But for the marquee and the khaki it might have been a gipsy encampment. After nearly two months of doodle-bugs in London River the battle headquarters was a haven of peace, and I had a good night at last.

Yet that night 'the Chief' (as his followers called him) ordered Falaise, not so far away, to be shelled for the first time, and the famous 'pocket' began to close.

Here is another of the secrets. One is inclined to imagine the headquarters of a great general in time of battle as the scene of feverish activity and even noise—staff officers bustling about, telephones ringing everywhere, dispatch-riders roaring in and out, pigeons

banging into cages, multitudes of clerks and orderlies—and reporters.

For all I know, there may be such goings-on elsewhere. But they
were not to be found at Monty's Tac. H.Q. For he considers that the
job of a supreme leader in the field is to *think,* and he insists on having the time and the conditions for thinking.

From which two things follow: he will not be bothered with a
mass of detail, and he will not be surrounded by a crowd. The
officers about him, day and night, are his own small, chosen, and
charming personal staff. The heads of departments, with all their
necessary routine and retinue, are elsewhere. But the Chief of Staff,
Major-General de Guingand, and the Chief Administrative Officer,
Major-General Miles Graham, could visit Tac. H.Q. at any time
they liked, and could stay the night there whenever it was more
convenient for them to do so. The heads of branches and departments were sent for as necessary to come forward and see the Chief.

I have seen somewhere some criticism of these arrangements—
'Monty shut himself apart, could not be got at,' and so on. It is not
for me to plunge into military criticism, but on general principles I
should say, as I said about Mr. Churchill in the debate of 1942: 'If
you have a great leader in whom you believe, for God's sake let him
do his work in the way in which he believes.'

Mr. Churchill, as we all know—and with what results!—was always giving his great mind and vast experience to faraway details;
and there were those, I believe, who complained of that. Even if
they had been right they would evidently have wasted their breath.
As well expect an eagle to sit still. Monty reduces every problem to
'principles' and leaves as much of the practice as he can to others.
His detachment was deliberate and scientific. The plans are made,
the orders given; the generals and the staff work out the details and
execute them. But he knows that his subordinates will set about any
particular task according to *his* principles—principles of action in
which all those under him have been so thoroughly instructed that
they are almost second nature. I was privileged to see his principles
of battle set out in *High Command in War*—and a masterly document it is.

So, once the task is set, the Chief can get thinking again—or write those letters home. And so, that night, while he was devising and executing perhaps the bloodiest slaughter of the war, we dined in surroundings like the last act in *Peter Pan* and talked about the House of Commons and the doodle-bugs.

But I do not wish to suggest the picture of a general sitting very far back in comfort, and letting things go hang. Far from it. Even the intrusive details, though they are kept at arm's length, are within easy reach, as I saw that evening.

We dined in the marquee, the Chief, Colonel Dawnay, and two merry and devoted young A.D.C.s, Captains Henderson and Chavasse, both Military Crosses, and a Canadian, Lieutenant-Colonel Trumbull Warren. I saw much of that mess thereafter, abroad and at home, and I cannot imagine a happier little community. There was youth in the air. Nor did austerity command the meal.

After the nine o'clock news, we went to the map-caravan, 'to hear what the boys had to say.' This is the regular routine. The 'boys' are the team of liaison officers—British, American, Australian, Canadian. They have spent all day visiting various sections of the 'front' —driving immense distances in jeeps—a tough job in the winter, a wearing and sometimes perilous one in any weather. They are all good soldiers, picked for intelligence and fortitude—and tact. While we dined, they have been chalking the latest dispositions on the talc that covers the great maps on the wall. Now each in turn comes forward and tells the Chief what he knows.

'The Twenty-first are through the wood. It's a bit sticky by the windmill. This bridge is "blown," but they hope to bring up "Ducks." Forty-fourth Div. will attack at 0400.' And so on.

The Chief asks a few questions, strokes his chin, does a few 'H'ms,' but makes few comments. It might be somebody else's battle. The news is about his own chosen men, using his ways, and so there is nothing much to say. But in this way, without fuss, he has a finger on every pulse at the front.

When the last 'boy' had gone, Monty said, 'That map's no good to me. Come and look at this one.'

'This' was a smaller scale map where you could see the big picture better. He showed how the 'pocket' had begun, and—with one exception—accurately indicated the end: how he had 'loosed' the Canadians southward, and how, that night, the north-bound force would be turning up through Alençon and Argentan. 'To-night,' he said, 'I have ordered Falaise—the road here—to be dominated by shell-fire.' Falaise had not, so far, been in the news, and I remember saying, 'Falaise? Didn't something happen there?' Monty thought so too, but neither of us could remember that William the Conqueror was born at Falaise.

Finally he put a finger on the map to the east of the pocket. 'There,' he said, 'I drop my air-borne troops.' And one saw the picture, the last gate shut.

But in all this there was no bombast—no triumphant, 'We've got 'em in the bag!' I shall never forget what he did say. A classic utterance, I think; and he said it twice, as he says so many things. 'It will be very interesting to see the outcome.' And again, as we stepped out of the caravan into the fairy forest: 'It will be very interesting to see the outcome.'

Two or three days later, after a night afloat in the Mulberry Harbour at Arromanches with my old chief, Lord Teynham, I was back in London River. Naturally, I said no word to anyone; but, naturally, I read and listened to the news with an almost proprietorial interest. When people wondered whether the 'pincers' would catch and crunch the Germans, I thought I knew the answer, the airborne troops. And I waited eagerly for the big event. It never happened, as you know; and there were some complaints by chair-borne critics that too many Germans were allowed to escape from the pocket. Perhaps the ground was not considered suitable for the 'airborne' effort, or the battle was too confused for such an operation, or the troops were wanted for other work. I do not know, and have never inquired.

But I remembered that night a long time later when I read a notorious war-book by an American, whom I will not name. Some of the book may have been fair and truthful for all I know, but it was certainly charged with malice against Monty. For one thing, it said that the Field-Marshal was a small man, but so puffed up with pride that he had special padding in his boots to make him look taller. And there was a nasty tale about the Falaise pocket and the air-borne troops. Some one in the American Army—an engineer, I think it was, although it may have been a doctor—had the big idea that the two air-borne divisions training in Scotland might be used to close the pocket. This brilliant notion, according to the author, was sent up to the highest 'levels' of the American Army, and there commended. It was sent across to the British Headquarters Staff, who thought it wonderful. General de Guingand, the Chief of Staff, made haste to the Bois de Cérisy, and was seen walking, confident and gay, to Monty's caravan. He came out despondent (one got the impression that he came out on all fours). For the 'Chief' had turned the big idea down. And so, of course, too many Germans escaped.

Well, if my flying visits cannot be justified in any other way, at least they enable me to say that that important accusation was nonsense. Whatever the source of the scheme, it is certain that that night —9 August 1944—the Field Marshal thought it good and intended to use it. There were other bits of nonsense in the book, with which I will not worry you.

Great men, like great trees, must have little legends, like creepers, climbing about them. Even after El Alamein, some clubs were saying, 'Only a showman—conceited fellow,' which was much resented by his friends, and, I should say, by his soldiers. For one thing, no one can be a 'showman' unless he has something to show. For another thing, I am sure that the things the whisperers had in mind at that time were done deliberately for a purpose. When he took high command the Army had little to show and few to show it. It was uncertain of its own, and low in others', estimation. Where is it now? Monty, I feel, blew the Army's trumpet, not his own. It was not in conceit, but confidence that he said, so quietly: 'It will be very interesting to see the outcome.' And what are we to make of that astonishing opening to his Order before Alamein:

The battle which is now about to begin will be one of the decisive battles of history. It will be the turning-point of the war. The eyes of the whole world will be on us, watching anxiously which way the battle will swing. We can give them their answer at once: 'It will swing our way.'

That is the language not of conceit, but genius.

Then there is the legend of the 'grim martinet,' the inhuman, humourless ascetic, who does not smoke or drink, who reads the Lessons, and quotes the Scripture in his Battle Orders. Well, there is a strong spiritual quality—why not?—but he did not call upon the name of God in vain or, as so many of us do, in times of trouble only. I have never been under his command, so I have never seen those keen blue eyes ablaze with anger (and a formidable experience that must be). Certainly, after a little time in his company, you go away thinking that you must try to be better and bigger. But I will not agree that this is a grim or humourless man. He does not drink because he does not like it, and no doubt in the way of duty he is severe about this department of conduct—so is the Navy. But, at a dinner in London, though he swills his orange drinks, his staff may have what they like; and in the mess, in Normandy or Germany, I was never the only one at the wine.

He goes to bed at nine-thirty, if he can, but does not expect the whole world to do likewise.

About smoking, he is more severe. I do not think I ever saw one of his personal staff smoke in his company. Therefore, when we sat talking after breakfast in the mess, I used (with a heroic effort) to defer my first, and finest, pipe of the day till we were outside. But often he has said suddenly: 'Smoke your pipe, Alan—smoke your pipe'—a still more heroic effort, I believe. I do not wish to overdo it and suggest that he is a wit; but there is plenty of quiet fun, and this is not reserved for the rosy days. At Lüneburg, much later, one of his staff told me that he had never seen the Chief 'more magnificent' than he was during the Rundstedt offensive in the Ardennes. At the height of the crisis—and it *was* a crisis—he would come down to breakfast and say, 'This is awkward. We can't go out through Dunkirk this time—the Germans are there.' When things are bad he is at his best.

At the risk of shocking some of his admirers, I must record that the mess betting-book at that time was full of entries like this:

General Eisenhower bets General Montgomery that the war with Germany will end before Christmas 1944.

General Montgomery bets General Freyberg that the war with Germany will not be over by . . .

The first was highly interesting, for I knew that Monty thought the war ought to end in 1944. Yet he took the bet.

After all, how could the man of the legends lead so many men, without losing a battle, from Cairo to Lüneburg Heath? When we drove about Normandy, one sunny afternoon, I wished that the whisperers could be there as well, if only to see his soldiers salute him. He took with him a bundle of old *Times* newspapers, and a mass of cigarettes. He would toss a *Times* to an astonished traffic-control man, or press several boxes of fags upon the sergeant of a road-gang. But, apart from these benefactions, it was a stirring thing to see the impact of his presence upon all who happened to see him. Half-naked pioneers, sweating with picks at the side of the dusty road, would look up and recognize and lift their heads high, and salute, sometimes with the most odd contortions, as if to say: 'This is *my* special salute for *my* general.' One realized what saluting is for.

Next day, over a long Cook's tour round the front in a jeep with young Henderson (I claim to have been the first sailor over the Orne) I got, still more strongly, the impression of a single binding driving electric force. I vividly remember the 'back-areas' in France in the First War. Here, it seemed to me, there was more order and less lounging, better traffic control and fewer 'jams.' (It is true that there was much less shelling than was customary in my day; and the new bridgehead over the Orne was as quiet as Kew.) The day before, the Poles had gone into their first attack, and, through too much impetuosity, I believe, had made a mess of it. That evening Monty said, '—— rang up and wanted me to give the Poles a pat on the back. I said, "No, give the Poles a kick in the pants. They'll do better next time." ' I believe they did. No one wanted a second kick.

Monty is interested in everything, and wants to know what you are doing, and why. But he has not the habit of some big soldiers, who shoot a series of questions at the civilian so fast that he has no chance to answer any, and then state their own opinions. If Harriette Wilson is to be believed, the Duke of Wellington was rather like this. But Harriette knew how to deal with him:

As I was one day taking a solitary drive up the Champs Elysées, on my road to the Bois de Boulogne, the Duke of Wellington galloped past my carriage. . . . In another instant he had returned and was at the side of my carriage.

'I thought it was you,' said Wellington, 'and am glad to see you are looking so beautiful. I'll come and see you. How long have you been in Paris? When may I come? Where do you live? How far are you going?'

'Which of these questions do you desire to have answered first, Wellington?' I inquired.[1]

Monty can listen. It is true, you do not argue very much with him, but he listens till he is sure that you are wrong. And everyone in sight, of course, is very much managed, even a guest. In November the *Water Gipsy* went into dock, I paid another visit to the mess, and flew to Brussels with the staff in the *Dakota*. We landed at twelve, and at lunch Monty said, 'At two o'clock, Alan will go to Antwerp. To-night Alan will play the piano.' The mess, for a few days, was in a rich man's beautiful house with a fine drawing-room and a Grand. Punctually at two I left for Antwerp—which, with V.1s and V.2s descending together, was quite like home, only worse. A few minutes later a doodle-bug fell 100 yards from the headquarters. Monty was telephoning by a window, which came in; but he was unhurt. That night he was very gay, and kept saying that Alan must play the piano. I duly played some of the old English choruses, and my one 'piece,' Handel's Largo. Suddenly, the grim martinet came to the piano, and, to the delight and surprise of his staff, burst into song. He sang an old song of several verses. I vamped an accompaniment, and was too busy with that duty, and too much astonished by the event, to take in the words. Now I cannot even remember the name of the song. Next day Lord Trenchard ('Boom') arrived, and in the evening we called for the song again. But now the Field-Marshal was shy.

I have never motored so much, or so painfully. 'Alan will go to Aachen in the jeep.' 'Alan will go through Antwerp and try to get to Middelburg.' Poor, flooded, beautiful Middelburg, at the far end of Walcheren Island. We got there, marvelling how the Canadians, fighting along the dykes and through the floods, had got there a few days earlier. I heard, too, the sad fate of the 52nd (Lowland)

[1]*Harriette Wilson's Memoirs*, p. 573 (Davies).

Division, who, having been specially trained for mountain warfare, were conveyed at last to Walcheren in small boats and flung into this battle of the swamps. Lieutenant-Colonel Warren, the Canadian A.D.C., wanted to reach Flushing and report to the Chief upon conditions there. We started off down the narrow, muddy towpath, all roads being flooded. I should have liked to see Flushing too, but what with the canal on the left and the mine flags in the bank on the right, I did not mind very much when the attempt was abandoned. All these trips, apart from their interest, were highly instructive to a water-borne Member of Parliament. I shall never again let anyone say that staff officers in the Army have a soft job. A long ride in a jeep in winter-time must be about the coldest method of motion devised by man. And they were doing it every day—and many a night—dodging always great columns of lorries, huge tank-carrying vehicles and guns, not to mention the invisible Belgian cyclists—and mine warnings—at the side of the road. Though on the water I count myself a pretty brave boy, on the road I expect death at every corner, even if there are no tanks or artillery or mines about; and on these trips I ought to have had innumerable heart attacks. But the driving was wonderful. I saw one smash only, in many hundreds of miles. And my chief memory still is of the back of a square shaven neck and a close-cropped head as steady over the wheel as the Rock of Gibraltar, under whose protection it was impossible to believe in danger. That steady, skilful head, I suppose, is now directing, not less surely, though not so swiftly, some London bus. Good luck to it!

We moved from Brussels to a little house in Holland, of which (apart from a lot more motoring—'Alan will go up to Nijmegen and suitably salute the Rhine') I have two special memories. No one who hears Monty speak or reads his military writings can fail to wonder at the clarity and neatness of his mind. As I have said, he likes to reduce everything to a few 'principles,' neatly subdivided into (a), (b), and (c). When you read these principles, you think: 'Well, that is good—but pretty obvious, after all.' But ten minutes later you may be hard put to it to repeat a single one of those 'obvious' principles. In 1948 he received the Freedom of the Borough of Hammersmith, and addressed a mass of my fellow-citizens in a cinema, with the Mayor and Corporation in extraordinary session on the stage. He was born not far away—in Chiswick—and he got 'a lot of laughs,' as we say in the theatre, about his early days in the neighbourhood. The final plans for D-Day were made in Hammersmith, at St. Paul's School (his own old school), and the new Freeman, thanking the citizens for their wild welcome, recalled with effect the many letters they had written to him in those days, saying, 'Please go away. You're bringing bombs to the borough.' If it be true, as the club critics say, that Monty was not endowed with a sense of humour, all I can say is that he has picked one up somewhere. And he is quite thorough enough for that. Now he might well have contented himself, and us, with a general address on goodwill, hard work, patriotism, or what he would. But it was a Local Government occasion—a whole local authority were on parade just behind him, and he had taken the trouble to study local government. He had been reading, I think he said, a book by Mr. Herbert Morrison. What is more, before the astonished Mayor and Council, he began to analyze and resolve the problems of local government. I heard with delight, in the new context, the familiar phrase:

'Now, the principles of local government, it seems to me, are these. First, . . .'

I forget how many principles of local government there were—I think about five; nor can I remember what they were. But they struck me then as sound and exhaustive, and I do not think the Mayor and Council would have quarrelled with a word.

That is an 'away' match; now for one at home. To this little house in Holland came a party of seven London editors. I was to fly home that morning, but Monty said I had better help him to receive my 'friends from Fleet Street' (I did, in fact, know two of them). Monty received them very graciously and sat them down in a row in front of the desk in his little room. But this headquarters was no Bois de Cérisy. It was a small house on a main road; the heating system did not work yet; the weather was wet and dismal; and Monty's room was always full of the rumble of tanks and guns and lorries. Doodle-bugs roared over now and then for Brussels. But the canaries and the goldfish were on parade as well, and the canaries did their best.

At that time everyone in England wanted to know what was to happen next. The Allied advance seemed to have spent itself. Arnhem was over. When should we cross the Rhine? How about Eisenhower? In what state were the Germans? The editors, I am sure, were bubbling over with sagacious questions. But, before one of them could open his mouth, Monty said smoothly, 'I wonder, gentlemen, whether you would care to hear the story of this campaign, so far?' Some eager gentleman said incautiously, 'Yes, sir,' and away he went. I think he went back as far as St. Paul's School. I knew most of the story already, and they probably knew more, but it was a fascinating performance. And, of course, while he was telling the long heroic tale, nobody could intrude with awkward questions about Eisenhower or the Rhine. The Rhine? He had them pinned down behind the Orne. At last, after about forty minutes, some editor managed to get in a direct question. Monty countered with a disquisition on various themes—the German generals, the character of the German soldier, the construction of tanks, the principles of warfare. He had not a note. There was noise and interruption all the time. But nothing disturbed the flow. 'There are three points,' he would say. 'The first point is——' Just as he got to Point 2 someone would ask for a window to be shut, there was a rumble of tanks, or a canary burst into piercing song. But Point 2 came calmly forth. During Point 2 Colonel Dawnay would come in with a message, for a battle was going on. By the end of these little whispers you or I would completely have forgotten what Point 3 was going to be. Not Monty. Out it came: 'Now Point 3 is this——' Simply as an example of speech-making it would have commanded my admiration in a long-schooled Cabinet Minister. But this was a soldier—who had just begun a battle.

After about an hour, I was extracted and put on the plane, so I do not know how the conference ended. But I will bet he charmed and exhausted them, told them nothing, and sent them away rejoicing.[2]

To complete the picture of the 'inhuman martinet,' I must relate,

[2]Years later, in 1949, a British correspondent described how the Field-Marshal dealt with a 'battling host of American reporters, photographers, etc.' when he arrived in the Hudson River: 'Monty disarmed, scattered, and routed them with ease, left them wondering what hit them, with his new brand of charm.' But it is not 'new.'

I think, what had happened earlier. As I have said, a small battle had begun very early that morning—it had been postponed for a few days because of the weather—a battle, I gathered, to clear away the last pocket of Germans on our side of the Meuse. After breakfast—as the great Damon Runyon might have said (and it is a fairy story deserving special treatment, I think):

I am sitting in the ante-room, rather cold, reading the newspapers, when who comes in but the Field-Marshal, bearing a bottle of brandy across his breast, like a bride with lilies.

'A bottle of brandy' [he says], 'captured from the Germans. A present for Gwen [who is my ever-loving wife]. Would you like it? Would you like it?'

Now, as a matter of fact, brandy is one of the very few drinks with an alcoholic foundation which I do not value very highly. I do not mean that I am unable to swallow it, but I do mean that if I am asked what drink I would choose to accompany me during a protracted visit to a desert island, brandy would be quite a way from the top of the list. But my ever-loving wife has no objection to harbouring brandy in the home, and I am thinking it is a much more sensational present than the bottle of red wine I have bought for her in Brussels. In addition, it is not every morning that a guy is fitted up with a bottle of brandy by a teetotal Field-Marshal who has just begun a battle, and I am so moved by the scene and spectacle that I cannot think of any suitable response. I say weakly, 'Thank you very much, sir.' And then, because I think I have not played my full part in the conversation, I say: 'I wonder what the Customs will have to say about this, sir?' But there is a little more in what I say than keeping the conversation alive, because I have just remembered that the little guy called Henderson, who is one of the Field-Marshal's A.D.C.s, has said to me in Brussels, 'Do you like Bols?' and I have said, 'Yes, I do like Bols' (which is a kind of Dutch gin, very good, they say, for the backache). So he says, 'We have captured from the Germans huge quantities of Bols, to which, if the truth must be revealed, we are not extremely partial. We will give you a bottle.' So he gives me two great earthenware bottles of this Bols. And I am thinking that what with the two Bols and the bottle of red wine and the Field-Marshal's bottle of brandy I am likely to be taxed like a wine-importer on my arrival in Old England, though it is true that I have also acquired some toys for some of the seven grandchildren and these—who knows?—may soften the heart of the Customs. While I am reflecting after this manner the Field-Marshal says, 'Oh, well, I will write you a letter' and scrams. I go up to my apartment and there is the nice little guy called Henderson, with the batman, which is a military man's man, and they are trying to thrust the two Bolses into my poor man's grip, which, what with the toys and the bottle of red wine, is not coming very easy. When I am sighted with the bottle of brandy they are discouraged somewhat, and it is decided after a few experiments that I will leave the bottle of red wine behind as a loving tribute to the Mess. At this moment who should sail in but the Field-Marshal himself with a letter he has just written in his own fair hand, and it goes like this: 'Mr. A. P. Herbert, M.P., has been staying with me as my guest. I have presented him with a bottle of brandy captured from the Germans. I hope the Customs will take a kindly view of this. I am sure they will. B. L. Montgomery, Field-Marshal.'

Now, once again, I am standing there like I have been hit by a hammer, because, believe me, by all the tales in town, this guy has as much loving-kindness as a goldfish and is by no means one of the Friends of Liquor. Moreover, this morning he is fighting a battle. I say, 'Why, thank you, sir'; but again I feel that I have not done justice to the situation. So I add, by way of a nervous crack, 'I suppose, sir, you could not add a footnote about these two bottles of gin the boys have given me?' and I look down at the two guys still in a clinch with my small grip on the floor. The Field-Marshal takes one look at the scene, and he says 'What, gin? What, gin? Well, I'd better write you another letter.' And I am telling you, on oath, if you insist, that he goes out and writes the letter again, with a new piece about the Bolses. After that, I think I will not say any more, for fear he will give me a case of champagne and send a telegram to King George.

Well, I come down at the airport in an Anson machine that bounces so many times I think we are going to start again, and here I am, half-deaf, before the Customs. Two of the Customs guys know me because they have served on the river. The chief guy gives me a loud 'Hallo' and asks if I have anything to declare. I say, 'Why, yes, I have something rather special to declare,' and I show him the letter. He grins and shows it to his colleagues, and they read it and grin and chuckle like mad. 'Well,' says the chief guy at last, 'I guess that will be O.K., Mr. H., seeing it's all presents. But,' he says, and I see very well where this cunning old guy is steering, 'I expect we'd better keep this document, hadn't we?' Now, if it is me, I would much rather keep the document and pay the duty, or abandon the cargo of liquor. But I think, if I do this, I am making a vain thing of the Field-Marshal's care and trouble. So I hand over the document, and I am telling you that there is some Customs guy who has the finest autograph of any field-marshal since field-marshals were invented.

To someone who seemed to believe in the 'grim martinet' legend, I told this story; he then professed to be a little shocked. 'Well,' I said, 'you can't have it both ways.' But they do.

37. Big Bangs

In September the Canadians were storming along the coast of France, our doodle-bug log was less busy, and we looked forward to an end of the Things. The last mentions of the V.1 I can find are for 18 September—'Doodles—2 or 3—seemed to be coming from N.E.' (the Hague, I suppose), and 18 October—'1 Doodle.' '1 Doodle!'—poor little thing. But on 8 September we had begun to record 'Big Bangs,' for a new plague had fallen on the patient Londoner—the V.2 rockets. These continued, off and on, for the next five months. Here, again, it seemed to me, the enemy did pretty good practice. The first one we heard in London fell in Grove Park, Chiswick, and the next at Chelsea, not very far from Westminster. The first 'bangs,' it was whispered officially, were caused by exploding gas-mains or delayed-action bombs. Presently so many gas-mains were exploding that it became a Metropolitan joke, but it was not till 2 January 1945 that the brutal word 'rocket' crept even into our confidential 'log.' Always, before that, it was 'bang' or 'big bang.'

The V.2s, no doubt, were intended to be still more terrifying than the V.1s, because there was no warning; but for that very reason, I think, they were not. No warning is better than continual menace. You did not have to watch one across the sky and wonder where it would fall. There was a sudden bang, a slow column of smoke, and ruin in some small street, but unless you were near that street, you forgot about it.

We were in dock for three weeks in the New Cross-Deptford area, where there were many, and some terrible, 'bangs.' But, even there, they were not always in the mind as the doodle-bugs had been.

I did some more amateur map-work on the 'bangs,' and I announced at last that our home at Hammersmith was 'on the main line' of the rockets. They came, I had heard, from somewhere near the Hague, and a line from the Hague to Westminster led onto the first 'gas-main' in Chiswick, I reckoned—and we were very near that line.

Sure enough, on the night of 1-2 January 1945, a rocket fell on the river bank, almost opposite, and less than 300 yards away. I had special leave to celebrate the thirtieth anniversary of our wedding, and friends had been singing round the piano by the front window till 0200. If it had fallen during the revels we should all have been cut to pieces, but it waited, fortunately, till 0340. The blast swept over the river, tore through the house (hardly touching our neighbours), and plucked great holes out of the roofs of the small houses behind us. But it did not even wake me. (I was sleeping at the back of the house, I should add, and my wife in the front: and they did say that the nearer you were to a rocket the less noise you heard!) I woke only when I heard my wife on the landing, saying calmly, 'Alan, come and look at me.' I went, wondering, and found her in a roomful of plaster and glass, but none the worse, thank God, and smiling still. Smiling, indeed, for though we had seen many a nasty blitz through together on my leave-nights, it was an old joke that I was never there on the really big nights of Hammersmith and Hammersmith Terrace. Now, at last, there I was for our first rocket. All the windows—and the frames as well—were blown out for the fifth time. And I slept through it!

All I could say was: 'Well, I told you we were on the line.'

In the same week, I see, though our victorious troops were facing the Rhine, we recorded the fall of twenty rockets on London. But that was Hitler's last attempt upon my brave lady and her home— and about time too! She had had five and a half years of war and loneliness in London. She had had a bomb on the water at the end of the garden, and another, not far away, on the other side of the house; two incendiaries on the roof and another (at the same time) in the front-room window by the hall. On that occasion, legend has it, a neighbour knocked on the door; my wife opened it with a charming smile, and said, 'It's all right. I know. The house is on fire.' She and two good neighbours put all three out. She had had many a hair-raising ambulance drive through the black-out and the blitz, with screaming casualties behind her. When she was not doing that, or waiting for duty in a damp station with a glass roof, she was defending our tall house alone in the noisy night. Somehow, almost alone, she kept the house going all the war, dealt with my correspondence, grew vegetables for the King in the little flower-garden, and provided miraculous meals when hungry sailors appeared on leave. She lost all her windows time and again, and lived in the dark behind cardboard, or in the cold when the cardboard went. She would not go away, as many did, but stayed like a lighthouse of faith and fortitude among poorer neighbours who could not go. She had guarded a daughter, pregnant with twins, for five weeks of doodle-bugs roaring over and falling not so far away. And now, when surely the serious war is over at last, she celebrates her wedding-day, her ninth wedding-day in war-time, fate sends a rocket, does its best to destroy her, and leaves her windowless in winter once again. And her husband sleeps! But still she smiled. And so did I. Of course we did. For how fortunate we were, after five and a half years, to be alive together in an old house still standing, on our ninth wedding-day at war! Still, I hope she has no more wedding-days at war, for she does not deserve it. No more, I know, gentlemen, do your heroic wives. I cannot tell their stories for you—but I salute them. It may be said that what they did and suffered is very small stuff besides the terrific tales of 'the few,' the fighting men, the 'resistance' men, the prisoners, the spies—or beside the horrors of Hiroshima. But all these things were done and suffered by millions for a very long time, and it may be well to record them, for we forget so soon.

38. Up the North Sea—But Why?

In March 1945 the *Water Gipsy* was 'paid off.' We 'returned to store,' reluctantly, our dear little guns and compass and charts and duffel-coats and signalling-lamps and all the accumulated battle-gear of five years, and took the naked little ship to Twickenham. I said a sad farewell to Tom Cheesman and Dan O'Connor, the last crew of the *Water Gipsy*, who went back, a little sadly, too, I think, to sea-fishing and plumbing, respectively. I was now practically a free man again, but my wretched sense of duty, or itch for activity, whichever you will, prevailed, and so I lost the chance of a lifetime. At the Royal Ocean Racing Club, and elsewhere, I had met many of the fine fellows who worked for the Admiralty Small Vessels Pool. These were civilian yachtsmen of all ages—but mostly more than middle. Their job (voluntary) was to take over new 'small vessels' of any sort and shape from the builders and deliver them to the port where the Navy wanted them. They did many fine and uncomfort-able feats, these civilian sailors. Some were sent to the States and brought their small charges, not in convoy, across the Atlantic. One of the regulars, named Holland, had promised to sign me on if ever I were free, and in April he had to take a small M.F.V. (Motor Fishing Vessel) from Brightlingsea to the Forth. He agreed to sign me as mate, and I was excited about going to sea in an active capacity at last. But, a day or two later, I had another invitation to visit Field-Marshal Montgomery, then roaring across Germany. I had a feeling that this was an invitation to see the end of the German war, and so it was. If I had gone I should have seen the surrender of the German generals; and, afterwards, the personal staff told me they wished they could have had some 'outsider' there to witness those tremendous days. Any sensible man, I suppose, would have asked to be excused from the job for which I had, quite unnecessarily, volunteered. But, 'Duty!' I said, poor fool, and away we went to Brightlingsea instead of to 'Tac. H.Q.'

The Motor Fishing Vessels were built in three sizes—90 something feet, 60 something feet, and, I think, 43 feet long. Ours was one of the baby class. She had no name, and it is just as well, perhaps, that I cannot remember the number of the beastly little ship. She was beamy, and a fine sea-boat, as we discovered later, but with no cargo, and not much ballast, she was as light as a cork and tossed and rolled like a sinner in Hell. The permanent thing against her was that—for reasons which will be explained—with her one Diesel engine going full out she was still almost immobile. The immediate thing was that she was half full of water; and even the engine-room was awash. She was to be taken to Grangemouth at the top of the Forth, and through the canal to the Clyde. From there she was to be shipped to the Far East—Rangoon or Colombo or Japan—for harbour service, and I often wonder to what unhappy harbour she got, if any.

We were a crew of six. There was a young engineer, but I, at fifty-four, was the baby of the 'deck department.' All the others, I think, were over sixty. Colonel Blewitt, a very fine seaman (and fellow) was the perfect bo'sun: he knew about everything, worked like a beaver, and spliced like an angel. There was another gallant colonel whose name I forget, and he was nearer seventy. The cook, a good cook, but no seaman, might have been any age. Yachting, at the best, demands muscle and hard work, and a ration of vigorous youth, for carrying, loading, rowing, pumping, and so on, is desirable. This voyage, it was clear, would be no picnic—not that anyone expected that. Even with the help of the Navy, it took us two days to get the water out of that fishing vessel, load her with stores, and start her on her tropical career.

On a calm day, we moved as far as Harwich, about twenty miles, at the speed, it seemed, of a glacier. Her slowness was something miraculous, and we marvelled at it. For in the spacious engine-room the Diesel 'power-unit' roared away with perfect efficiency, and it commanded, if I remember rightly, the power of sixty horses. Nevertheless, with a smooth sea and a slight tide under us, the same shore feature seemed to be abreast so long that we suspected a mirage. Infant fish came up, had a good look, and strolled ahead. When we passed a jelly-fish we cheered. All the time she made water like a swimming-bath, and always one of the old men was breaking his back at one of the bucket-pumps—one of the most odious forms of physical activity. Still, it was fine; Blewitt was happy putting eye-splices into our tough new warps, and I (between pumpings) studied charts and courses.

At Harwich the Protectress of the East was solemnly degaussed (against mines). At Lowestoft I gave a lecture about Parliament. Here it was decided that the vessel was insufficiently sea-worthy and must go into dry-dock for caulking. By the time we got into dry-dock we had been eight days in the absurd ship, we had done sixty miles, and there were more than 300 to go. The weather had gone bad, with northerly winds, and at this rate it might be months before we saw the Forth. Our skipper, a professional man, could not spare much more time and, with the Navy's consent, handed over his command to me. The moment the dock was dry I went down and inspected the propeller. I do not pretend to know much about propellers, thrust, pitch, 'slip,' and all the rest of it, but this affair seemed simple enough. The M.F.V. had a very wide stern-post and a very small propeller. The ends of the tiny blades only just cleared the stern-post. However hard the engine worked the screw was whizzing round in an area of dead water. This was surely a mistake, and I rang up the builder at Brightlingsea. He agreed that, by the original design, the ship should have had a different engine and a bigger propeller, but for some complex reason he had been instructed to fit her otherwise. No one seemed to think there was anything to be done about it now, so, at least well caulked and dry, we put to sea again.

Though I wished that their Lordships had provided a nobler

vessel, I was very proud to have a command at sea, under the Admiralty, at last; and after five years of the river I found navigation at sea comparatively easy and free from care. The swept channel was well buoyed all up the coast; the Admiralty provided a list of the buoys, with latitude and longitude, and all the mariner had to do was to mark their position on the chart, and lay his courses from buoy to buoy. As long as you remembered about the magnetic variation and did the right thing about it, all was well. It did not matter if you strayed from your course a little while eating a sandwich at the wheel. We met many ships, but feared no collision, as they kept their steady course. In the river every vessel or craft in sight is an anxiety, for who knows what any of them will do next, and the helmsman can seldom relax. Moreover, the North Sea is not littered with fixed obstacles, with barge-roads and moored hulks and piers and bridges and dolphins and ferry-steamers, and tugs with long tows straying across the fairway. And though the tide may be an enemy it cannot sweep you to disaster at a moment's notice (if your engine fails, for example).

Still, to be quite carefree, you must have reasonable power—and weather. As near as we could judge, we had about five knots of our own, and, with the tide under us and no head wind, might hope to make seven. That was optimistic, for later, in Yarmouth Harbour, I conducted an unofficial speed trial, and found that our mean speed, in slack water, was four knots.

We were warned—I forget if it was an order—against night-steaming, for the E-boats were still about. Still, when there are plenty of harbours, even a four-knot tub can crawl from port to port in the daylight hours. But our big problem was the same as King John's—the crossing of the Wash. From Great Yarmouth, the last harbour on the Norfolk coast, to Great Grimsby, in the Humber, was more than 100 miles. Suppose, with a fair tide (a rare phenomenon, in our experience), and no head wind, we covered forty-two miles in six hours and in the next six hours we made about one knot or even two, we should still, after twelve hours' steaming, have fifty miles to go. So our plan had always been to take two bites at the voyage, and spend a night at the little village of Wells, twenty miles west of Cromer. It appeared from the North Sea pilot to be one of those delightfully complicated little havens which 'dry out' at Low Water, and even when the sands are covered have to be approached by a twisting channel from a buoy well out to sea. Still, if we got there near High Water, and in daylight hours, a pilot, we were told, would meet us. But the time of High Water was getting later and later in the afternoon, and so we had chafed increasingly against the Lowestoft delays. The day we got away, it blew pretty hard from the north; we moved like a sea-snail, and by dusk we had not even reached the turn of the coast below Cromer, so we turned and entered Great Yarmouth in the dark— of which, not having been there before, and, having studied with awe the Pilot's remarks about the tidal currents,[1] I was a little proud.

The next day—because of the time of High Water—was our last possible chance of making Wells in daylight, just before dusk. We slipped out of harbour just before dawn—and just astern of a midget submarine. It was calm enough then, and we had strong hopes of getting the accursed little craft a little nearer to Rangoon or the Philippines. But our usual luck held, the wind worked up all day, and in the afternoon, when we were round the Cromer corner at last, and nearly up to Cromer, it was blowing a full gale from the north-west, dead ahead. Before us lay the rough and raging Wash, the tide was foul as usual, we were making about one knot, the ship was standing on her head now and then, the Humber was seventy miles away, and Wells about twenty. I suppose that any sensible man would have turned back long before. But among my major vices is tenacity. It is, I suppose, akin to the old Oxford weakness for lost causes. You hold on confidently, believing in the right and so on, when all the wise spectators know that you are beat. But I had, I hope, some reason on my side. The tide was due to turn pretty soon. That wretched little slug of a ship was revealing herself as a fine sea-boat. She plunged, and rolled, and stood on her tail, and we were flung about the Chart Room like elderly

[1]"Vessels entering the haven at High or Low Water by the shore experience the disadvantage of the full strength of the stream setting across the entrance, and into or out of the haven. The south-going stream, being deflected past the entrance of the haven by the projection of the North Pier, enters the harbour as an eddy from the southward. During freshets, the rate of the stream at the Brush quay is occasionally 6 knots, but at ordinary springs from 3½ to 4 knots.'

peas. But always she rode the great waves with an air, as comfortable as a cork. I formed a sudden affection for her, and felt she could go anywhere. In theory, there was still a chance of reaching the Wells buoy before dark, though then, it was true, we should have to turn south, with this grim wind and sea on our beam, which would be nasty. Well, if that failed, we could go on plunging across the Wash, perhaps, in our navigable cork, till we made the lee of the Lincoln coast. Here we were, after thirteen days, only 100 miles from Brightlingsea, and I wanted to get on. Also, I kept thinking, why the Hell am I steering a useless M.F.V. towards the Wash in a nor'-wester when I might be with Monty seeing the end of the war? My gallant crew made no comments or suggestions, and I believe I should have held on—and perhaps drowned us all. But when we were nearly abreast of Cromer, the signal station on the cliffs began blinking at us. I read 'RETURN TO YARMOUTH,' and was glad I had spent so much time practising Morse. Wells had telephoned, I heard later, to say that it was quite impossible for us to get in there—if we got there. We turned and were blown back to Yarmouth in good time.

The next day we tried again, but conditions were not much better, and, on my good behaviour now, I gave up and turned before we rounded the corner. I then held my 'speed-trial,' reported the result to the Admiral's staff and asked for advice. Wells was out of the question for about a fortnight, and, failing calm weather or a new propeller, our job looked like a life sentence. It was no part of the Admiral's duties to fit new propellers to Motor Fishing Vessels. But my old friend Commander Chapple was in port with his flotilla of (mine-disposal) trawlers, for which the *Water Gipsy* had done a little work in London River. Through him it was arranged that we should be *towed* to the Forth by one of two mine-sweepers who were bound north for Scapa Flow. And it was so.

'Towed' indeed—for 300 miles! It may sound a lazy way to finish a journey; it may even sound fun. But it is not exactly that. Ask your dog when you take him for a harnessed walk. The first day was fine. Our astonished little M.F.V. found herself bounding over the sea at more than ten knots, and the man at the wheel had to watch her like a cat. The waters which we had three times attempted so painfully and vainly were now smooth and blue, and even the fearsome Wash was gracious. We made Bridlington before dusk, 120 miles, and anchored south of Flamborough Head.

The next day there was more rough weather from the north, and it was a job to steer her. She danced and tugged like a puppy on the lead. We went into North Shields for the night. It was good to survey so much of the coast of England in this way, famous headlands and hills and smoking cities which had before been no more than names on the map. But the farther we went, the more crazy it seemed that we had ever attempted to cross all those miles of tidal and windy water in a bouncing tub with no more than four knots of her own. On the third day the wind had shifted to the southward and we had a following sea. That was the devil of a day and a tough test of the old gentlemen. When the big wave came up astern it tossed the little ship ahead and the tow-rope slackened and dipped to the sea. She fell back then, and, the mine-sweeper charging ruthlessly ahead, the line tautened and there was a sharp, alarming jerk as the rope took our whole weight suddenly. Brilliant spray spurted all along the line then, and, if the sun shone, there might be a million little rainbows, and it was beautiful. But we were not bothering about beauty; we were wondering how long our tough new line would stand the strain. Five times, that endless and strenuous day, the tow-rope parted; and in the end we pulled one of the mine-sweeper's strong bollards clean out of her deck. When the line went, the ship, without way on her, rolled and wallowed wildly, intolerably. In these conditions the old gentlemen had to haul in perhaps seventy or eighty feet of heavy wet, new intractable rope. It would not coil easily like old rope. As it came in, every fathom an effort, an agony, it piled and twisted itself into enormous insoluble 'snarls' on the fo'c'sle head. Blewitt was magnificent, indefatigable; and the other colonel did all he could. I darted out and lent a hand when I could; but, as well, I had to semaphore to the mine-sweeper, reeling precariously on the see-saw deck, watch the wheel and signal to the engine-room. When all the line was in we would crawl up to the mine-sweeper and, rolling alarmingly under her quarter, start again. Blewitt dug out massive new ropes from the fore-peak; he cun-

ningly bent together the ends of the old ones. In the end, we had
to borrow from the mine-sweeper. When the murky dusk descended,
making the strange hills and mountains of Scotland look less hospitable still, we were heaving and sweating on the fo'c'sle head
for the fifth time, like Laocoön among many serpents of wet, cold
rope. The Captain and the crew of the mine-sweeper were amazingly
patient. They were on the King's business, and now I kept wondering why they did not leave us to waddle along alone. But long
after dark they faithfully brought the old gentlemen, exhausted
but happy, to Methyl.

The next day we made our own way through a labyrinth of buoys,
booms, and guard-boats to Leith. It was Sunday and the pubs were
shut. The next day we slowly but proudly passed under the great
bridge and saw the fine ships of the King, and so to Grangemouth
Docks. It was Monday and the pubs were shut. But there we were.
After three weeks of uncomfortable effort, we had duly delivered
our ridiculous charge (and, but for the tow, it might have been
three months). The small dock to which we were directed was full
of her sister-ships, but those who brought them there had gone.
We were asked if we would carry on and take our ship through
the canal to the Clyde. But here, I am glad to say, I said to Duty
and Tenacity, 'Enough!' I said that I had a fellow-feeling for the
mariner who would have to handle our ship in Colombo Harbour,
the Philippines, or Japan, and I would do nothing more to speed
her passage to the unfortunate East until she had been given a
man-sized propeller, or otherwise made reasonably mobile. Besides,
we all seemed to smell the end of the war—and how right we
were! That very morning the 'act of unconditional surrender' had
been signed—and we wanted to be back in London for lighting-up
time—especially as, whatever day it was in Scotland, the pubs, it
seemed, were always shut. We caught the night train from Edin-
burgh and arrived in London at dawn on V.E. Day—8 May. A
neat piece of staff-work by the gods, as far as we were concerned.
And I could say at least that I had been busy for the King (however vainly) till the last moment of the struggle. But, of course, I
should have been on Lüneburg Heath, seeing Victory itself.

39. V.E. Day—and After

Still, it was stirring enough, and far more proper, to be sitting in the House of Commons and waiting for Mr. Churchill to come and tell us the tremendous tale we knew already. For the humble Member of Parliament who has suffered disillusion, discouragement, or boredom there and wonders often why he ever came into the place, such great State occasions are a powerful restorer of conceit and contentment. The Coronation, the Wedding, the Abdication, or the death of Kings, the making of war and peace—he has a right to walk in and sit in the front row (or nearly). He is somebody, after all. I frankly confess to this human weakness, though I have long been free of any itch to be present at theatrical 'First Nights.' And for those who had heard the 'blood and sweat' speech, and the Vote of Censure debate of July 1942, this was like the curtain to the Third Act of a highly satisfying play. My mind went back still further, to a wet November Sunday in '33 or '34, when I had the honour to lunch at Chartwell. Mr. Churchill then was still 'in the wilderness' and looked like being there for ever. But he was writing *Marlborough;* he had his dear wife and children, his painting, his bricks, and his birds on the lake. Though he was sadly concerned about his country and those in charge of her, he talked like Cincinnatus and tried to persuade himself that, with so much to keep him happily busy, he should not worry because he was not wanted. 'It is easy,' I remember him saying, 'to exaggerate one's own importance.' That day, much as I loved and honoured him, I would have laid any odds that he would never be Prime Minister. He was under the same 'hoodoo' as his father. Yet—here he was.

But he was not. He was late. If the historian peeps into our Official Report of the House of Commons, for that great day of Victory, 8 May 1945, he may be surprised to see the following:

PETTY-OFFICER ALAN HERBERT: When do His Majesty's Government propose to proceed with the Outlawries Bill?

HON. MEMBERS: Answer.

SIR J. ANDERSON: We fully understand the implications of that question, and my hon. and gallant Friend knows as much about that matter as I do.

'Incurable frivolity,' the historian may say, but it was not. Mr. Churchill had been broadcasting to the nation, and the British Empire and Commonwealth. There had been some mistake about time, and he was late. Questions were over: some questions had been put to Sir John Anderson about the course of future 'Business,' and he had dealt with that. Still no Prime Minister. The House of Commons, like Nature and the B.B.C., abhors a vacuum. If the appointed thing does not happen, it must go on to the next thing, or adjourn. All that Members could do now to fill the hiatus was to ask further questions about the 'Business of the House,' and in the excitement of the hour it was difficult to think of any. The Third Reading of the Water Bill had been announced for Friday, and Sir Jocelyn Lucas asked: 'Is not water unsuitable business this week?' My Outlawries Bill went well. This is the Bill which is formally read at the beginning of each Session, after the King's Speech. It is supposed to preserve the right of Members to discuss what they will, whatever the topics put into the King's Speech by the Ministers. In fact, it does no such thing. The Bill is not printed, and nobody has ever seen the text of it, though it is believed to be designed 'for the better prevention of clandestine outlawries.' It is, in fact, a sort of fairy. As Members seemed to have dried up again, I returned to it, and Sir John Anderson, who has a slow delivery, well fitted for such an emergency, responded with a noble piece of gagging:

PETTY-OFFICER HERBERT: Further to my point on Business; and arising out of the most unsatisfactory answer, may I ask by what Minister of the Crown the Outlawries Bill was, in fact, introduced, and why it is that such an important Measure, the first Measure considered in a new Session, is not on the Order Paper: and further, may I mention the suspicion that this Bill was in fact introduced by one of the Clerks at the Table, and much as we love them, have not things come to a pretty pass if public Bills are to be introduced by the Clerks at the Table without the sanction of the House?

SIR J. ANDERSON: I thought I was in a position to deal with any matter likely to be raised on the spur of the moment by hon. Friends, but my hon. and gallant Friend's ingenuity has, I must confess, for the moment got the better of me. But I will consult with my right hon. Friend the Home Secretary, who seems definitely to be involved in any question of clandestine outlawries, and perhaps I shall be able to satisfy my hon. and gallant Friend, either privately or in answer to a Question, if he chooses to put one on the Paper.

But still no Prime Minister. Three other Members spun out the queer curtain-raiser for a minute. Sir Herbert Williams asked:

Can the right hon. Gentleman state when the Bill introduced in another place, dealing with Select Vestries, will be brought to this House?

SIR J. ANDERSON: No, sir, I do not know.

Then he came from behind the Speaker's Chair, and we all went mad. Even *Hansard* went a little mad, for the headline

GERMANY (UNCONDITIONAL SURRENDER)

is in the largest, thickest capitals I have ever seen in that grave publication.

After telling the story, Mr. Churchill gave warm thanks to the House of Commons,

which has proved itself the strongest foundation for waging war that has ever been seen in the whole of our long history. We have all of us made our mistakes, but the strength of the Parliamentary institution has been shown to enable it at the same moment to preserve the title deeds of democracy while waging war in the most stern and protracted form. I wish to give my hearty thanks to men of all parties, to everyone in every part of the House where they sit, for the way in which the liveliness of Parliamentary institutions has been maintained under the fire of the enemy and for the way in which we have been able to persevere—and we could have persevered much longer if the need had been—till all the objectives which we set before us of the procuring of the unlimited and unconditional surrender of the enemy had been achieved.

Then he 'begged to move'

That this House do now attend at the Church of St. Margaret, Westminster, to give humble and reverent thanks to Almighty God for our deliverance from the threat of German domination.

'I will go first with the Mace,' said Mr. Speaker. 'Then I invite Privy Councillors to follow in fours . . . and then the rest of the House will fall in behind.'

So we all marched over, bare-headed in the sun, through the cheering crowds. And would that we were all as well together as we were that day!

The whole of that most moving service is set out in *Hansard*, with the names of the twenty-one fellow Members whom we remembered. I thought especially of the gallant Arnold Wilson, who at the age of fifty-five insisted on becoming an R.A.F. machine-gunner; and young Ronnie Cartland, in whom a fine bright flame was put out; and Victor Cazalet, and George Grey, who made that brave speech about Tanks in a Secret Session; and Bob Bernays, who gave up a safe job as Regional Commissioner to join the Army, for which, a psychiatrist told him, he was quite unsuited.

We sang 'O God, our help in ages past,' and

At the conclusion of the Service, THE SPEAKER, *preceded by the Sergeant-at-Arms bearing the Mace, left the Church by the West Door.*
Whereupon, the bells of St. Margaret's Church were rung, in celebration of Victory.

We do these things well.

40. To Lüneburg

A week later there was the victorious Field-Marshal, in full flower, at Claridge's again, with two or three of the happy staff. We flew to Paris in the *Dakota* and saw some fine and unforgettable scenes. Monty waiting alone, in the sunny centre of the quadrangle of the Invalides, for General de Gaulle to come. The huge figure of Napoleon, in the shadow, looked down upon him, but small clambering boys sat on the arms and shoulders of the great Napoleon to see the British general, who, after all, had gone as far and fared better. He looked more like a shy schoolboy himself than a conqueror, a small embarrassed head prefect, waiting for the head master, who was surprisingly late. The tall De Gaulle came, at last, and embraced him right and left, and invested him with the Grande Croix of the Légion d'Honneur. The band played, and we all felt like embracing somebody too. In the streets Napoleon himself, if he had won the Battle of Waterloo, could hardly have had a more rapturous, rosy reception than the Parisians gave 'Montee.' In the Champs Elysées the car could move no faster than my Motor Fishing Vessel. He could have walked for miles on the adoring heads. Duff Cooper, British Ambassador, made a speech in perfect French, and even Monty, in his speech, gallantly performed a brief passage in the local language. In the evening, when the long day's programme was done, the French still crowded the street and courtyard outside the British Embassy and refused to leave. Someone took the Field-Marshal onto a balcony to placate and disperse them if he could. *'Merci,'* he said briefly. *'Et maintenant —allez-vous en.'* 'Alan,' he said afterwards, 'they tell me I said the wrong thing. What should I have said?' 'What did you say, sir?' 'I said, *"Allez-vous en."* That means "Go away," doesn't it?' 'Yes, sir.' 'Well, that's what I wanted. And that's what they did. I think my French must be pretty good.'

We flew on to Lüneburg Heath, the scene of surrender. It was exciting to see the old caravans again (especially Rommel's) which had come from Alexandria (or near it) to the heart of Germany. But there was no lounging in the camp of caravans. To the windy heath came the heads of all departments with pressing problems of Occupation, and Administration, and Intelligence—Himmler— William Joyce—Mrs. Joyce—'non-fraternization'—agriculture and food—the prisoners—the Russians. I was kept busy too. 'Alan will fly over Hamburg and the Kiel Canal.' 'Alan will go to Lübeck to see if our yacht is any good.' (The mess had acquired a small yacht and we did a day's drifting in the Baltic among the wrecks. Later, on a windy day, they took the Field-Marshal out, I believe, and nearly drowned him.) In my guest caravan (which had the cosy feeling of a cabin at sea) I worked hard at my Election Address and wrote 6,000 words, which were kindly typed by two astonished sergeants. Monty was finishing his *High Command in War,* and we exchanged criticisms. His, you will not be surprised to hear, were more useful than mine. All the political parties, I gathered, were then 'approaching' him, but he said very firmly that he did not want to go into Parliament. I told him that he could hardly avoid that, for he would certainly be made a peer. He did not seem to have thought of that. At that time, I believe, if he had been allowed, in slight reward, to choose his future for himself, he would have said, 'Head of an Oxford College—with a garden.' His Latin verse might not have been up to standard, but if clarity of mind and command of character—and language —are useful to the young it might not, I thought, be a bad appointment. And, after all, he is an Honorary Doctor. Cambridge has set two fine examples of this kind, but whether Oxford will ever follow I cannot tell.

One day we drove in to Hamburg to lunch with General Ritchie at the headquarters of 12th Corps, and the Main Brace gave trouble again. The damage we had done to that great city was terrifying to see, but what struck me most was the dock area. Here, though almost everything for many miles was as flat as the shore of our Surrey Commercial, almost all the innumerable little dockland road-bridges seemed to have survived, and there was never a pause. As we sped on towards the suburbs, the Union Jack fluttering bravely on the bonnet, I looked down to the water and saw two White Ensigns among the warehouses. They were the first two ships of the Royal Navy to reach Hamburg, a mine-sweeper and, I think, a sloop. Monty had explained proudly that he had accepted the surrender not only of the German Army, but the naval and air forces as well, and he was, I gathered, in supreme command of everyone. So I drew his attention to the ships. He said, 'After lunch we'll go and see them'; and an A.D.C. was sent ahead to warn the Navy. On the way down I said, 'If you're the Lord High Admiral, sir, and these are the first two Navy ships to get here, you ought to say, "Splice the main brace," don't you think?' 'Splice the main brace?' said Monty. 'What is that?' I explained, in good faith but, they say, in error. We were met by a captain ('the Commodore'), to whom, as we walked down the quay, I confessed the suggestion I had made. 'That's all right,' he said; 'the only thing is, I'm not sure we've got enough rum.' The crews of the two ships were at their stations, ready for the Field-Marshal's inspection. I felt deeply embarrassed, for Monty always made me visit him in my uniform (to save permits and explanations), and I could imagine the kind of things the sailors were muttering about the queer-looking spectacled P.O., 'sculling about' in his No. 1s astern of the Field-Marshal. I slipped away from the party as soon as I could and hid behind a ventilator till the inspection was over. Then both crews fell in on the quay and Monty addressed them from one of the ships. At the end, to my delight, he said something like this: 'I am in command of all the King's forces in this area, including the Navy. I am told that I ought to say "Splice the main brace." I should like to say "Splice the main brace." I do say to the Commodore, if I may, "Splice the main brace!" ' The Commodore saluted and said, 'Make it so.' The crews gave the Field-Marshal a hearty cheer as he left, and I was sorry I could not tell them that it was the queer-looking Petty Officer they had to thank. I have often wondered whether Monty, after that, made a habit of 'splicing the main brace' (as he does of asking for half-holidays at schools), and, if so, what the Admiralty thought. I now know the answer.

The First Sea Lord complained to the War Office that I was not entitled to 'splice the main brace' and asking that I be told not to do it again. I was duly told! I then wrote to the First Sea Lord (Andrew Cunningham) and apologized for breaking the rules. He wrote back a very nice letter. I have not offended in that respect again! You can use this in your story if you like.

Yours ever,

MONTY

The Field-Marshal might well have reproached me for leading him, though innocently, into error and rebuke: but he never did. I still feel that, in the very 'exceptional circumstances,' he was hardly used: but I must not bandy words with their Lordships. I had failed, it seems, to perceive the difference between an 'extra issue' and a 'special issue,' and I apologize.

41. 'Demob'

The demobilization—smooth, efficient, considerate, and just—was a wonderful deed, and it is odd to think that a Government containing so many cruel and clumsy Tories could have conceived and put it through. It must, I think, have been some jester in high places who sent to me, alone of my crew, the Industrial Resettlement Questionnaire. It was mercifully brief, and had two questions only, but I felt that they should have been addressed as well to my mate, Tom Cheesman, fisherman, and my 'stoker,' Dan O'Connor, sanitary engineer. Here they are (to the best of my recollection), with my answer:

(1) What was your occupation before the war?	*Author and Member of Parliament*
(2) Briefly describe the character of your work.	*Good*

My officers passed it on, so I suspected a conspiracy. But perhaps it was this odious levity that brought upon me the ordeal of my 'passing-out' medical examination. We were all borne on the books of H.M.S. *Pembroke,* and would have to go to Chatham

Barracks for the final business of discharge. But it was conveniently, considerately, arranged that many 'ratings' should have their 'medical' on the Admiral's floor of the Port of London Authority Building on Tower Hill. An ordinary office-room was handed over to the medical officer and his staff. About twenty 'ratings' sat in a queue on benches in the corridor outside, and I was last in the queue. The other sailors were all 'square-rigged,' took off their jumpers, and sat in their white singlets. Not wanting to fall behind, I took off my jacket and jersey and sat (for about an hour and a half) in 'shirt-sleeves' and braces. Up and down the corridor there passed before us the ordinary traffic of the Admiralty—Captains, Commanders, heavy with care and papers, Wrens, demure or dimpling, severe Wren officers, tall superior Paymasters, Messengers, Writers, Dispatch-riders, a few civil servants, and civilian workers, the Admiral's Secretary, the Chief of Staff, the Admiral himself. From time to time some officer would recognize me and kindly stop for a chat, in this style:

'Hullo, Herbert—what are you doing?'

Me (standing to attention): 'Being demobilized, sir.'

'Oh? Jolly good show! How's the old *Water Gipsy?*'

'Paid-off, sir. Up at Twickenham.'

'Well, I expect you'll be glad to get back to Westminster?'

'Yes, sir.'

'Well, do what you can for the Navy.'

'Aye, aye, sir.'

'Well, good-bye, Herbert, if I don't see you again.'

'Good-bye, sir—and thank you.'

After several friendly exchanges of this kind, I arrived at last at the top of the queue, and slipped my braces off my shoulders. I undid my collar and loosened my black tie. I entered the little room, and the medical orderly at once thrust into my hand a long vase, looking very much like one of those tall glasses of lager beer.

'TAKE THIS AWAY,' he said bluntly. 'AND BRING BACK SOME OF YOUR OWN.'

I went back into the corridor. This sort of thing had happened to me many times during my nine years in the Navy, but never in such surroundings. The nearest place at which I could obey my orders was about fifty yards away. I set forth at a dignified pace. My tie was hanging down, my braces were hanging down; my trousers were not too secure, but I held my vase stiffly before me, elbow to the ribs, as if I were carrying a rifle 'at the slope' (on the wrong side), and marched ahead.

'This,' I thought, 'should teach elderly Members of Parliament to take a commission when they get the chance.'

I met sailors, who said, 'Well done, P.O.!' which I resented, for what I carried was nothing to do with me.

I met Wrens, who, whether demure or dimpling, glanced at me and my burden and averted their eyes with a secret smile. I thought that perhaps my drill was ill conceived, but I did not know what to do with the damned thing. To hold it behind my back would be to attract even more attention. I compromised, and lowered my hand till the vessel was nestling against my leg, on the starboard side, and I continued the voyage, more stiffly still, as if I were marching 'at attention' (and suffering from cramp).

Then I met officers I knew, hurrying along with papers. They did not see the vessel. They saw their queer friend the Petty Officer, M.P., walking along the corridor in his shirt and trousers, with his braces hanging down; and, with an easy grace, and the most kindly intent, as if this was the most ordinary sight in the world, they stopped and said: 'Hullo, Herbert. What are you doing?' 'Being demobilized, sir,' I said, standing very straight and easing the vessel a little aft, behind the legs. 'Good show! I wish I was. . . .' 'I expect you'll be glad. . . .' 'Yes, sir . . . Westminster. . . .' 'Yes, sir . . . *Water Gipsy*. . . .' '. . . remember the Navy?' . . . 'Aye, aye, sir. . . .' 'You know what Baldwin did?' . . . 'Yes, sir . . . there was that sixpence. . . . Yes, sir. . . .' 'And then they let us down.' . . . 'Yes, sir. . . . Well, good-bye, Herbert.' . . . 'Good-bye, sir—and thank you.'

After three encounters of this kind, I came to harbour; and, after the nervous strain, I was agreeably surprised to find that I was able to execute the second part of the order. On the journey back, there were two more affable conversations. Now I felt a little more easy; at least I was carrying 'my own.' But I was surprised that the doctor, when I saw him at last, discovered no signs of shock, or any pension-worthy neurosis.

I went through the final stage at the Royal Naval Barracks, Chatham. All was done with wonderful efficiency and kindness, and when I walked out in my 'demob suit' with a gratuity and a great envelope of papers to assist me back to civil life, I said good-bye with sadness to the Navy, and thought kindly of the Government which had ordered all these difficult things so well.

42. The Rude Parliament

The triumphant surge of Socialism into the House of Commons was something to see. An old Conservative Member was said to have remarked indignantly: 'They look like a lot of damned constituents!' So many old faces gone, so many hundreds of new ones —I think I know how he felt—as if the Athenaeum or the Carlton Club had been suddenly invaded by a swarm of irreverent strangers from the Savage or National Sporting Club. And their friends and relations were swarming in too—eager for tea, for seats in the Gallery, for a conducted tour round the People's Parliament—*their* Parliament now. The Central Hall, for a month or two, was like Hammersmith Broadway. I was delighted at least to see the long queues for the Gallery stretching into the open street, for I had lectured so often about the virtues of Parliament and chided thousands for calling it the 'talking-shop,' the 'gas-works,' and so on. Those queues, that wide new interest in the place, have continued, I believe, ever since. So far, so good. But in the telephone-box opposite the Members' Smoking Room, on the first day, I read, scribbled in pencil, on the asbestos wall, '10,000,000 TORIES MUST BE WRONG.' I looked with wonder, though in one of the Members' lavatories I had just seen the 'Hammer and Sickle' drawn on the dusty side of a cistern. The next day someone had scribbled out

'MUST' and written 'CAN'T.' Next day 'MUST' was back again. Then someone wrote a long pompous message drawing attention to the undesirability of scribbling on the walls of telephone-boxes, and at last the whole fascinating exhibition disappeared. A small thing, perhaps, but that was the nasty note on which the 1945 Parliament began, in and out of the Chamber. I did not condemn, so strongly as others did, the singing of the 'Red Flag' in the Chamber—poor song though it is. The Socialists were provoked by some Conservative beginning 'For he's a jolly good fellow!' in honour of Mr. Churchill. But what a pity they could not join in that old English ditty on that occasion! After all, with that great man on the bridge, we had all come safely and surprisingly to that harbour together. It was in my mind—and, I am sure, in the minds of many—to pipe up 'God Save the King,' a song we all could sing. But the King's name, I remembered, must not be invoked in the Chamber (an ancient rule); and, apart from that, I felt—wrongly, I hope— that the air of the House was not fit, and ready, just then, for such a solution. That, at least, was my sad impression of that great day when, after six years of struggle against an enemy determined to destroy it, a victorious, freely elected Parliament met again at Westminster. Arrogance, almost the worst of spirits, was in the air.

Arrogance, I am sorry to say—for I am doing my best to be fair —remained, a continual poison, till the end. At the beginning much could be forgiven—and was. Physically, that mountain of triumphant new men on the Government side could not be anything but overwhelming, especially in the early days, when they all sat in their seats as punctual as priests, and as ready to cry aloud when the High Priest gave the word. There were so many of them that they overflowed, quite properly, onto the other side. But then Opposition speakers were disconcerted to hear jeers and hostile interjections coming from behind them. This again could be forgiven on the ground of inexperience, ignorance of Parliamentary niceties. It was, and it was corrected. There was, of course, a mellowing of manners. There were quiet times on unimportant business; there were even compliments across the Floor. But I never liked the few professional interrupters, who sat in their places, doggedly, for hours, waiting for a chance to cry 'Nonsense' or 'What about 1926?' (the longest speeches they ever made). I hated to see a mob of such men yapping incoherent insults at Mr. Churchill, like rats squealing at a lion in his cage. He did not care—indeed, as a rule, if he could hear what they said, he got the better of the exchange: but I cared—for the credit of my countrymen and fellow Members. And whenever there was a big debate, there was such a *concerto* of nastiness, and hate, and imbecile yelling, that I thanked God many times that I was an Independent and could sit silent without disloyalty. I suppose that all Parliaments are entitled to be rude—and perhaps ought to be. Mr. Lloyd George, his son Gwilym has often told me, used to say that the debates of our time were shockingly polite and anaemic. I have been rude myself (though very seldom in interruption). But, to my mind, there is a distinction between a rudeness founded on principle, and a rudeness that springs from personal aversion or class hatred ('We are the masters now!' 'Tory vermin,' and so on). May I put it in this way? I do not believe that if Mr. Churchill and his men had won such a smashing victory at the polls they would have sought to 'rub the Opposition's noses in it.' Indeed, though they had suffered months of violent abuse, and years of insult in the Yellow Books, they began the Parliament with great restraint and quietness. I began my first speech (on Private Members' Time): 'Like all of us, I am most anxious that this new Government should start their difficult voyage with a fair wind and a willing crew,' and I think that was true of 'all of us.' The victors were entitled to their elation, but they would have arrogance as well, to which no man is entitled. Two months later, I see, I began a speech (on the Supplies and Services [Transitional Powers] Bill) in very different style—but it was not my fault, nor the fault of the wicked Tories:

I had not intended to intervene in this debate to-night, but if I had had even less intention to speak, that modicum of intention would have been greatly stimulated and increased by the animal cries I have heard from the other side of the Committee when humble private Members on this side have ventured to do what is their duty—to offer such foolish thoughts as are in their minds. . . . The Fuehrer has spoken, the howling down of the Opposition has been tried . . .

Hansard records 'Laughter' only when the speaker refers to it. Here is an example. I said:

However many blessings right hon. Gentlemen opposite bestow on this country, and I think they may bestow a great many, because I am not a partisan.(*Laughter.*) That is the kind of foolish laughter which will get hon. Members into great trouble before they have finished.

If the Conservatives, in the end, became just as rude and bitter, it was in sheer self-defence.

Some of this sour spirit crept into corners of the Smoking Room, even that neutral territory. I found it very tiresome when two good fellows could not talk for two minutes without some party quip or jeer. In the end, I am glad to say, I made some good friends on the Labour side as I had in my first Parliament; but it took longer.

43. Bills on the Floor

The first tussle ('Division No. 1') was about Private Members' Time. It was disappointing, just after the Victory of Freedom, to have all our rights taken away again, especially as the Session was to last about fourteen months. The excuse now was the Government's great legislative programme of reconstruction. Mr. Eden, Mr. Churchill, the Father of the House (Lord Winterton), W. J. Brown, and others spoke against the ban, but in vain.

I had been working very hard, and had eleven Bills ready, in case the old story should be heard that the private Members had no ammunition. They were not mere names, or dummies, but fully drafted. They were:

A Legal Aid and Advice Bill.
A Judicial Appeals Bill.
A Decree Nisi (Abolition) Bill.
A County Court (Extension of Jurisdiction) Bill.
A Law of Slander Bill.
A Sunday Entertainments Bill.
A Fair Voting Bill (Proportional Representation).
A Hotel and Restaurants Bill.
An Air Advertisements Bill (to prohibit them).
An Education (Latin and Greek) Bill.

A Betting and Bookmakers Bill (my old Bill of 1936).

Not only the 345 new Members, but many others, had never seen our ancient rights in action, and it was necessary to explain them, and our pride in them; but they were not easy to impress.

'A man called Samuel Plimsoll,' I reminded them, 'who wrote the Plimsoll line on all the ships of Britain, began his great career of reform by producing—unsuccessfully, it is true—a Private Members' Bill in this House.' I do not think they laughed at that. But they laughed like anything when I suggested that there were things to be done as important and popular as the socialization of the Bank of England.

I reminded them of my own good fortune, and the contribution that Labour men had made: 'I am not boasting, but I am trying to tell hon. Members what is the scale of these things that we are asked to throw away. . . .'

'Private Members' Bills also bring about a charming camaraderie between the Members of one party and another.' They laughed; they could not imagine it. Camaraderie with Tories? 'I had most ample support from Members of the party on the benches opposite . . . and I shall always be grateful for it. On such occasions Members of all parties get together.' They laughed again. So I said: 'Well, if I were to introduce a Bill to abolish the *decree nisi,* I feel sure it would find a great many supporters on the benches opposite.' And indeed, a year or two later, the Labour Lord Chancellor, the excellent Lord Jowitt, did, by administrative action, practically abolish it.

The odd thing was—and I was duly thankful—that nobody laughed when I flung my eleven Bills on the floor. I suppose, by then, I had persuaded them that I had something to say, and meant what I said:

Lastly, these Standing Orders which we are asked to suspend, are part of the great apparatus of Parliamentary freedom for which we have been fighting. What was the first thing we did this afternoon? . . . We gave a First Reading to the Outlawries Bill, a most extraordinary proceeding. It is a Bill not recommended or introduced by any Members; it is not printed, and it is quite impossible to find a copy of it in the Library. I am not laughing at it. It is a very serious thing. The

purpose of that queer procedure was to establish the right of this
House to discuss what it likes quite apart from the programme of
legislation laid down in the Gracious Speech.

This Motion is taking away a right which we laboriously established
this morning. Hon. Members opposite are against monopolies. Do
they suggest that the Government have a monopoly of wisdom? I am
sad about this. I have worked very hard. Hon. Members may laugh
at my little Bills, but I believe they will be a little more popular with
a great many people than some of the proposals which will later be
laid before us. . . . Look at what this House is doing to me after all
the things I promised to my constituents, and all the things I have
promised to the constituents of other hon. Members. I get a hundred
letters a week, not from my own constituents but from poor people
who are worried about their divorces. (*Laughter.*) There is no laughter about this. They write also about the Poor Persons' Procedure.
I have a Bill here dealing with the provision of legal aid and assistance
for the poor. That is something fundamental, but there is not a word
about it in the Gracious Speech. What am I to say to all those people
who write to me? I must tell them to stop sending their letters and to
save their stamps, because I can do no more to help them if this Motion
goes through; I might just as well be a Member of the German Reich-
stag or a stuffed exhibit in the Natural History Museum. If the House
will not have my Bills on the Table I cast them on the Floor, as a
monument to Parliamentary liberty and a challenge to despotic power.

This, I dare say, was a crazy melodramatic thing to do, and as
I tossed the bundle into the middle of the Floor, I thought, 'This
will be the biggest laugh for centuries.' But there was no laugh—
not a sound.

While I continued, more mildly, asking for some compromise or
concession, I was thinking—so many ways can the mind work at
once—'How the devil can I get my Bills back with dignity?' I finished with a prophecy which was sadly true: 'If this Motion is
accepted to-day I believe that next year the right hon. Gentleman
will come forward with some other reason why Private Members'
Time should be taken, and not only in this Session but in all the
Sessions.'

Mr. Herbert Morrison was polite and complimentary ('a very

interesting, witty, eloquent, and quite relevant speech'), but he was adamant. Wc fought the same battle every Session, and got nothing till 1949. But every battle helped to keep the cause alive.

Sir Jocelyn Lucas picked up my Bills and handed them to me—an anti-climax, I thought. But nobody saw.

44. A Tale of Bravery

'Aug. 31—Began Big Ben,' says the little diary. The election over, the new Parliament in recess, I turned to the theatre again, to which I had given no more than a wistful thought during the war. This is not a theatrical record, but during my Parliamentary time I wrote the words for six musical plays (all for Sir Charles Cochran), and, except during the war, the theatre was always a comforting link with my past, and proper, life. I do not see how, in these days, a Member of Parliament could write a novel worth reading, for this requires calm and concentration, sustained, continuous toil. But between Parliament and the stage there is an evident affinity. Spasmodic effort, sudden spurts, brilliant improvisations may have big results. Neither is a whole-time one-man job like a novel, so one can dart from one to the other with fair success.

'Sept. 15—Finished First Draft Big Ben,' I see. Sixteen days—lyrics and all. On the 'first draft' I work like a madman, day and night, till it is done. 'Sixteen days!' you may say. 'An easy way of earning income-tax.' But that is only the beginning of 'six months hard.' Apart from anything the producer has to say, the composer—in this case my very good friend the brilliant Vivian Ellis—now begins to tear the thing to bits. Which comes first, so many say, the words or the music? The answer is—both. Wherever he can—

and it is much more convenient if he can—the composer sets the
words as written, subject to slight alterations for singability, suitable vowel-sounds, and so on. But sometimes the musical scheme
which the words suggest to him is too small to contain all the words,
so I must 'cut' somehow; or it is too large for him, and then
I am given four new lines of music to provide with words, which
takes as long, very often, as the writing of a whole song. Then he
will be independently inspired to three or four tunes to which I
write the words. In three of the 'hits' of *Bless the Bride* the music
came first. You may remember a song called 'Ma Belle Marguerite,'
sung with great effect by M. Georges Guétary. It was supposed to
be 'an old French song,' and many kind critics seemed to think that
it was. Not at all. Before we ever heard of that fine artist, M.
Guétary, Vivian Ellis rang me up from Chappell's, where he has
a telephone by the piano, and said, 'I think I've got a good tune.'
'Play it,' I said, and over the telephone came a lively tinkle, like
cow-bells far away. 'Fine,' I said, 'but what a job for me!' He sent
me a 'top-line,' and I wrote a song, partly in French, about a donkey,
with bells on it, I know not why. Everybody seemed to like it, but
'C.B.C.' said: 'Haven't there been a lot of songs about donkeys?'
I could remember only the 'Dear little donkey' duet in *Véronique*,
but during the war, it seemed, there had been a 'Donkey's Serenade'
in *The Lisbon Story*, which I, occupied on the river, had never heard
of. So I scrapped the donkey and wrote another song, all in French,
about a tired soldier who was always calling upon his captain to halt:

> *Mon brav-e Capitaine-e,*
> *Arrêtez, s'il vous plaît!*

But the Captain would never halt, even when Madeleine-e was
waving from the window. It was very sad. Nobody said much about
this, one way or another, and at last I was asked to try again. I said
I would try once more—but no more, for I was tired of the task,
and so 'Ma Belle Marguerite' was painfully born. Ellis wrote three
or four tunes for another song before he was satisfied. I think we
earn our money.

We also earn many shocks and sorrows from which the novelist
is spared. The first night of *Big Ben* had a true *I Pagliacci* flavour.

All through rehearsals, all through the twelve weeks' successful tour, Sir Charles had been very ill. That brave man is nearly always in pain with arthritis, and now he had nasty internal trouble as well. Yet he followed the play to Scotland and all round England, an attentive eye on everything, as usual, words and music, scenery and shoes, the actors and the band. At the last dress-rehearsal in London everything went wrong: the scenery jammed for half an hour, one of the leading ladies fell on the stairs and came on in tears with a swollen ankle and a plastered knee. 'C.B.,' very sick himself, insisted on hobbling up to the dressing-rooms well after midnight. And the next morning the doctors decreed that he was too ill to attend his own first-night—his 'comeback' after the war. It was a 'brilliant' night. Royalty, the Prime Minister, Field-Marshal Montgomery, some of the Cabinet, many from the House, were there. The show went well. But I had this sad, secret letter in my pocket, and all the evening I had small pleasure, wondering how he was. In the interval, when merry friends cried, 'Where's "C.B."?' I said, according to orders, 'He's fine! Upstairs' (or 'Downstairs,' as the case might be). And at the end I had to go on the stage and face the wall of light, and break the news. They took him to a nursing-home, and the next night, at midnight, the Press Association rang up about a rumour that he was dead. Next morning the B.B.C. rang up and said that they had heard he might die at any moment. I said I did not think it was as bad as that. They said that that was their information: the public had had no warning and would be shocked, and they had nothing ready. Would I prepare and record a three-minutes' 'obituary notice'? Five o'clock would be convenient. I said that I had arranged to go and see him at six: it seemed a little ghoulish to pronounce his obituary just before. But they insisted, and after a miserable afternoon of composition, I did it—the most distressing job of my life. The tough old gentleman had a tough time, and now, as I have said before, he has only one kidney—but he has three hearts. A fortnight later, a hot August afternoon, Vivian Ellis and I sat by his bed. He was very weak. The critics, as usual, had given us a 'mixed reception.' Old Mr. Agate had been spiteful, as usual, and had even repeated his pompous opinions at the sick man's bedside,

for which I will never forgive that malignant ghost. 'Business' was
not too good. Though the tour had been a success, it had made
no money (for the theatres were too small). Vivian and I, apart from
all that, were by no means sure that he was out of the wood yet,
and were, not unreasonably, in low spirits. Suddenly the sick man
said, 'I want you two to write another play for me.' Such courage
commands devotion and obedience. A few days later, on 21 September, I began a new piece, and I finished the first draft on 11 August
—three weeks again. That piece, so strangely, so stoutly commis-
sioned was *Bless the Bride,* which ran for more than two years in
London, came off in very good condition, and is running round the
country still. 'Say not that courage naught availeth. . . .'

Critics and theatre-folk are often heard to say, when a play does
not go well, that they cannot understand how experienced men can
ever have put it on with hope of success. This, with great respect, is
to forget that the theatre is about the most incalculable of human
enterprises. It is like wondering why Eisenhower chose rough weather
for D-Day. Not even Monty, I think, could command success on the
stage. *Tough at the Top,* which followed *Bless the Bride* at the
Adelphi, was a good example. Cochran, Lord Vivian (his partner),
Ellis, and I all thought it was—or would be—a better show than
'the Bride,' and one or two critics said the same. Ellis's music,
though not perhaps so 'popular,' had a new maturity and distinction, and my 'book,' I still think, was a worthier work. One very
rude critic thought that I had 'not taken trouble' or, perhaps, was
'despising the public'—but these are crimes I have never committed.
We had the famous designer, Oliver Messel, and the same most able
producer, Wendy Toye. The singing and the band were fine, and
there was sufficient fun, though I say it myself, especially from that
brilliant young comedian, Brian Reece. But it came off after five
months, and lost I know not how much money. True, it opened in
July and suffered twelve weeks of an unprecedented summer. True,
it was far too expensive, and Heaven knows how long it would have
had to run to show a profit. True, it had an 'unhappy' ending, and
a not very attractive title. True, I wrote the play for Lizbeth Webb,
and she was not engaged. True, some of the critics were not very

kind. We were much abused for going to 'Ruritania': but a few months later nobody complained of that magician, Mr. Ivor Novello, going to 'Ruritania.' But I am not complaining. They were not much kinder about *Bless the Bride;* and they, and all things, can be survived if the total effect is right. Evidently, somehow, it was not. And I am only concerned to show that the best of producers can make no bets in the theatre, which is one of the big arguments against the Entertainments Tax. You can see the same thing in the House of Commons. A Minister opens a debate, calm and complacent. Something, wholly unforeseen, is said or done, and the day ends in uproar. This was my thirteenth musical production. It was the first time I ever 'had my name in lights'; and, when I saw them, I said to a friend, 'I'm sure it will be fatal.' That is as near as I can get to a rational explanation of a melancholy mystery.

The theatre is a fascinating but disturbing mistress. You sigh for her when you are not with her, but she is an endless worry when you are, even if she smiles. If you write a book, the critics may like it or not, the public may buy it or not. But you do not see the public *not* buying it; you do not see or hear them disliking it. Nobody can boo, or go out ostentatiously in the middle of it.[1] Nor, if it fails, are you likely to ruin your publisher, or throw a great many people out of employment. A book is not, like a play, the prey of chance and circumstance outside your control—sickness, accident, faulty casting or direction, bad weather. It stands, or falls, by itself. How often have I sat in the stalls, at a difficult stage of rehearsals, and thought:

Everything seems to be going wrong. Fifteen or twenty thousand pounds have been spent already on the production, and it will have to run 'to capacity' for six months before it begins to show a profit. Sixty good people are employed upon the stage, twenty or thirty behind it, twenty-five in the band. Fortunes, reputations, livelihoods, depend upon this affair. There are many others engaged in it, and all that goes wrong cannot be put down to me. But still, it all began far

[1]But Sinclair Lewis told me this story. Crossing the Atlantic, he saw an old lady on deck reading his latest book, about which there had been some hot discussion. By the number of pages she had read, he had judged that she was approaching the shocking passage which had caused most trouble, and he thought he would keep an eye on her, to see how it would affect her. Presently the old lady rose up, walked firmly to the rail, and flung the book far into the ocean.

back when I sat down in Cornwall and wrote upon some fair white paper: 'ACT ONE, Scene One.'

What a responsibility!

If you write an unsuccessful book, it is a pity; but by that time you are busy on another. If a play is harshly received, or even has a faint aroma of failure, you go about London feeling like a leper. Even if it looks like a success it is always jogging your elbow, and saying, 'Quite sure?' You have survived the agonies of rehearsal ('All seems pretty well, but what would happen if the baritone falls under a bus, or the leading lady's "throat" continues?'), the emotional ordeal of the First Night, the un-Christian insults (as you think) of ignorant and jealous scribes. 'Business' is pretty good. You stroll into the theatre, to see how things go, or simply, let us confess, to enjoy yourself. It may be a vanity, but it is a pleasing thing to make people laugh, and a thing more pleasing still to hear them laughing. I weary very soon of listening to my own dialogue, but I never tire of listening to my composer's music, especially a song that the public seem to like as much as we did. Well, the house is full. But the leading lady —or, worse, the 'comedian'—is 'off.' The valiant understudy does well, but not well enough for you, and you go into the bar for comfort. A strange man totters in from the stalls, panting, as if he had just escaped from the Gestapo. 'Give me a brandy,' he says. 'This is the lousiest show I ever saw!' He is only one out of two thousand, perhaps, but he is discouraging. You go round 'behind,' to show the company you have not forgotten them. The leading lady is in tears: her throat is worse and 'the Income Tax' has upset her. (But this is nothing. Within a few months of the opening of *Big Ben* both the leading ladies departed to have babies.) The baritone is reproachful: he should have had a better song. The comedian still thinks he should have a funnier exit-line in Scene Three; you still think he says it wrong. Someone else has had a searing row with the stage-manager, and you hear both sides. Then, one day, there are gaps in the stalls. Receipts are 'down' on last week. Nobody can understand it, and all the good old reasons are discussed. It is very bad weather, or it is very good weather. It is the fog, the snow, or the sunshine. It is just before a public holiday, when people are saving up their money; or just after a public holiday, when they have spent all their money. It is the Christmas shopping season—or election time—a time of national mourning—or national rejoicing, when the Government is giving free shows in the streets. Every morning a 'return' of last night's receipts arrives by post—anxiously compared with the week before. Every day somebody writes to say that he loved the play, but he couldn't hear a word—and *can't* you do something about this or that? The thing is nagging at you all the time. A book keeps quiet.

Against all this, you have some respectable pleasures not enjoyed by the novelist, high and dry and undisturbed in his study—the pleasure, for example, of communal effort, of working with a team. This is very good for you. In no other industry, I suppose, are the different levels and departments so close together. The stage-hand, the electrician, who are never seen, the chorus-singers and small-part players, are as keen upon the common business as the manager, stars, or author. The property-man or linesman is no less proud of success and even more resentful of unjust (as they think) criticism. It is their show too. When the fortnight's notices go up at last, and the play is under sentence of death, we are moved by more than loss of money or employment. It is like the breaking-up of a happy family or regiment. We have shared many toils and trials and emotions. The painted scenery has become a common home. The costumes and characters have taken on a kind of reality. There is no cause for tragical thought—except, perhaps, for the bold men who have risked, and lost, their money. In a few weeks, perhaps, the golden girls will be pattering and chattering up the stairs of another theatre, as merry as ever. But there is much food for honest sentiment. The living unity that we built up together is to die, and tomorrow we shall be sixty or seventy separate individuals again, sharing nothing but memories. So we are inclined to weep a little. But there are still the songs and the music. And we can gather round the family piano and croak the tunes again and wistfully revive the old days, Miss X and Mr. Y, and the happy crowds. This is something. I do not think that any novelist sits down and sentimentally reads his forgotten books.

Happy the writer, I think, who can bite a bit—if it is only a little bit—from both these worlds. Happy, indeed, if he has the fortune to serve two such luminous masters as Sir Nigel Playfair and Sir Charles Cochran. I was highly delighted when His Majesty honoured 'C.B.' with a knighthood. But, if I had been Prime Minister, it would have been the 'O.M.'

45. Snub for King James

On 12 October 1944 Mr. D. N. Pritt, on the House of Commons (Redistribution) Bill, put down an amendment attacking the University seats, which had been excluded from the Bill by the agreement of all parties. His last words were:

If we did not have University Members, and anyone were to propose that we should have, it would be very difficult to find any argument in favour of it.

I was called after him, and was able to cap his concluding remark. The week before I had gone across to Dieppe in a trawler. In a café a British officer introduced me to some Frenchmen as 'M. Herbert—*un député Anglais.*' That did not excite the Frenchmen very much: but one of them said politely, 'What part of England do you represent in the Chamber of Deputies, M. Herbert?' I drew myself up and said proudly, '*L'Université d'Oxford.*' At once they pricked up their ears. '*C'est vrai?* The universities are represented in the Parliament? *Très gentil—très moderne!*' One of them called another over, and, with sparkling eyes, told him the big news. 'M. Herbert in the Chamber represents the University of Oxford. All the universities are there.' '*Mais oui?*' said the other. 'Ah yes, that is the "reconstruction"—yes?' To them the arrangement seemed, not an antiquated 'anomaly' but something highly enlightened and 'progressive'—as indeed it is—something, moreover, which an advanced democracy might well think worthy of inclusion among its measures of postwar reform.

Official Labour was then abiding by the unanimous conclusion of the all-party Speaker's Conference that the University seats should be preserved. So Pritt was defeated by 152 votes to 16.

But his day was to come.

March 16, 1948 should be marked in black—or perhaps red—in the diaries of University men and women, for that was the decisive day in the slow and treacherous strangling of University Representation. There voted, for Mr. Churchill's amendment to preserve us, 198; for the destroyers, 328. Five Independent Liberals voted against us, and only two, I am sorry to say, for us (one of the two was that monument of good sense, Gwilym Lloyd George; his sister, charming Megan, was in the other lobby. Where, I wondered, would Papa have been?). One Labour Member, Mr. Skeffington-Lodge, bravely voted against his party.

The debates were able, obstinate, and bitter.

Arthur Salter, Kenneth Pickthorn, John Anderson, Harry Strauss (and others) stoutly developed the charge that the thing being done was done in breach of an honourable obligation binding the Prime Minister and other Ministers who had been members of the Speaker's Conference; and those accusations were firmly, but feebly, resented. I never heard a good answer, but I thought too much time was given to this.

Certainly far too much was given, as usual, to the personal qualities of University Members, past and present.

The missionary, I imagine, does not bother to accuse the cannibal king of unethical conduct, and the cannibal king does not inflict upon the missionary an abusive speech about his character and ancestors before he pops him into the pot. But it seems impossible to discuss this constitutional question without the intrusion of 'personalities.' Even Oxford's quarrel with Mr. Gladstone in 1865 was used as an argument against the representation of Oxford in 1948.

I saw one letter from a Member to a constituent in which he said that the University Members were 'men of narrow outlook' and included 'two of the worst snobs in the House.' In the debates it was said that we were poor attenders, that two of us were confessed Tories, and the others Tories in disguise, some of whom had gone so far as to vote against the Government. One Member (a University man) said, 'So I divide the University Members into two sorts—the spineless ones and the party advocates. I want to see the open party Members in this House; I do not want the spineless ones.'

Mr. Woodburn, on the other hand, Secretary of State for Scotland, in two extraordinary speeches, took the opposite view. 'When the universities can be used to retain purely party Members' (Mr. Walter Elliot and Mr. Henry Strauss) 'without their having a specially independent character in this House, then I suggest that that is a breach of the arrangements we came to in the Speaker's Conference.' It came almost as a warming compliment when one Member said of us, 'I should have thought, on the whole, one could say they were typically average hon. Members of this House and of neither more nor less distinction.'

In fact, I think we were a pretty good lot. Three of the twelve were Privy Councillors—no mean proportion; and first-class University degrees are not necessarily a proof of incompetence. But here is a little evidence from an impartial observer, the Parliamentary correspondent of the *Manchester Guardian:*

Whatever may be said for or against the abstract justice of one man, one vote, there is no denying that the sacrifice of University Representation to the principle means a sad loss to the House of Commons on the personal side. There was hardly one of the university members in the late Parliament who did not bring a strong individual flavour to its debates, and several of them acquired considerable authority, while one, Sir John Anderson, achieved eminence. . . .

All this is nice to read, but in public debates in the House, whether we were being described by our friends as paragons of intelligence and independence, or whether, provoked by these praises (and I did not wholly blame them), the other side were representing us as horrid partisans, men of narrow outlook and inferior industry, I found it equally embarrassing. When this sort of talk began I felt that we should all walk out and leave the others to dissect us.

It was irrelevant as well as embarrassing. The only question is: Should the universities be represented or not? If they should, they should be free, like others, to choose whom they will, independent or partisan, poet, professor, or pugilist. If, in fact, they sometimes choose outstanding men of lively mind and large experience, that is a happy accident. But no one is entitled to insist upon it.

I have nothing to add to the words which Arthur Salter and I used in our farewell letter to *The Times:* 'A most stupid and spiteful act.'

46. To the Argentine

The International Confederation of Societies of Authors and Composers held its Fifteenth Conference (*Congreso*) at Buenos Aires. I was privileged to be one of the British delegates. I went there on the good ship *Highland Brigade,* and returned in the good ship *Andes,* both of the Royal Mail. Instead of writing, I played with my sextant and my sums and studied the stars; and swam and lay in the sun till I looked like a Brahmin. I wrote the words for 'Crossing the Line' and persuaded Sir John Balfour, our new Ambassador to Buenos Aires, to take first 'dip.' I love this life, and I think if I were rich, I should buy a great ship and steam up and down across the Equator, between 20°N. and 20°S., for ever—well, for a long time.

Though I spent ten days in Buenos Aires and two nights at Rio, I shall not attempt a description of the South American Continent.

We were the guests of the Argentine Government, so I must make no political comments: but I may, I hope, relate the tale of Sir William Walton. Our ship was late, so I did not have the honour of meeting El Presidente Perón or his lady, Señora Eva. But I saw them glittering far off at a 'gala performance' at the magnificent Teatro Colon (about twice the size of Covent Garden), and 'on the air' I heard them address the multitude in the Plaza. It was the anniversary of the day when the *descamisados* ('shirtless ones') 'stormed the Bastille' and carried General Perón from prison to power. There was no doubt now about his hold upon them. They had come to the capital in special trains and lorries from all over the country. It was a public holiday, of course; and at the end of the speech El Presidente declared the next day, Monday, a public holiday. The previous Tuesday, on which my ship arrived, had been a public holiday—the Day of the Race (Columbus Day elsewhere). So that was three public holidays in my first seven days. And holidays there are holidays for all. Not one waiter, barman, porter, or chamber-maid was on duty at any hotel, restaurant, or club. Not one, I think, would dare. The meeting and the speeches were strongly reminiscent of the style and method of Herr Hitler. The General would make some short, sharp remark. *'Abajo los oligarchos!'* ('Down with the oligarchs!'), and then the crowd, not content with cheering, would chant, 'Perón! Perón! Perón! Perón! Evita! Perón!' Another loud cry: 'They shall not defeat us!' and the crowd chanted again. Some-times a section would break into a song. It must be most exhausting, both for speaker and audience, and it takes a long time to say very little.

But this was for the populace in the Plaza. When the President, early in the morning, did the authors and composers of the world the honour to open their Conference, I was told, he was urbane and charming; and the speech, which I read, had many kind references to *La Libertad* (Liberty). But even there the audience thought it right to chant 'Perón! Perón! Evita! Perón!' at the end.

Our own Mr. Leslie Boosey, the music publisher, who for many years had done wonderful work as President of the Confederation, briefly replied, and thanked El Presidente.

Sir William Walton, the famous composer, was one of the British delegates. He was standing at the back, and at the end he told me he had two thoughts. One was, 'When in Rome, do as Rome does,' and the other was, 'Speak for Britain.' So he called out, *'Boo-*sey! *Boo-*sey! *Boo-*sey! *Boo-*sey!'

This, I believe, was not well received in any quarter.

May I, Young Man, for international conferences, modestly com-mend my 'Own Interpreter' trick? Nowadays, at the serious meetings, they may have this magical Nuremberg-each-way-head-phones-interpreter arrangement. But one evening there will be a Farewell Banquet, at which this machinery is not available, and you will be ordered to make a gracious and amusing speech to an audience very few of whom understand your language. Your countrymen will laugh, if they can (they have heard all your jokes and stories before); but (even if you produce a new one) in that crowd of wondering foreigners their laughter will sound as small and rare as the kisses of fish or the compliments of two Communist leaders in the Balkans. Then some interpreter gets up and whispers inaudibly, and uncertainly, into the microphone: 'Mr. H. has said that he is in favour of the sentiments the most profound, etc.' And no one, quite rightly, pays the smallest attention.

The Fourteenth Conference was held in London. I was 'told off' to make a speech at the ultimate feast at the Mansion House, and I thought I would try a new, and rather perilous, drill. I had a little French, and more than half the delegates had more, so I composed a speech in alternate English and French couplets—the French (pretty roughly) translating the English—this sort of thing:

> *To-night, if you'll forgive me, sir,*
> *I am my own interpreter.*
> *Pardonnez-moi—ce jour de fête,*
> *Je suis, moi-même, mon interprète.*

Most of it was better than that, I think, and it went pretty well. And now, it was suggested, I should be ready to do a similar performance in Spanish. The weak point was that I knew about two words of Spanish only.[1] But I got three of Hugo's admirable little paper books, and studied them, now and then, for a fortnight. In the second week I began my speech, and it was ready before we sailed. Almost everyone in the ship had a go at it, Argentines, Uruguayans, Paraguayans, and His Excellency Sir John Balfour, who is a master of many tongues. We added a couplet or two, and made some small corrections, but at the end it was little different from the speech I had composed after a week of Hugo, who deserves full marks. Here it is:

[1] 'Cerveza'—beer; 'muchacha'—girl.

ORAÇION INGLESA Y ESPAÑOLA
DE
A. P. HERBERT

Poet and politician I: as such
It well may be that I have talked too much
Como poeta—y como diputado—
Yo he hablado—quisá—demasiado.
At all events, a law has just been passed
By which, quite soon, I'll have to speak my last.
Una ley mi país ha pasado
Por la que, pronto, estaré eliminado.
Not much encouragement, you'll understand,
To making speeches in a foreign land.
No tengo, pues, mucha tentación,
En otro país de hacer oraçión.
But still I feel a duty to suggest
Some of the things that bubble in my breast.
Pero quiero dar expresión
A lo que siento en mi corazón.
You may inquire the reason, I suppose,
Why I am not addressing you in prose.
Preguntarán ahora una cosa,
Por qué el Inglés no les perora en prosa.
Because—and this should comfort the reporter—
Verse is or ought to be, a good deal shorter.
Porque, cosa que mucho les importa,
La poesía debiera ser más corta.
How many words the statesman flounder through
To say what poets would express in two!
Cien palabras de los políticos
Sabe el poeta comprimir en dos.

Behold, O World, a sight not often sighted—
The Kings of Music happily united!
Mira, O Mundo, a esta compañía,
Reyes Unidos—sí!—de la Armonía!
Music and Poetry, most fruitful match—
What eggs they lay—how busily they hatch;
La Poesía y la Música—
Boda feliz, y fertilísima!

We do not labour to destroy our sons
With bombs, torpedoes, hand-grenades, or guns.
No fabricamos nada destructivo—
Bombas, cañones, o alto explosivo.
It is our happy, honourable place
To fashion gladness for the human race.
Nuestra gloria, nuestra gana
Es de deleitar la raza humana.
A little tune, a simple word or two
May do what Parliaments can never do.
Arias pequeñas, verso de sentimiento
Harán, tal vez, mas que el Parlamento.
Poor poets, rich composers, we all know
A certain cure for almost every woe.
Poetas pobres, ricos compositores
Sabemos disipar muchos dolores.
Is the old world as worried as a debtor?
Play it a tune, and it will feel much better.
Toda la tierra esta apesadumbrada?
Y bien—que la Música sea tocada!
When it appears that nothing's going well
A song is more consoling than a shell.
Por evitar las tribulaciones
Más valen canciones que cañones.
If Russia keeps her negative position
You need a poet, not a politician.
Y si el Ruso es siempre crítico
Vale más el poeta que el político.
Behold, O World, a sight not often sighted—
The Kings of Music happily united.
Mira, O Mundo, a esta compañia,
Reyes Unidos—sí!—de la Armonía!

Buenos Aires (no truer name could be)
We'll not forget your hospitality.
Buenos Aires—buenos en verdad—
Recordaremos su hospitalidad.
The Argentine, a silver shining star,
From our small sky will not be quite so far.
La Argentina, estrella luciente,

En nuestro cielo brillara firmamente.
A happy land of beauty and the bold,
The face of silver and the heart of gold.
Doncellas rubias y suelo moro,
Cara de plata y corazón de oro.
Ladies with flowers in every glance they fling,
So that the streets are like a lawn in spring.
Damas de ojos tan encantadores,
Que cada calle es un jardín de flores!
We live, the two of us, beside the shore:
We ask to live in peace—and not much more.
Ambos vivimos al lado de la mar,
Ambos queremos en la paz durar.
You have, my friends, what I should like to take:
You want the sterling—I must have the steak.
Aquí tienen lo que yo quiero:
Busco la carne—ustedes el dinero.
And British tummies never should forget
How much to Argentina they're in debt.
Y el estómago Inglés se siente
Muy agradecido al gaucho valiente.
So, hand in hand, we'll climb the lofty slope,
Old England and the Argentine, I hope.
Juntos subimos por la Cordillera,
La Argentina y la Inglaterra!

(to the Chairman):

Good sir, good friends we must forever be.
In vino veritas—so drink with me.
Señor, llámame siempre su amigo.
In vino veritas—bebed conmigo.

Unhappily, there was no banquet; but I fired off the *oraçion* at a gathering of Argentine writers, and they seemed to like it. One of them, a poet, saw me off in the *Andes,* and kindly gave me a volume of Spanish poetry and a Spanish Rhyming Dictionary. But it is not my favourite language for light verse. It has too many long words like *demasiado* (too much)—which take up half a line. French is much easier.

You, Young Man, may not have the time for light verse. But you can still be your own interpreter, in prose.

Then, for similar occasions, or long Parliamentary missions, may I recommend the Speech Sweepstake? I naughtily invented this in 1925 when I represented *Punch* at the Third Imperial Press Conference at Melbourne. For three months we travelled round the mighty continent, making, or suffering, speeches. Many a day we had speeches all day—at breakfast (after a night in the train), at lunch, at tea-time, and at dinner. The strong men who live in the great open spaces delight in speeches. We took it in turn to make our own, and there were many good ones. The late Lord Burnham was our excellent leader and had to speak everywhere, poor man. There was John Astor, proprietor of *The Times,* with a quiet but delightful turn of humour, and a young man called Anthony Eden; Sir Harry Brittain, Sir Frank Newnes, Lord Iliffe, and others. But all the speeches must be, more or less, the same, and no one could avoid repeating his pet jest or story. We became stupefied with speeches, half-mad with speeches. The Speech Sweepstake was a great relief, though it had, no doubt, the nature of a giggle in church and received due frowns from some of our seniors.

You 'draw' (as you draw for horses in the Derby) for the main speakers on the toast list. There is a prize for the Longest Speech and another for the Shortest Speech. If the entrants are numerous enough you can have also a Special Prize for the 'Best Remark,' or the 'Worst Cliché.' The point is that, however long, dull, familiar, or numerous the speeches, the interest of the 'sweepers' is closely held till the very end of the banquet. So the speakers should be grateful. In fact, they seldom are; and, as a rule, if they hear about the game, they resent it. The timekeeper must be careful not to let Mr. A., the speaker, see him referring to his watch, for this throws Mr. A. into a frenzy. Besides, it is unfair to the man who has drawn A. and hopes that he will win the 'Longest.' But a little mild cheating adds to the fun and does no harm. Mr. A., shall we say, has spoken for twenty-one minutes and looks like a winner. Mr. B. does eighteen, but begins to flag. 'The hour is late,' he says; 'I must detain you no more.' Instead of the customary sigh of relief, he is surprised and delighted to hear a loud voice cry, 'No, no! Go on, sir! Go on!' (This is from the holder of Mr. B.) 'Well,' says Mr. B., 'I did want to say a word about immigration. Last year, as you all know, there were twenty thousand immigrants from——' *'Forty thousand!'* cries the loud voice. Mr. B., taken aback, looks for the Voice, and says, 'Twenty thousand, I think you will find, sir. Some mistake, I am sure. In fact, I think I have the figures here.' He finds the figures, and reads them out, and there is great applause. Mr. B. has now got his second wind, makes a few more points he had thought of leaving out, sails on into a peroration and easily qualifies for the Longest Speaker. In such disgraceful fashion I have seen good money won.

All this can make a dreary banquet as exciting as a horse-race. I have even seen the last speaker, who was fancied for the Shortest, come out and win the Longest at the post.

The Best Remark is sometimes difficult to judge. But here is a good, and true, example. There was a great State Dinner to the Imperial Press at Wellington, the capital of New Zealand—white ties, decorations and all, seventy journalists from all over the Empire, a very solemn occasion.

Mr. Pomare, the lively Minister for the Maoris, made a speech, in which he said:

People often ask me to what I attribute my success in life. I tell them that my great-grandfather ate the first Presbyterian missionary to land upon this island; and I attribute my success in life to the Scottish blood in my veins.

I won a good prize for that.

47. 'We Could Not Risk It'

I must complete the long story of Newfoundland, as briefly as I can. After all, it concerns the death—I think the murder—of a Dominion.

In 1948 the Newfoundlanders by a 52–48 per cent majority—78,000 in a poll of 150,000—voted for union with Canada. Mr. Mackenzie King, when Prime Minister of Canada, had stipulated that the Newfoundlanders should indicate their will *'clearly and beyond all possibility of misunderstanding.'* As I pointed out, you cannot alter one comma of the American Constitution or even one of the Rules of Cricket without a two-thirds majority. But now this narrow verdict was considered sufficient; and Whitehall and Canada had charged ahead.

The King's speech, on 26 October, said: 'Legislation will be laid before you to give effect to whatever decisions may result from the negotiations for admitting Newfoundland to the Canadian Confederation.'

I returned from Argentina in the noble S.S. *Andes* (Captain Casey) on 6 November. The following week three fighting Newfoundlanders arrived in London with their Petition to the House of Commons, and a great bag full of signatures. They had, they said, 50,000 names, and before they left they had issued a writ against the

Commission of Government. They did not expect to do any good in the Newfoundland courts, but they hoped, in the end, to reach the Judicial Committee of the Privy Council.

They were fighters indeed, and very good company. The leader was a quiet businessman, Mr. Frederick Marshall. Then there was Mr. Peter Cashin, a former Finance Minister (and full of figures), and Mr. John G. Higgins, K.C., a constituent of mine and a fine lover of Oxford, with a poetic soul. These two were of Irish blood and could not always be described as 'quiet.' They loved a song. All three had been Members of the Newfoundland Legislature in the old days, and all three had worn the King's uniform in one or other of our wars.

I studied the sheets of names in the big bag. It was a wonderful feat, I thought, to have collected 50,000 signatures—and they said that but for a strike on the railway they would have brought more. It is one thing, as I know well, to get fifty men into the Lobby when the bell rings, but it is quite another to go about the House and persuade fifty men to sign their names to anything—even if it is the Ten Commandments. And these names had been gathered in innumerable far-flung villages round 6,000 miles of coast. I saw the names of many outports we had visited, and many of the names of Old England—the Pilgrims, Grenfells and Loders. On one page, as I told the House, I saw Tarrants and Turpins, Blakes and Drakes, a Samuel Butler and a William Churchill (who made his mark). It was a moving thing to see those thousands of simple scrawls, and I felt that there was something very solid behind them.

(While they were preparing the Petition, by the way, it was arranged for an appeal for signatures to be made on the radio. At the last moment the Commission of Government forbade it. But two Commissioners had been permitted to use the radio to obtain support for Confederation. Mr. Gordon-Walker frankly admitted to me that the facts were as I have given them, but I never heard any defence of this queer exercise of partial power.)

I asked the Prime Minister to receive my friends. He said, very rightly, that first we should see the Secretary of State. I took them to lunch at the House of Commons. Mr. Noel-Baker, by chance, passed our table and I introduced them. It was not a very cordial encounter.

On 23 November 1948 I presented the Petition to the House. I had never presented a Petition before, and even this, Young Man, is not so simple as it sounds. It must be written (not printed or typed). It must be free from 'interlineations or erasures.' Every signature must be followed by an address. It must conclude with a 'prayer,' and the prayer must be repeated, at the head of each sheet. The Petition must be respectful, decorous, and temperate in its language. Our language passed the officials' kindly scrutiny (though there was a little doubt about the word 'protest'). Our script was beautifully done, but some small error had been found in a date (an 8 for a 6), and if this was corrected the whole thing might have to be done again. (I forget how we got over that—either we were let off or we left the error in.)

When you present your Petition you can either make a brief speech of explanation or, 'if required,' the Speaker can instruct the Clerk to read the Petition to the House. One point of this is that it is then printed in *Hansard,* but since this business takes place in Question Time, you gain no great applause from the Speaker, or anyone else. But there were my 'Three Musketeers' goggling from the Gallery, and I thought that, having come so far, they deserved it. The Speaker said: 'I know that it is a short one, but not only that, I realize that there is some importance attaching to it by many in the Dominion of Newfoundland.' And it was so.

How proud, how thrilled, they were, to set their names to the historic scroll in the panelled room off Westminster Hall, to hear the words of Mr. Speaker, and to see me carry their Petition to the Table! I was proud too. It showed once more what strength and soundness there is in some of the ancient customs we take for granted, or disregard, or even belittle. These honest patriots believed without pretence or doubt that they had been hardly used by the King's Ministers. They had reminded me often of the words of the last Newfoundland Prime Minister, Mr. Alderdice, in 1934:

We trust implicitly in their [the Ministers of the United Kingdom] honourable intentions, feeling confident that a full measure of Responsible Government will be restored to the island when we have again been placed upon a self-supporting basis.

They thought sincerely that that honourable trust had been abused, and now they had come 2,000 miles to make their 'humble prayer' to the fount of power and justice, the House of Commons. It was to them a tremendous event. It should, I think, have had a powerful effect. But as I dropped the Petition into the bag behind the Speaker's Chair, I was sadly aware that very few would be likely to think of it again. Still, it had advertised their presence and their plea, and there it is, for history to read, in *Hansard*.

Disillusion, I fear, must have begun to touch them that very day. I had acquired a very keen and useful ally in the House of Lords— Lord Sempill. We had arranged a meeting upstairs, in Room 11, that evening, at which the Newfoundlanders could address any British legislators who were interested in their fortunes. They wanted it, and it was right; but I did not expect much. There are so many Committees, so many meetings, so many things to do in that House (apart from attending the debates in the Chamber), it needs a Smuts or a Spaak or a deputation from the stage to draw a good audience at 5 or 6 P.M. So often, with sympathy, I have seen eager folk come in from outside, excited by the chance, the privilege, to address the Members, and sure that their righteous cause will sweep like wildfire through the place. They find a bleak, empty room, a cross between a schoolroom and a Gothic waiting-room, with Gothic windows and a portrait of John Wilkes—and less than a dozen Members. And the Members, who have two or three different appointments or invitations at the same time, keep coming and going. They simply rise, with wooden faces, in the middle of a sentence, and go out. Or they open the door, take a look round, and, with an expression of horror and alarm, disappear. We are accustomed to this; the outsider is not. We were lucky, and had between twenty and thirty, from all parties. Peter Cashin made a powerful and eloquent speech, which, at great expense, we had 'roneoed' and distributed.

He very properly reminded the Members that Newfoundland's original default partly arose from

her voluntary sacrifice made in the 1914–18 war, when in an excess of patriotic generosity she undertook to equip and put in the field a regiment of Newfoundland Infantry. It is estimated that of the total National Debt of one hundred million dollars at that time, approximately forty million dollars was the direct result of our war expenditure.

On the subject of finance, and economic prospects, he condemned

the highly improper arrangement whereby the Commission of Government ceded to Canadian and American interests the great wealth of newly discovered iron mines in the Labrador possession. It is estimated that the value of these high-grade iron deposits is in the vicinity of two or three billions of dollars. And that, through the maladministration of the Commission, Newfoundland revenues had been permanently deprived of an annual income of around two or three millions of dollars. In short, if a people's government had been in control of Newfoundland in accordance with the terms of the 1933 Act, she would be to-day *one of the most prosperous little countries in the world*. It is worth remembering this, because the basis on which we are now asked to surrender our country to Canada is that we were not as a country able to carry on alone.

But the speech was too long for the occasion, and the audience dwindled. Still, I saw good signs of sympathy, and we had made a fair beginning.

But even that evening I heard the kind of 'personal remark' by which, sometimes, we excuse ourselves for making a dubious political judgment. I was told that my friends were 'tough guys,' 'typical Irish politicians,' and so on. To which I replied that certainly they did not speak with the accents of the Carlton Club, but few Newfoundlanders did, for it was a tough country to live in. Further, I added, tartly, that Canadian politicians were not noticeably anaemic and that there was no reason to suppose that Confederation with Canada would refine and purify the personality of Newfoundlanders.

I put a Motion on the Order Paper, supported by Members of all parties,[1] as follows:

[1] Mr. Gammans, Mr. Grenfell (Labour), Mr. Hopkin Morris (Liberal), Mr. Baxter, Lieutenant-Colonel Sir Thomas Moore, Mr. Rhys Davies (Labour), Captain Marsden, Sir Jocelyn Lucas, Mr. John Crowder, Professor Savory, Sir Patrick Hannon.

Newfoundland (Liberation). That this House, having taken note of the facts set forth in the humble Petition of certain Newfoundlanders presented on 23rd November, calls upon His Majesty's Government to introduce without delay a Bill to repeal the Newfoundland Act, 1933, and to restore self-government to Newfoundland, so that an election may be held in May 1949, after which the people of the island, through their own elected Legislature and Government, may determine their future, whether by way of Confederation with Canada or otherwise.

No invitation came from Mr. Noel-Baker. They were hurt, and I was indignant. After all, these men had been in the Commonwealth capital for nearly a fortnight; they had presented a Petition to the House of Commons; they represented 48 per cent of the voters of an island for which the Secretary of State was responsible; and even if they were politically repugnant, they deserved, I thought, a little personal attention from the Minister, Secretary of State for *'Commonwealth Relations.'*

On 25 November I was invited to a lunch at 10 Downing Street in honour of some foreign delegation or other (I forget who it was). Saying good-bye to Mr. Attlee, I managed to slip in the remark that the Newfoundlanders had not yet seen Mr. Noel-Baker. Mr. Attlee, like a good Prime Minister, is a man for remembering details, and the next day, I think, a polite invitation came. It may, of course, have been a coincidence, but that, Young Man, is the queer kind of way in which things get done in this queer world of government.

Not that anything got done on this occasion. My great hope was still, while pursuing justice, to preserve the peace. I was by no means spoiling for a fight with the British—and the Canadian—Government. I hoped to persuade the Secretary of State that what we proposed was the best for everyone—including himself—and need not prejudice the cause of Confederation. Repeal the Newfoundland Act, 1933, restore self-government, and arrange for a General Election as soon as the snows cleared (my three friends and I had even fixed the date—Wednesday, 4 May). If the Confederate Party were successful, well and good: the Newfoundland Prime Minister could send his delegates to Ottawa to negotiate with the full authority of the people. And when the terms were brought back to St. John's, they could be properly debated—yes, and if necessary, rejected. If the Responsible Government Party won the election, very well; the island, it seemed, was now quite capable of carrying on under her own steam. Or, if not, she could turn to Canada later. What was the hurry? In either event, we should avoid unpleasantness in the British Parliament, and bitterness in Newfoundland. No one could say, then, that we had gone back on our word.

Mr. Noel-Baker kindly gave us an hour or more, and listened patiently. The proceedings were confidential. They were also fruitless.

Months later, one of my supporters asked one of the Minister's colleagues, 'But why on earth *don't* you do what "A.P." suggests? What's the objection?'

'We can't risk it,' said the Noble Lord.

In other words, they were by no means sure that the small surplus of votes might not shift the other way, against Confederation.

They could not risk giving the Newfoundlanders a chance to settle their own future in their own Parliament.

This, I think, is the heart of the indictment.

The Terms of Union were debated in the Canadian Parliament for a fortnight. In Newfoundland they could not be debated at all. They were 'approved' by the Government of Newfoundland, which meant seven men appointed by Whitehall, *four of whom were Englishmen.*

The Newfoundlanders' appeal was lodged with the Judicial Committee of the Privy Council in London, the ultimate fount of Commonwealth justice, just before the British Government Bill was introduced. But Whitehall and Canada were in a hurry, and would not wait to hear what the lawyers had to say. His Majesty's Government went further and tried the case themselves. 'We take the view,' said the Attorney-General, 'that the action was a frivolous and vexatious action.' Yes—but who are 'we'? The defendants!

In the Canadian House of Commons, though there was unanimity about Confederation, Mr. Drew, the Leader of the Opposition, led seventy-four Members into the 'No' Lobby on the final resolution, to mark their disapproval of the 'quite improper' procedure.

In London the Conservative Opposition would not oppose, uneasy though many of them were. 'The right thing done in the wrong way,' everybody whispered. 'A rape, for example,' I said. No one of importance went on to say: Why not do it in the right way?

So I could get only sixteen stout fellows to support me. But we went down fighting. This was my last assault:

Here, in the House of Commons, we are discussing the affairs and the future of Newfoundland, and the terms in the Bill. To-morrow in the House of Lords there will be more Parliamentary discussion of the Bill and the terms. For sixteen days in the Parliament of Canada these Terms of Union were discussed. There is nothing to stop the Federal Parliament in Australia or the State Parliaments from discussing in an airy way to-morrow this great union between Canada and Newfoundland and saying: 'These terms seem to be very favourable and fair.' In New Zealand and South Africa they can do the same, and in the cold air of Hobart or the hot sun of Queensland. They all have Parliaments. There is only one place in the whole Commonwealth where there can be no Parliamentary discussion of these terms, and that is in the Dominion of Newfoundland. Let us sweep away all the legal arguments and the quibbles; this does not seem to be a democratic thing which can be adjusted to our ideas of law or of fact in this Empire. Therefore, if I only have one man with me, I am going to ask the House of Commons to divide with me in favour of this Amendment.

On 1 April 1949 the Union was inaugurated in Ottawa and Saint John's. In Saint John's there were some black ties and flags at half-mast, and in a certain office in Whitehall I expect they had a bonfire.

But I hope with all my heart, as I said on the Third Reading, 'that this affair will go much better than I feel and fear, and that this Union, which has been so queerly and somewhat unhappily solemnized, may be consummated more smoothly and satisfactorily, and that this fine couple will live happily ever after.'

God bless Canada, and her new Province!

48. Writing to *The Times*

In my youth I wrote a long satirical poem called *The Saviours,*
about the kind of people who write letters to *The Times.*

I read that to-day with some amusement, for I have long been an
addict to the vice myself. Indeed, I would now, in Parliamentary
language, 'beg to leave out "vice," and insert "virtue" '—or perhaps
'adventure.' We may laugh at those who are always 'writing to the
papers,' but it is a very big thing that they can, and do. Few, I believe, 'write angrily to *The Times*' in Russia. Even here, you may
have a vote, you may have a Member, you may have a trade union,
you may have your chosen party in power; yet there may be many
things that you think should be said, and no one is saying. But you,
not a Member of Parliament, not even a Lord, can 'write to the
papers' and say them. This 'Freedom,' in recent years, has noticeably
expanded its appeal and area. *The Times* may still be the favourite,
but the *Daily Telegraph,* the *Sunday Times,* and *Observer* have fine
and well-filled correspondence columns; and the earnest citizen can
write even longer letters to the thoughtful weeklies. The 'popular'
papers now provide similar safety-valves for their readers' indignant
steam. 'Brickbats and Bouquets'—'Live Letters'—'What You
Think,' and so on. It is a good institution; and the readers who fill
so much space do not, like greedy journalists, expect to be paid. If I

had been paid for all my contributions to *The Times,* I reckon I could buy the proprietor's yacht (in which I have had some happy voyages for nothing).

Apart from the general duty of every citizen to save his country if he can, I commend the practice to the young Member of Parliament who has some lone or unusual campaign in mind. When the day of battle comes, the words on the Order Paper may be most unexciting, and indeed meaningless to many:

Page One, Clause 2, line 27, after 'accordingly' insert 'save as provided by paragraph (*b*) of sub-section 2 of Section 89 of the principal Act.'

or

Page Fourteen, Clause 29, line 3, leave out the second 'not.'

Or there may be nothing on the Order Paper at all. If Members have no notion what your great crusade is about they will stay in the Smoking Room or elsewhere, and when the Division Bell goes they will vote as the Whips direct them, however much they love you. So it is a good thing to let them know beforehand something about the monstrous injustice or brilliant reform which is agitating you. The party Member, I suppose, can tell a party meeting about it, but the party may be against him, or have no strong views—on Entertainments Tax, for example—and he may still require support outside. The Independent can only nobble his friends in smoking-rooms and corridors, where all conversations consist mainly of interruptions. A good letter to *The Times* is much more likely to get intelligent attention. It is true that in this way you may put off as many as you persuade, and your enemies may make hot shot from your letter, but no one who really believes in his cause will be afraid of that. Still, it is, I confess, an anxious and exacting life, running a correspondence in *The Times.* You have offered yourself as a target in a world of learned and expert men, and one brief, witty reply may blow you to pieces. I try to do all things as well as I can, but I believe I have given even more care to my letters to *The Times* than to some of my professional writing. This is natural enough. There may be any number of excuses for error in a paid article. It was, no doubt, a misprint;

the sub-editor, cruelly and ignorantly, cut the thing about; the editor, held down by tyrannical proprietors, refused to print the fundamental argument; and, in general, the paper, which has paid for the article, is responsible. But in the correspondence columns you are naked and alone. Nobody asked you to Save the World, or Newfoundland, or anything else. Any error you make is 'gratuitous' (in every sense) and unprovoked. What you say is not (unless you are libellous) the editor's fault. Indeed, for all you know, he may be sitting back and chuckling about your discomfiture to come.

So every sentence, every word, is a worry. How I fuss! Even after I have left my torpedo at *The Times* front door, I read in the Underground the carbon copy and wonder if it is quite so explosive and shattering as I thought. Is it too long? Are the facts right? Is the argument clear? Will that phrase be frowned upon by the masters of English? And then, of course, will it ever be printed, this unanswerable weapon, this atom-bomb of public argument? Next morning one opens *The Times*—oh, so casually! The letter is not there. That could hardly be expected. But still, some of the spice has gone out of the day. Another twenty-four hours must pass before the World can be Saved. Still, it is just as well, perhaps, for now there is time to consider and correct that dubious point or phrase. And here is some practical advice, Young Man. The Correspondence Department reach the office about 4 P.M., and, thereafter, if you telephone, they will courteously note your corrections. But let them not be too numerous, and go carefully. Do not, for example, assume that you are going to be printed. No, no; the formula, I fancy, is: 'My letter about Agriculture. In case the editor thought of using it, I wonder if you could make two small corrections?' That is the kind of approach. But the next day there is no letter—nor the next day either, and life is pretty grim. It seems incredible that they should want to drag out that dreary correspondence about University teaching or the trial of some damned Cardinal in the Balkans, when they have your letter about Agriculture waiting to bring prosperity to the planet. But the next day, there it is. How pleased you are—and how rosy is Man's future! You are surprised, as you go about the town, to meet many men who have not read your letter. Nor has any evening paper thought fit to write a leading article about it. But those who matter will have read it, no doubt; and two days later there are two answers in *The Times*. One seems to be on your side, but goes off on a side-issue. The other, which is against you, is evidently the work of an imbecile. The next day there is another, by a man who seems to dislike you and does wild illogical injury to your argument. This is grand. You go about all day with a burning sense of injustice, but this is far better than being ignored. It is bad when nobody answers and your 'correspondence' dies like a May-fly after a single shining day. Now you can reply to this ignorant, malignant fellow, and perhaps pop in some of the points you left out, for the sake of brevity, the first time. But now, Young Man, be careful. Now that you have seen how low the human race can descend, you may be tempted to let go, to discharge at once all the guns you have been masking. Do not do that. Restrain yourself. Keep the note of polite and quiet irony. Assume (though it seems unlikely) that your opponent is a human being too. And now it is no bad thing to spread the thing a little. Toss a few red herrings about, for these may bring in other correspondents who are quite uninterested in your central theme. Your friends will then write to say that the herring-chasers have completely missed your point, which is a sound one. Keep something up your sleeve, too, for you may want to discharge a third letter. Indeed, you may have to, if the thing is to be kept going. Personally, I like to see a good 'bang-bang' correspondence between two tenacious citizens, who both live in London, so that the deadly 'answer,' delivered by hand, appears hot the next day. It is a flaw when the second fellow lives far away in Yorkshire and his reply falls like a spent bullet three or four days later. After a few days of this you will be worn and weary. You have neglected your work. You have got Agriculture on one side of the brain, and on the other a growing distaste for the subject. You no longer hope that the other fellow will be at you again; you hope he has had enough. But persevere. For—who knows?—it may work up to a leading article, and that is Game, Set, and Match! After that, when you rise up in the House, you are a lone wolf no more. Always, by the way, put 'House of Commons' at the bottom of your letter, to show that you are a Member of Parliament, though Parliament is in recess and you have not been near the place for six weeks.

During the divorce affair I had many a brush with Bishops in the public sheets, and many important misunderstandings were, I believe, corrected before the Bill was ever debated. I remember especially a very heavy engagement with the Bishop of Gloucester in *The Times,* and a most odd encounter with the Bishop of ——— in the *Daily Telegraph.* About teatime, one day, I was at the Turkish Baths in Northumberland Avenue (where I used to meet Mr. Bevin and Mr. Bevan *in puris naturalibus*), in the small room where you could sweat, and smoke as well. There were a few dank newspapers lying about, and suddenly my eye caught my name in a sodden copy of that morning's *Daily Telegraph.* It was from the Bishop of ———. I forget what he said, but it seemed to me to be un-Christian and personally insulting. I was very hot, and 'sweating profusely,' as a man should be in a Turkish Bath. But he should also, according to the rules, be relaxed and ruminant, forgetting the cares of the outside world. I was not. I was enraged. I muttered phrases about 'turbulent prelates,' dried myself, and, still stark naked, marched through the swing-door into the little lobby, where there was a telephone. I rang up the *Daily Telegraph* and asked for the editor's secretary. Her name, I think, was Silver and she was very helpful throughout. 'Can I,' I said importantly, 'dictate a letter to the editor about the Bishop of ———?' 'Certainly,' she said. 'Go ahead.'

I began, I remember, pretty strongly:

Sir,
    The Bishop of ——— has the effrontery to . . .

But by then I had started sweating again. I received a sharp electric shock and dropped the instrument. Many men, at that point, would have given up the notion of telephoning a letter to the *Daily Telegraph* from a Turkish Bath about the Bishop of ———. Not I. I went back to my towel, dried myself thoroughly, returned to the instrument, and captured the obliging Miss Silver again. I explained to her the situation in which I found myself and begged her not to desert or think ill of me if electrical phenomena should silence me again. She charmingly understood and agreed. There was, I think, only one more interval for drying. We got the whole letter through, and it appeared next morning.

In 1949, too, if I may be permitted one more bit of boasting—and it is a pretty big one—I silenced Mr. Bernard Shaw.

After the debate on Mr. Follick's Reformed Spelling Bill (defeated on Second Reading by three votes), Mr. Shaw wrote to *The Times*. We are used to the great man's superiority to other men, especially the half-witted citizens who inhabit the House of Commons. But he now spent a haughty paragraph on me, and ended with a challenge which could hardly be ignored. Mr. Shaw wrote:

In the debate Sir Alan Herbert took the field as the representative of Oxford University, the university of Henry Sweet, greatest of British phoneticians. After debating the stale tomfooleries customary when spelling reform is discussed by novices and amateurs, he finally extinguished himself by pointing out that a sample of Mr. Follick's spelling saves only one letter from the conventional Johnsonese orthography. This was the champion howler of the debate. I invite Sir Alan to write down that one letter, and measure how long it takes him to get it on paper, and how much paper it covers: say a fraction of a second and of a square inch. 'Not worth saving' is his present *reductio ad absurdum*. But surely a University Member must be mathematician enough to go deeper. In the English-speaking world, on which the sun never sets, there are at every fraction of a moment millions of scribes, from bookkeepers to poets, writing that letter or some other single letter. If it is superfluous, thousands of acres of paper, months of time, and the labor of armies of men and women are being wasted on it. Dare Sir Alan now repeat that a difference of one letter does not matter?

The rest is poppycock. . . .

I replied:

SPELLING REFORM

THE LONG AND SHORT OF IT

To the Editor of The Times

Sir,—'Dare,' indeed? I eagerly accept Mr. Bernard Shaw's challenge. I still think nothing of one letter (in 31 words) to be saved (perhaps) by the Follick plan, however many millions are now writing or printing it. Nor am I worried about the millions who are spending time or space this morning on shaving their chins or spelling God with a capital G.

I am sorry to say, by the way, that I may have been too generous about that one letter. I have again done the long title of the Bill into

Follick English, as I understand it; and this time I make the scores equal (145 letters). I may be wrong: but look, sir, at the following phrases, set down at random:—

'The United Nations need a philosophy.' (31 letters)
'Dhe Iunaited Neishuns niid ei filosofii.' (34 letters)
'No sage is as wise as he looks.' (23)
'Nou seij iz az waiz az hii lwks.' (24)
'You are going round in a circle.' (25)
'Iu ar gouing raund in ei serkel.' (25)
'No elephant is a Socialist.' (22)
'Nou elefant iz ei Soushalist.' (24)

Here, if Ai hav dun it rait, Mr. Follick is six letters down. It is easy to see why. He pulls out the 'ph' from 'elephant' and says 'What a good boy am I!' But what does it profit a space-saver if at the same time he spells 'go' 'gou' and 'a' 'ei'? Now for the time-saver. See what he has done (above) to such words as 'United,' 'Nations,' 'circle,' and 'Socialist.' Such words, at present, are easily apprehended by millions of the Latin (and the English) speakers. Let Mr. Shaw, the great mathematician, consider how many trillions of important seconds are going to be wasted by Frenchmen, Italians, Spaniards, and Americans wondering what on earth the English mean by 'serkel' or 'neishun,' which are related to nothing they know, and do not even represent phonetically the way we say 'circle' and 'nation.' As for our children, Mr. Shaw and his like are distressed by the time spent in teaching them that 'nation' and 'national' are not pronounced the same way. But how much time shall we have to spend on teaching them that 'neishun' and 'nashunal' are really the same word and spring from the same root?

Of course, as I said in the debate which Mr. Shaw seems to have read, you can save paper space (though not, I think, much printer's or student's time) if you have a thoroughgoing phonetic system with an enormous alphabet and a lot of weird signs that make the printed page look like a bowl of tadpoles. Both Mr. Shaw and Mr. Follick, I gather, shrink from this. But Mr. Shaw and others want to use several of our present letters upside down. Imagine the trouble of teaching a child to write 'c' or 'e' upside down! How many adults are likely to do it efficiently? And in print, as Sir Harry Johnston has remarked, how should we be sure that it was not a printer's error? The reformers, it seems to me, are in a dilemma which they will not face. Either they save no space worth mentioning, or they make the page repulsive and the sense obscure.

Going back to the challenge, even if I were persuaded that Mr. Follick was going to save that one letter, I should not be impressed. What is the hurry? If we wish to communicate swiftly we have shorthand, Morse, the telephone, and loud-speaker. The printed page is read at leisure: and other qualities get marks. We could save much time if we all wore beards and no collars. It would save time if Black Rod ran up the floor of the House without the stately gait and bows. We could save street-space if the Colonel marched in column of threes and there were no intervals between the companies. We could save paper if we cut out stops or ranthewordstogetherlikethis. All books, no doubt, could be printed in shorthand, and all citizens compelled to learn it. But in all these cases there would be a loss to elegance and understanding and the pleasures of the mind and eye which no mere saving of time, space, or trouble could justify. For example, it does not upset me to see Mr. Shaw spell 'Labour,' 'Labor.' Let him carry on. What a wonderful saving! But suppose the one letter were the 'y' in 'you' (Mr. Follick wants to abolish 'y'). I do not find it any easier to write 'iu' (try it, sir); it is not so legible in cursive script and might be taken for 'in'; it does not seem to me to be quite the same sound; and I, for one, should miss the word 'you.' So, with due apologies to the children and foreigners, I hope that letter will be spared, not 'saved.'

Mr. Shaw should be almost old enough to know that you prove no case by shouting words like 'tomfoolery' and 'poppycock.' My own 'tomfooleries' I believe to be facts. From Mr. Shaw we get nothing but dogmatic assertion and vague invective. But I hope that the writing of this long letter shows my proper respect for our oldest writer. Mr. Follick wants to represent the 'aw' sound in 'paw' by the letters 'oo'; and I was tempted simply to say 'Pw! Mr. Shoo!' It would have saved much time.

I am, sir, your obedient servant,

A. P. HERBERT

Now, I thought, surely a thunderbolt will fall. But there was not a word.

49. Last of the Burgesses

You may laugh, if you like, at the 'dull dons'; but there is, I swear, no body of civilians that looks so gay, and gracious, as the University folk on their days of ceremony. The 'Burgesses' were charmingly included in the big occasions, royal visits, foundation-stones, new buildings, and the presentation of Loyal Addresses at Buckingham Palace, when Pall Mall taxi-drivers were astonished by loads of passengers in hoods and gowns. But I most enjoyed—though it alarmed me a little—the colourful pageantry of Encænia[1]—or Commemoration Day. The Doctors and the Masters of Arts invited assemble at the college of the Vice-Chancellor and there enjoy the Creweian Benefaction, which in my early days was champagne and strawberries. There are also the Honorands, the eight or nine distinguished persons who are to be voted Honorary Doctors of Literature or Civil Law by Convocation (or not). In anticipation of a favourable verdict they are already arrayed as Doctors. There was so much colour in the scene that I often thought of it as the opening for an opera—light or grand: the Doctors of Civil Law in robes of scarlet cloth with crimson silk sleeves and 'fronts,' Doctors of Literature and Science in scarlet cloth and dove silk, Doctors of Philosophy in

[1]'A renewal: a dedicatory festival.' 'The annual Commemoration Day of Founders and benefactors at Oxford University.' (O.E.D.)

scarlet cloth with sleeves of mazarine blue silk, and Doctors of Music (alone disdaining the scarlet) in white brocade silk with crimson satin sleeves and fronts.

Then the Registrar of the University (through all my time the most kind and capable Mr. Douglas Veale) marshalled us in column of twos, and we marched in slow procession through the streets to the Sheldonian Theatre. First the Chancellor (Lord Halifax)—or, more often, the Vice-Chancellor of the day, with a screen of bulldogs before him; then the High Steward (now Lord Simon); then either the two Burgesses or the two Proctors. Lord Hugh Cecil had laid upon his successors an almost sacred charge, to insist upon the right of the Burgesses to march ahead of the Proctors. Sometimes we did, and sometimes not: I am sorry to say we never fought about it. I was much more worried to find myself marching ahead of the long column of Doctors, including all the Heads of Houses, famous scholars, good and learned and venerable men who had been serving the University and spreading the light for thirty years and more. Also, I always felt a self-conscious ass in my unaccustomed mortar-board and hood and gown, as I muttered nothings to Arthur Salter beside me, and, with my long legs, tried vainly to keep in step. There were crowds all the way, as thick as the Lord Mayor's Show can gather, to see the 'Honorands' at the tail of the procession. What a day that was in 1945 when the great commanders of the war were —'for the sake of honour'—admitted to be Doctors of Civil Law— Eisenhower, Montgomery, Bernard Freyberg, V.C., Earl Gowrie, V.C., Admiral Lord Tovey, Field-Marshal Viscount Alanbrooke, and Marshal of the Royal Air Force Viscount Tedder! Oxford put on its very best that day. All traffic stopped for miles as the procession of heroes crawled across the city. The lights in the Sheldonian were the lights of Heaven—or Hollywood. Every seat on the floor was bright with a Master's or Bachelor's hood; no brighter were the summery girls in the galleries. Lord Halifax, a noble head above a brilliant gown of gold and black, was like an immense golden eagle in the Chancellor's chair. The warriors, the sailors, wearing their strange merry robes over their khaki and blue, their crossed swords and batons, their medal ribbons and golden rings, were frightened, I dare say, for the first time in their lives. The ordeal was severe. One by one, each of the great men had to stand forth and listen while the Public Orator, in Latin, read a graceful and witty speech in his praise, of which the victim did not understand one word. Then the great golden Chancellor above him, with a few more words of Latin, 'admitted' the new 'Doctor' into the bosom of the University. Then at last the reverent hush was broken and the academic audience roared like a football crowd. I remember Eisenhower standing very straight in the storm of cheers, a rugged monument of character, trying hard to keep the solemn face which, no doubt, was demanded of a Doctor, but relaxing at last into a shy schoolboy smile. Montgomery, too, was a grand, embarrassed Doctor of Law (but I thought we should have given him Literature). Then came that fine, shy Ambassador, John Winant, the Admirals and Lords of the Air. 'Oh, why,' I thought, 'is there no music?' It was a scene for Grand Opera. Wagner, or Elgar, perhaps, should have done the music. Chaliapin himself should have sung all the parts in this Blessing of the Heroes by the Queen of Universities, this fusion of the fighter, the philosopher, the scholar in the common triumph of civilized thought and behaviour, this salutation of the sword in the citadel of learning.

I remember, too, another Commemoration Day, when the Prime Minister, Mr. Attlee, and Mrs. Churchill were made Honorary Doctors. At the last moment Mr. Churchill arrived to see his lady gowned, and he marched at the head of the Doctors,[2] just behind Arthur Salter and me (the Proctors must have popped ahead of us that day). The speeches of the Public Orator (then Mr. T. F. Higham, of Trinity) and the prize-winning Latin compositions are all spoken in the horrid 'New' pronunciation (as I still call it after thirty-five years). *Vobis* was not 'vobiss' but 'woabeese.' But Lord Halifax, the Chancellor, stood firmly to the good old 'English' pronunciation of my youth. *Domini,* for him, was 'Dominye,' not 'Dominee.' As we marched out, I heard Mr. Churchill say something like this to some one: 'I'm so glad Edward [Lord Halifax] refuses to talk this Dago-talk. We should pronounce the Latin as we pronounce it every day, in our own language.' My heart was warmed. He went on with a favourite example of my own. 'After

[2]He was honoured in 1925 (Doctor of Civil Law).

all, we don't teach the young that the month of August is named after the Emperor "Owgoostooss." We say that August comes from Au——' The crowd saw him then and yelled 'Good Old Winnie!' He turned and made the V-sign, a pleasing sight in his robes and flat velvet cap. 'I think,' he went on, 'these two learned gentlemen should do something about it.' 'Good old Winnie!' I turned and said I had been denouncing the Dago-talk for years, and we had an animated discussion all the way to All Souls, myself walking sideways and Mr. Churchill punctuating every sentence with the V-sign.

Nor shall I forget the Encænia of 1949, the last we were to attend as Burgesses. On that day the University of Oxford did a very Christian thing. On the way up in the train, I learned that the two principal 'Honorands' were to be the Lord Chancellor (Lord Jowitt) and the Chancellor of the Exchequer (Sir Stafford Cripps), two leaders of the Government which had just destroyed the University seats. One was an old friend of mine, and the other an old schoolfellow, but I felt that this was almost an excess of the Christian spirit. When the Vice-Chancellor put my Right Honourable Friends to the vote: *'Placetne vobis, Domini, Magistri?'* ('Does it please you, Doctors and Masters of Arts?') I was tempted to say, on principle, but with a smile, *'Non placet.'* ('It does not please.') But they were our guests, as Arthur Salter said, and I was silent.

A graceful mark of the occasion was made. We found ourselves marching behind the Vice-Chancellor, ahead of the Proctors, ahead of the High Steward himself. Lord Hugh Cecil, we felt, would have been pleased by that, at least. But it was a melancholy march. In 1603 King James I summoned the first Burgesses to Parliament from Oxford and Cambridge. From Cambridge had gone, among many others, Francis Bacon, Isaac Newton,[3] William Pitt, Lord Palmerston, and Eldon Gorst.

Mine was the unworthy end of a list of more than fifty names,

[3]Mr. Kenneth Pickthorn, in one of the debates, made a delightful and characteristic interjection. Mr. Ivor Thomas had said in rather patronizing tones: 'At any rate the universities are beginning now to send better men to the House of Commons. . . .'

MR. PICKTHORN (Cambridge University): 'I would like to ask the hon. Gentleman whether he really thinks that I am an improvement on Francis Bacon and Isaac Newton?'

which included John Selden, Matthew Hale (Lord Chief Justice), Roger Newdigate, Robert Peel, Mr. Gladstone, Sir William Anson, Charles Oman, the historian, Lord Hugh Cecil, that fine thinker and speaker.

Now this ancient, unique and enlightened tradition was to die; and whether it was to die for party pique or a mathematical formula, it seemed a pity. Two of the chief murderers, in robes of honour, marched behind us, and as we turned the corner I looked across the High to University College, the old college of our principal constituent—'Attlee, the Rt. Hon. Clement Richard, M.A., and D.C.L.' Prime Minister.

Well, I can be Christian too, and I hope he will come to my house for the Boat Race again.⁴

⁴He did.

50. Swan Song

Sick though I was of speeches, I thought, now and then, towards the end of 1949, about my Parliamentary swan song. The Dissolution might come in February, or March, or even June 1950; but, in any event, there would be a chance—probably on an 'Adjournment' motion—for a final fling. I would, I thought, take trouble, and prepare, and give them of my best. It would be a speech in my old form and please them all. I should be witty, but profoundly wise. For once, even the Chair should have nothing to complain of—though the Chair itself would be in a melting mood, because it was my 'positively last appearance'; and though it remembered what an un-Parliamentary nuisance I had been so many times, the Chair forgave me. Tears came into my eyes when I thought of this oration. (And this is perfectly true, you unbelievers! Time and again, I have made myself cry with speeches, or parts of speeches, which I never, in the end, delivered. That is the sort of stuff we hard-faced humourists are made of.) The form and substance of this great speech varied. Sometimes it began most angrily and bitterly—'*Moriturus te saluto!*', but with what a difference! I should rub it in about the abolition of the University seats, and make that most stupid act a test of Ministerial wisdom. I should address ironical but blistering words to 'my principal constituent,' the Prime Minister,[1] who had destroyed his Member (and would,

[1] Attlee, Right Hon. Clement Richard, M.A., *Univ.*

of course, be 'in his place'). From that I should pass to my favourite enemy, the Arrogance, the *Hubris,* the Intolerable Conceit and Spleen of Ministers and their supporters; and a few deft classical and historical allusions would show what came of that. During this version of the speech the Conservatives and Liberals were rolling about in glee and rapture; the other side were mortified and writhing, but somehow (unusually) reduced to silence by the sheer power of the speech and, of course, by their own consciousness of sin. My old friend Herbert Morrison was white with impotent rage. The Prime Minister hung his head in shame—too much distressed to doodle. The little legs of the President of the Board of Trade fell off the Table and he had not the heart to lift the tiny feet again.

In other versions of the speech the tone was mellower, though the tune was the same. Similar things were said, but with such good humour, such flickering, summer-lightning wit, that none need blink or wince and all were happy. Herbert Morrison sat writhing but delighted. The Prime Minister was not so sure about it all, but doodled undisturbed. The little legs of the President of the Board of Trade fell off the Table again, but now because he was laughing uncontrollably. And the Conservatives and Liberals still rolled about in glee and rapture.

Then the speech (as a rule) became rather solemn. I was (after only fourteen years, it is true) a bit of an Elder Statesman, about to retire—and an Independent, too. A General Election was ahead, and I exhorted all parties to remember what they were—Britons, just Britons; men of the same breed and history, honouring one King and Flag—and Parliament men as well. What a pity if, on the platform, before the people, they forgot the common courtesies that Parliament had taught them. But not much of that. Then the speech finished with a modest farewell to the House, an affirmation of faith in the Parliamentary ways, a grateful salute to the Speaker, and perhaps a reference to the last words of my Maiden Speech: 'I am proud indeed to be standing in this place among the faithful Commons of His Majesty the King.'

All this part was a little vague. The one thing certain about the speech was that it remained outstanding for many years in Parliamentary memories. They would talk about it in the Smoking Room, that unique museum of memories, long after I had gone. I shall not miss the Chamber; I never want to make a speech again. But I hope my ghost will walk the Smoking Room. You must use the Smoking Room, Young Man. All the best men do—all the best Prime Ministers. Has not this humble person drunk there, and even argued, with Baldwin, Lloyd George, Churchill, and Attlee; with Austen Chamberlain and Eddy Winterton, Anthony Eden and Duff Cooper and 'Bobberty' Cranborne (the three who bravely resigned), the twin witty Olivers, Stanley and Lyttelton, Bevin and Bevan, John Simon, Jowitt, and Donald Somervell, three great lawyers, all judges now. All the warm full-blooded men go there; only the foolish laugh at the place, and only the cold men keep away. I never, I think, saw Neville Chamberlain or Stafford Cripps in that room. Almost everything that is said there is 'shop,' touching, in some way, the business of governing men. Here you may hear gossip that would shake the world, send Fleet Street into a fever, if it got out. But it is penned in by a stern unwritten tradition. Collins and Wright, the two faithful waiters who saw us through the war, were always in and out among us, and, in the ten years I knew them, must have heard secrets worth a fortune or two. They never got out. Here you may hear the first whispers of big shifts of opinion, plots, cabals, rebellions, that may end in the fall of Ministers or Governments. Here you may pursue your own little plans, suck the brains of the old on strategy and tactics and procedure, and secure, if you can, their signatures to your amendment or motion. Here the hot enemies of the Chamber have a drink and are friends again. Here you may see Ministers of the Crown, who have just, in the Lobbies, defeated Mr. Churchill by enormous figures, sitting respectfully about him while he lectures them upon the folly of their ways. Here, on the other hand, it is true, when feeling is high among the parties, you may see little pools of oil and vinegar, small hostile groups who mutter bitterly among themselves and throw dark glances at each other. There is more of that now, I am sorry to say, than there used to be, and I never like it. I am always saddened when some member of Party A comes up to a table where one of his own lot is sitting with some of Party B, and says: *'Hullo, Bill, you're in bad company.'*

It is meant as a jest, no doubt, but it has a rancid flavour and springs from a sour mind, where politics is all and all men are very far from being brothers. I prefer the little groups of real 'Parliament men,' who can relax and forget their creeds and factions, remembering only that they belong to a place called the Commons—men of all parties but citizens first, and blessed with a broad humanity. The tales they tell are never partisan or personal slights, but part of the common stock of Parliament men, memorable jests and retorts and orations. And someday, I thought, they would recite, with many quotations, the tale of 'A.P.'s Swan Song.'

But, alas, as you may have gathered from this narrative, it is not for a back-bencher to design what speeches he will make, or when. As Fate would have it, the last speech I made was in defence of a Herbert Morrison Motion and won far more cheers from Socialists than Tories. I was—and am still—on the Council of the Festival of Britain, 1951. On 23 December 1949 a Festival of Britain (Supplementary Provisions) Bill was down for Second Reading. The main theme was the Festival Gardens in Battersea Park, about which the Conservatives were known to be dubious (and it may still turn out that they had good reason). My old friend, Gerald Barry, Director-General of the Festival, had rung me up and implored me to speak. So had Tom Macpherson (Labour Member for Romford), the new Father of the water-buses, for, he reminded me, there was provision for new water-bus piers in the Bill, and I must be keen about that. So I was. But that morning I did not feel like festivals or fun. I had taken some of the family to the theatre the night before; they had kept me up late, and I did not feel well. Three days later, *Tough at the Top*, though it had had a five months' run, was coming off disappointingly, indeed disastrously, too soon. I had not had a very good year. I had lost my seat; I had lost the great battle of Newfoundland; I had written no book; and my new play had been, comparatively, a failure. Now they wanted me to make a speech about Fun and Games, and all I wanted was a Turkish Bath. However, the twin fiends Duty and Tenacity intervened once more, and in I went. I had nothing prepared, but I took some old notes about the fatal forties which I had used once or twice in after-dinner speeches.

After all, the forties were nearly over, and I should never be able to use them again. In the Speaker's Court I met the charming little Lady Megan Lloyd George, also on the Council and bound on the same errand. She said that she would speak, and I thought that that would probably be enough. I should get away quite quickly to my Turkish Bath. Then in the Lobby I met Mr. Robert Hudson, who was leading the Tories and told me that they were going to vote against the Bill. Mr. Herbert Morrison came across the Chamber and hoped that I would speak. I told him I had a headache, but he only laughed. The House is as exacting as the Brigade of Guards, and I felt that if I did not speak I should be guilty of desertion.

I suffered the pains of the Torture Chamber.[2] Mr. Barnes, for the Government, was long but dull. Hudson, for the Conservatives, was wildly gloomy about the whole affair. But Megan Lloyd George made one of her twinkling, capable speeches, and Mr. (now Lord) Wilmot, also on the Council, was equally good on the Labour side. It was the sort of debate I generally enjoy, where the parties are not automatically arrayed against each other, and speeches can actively influence votes. But I thought that everything had been said, and what could I say now? A back-bench Tory was gloomy too about the Festival Gardens, but did not say that he was going to vote against them. I thought that what was wanted was a change of mood, a lift of the spirit, which I ought perhaps to try to supply. But how? I had nothing prepared except the notes of my stuff about the forties; and that, for all I knew, would be held irrelevant and out of order. All this is to suggest once more that Members of Parliament do earn their money. It was, almost to the day, fourteen years since my Maiden Speech, and I swear I was as nervous as I had been then. Then, indeed, I had been eager to speak, and now I had no such itch. But Tom Macpherson (Labour) said some nice things about me, 'the great champion of Thames water-buses and boats on the river.' This was a cue that could not be ignored, and Frank Bowles, Deputy-Speaker, and a good friend, called me next. My swan song took nine minutes only, but, I am glad to say, it made them laugh a lot. I ended:

[2]See the 'Torture Chamber,' p. 47.

I had hoped that the Conservatives would not vote against the Bill, so that we may present a united front of the House towards this scheme. That will be a very pleasant thing.

May I say how disappointed I am at some of the talk in some of the papers—this very gloomy talk, with petulant letters saying, 'What, after all, have we to celebrate?' Surely right hon. and hon. Members on this side of the House, at least, will agree that if, in 1951, we have survived five years of war and five years of His Majesty's Government, then even they will have something they will like to celebrate, to dance and sing about. 'Faith,' I think Mr. G. K. Chesterton said, 'is the capacity to believe in that which is demonstrably untrue.' If that is the only sort of confidence we have in our future, then let us have that.

I think there are other causes. I am no historian, but if the House will bear with me for one more minute, I will present another historical reason why we should celebrate, not only with the main Exhibition but with the arrangements set out in this Bill. After all, we are emerging from the murky forties into the fifties, and it has been pointed out to me by a better historian than myself that the forties have always been a pretty wretched sort of decade. A hundred years ago there were the Hungry Forties, with the whole of Europe in chaos and revolution, with the Communist manifesto, with crowned heads falling everywhere and rulers taking refuge in this island, and with the Chartists massing on Kennington Common. However, after that period we emerged into what was almost the most prosperous, happy period in this country's history.

In the seventeen-forties, I think, we were at war with France, Spain —and Scotland. A predecessor of mine in this House, Sir Charles Oman, records that when Charles Edward arrived at Derby

> Panic prevailed in London, the King's plate had been sent on shipboard, the Bank of England had paid away every guinea of its reserves, and the citizens of London were fully persuaded that they would be attacked next day by 10,000 wild Scottish clansmen.

In the sixteen-forties there was civil war and King Charles I had his head cut off. In the fifteen-forties, I see 'The time was a very evil one for England.' King Henry VIII was marrying too many women, executing too many men, and persecuting everybody else. I need hardly add that we were at war with Scotland, and France as well; but the historian adds, rather woundingly, that 'the French War was far more dangerous.' In the fourteen-forties we had a weak king, King

Henry VI. We were at war with France, and we were gradually losing everything King Henry V had won. In 1431 we had burned Joan of Arc—and our publicity on the Continent was not good. In the thirteen-forties we were at war with France, and the Scots invaded the North of England. Also, a small detail, there was the Black Death. In the twelve-forties we invaded France. In the eleven-forties we were ruled by an unpleasant woman called Matilda and there was civil war all the time. In the ten-forties we were invaded by the Danes.

Now, whatever else may be laid at the door of His Majesty's Government, we are not now at war with France or Scotland or even Denmark, and I do not think that we shall be in 1951; and my hope is that in some way we shall emerge from the nineteen-forties into the fifties in such condition that we shall be justified in celebrating. But if not, even if we are going down, it is not the habit of the British Fleet—and again I am sorry that the Admiral, my hon. and gallant Friend the Member for South Paddington, is not here—to haul down the ensign when about to begin a doubtful engagement. On the contrary, each ship flies two or three to make sure that one shall be seen. It is in that spirit, I feel, that we ought to go forward with this bold, imaginative, attractive scheme, and show, whether we go up or down, that we can be gracious, gallant, and gay.

'*Loud cheers*,' said *The Times*, and I was told by a friendly Minister that 'I had changed the whole course of the debate.' I can't say about that, but I know that Herbert Morrison made a very conciliatory and persuasive speech and the Conservatives did not vote against him after all. So I did feel that, at least, I had played the part of the child in the pictures who helps to bring Daddy and Mummy together—a fitting part for an Independent, singing his swan song, though he did not know it.

Parliament was prorogued in December and never met again, though we had been summoned for 24 January. So those, by chance, were the last words I said in the House:

Whether we go up or down, let us show that we can be gracious, and gallant—and gay!

It was not quite what I had planned. But I am content. The Ayes had it.